Why God Allows Evil

Why God Allows Evil

A Former Atheist Discusses a Resolution
of the Problem of Suffering

Daniel Parks

Mill City Press, Maitland

Copyright © 2017 by Daniel Parks

Mill City Press, Inc.
2301 Lucien Way #415
Maitland, FL 32751
407.339.4217
www.millcitypress.net

All rights reserved. No part of this publication may be reproduced, stored in a retrieval system, or transmitted, in any form or by any means, electronic, mechanical, photocopying, recording, or otherwise, without the prior written permission of the author.

Unless otherwise indicated, Bible quotations are taken from The NIV Study Bible, New International Version, Copyright © 1985 by Zondervan Bible Publishers. Used by permission. All rights reserved.

Bible references other than NIV quoted by permission in this book are as follows:

NASB. From the New American Standard Bible, © 1960, 1962, 1963, 1968, 1971, 1972, 1973, 1975, 1977, 1995 by The Lockman Foundation. Used by permission.

NLT. From the Holy Bible, New Living Translation, copyright © 1996, 2004. Used by permission of Tyndale House Publishers, Inc., Wheaton, IL 60189 USA. All rights reserved.

KJV. From The Holy Bible, Old and New Testaments in the Authorized King James Version, copyright 1985 by C. D. Stampley Enterprises, Inc., Charlotte, NC. Used by permission.

ISBN-13: 978-1-63505-625-9

Printed in the United States of America.

Acknowledgments

I am thankful for David Theodore, who has given freely of his time to read the entire manuscript and make numerous and insightful comments. The manuscript was substantially improved by his critiques, but the final product remains my own and may or may not reflect his views. I am also thankful for several others for their comments on portions of the manuscript: Stuart Harrison, Brenda Kuhlmann, Alicia Johnston, Haydn Piper, and my wife. Not least of all, I am thankful for incredible support from my wife and daughter.

1

My Journey into an Investigative Study

1.1 An Atheist Who Became a Christian and Later Became an Atheist Again

I grew up in a nonreligious home. I had no Christian[1] influence growing up except perhaps a televised movie that I had seen a few times on the life of Jesus, or a little interaction with my childhood friend's Catholic grandmother about Jesus or life after death. There were a few other occasions when I heard a Bible message (e.g., at a wedding), but I don't recall being either interested in it or impacted by it.

The same is true of my young adult life. After I had graduated from high school, I joined the US Navy and served as a hospital corpsman at the National Naval Medical Center in Bethesda, Maryland, a suburb of Washington, DC. While stationed there, I eventually learned that one young lady I dated, Ebalina, was a Christian.

Ebalina lived with her parents while she pursued a college education. I soon discovered that she was avoiding spending time with me on the weekends, and when I pressed for a reason, she told me that she regularly observed "the Lord's Day" with her family. Spending any time with her on her worship day meant that I would attend church or visit with her in the company of her family. She invited me to church. I attended, but only two times (both times hungover from partying the night before). I didn't feel particularly impressed by the church group discussions, or the sermons, and I certainly had no intention of becoming a believer.

We eventually parted ways, and about a year later I met and dated a young Navy sailor who was stationed with me at Bethesda. She wasn't a practicing Christian and didn't bring up the subject of religion. She had been baptized when she was fifteen years old, but had since fallen away from her faith. While we dated I became aware of her Christian past, but there really wasn't any significant discussion about God. We were the typical young, secular-minded types, working and enjoying life with no thought of the deep mysteries of life, or of God, sin, or salvation. Two years later we were married. Shortly thereafter we were honorably discharged from the Navy, and we moved to the Phoenix metropolitan area of Arizona.

We settled into an apartment in Chandler and got jobs. We each had aspirations of getting college educations, but hadn't yet decided on career paths. A few years into married life, I found myself continually feeling that life was meaningless. And no matter what I did, the feeling didn't go away.

Then one Sunday morning in the spring of 1991 I watched a television show that discussed archaeological finds that correlated with the Bible. Archaeology interested me, so I watched the show. At the end of the program, to my surprise, was a brief presentation of the gospel and prophecy of the return of Christ. I was particularly impressed by the love of Jesus and the message of his return. Suddenly I felt a sense that if God existed, life would seem meaningful. I wanted to find out what the Bible had to say about God, the afterlife, and prophecy, and I was determined to seek the answers. I recall that while sitting there on the couch I informed my wife that I would be attending church. She could join me, or stay home, but I was going just the same.

We went to the first available church Bible study and worship service. My wife apparently thought it was a one-time thing, because the following week she was surprised when I asked her if she was going to church with me. It was at that point that she believed I had been serious.

We went to church every week. Like a sponge, I soaked in all of the teachings. Within about six months I had read the entire New Testament and much of the Old. I attended Bible classes, and after about eight months, my wife and I were baptized.

My faith was strong and my Bible knowledge grew rapidly. Noticing my faith and growing knowledge, church leaders had me serving in various church positions and activities. I taught Bible classes to young adults. I regularly assisted with the worship service. Sometimes I would read from the Bible to the congregation; other times I led in the congregational prayer, or announced upcoming church events. Being a shy introvert, I was nervous about speaking to a large group, but I gradually got over it, in part because of faith that I could "do all things through Christ who strengthened me."[2]

Only twenty-two months following my baptism I had been ordained a deacon and delivered my first sermon to the church. During the next few years I fairly regularly taught Bible classes, and several times a year I preached a sermon. Then I was ordained an elder. I recall many times being asked if I had considered becoming a pastor.

My wife and I bought our first house, and in October 1996 she became pregnant with our daughter. I was working and attending college. On the evening of December 22, while we were traveling to Oklahoma to spend Christmas with my wife's parents, I became ill.

It started with flu-like symptoms, which lasted a couple of weeks, followed by a chronic condition that entailed a decreased ability to react to stress, chronic fatigue, a dysfunctional immune system, difficulty getting restful sleep, and irregularity of mood and emotions. After seeing several kinds of doctors and undergoing many tests during a span of several years, eventually the conclusion was that I was suffering from an obscure condition recognized as hypothalamic-pituitary-adrenal (HPA) axis dysfunction.

The hypothalamus, pituitary gland, and adrenal glands work together to regulate stress response, the immune system, energy levels, sleep, mood, digestion, libido, and metabolism. The axis of the three organs consists of hormone secretion and stimulation of the pituitary gland, which stimulates the adrenal glands, which secrete hormones in a chemical feedback loop to stimulate the hypothalamus and the pituitary gland. If the axis operates properly, the immune system and the other functions all work for a healthy life. But if the axis suffers dysregulation, due to a genetic predisposition and a stressful situation, the immune system can be compromised for an extended period of time. A long-term compromise of the immune system leaves the body exposed to infiltration of a virus (i.e., Epstein-Barr virus). The combination can be a "perfect storm" for dysfunction of the HPA axis, and that entails a dysfunctional immune system, chronic fatigue (both physical and mental), difficulty getting restful sleep, memory loss, difficulty concentrating, fluctuation of mood, headaches, low-grade fever, aching muscles and joints, low blood pressure, environmental sensitivities, and falling prey to frequent infections. A problematic digestive track adds to the issues of the dysfunctional immune system, fatigue, and constipation. The partial loss of ability to react to physical and mental stress alone limits a person's response-ability at home, at school, and at work.

Certain foods make the problems worse, especially if eaten with any regularity. These include foods made with yeast, white flour, most all grains (bread and pasta), foods with added sugar, foods high in fat, fried foods, shellfish, processed foods, junk foods, and stimulating drinks such as coffee.

As is often the case, especially during the first few years, my condition was improperly diagnosed. This is because routine medical tests are not able to detect the problem. After first ruling out hypochondria and psychosomatic illness, the diagnosis of medical doctors was depression. It wasn't until years later, and the involvement of naturopathic doctors and practitioners of Chinese medicine, that depression, or any other mood disorder, was ruled out.

My Christian friends prayed for my healing, but my condition continued. I called for special prayer and anointing with oil by my pastor and elders. No change. I prayed for understanding. I meditated to try to figure out what lesson God would have me learn, or what good he would bring out of it. But I could not see any divine purpose for it. The years passed, and my wife and I continued to suffer.

I eventually came to realize that no amount of pleading or begging to God would make any difference. There did not seem to be a God who would listen. I felt spiritually crushed, ruined, and nearly drained of hope. Sometimes when the fatigue was significant, my will to live would fade in and out. I saw no point in God allowing me to suffer as I was. I saw no way for God to bring any good out of it. It just made no sense. I gradually lost my motivation to study my Bible, or spend time with Christians, or pray.

My suffering from this took a hard toll on me physically, mentally, and spiritually. There was not one area of my life that was not without difficulty and suffering. As is often the case with people with HPA axis dysfunction, my marriage and friendships became about as dysfunctional as my HPA axis. Often I wasn't able to participate in activities with friends or with my wife and daughter. They didn't understand what I was dealing with. Christian friends and family sometimes avoided me, talked about me derogatorily, or even insulted me. Later came bankruptcy, divorce, and nearly complete wreckage of my life.

My Journey into an Investigative Study

Several years later my health improved, primarily due to Chinese medicine and a strict diet. But by that time I no longer believed in God. Because of my suffering, I was perplexed as to why God would allow so much evil and suffering in the world. Why no apparent intervention? Why all the unanswered prayers? If God is powerful enough and knowledgeable enough to make anything happen, and good enough to want only good things to happen, then why do bad things happen? Why are there so many cruel and violent people in the world? Why diseases, birth defects, storms, earthquakes, animal attacks, etc.? With all the apparently pointless or meaningless evil and suffering in the world, if God existed, he could not be perfectly loving and good. Such a God would not sit on his hands and watch innocent little children suffer intensely without any response to their cries.

Discussing such things with friends and acquaintances led me to read of the many perplexing and distressing challenges made against Christianity. I hadn't realized that there were so many. One such challenge was presented by agnostic Bible scholar Bart D. Ehrman in his book *Misquoting Jesus*.[3] According to Ehrman, the New Testament manuscripts contain a few hundred thousand alterations made by scribes. Most are said to be unintentional copy errors, while a few are said to be *intentional* changes. In some instances, the original meaning is changed. I reacted by thinking that the church had tampered with the Bible, which added to my doubt about its credibility and authority.

Another challenge to Christianity came by way of the claim that some of the Bible teachings about Jesus are not historical, but actually mythical conceptions adapted from the "mystery religions" of Mediterranean polytheism to give Jesus divine status. According to the authors Timothy Freke and Peter Gandy of *The Jesus Mysteries* and *The Laughing Jesus*, many of the New Testament teachings about Christ are prefigured by the conceptual myths of a dying and resurrecting god-man found in Egypt (Osiris), Alexandria (Sarapis), Greece (Dionysus), Asia Minor (Attis), Syria (Adonis), and Persia (Mithras).[4]

Perhaps the most talked about of these god-men is Persia's Mithras, of whom it is said was a great teacher, was born of a virgin in a cave on December 25, had twelve disciples, promised his followers immortality, performed miracles, initiated a communion-like meal, was hailed as the way, the truth, and the life, sacrificed himself for world peace, and was buried in a tomb and resurrected three days later.[5] The inference drawn by many about this is that nearly all of the history attributed to Jesus in the New Testament is borrowed pre-Christian myth. By the time that I learned about this, I had little belief in the credibility of the Bible.

The thing that finally extinguished it, though, was my conclusion drawn from studying the theory of evolution. Years before, my Christian friends had assured me that Darwinism could easily be explained away as flawed, and/or it was the product of atheist scientists under the influence of the devil. So I had believed Genesis taught that the universe and all of Earth's life forms came into existence instantaneously during six sequential twenty-four-hour days of creation roughly six thousand to twenty thousand years ago,[6] and that all disease and death are the results of original human sin.[7]

But on the way to becoming a nonbeliever, I took a *real* look at Darwinism (neo-Darwinism) and the mainstream cosmological and geological estimates for the age of the universe and Earth. The evidentiary data was incontrovertible. The universe is roughly thirteen to fourteen billion years old; Earth is about 4.55 billion years old,[8] and life has existed on Earth for the past 3.8 billion years.[9] Geologists, including most Christian geologists, are overwhelmingly in agreement that about 4.55 billion years is the most acceptable age of planet Earth.[10] Today the case for common descent is very strong as there are numerous integrated lines of confirming evidence from a wide range of scientific disciplines (albeit with gaps in understanding of the mechanisms of evolution).[11] Further, the fossil record unmistakably shows that animal disease and death occurred for millions of years before Adam could have sinned[12] (refuting the claim of some creationists that animal death occurred as a result of Adam's fall into sin).

Not only did science seem to discredit the Bible, but it also eliminated the need for a creator. As stated in the textbook *Evolutionary Biology*, "By coupling undirected, purposeless variation to the blind, uncaring process of natural selection, Darwin made theological or spiritual explanations of life processes superfluous."[13] Needless to say, the Genesis creation narrative that I had believed appeared refuted, and the world no longer seemed to reflect the handiwork of God.

Another problem for Christianity came by way of new theories that seemed to explain away the claim that Jesus was resurrected-translated. A central tenet that would authenticate Jesus' divinity is the event in which his crucified body, which had been dead for nearly forty hours, was miraculously transformed into an immortally-living supernatural body.[14] Refuting explanations include that Jesus was never crucified, that Jesus didn't die from the crucifixion, or that Jesus never survived the crucifixion. There is even a claim that Jesus' bones had been found. The challenge to Jesus' resurrection-translation added fuel to my doubt about God's existence.

Another problem was the Old Testament portrayal of God as immoral (by Jesus' standard) for commanding humans and angels to exterminate large numbers of people, including innocent children and livestock (or causing natural events to kill multitudes). Examples include: God's command to kill the Canaanites, the Amalekites, and other peoples (Deut. 20:16-18); God's killing all of the first-born children in Egypt (Ex. 11); and the killing of many thousands in a flood (Gen. 7:11-12, 17-23).

Another apparent portrayal of a cruel and unloving God was in the idea that God consigns a multitude of people to everlasting punishment in hell, even if the only sin committed is unbelief in a gospel story that had never been heard. This seemed inconsistent with a good and just God. The Bible says God is caring enough and powerful enough to make knowledge of the gospel accessible to all, yet it seemed that he hadn't made it accessible to the billions of people who died without ever learning of it. It didn't seem fair that people should suffer the eternal punishment due to the misfortune of being born in the wrong place and time. Doesn't God love and care for even his enemies? I asked. Doesn't he want everyone to be saved? Then why, I wondered, would God *not* make sure that every nation and tribe is informed of his gospel?

After reading material on these challenges (and several others), it seemed to me that it was unreasonable to continue to believe in the God of the Bible. There appeared to be too many theological inconsistencies, too many reasons to distrust the Bible, too few miracles, and too little evidence of the existence of God. I gave up any trust in the truth of Christianity.

Other religions also seemed unbelievable, as there was less evidence claimed by their adherents to substantiate them. At least a viable argument could be made for many of the historical claims of the Old Testament and the claims of Jesus Christ and his apostles. But this was not so for Hinduism, Mahayana Buddhism, religious Taoism (Daoism), Jainism, Baha'i, Sikhism, Zoroastrianism, Wicca, or Islam. For example, one of the problems in Islam is that none of the claimed fulfillments of the prophecies in the Quran[15] can be legitimately verified. All in all, I didn't find any evidence in history or prophecy or even in my personal experience on which to place my faith in non-Christian religions. Therefore, an atheist-Darwinist theory of the universe and humankind seemed most probable.

While an atheist universe seemed likely, I was open to the possibility of deism. Deism is the belief that the universe was created by an incredibly powerful god who has no involvement in what occurs on the planet. His noninvolvement is because he no longer exists, he lacks knowledge of our existence, he is unable to interact with us, or he does not care about us. Deists typically do not believe in the inspiration of the Bible or other kinds of supernatural occurrences (except for the creation of the universe), although deists are divided on whether there is an afterlife or a soul that survives the death of the body. Some deists believe in a resurrection, while others believe in reincarnation, and still others believe at death we cease to exist.

Even so, there wasn't any evidence on which I could place my faith in deism. More probably, I thought, there are no gods, and we are an accident of nature and the "uncaring process of natural selection." So I let go of the belief that God or deities exist. I had become an atheist[16] again.

1.2 Atheism Never Promised Me a Rose Garden

According to atheism the entire universe is on course toward the end of its existence. Galaxies are moving farther and farther apart. The universe's energy is being used up. Eventually, all stars will burn out. All matter will collapse into dead stars and black holes. Whatever will be left of galaxies, stars, and planets will be without heat or light, drifting ever farther into absolute blackness. Obviously, every form of life anywhere in the universe will inevitably cease to exist.

Earth itself has a maximum of roughly five billion years left of habitability. The eventual death of the sun will ensure that every trace of life on the planet will one day expire. Anytime between now and then, any one of several cataclysmic events is likely to occur that could cause the extinction of humankind. Examples include large-scale volcanism, a supervolcanic eruption, an asteroid strike, a disease pandemic, a scientific accident, global nuclear annihilation, or an extreme ice age leading to prolonged global drought.

Nonetheless, the atheistic fact of an eventual end of the human race actually should not matter much to the atheist, because each of us is destined for extinction. This life is all there is, so at death there is no longer any thought about any of it.

The same is the essential end result if reincarnation is true. In reincarnation, the ultimate end is Brahman, nirvana, or moksha, "a blowing out of the candle of self," which is the end of a person's individual, conscious self.

However, while the individual, conscious self ends with the a final reincarnated life achieving Brahman, nirvana, or moksha, actually, in reincarnation a person's individual, conscious self comes to an end at death. This is because knowledge and memories acquired in one life do not extend into a subsequent life. While a few people report having memories of past life experiences, some of which have been corroborated[17] (but which can easily be explained away[18]), they tell of only tiny fragments, and are thus insufficient for continuity of the individual, conscious self beyond death.[19] Thus, reincarnation offers no real immortality beyond death, which is tantamount to the atheist view that this life is all there is.

This points to the atheistic reality that everything we are—everything we experience, think, or feel—all comes to nothing. Every trace of human effort to build civilizations, cultivate arts, or develop technologies will eventually be erased. Every good deed, every good cause, all the work to preserve legacies and provide for future generations—all will avail nothing and cease to be, as if they had never been made, as if we never existed at all. There will be no creature existing to give any thought to any of it, just mindless debris drifting aimlessly in pitch-black space from eon to eon.

This was my worldview as an atheist. It loomed like a dark cloud over my life, draining everything I did of a sense of meaning, purpose, or value. Now, looking back, I believe that the fundamental reason why was because in atheism there is no immortal life and no loving and good God.

If there is no immortality and creator, conscious life itself is an unintended occurrence that will end in absolutely nothing. As such, conscious life *itself* is without ultimate meaning, purpose, or value. In other words, there is no meaning, purpose, or value *of the existence of human life*; one may find meaning *in* life, but this is not the same as there being a meaning *of* life.

Moreover, since all life experiences are an inherent part of life, they too are without ultimate meaning, purpose, or value; however, one can experience a feeling that they do. The atheist can avoid the thought of the reality that life's existence has no meaning by occupying the mind with things that invoke feelings that carry a *sense* of meaning, purpose, or value. The atheist can fill this sense by getting caught up in relationships, intellectual pursuits, or projects that improve the living conditions of others.

This seems to be the solution proposed by atheists like David Mills and John W. Loftus. In chapter 1 of Mills' book, *Atheist Universe*, he suggests occupying the mind with meaningful and satisfying pursuits, such as relationships, the arts, intellectual projects, scientific inquiry, hobbies, games, and entertainment. Engaging in such things can bring meaning to life, Mills says.[20]

It is true that some atheists can get enthralled in these things and avoid a sense that life itself is devoid of ultimate meaning. But whether there is lasting happiness and joy in such pursuits is contingent upon a person being in good health or having enough money, good looks, or good fortune. It is only a matter of time before we lack one or the other.

Life has its ups and downs. Some circumstances in life are often not in our control. There are accidents, illnesses, poor decisions, unfaithful spouses, addictions, and the thing that catches up with each of us—age. With old age are arthritis pain, disease, and organ failure. Happy days will be less happy, and one day the ride will be over. So for many atheists, creating happiness is not practical.

I was fortunate enough to have a fair ability to occupy my mind with meaningful and satisfying pursuits. But I still sensed life's meaninglessness and it put a damper on my happiness every time someone said anything that reminded me that I was an atheist. Reminders happened often while in conversation with family or friends, while watching television programs or movies, or while driving past a church. Even trying to make future plans was a reminder. The reminders kept bringing that dark cloud back. I was too much of a thinker. So the old "occupy the mind" method to happiness wasn't working for me.

Mills might suggest that I was creating a "self-fulfilling prophecy" by making myself unnecessarily unhappy with my belief in the "propaganda" that happiness is impossible without belief in God and immortality.[21] He might also suggest that I could be "highly optimistic" and truly happy if I would just employ the right psychology.

However, regarding creating a self-fulfilling prophecy, Mills seems to conflate the difference between the shallow, temporary happiness that atheism offers, and the deep, permanent happiness that a theism offers. The best that atheism can offer for a happy life is wrought by the mind trick that eventually, for most of us, is not practical. But a true, constant and permanent happiness can be had *despite* life's problems, which comes from believing in an immortal life with God. This is what Jesus meant when he said that people can be internally happy while feeling externally unhappy due to unfortunate circumstances (Matt. 5:4).

I think deep down inside I knew that true and permanent happiness would only result from a worldview that offers an extremely high degree of meaning and value. And the only worldview that can plug this much meaning and value into the life through thick and thin is the theistic worldview of an immortal life with God.

With regard to employing the right psychology, I knew very well the power of positive psychology from books and many hours of life-impact training that I had received in years past. I was trained to recognize when I had slipped into negative thoughts and shift from thinking like a victim to accounting for what I was creating in life without finding fault in others or myself (accountability). I was quite capable of keeping myself from depression and negative behavior. And on top of that, I pursued purposeful endeavors (i.e., service oriented work and positive relations with family and friends). But at the end of the day, there just wasn't anything to feel "highly optimistic" or truly happy about.

Mills' book doesn't make a case against the high degree of meaning and value that can be had by believers. I doubt that a good case could be made. Rather, Mills merely points out that he has "known scores of Christians who led very unfulfilling lives, praying endlessly for 'miracles' that never occurred or waiting pitifully for Jesus' oft-delayed second coming." I'm not sure what he means by "very unfulfilling," so I don't know how to respond to his comment. But my guess is that every serious Christian would admit to having a more fulfilled and happier life believing in God than they would in rejecting that belief.

This, I think, is because nontheist[22] worldviews simply do not have anything near this meaningful and valuable to offer. They cannot even come close. The conception of the existence of God and immortal life contains too much meaning and value for atheism or nontheism to compete.

Atheist John W. Loftus' suggestions for atheistic happiness in his book *Why I Became an Atheist*[23] were no more helpful to me than those of Mills.

Although in chapter 24 he poses an interesting question: If there is no God and no immortality, who is better off, the one who believes in the existence of God, or the one who does not believe? (p. 413). Loftus thinks the person free of religious belief is "better off."

It is unclear to me what he means by "better off." If he means happier, then, as a fellow atheist, I did not see why this should be plausible. How could the idea of our accidental existence which ends in absolutely nothing bring enough meaning and value to life's existence and activities to generate deep, permanent happiness despite disadvantages, hardships, and suffering? It *didn't* seem to me that it could.

1.3 Why I Began an Investigative Study

One day I met with an atheist turned Christian who challenged me to engage in an investigative study of evidence argued to support the truth of Christianity. At that time, my reasons for rejecting belief in God were more emotional than intellectual, as I hadn't studied the issues thoroughly, or with any rigor. So while I believed that Christianity had been debunked, I didn't feel that my opinion had been grounded in much knowledge. I wasn't confident as to which side of the debate the evidence and arguments were the weightiest. I began to wonder if the evidence for atheism was as strong as I had thought. Was there any valid evidence that the Christian God was real that I wasn't aware of? What about all of the challenges against Christianity that the Bible isn't trustworthy, or that science had discredited the Bible's claim of creation? I then wondered, who *really* had the better arguments? What did atheism's *best* attackers have to say? What did Christianity's *best* defenders have to say about all of the tough challenges?

I was living a life of rejection of belief in God because it was my opinion that a reasonable and objective examiner of the proposed evidence and arguments should conclude that they pointed to a greater probability that there almost certainly is no God. But I was realistic about the fact that my study had been quite limited. I had read the opinions of atheists who had seemed to have studied the issues with objectivity and depth. But, I thought, perhaps I had made too many assumptions. I also had read very little of any Christian defenses and discussions of the issues because I thought their opinions would be filled with bias and blind faith. So I decided I would apply myself to an investigative study, listening to both sides of the issues objectively and examining the evidence presented and arguments made.

It would take effort and time away from fun activities and entertainment. But, an investigative study of this kind was an intellectual pursuit that had appeal to me. Why not? After all, Mills suggested that atheists occupy the mind with meaningful and satisfying pursuits. To me, this certainly was one of them.

Besides, if humankind is really an accident of nature headed to annihilation, I thought, whether my life was less fun from spending a great deal of time doing a rigorous investigative study didn't matter, because eventually I'd cease to exist. On the other hand, if the universe is a theistic one, with individual immortality, then such an investigative study would prove useful regardless of my sacrifices or what my conclusions on the issues turned out to be. If God really did exist, and I ended up in hell, I would at least feel some satisfaction (so I thought) in knowing that I had *really* searched for the truth of human existence or of any God. And I would see my eternal lot as the result of having given faith a truly fair chance that, despite my best efforts, just didn't pan out. On the other hand, if I ended up in heaven, needless to say, the reward for doing a years-long investigative study would be incalculable. Thus, it seemed that I had nothing to lose. I decided that I'd rather come to the end of my life having a knowledgeable belief that I could live with—whether nonreligious or religious, whether trusting in the existence of God or believing we're all a result of purely natural processes.

1.4 Study Objectives

The journey would require study in the areas of evolutionary biology, geology, astronomy and cosmology (ancient and modern), ancient cosmography (Near Eastern and Native American), archaeology, theology, theodicy,[24] the Bible, biblical interpretation (exegesis[25]), and the history of the formation of the Bible, as well as the study of non-Christian religions. It required study of evidence proposed from each side—the fossil record, scientific experiments, data and theories, the geologic column, scientific dating methods, flood geology, archaeological discoveries, historical evidence, ancient documentary evidence (biblical and extrabiblical), and claimed evidence of supernatural occurrences.

Where my "fire" for such an undertaking came from, I'm not sure. Maybe it was partly my desire to justify my rejection of religious faith. Or maybe it was a desire to confirm that the Christian position wasn't reasonable. Or maybe it was my unshakable desire to know the truth behind humankind's existence. Or perhaps it was my inquisitive disposition combined with my skills in critical thinking, evidence assessment, argument construction, and research acquired while a paralegal.

I'd judge the weight of the arguments and counterarguments based on my application of reason and the persuasive power of the arguments. I'd judge the weight of evidence based on where I would see it leading and on a preponderance (more likely so than not so) of the evidence,[26] and I'd draw inferences to the best explanations.

I believe I was fair-minded about it for a few reasons. First, at different times in my life I had been fully committed to both Christianity and atheism. As a former Christian, I would give the Christian side a fair hearing, and as a formerly trained lay-evangelist, I understood Christian doctrines and had substantial Bible knowledge. As an atheist, aware of the evidentiary challenges against the existence of God, I would approach my study with the opinion that Christianity had been debunked. Second, my highest objective was my pursuit of discovering reality, which was of greater interest or worth to me than finding out which side won a debate. As such, I would follow the evidence to wherever it would lead me. Finally, I wasn't emotionally (or financially) invested in being an atheist, so if I were to find good scientific and theological reasons to reject it, I felt un-entangled to do so. I was in pursuit of truth, to whatever end it would lead. I was willing to give Christianity's best defenders fair opportunity to convince me, if they could, although I didn't expect that to happen. I more expected that I would write a book about the debunking of Christianity despite a fair and deep investigative study.

I made a list of all of the challenges. In section 1.1 I mentioned some of the major challenges to my faith, but the following is the full list:

a. The Bible is not trustworthy with regard to history or doctrine because: (1) it contains many copy alterations by scribes that, in some cases, change the original meaning; (2) much of what it talks about resulted from infiltration of legends and myths; and (3) the church picked only the gospels and epistles that would be part of the canon (Bible) that upheld its made-up legend of the deity of Jesus Christ.

b. Basic Christian tenets were copied from earlier mystery religions of polytheism, such as the god-man who is born of a virgin, dies, and is resurrected.

c. The gnostic gospels are just as valid as the gospels of the New Testament and they teach of a very different Jesus and salvation experience, so we cannot really know who Jesus was or how a person is saved.
d. Supernatural events do not occur, as is proven by scientific explanation.
e. Scientific theories discredit the Bible's claim of creation because: (1) cosmological models show that there was no need for a creator of the universe; (2) Darwinian theory proves that life on Earth came to be without the need of a creator; (3) scientific dating methods prove that the universe and Earth are vastly older than the roughly six thousand to twenty thousand years of age that some Christians claim the Bible teaches; and (4) genetic ancestry has now traced modern human lineage to a group of about two thousand people who migrated out of Africa approximately sixty thousand years ago, so modern humans could not have descended from Adam and Eve.
f. Darwinian theory shows that billions of animals have died during the past eons; therefore the Christian claim that all death is a consequence of the original sin of Adam is disproved.
g. A worldwide flood as depicted in Genesis 6–8 is impossible because all plant life would have become extinct, which would've put an end to any animal and human life, in addition to several other logistical issues that make the flood story impossible.
h. There is no historical evidence to back up the Exodus story of the Old Testament.
i. The holy wars depicted in the Old Testament in which there is the slaughter of innocent children is not consistent with God's perfectly loving and good disposition.
j. Church history is full of violence and oppression by the church, which reflects a more man-made institution than a God-led people.
k. The synoptic gospels[27] do not claim that Jesus Christ is God; therefore, teachings about his divinity in the rest of the New Testament are likely due to a later legendary conception about Christ's divinity that Jesus never taught.
l. Jesus Christ did not actually fulfill messianic prophecies of the Old Testament.

m. The evidence for Jesus' resurrection-translation is flimsy and easily explained away.
n. The Christian atonement is illogical, immoral, or incoherent, and therefore absurd.[28]
o. God's nonexistence is demonstrated on the basis of the existence of evil, which, if God exists, is either logically impossible or logically possible but highly unlikely. Additional dimensions of the challenge from evil include arguments by divine silence, the suffering of innocent animals, suffering in hell, and the teaching of consignment to hell of people who have died without an opportunity to learn of the gospel necessary to be saved (the soteriological problem of evil).

1.5 Study Results

To me, some of the challenges had strength enough to make Christianity work hard to defend itself, while others, not so much. I was surprised to find some of the challenges supported by weak argumentation, and, in some cases, haplessly so (i.e., challenges a, b, c, j, and k, listed previously).

Another reason for the weak argumentation is a lack of education in theology and biblical exegesis (see chapter 10.2). In all of the challenges listed, all of the discussions of the skeptics of Bible passages fell short of having an adequate understanding of how to study the Bible or apply a legitimate interpretation methodology. This is especially the case regarding the book of Genesis, the Apostle Paul's epistles (letters), and the Bible's teachings on hell and salvation.

A third reason for weak spots in many of the challenges is a failure in reasoning or logic in the arguments (fallacious arguing). I found this to be particularly prevalent with regard to the challenge that God's nonexistence is demonstrated on the basis of the existence of evil.

Still, despite the weaknesses, some of the challenges were strong enough to make Christian defenses difficult. Among these were the ones that challenged claims of the supernatural (d), which included the claim of Jesus' resurrection-translation (m), the credibility of Genesis (e), and the existence of God in light of the existence of evil—the problem of evil (o). Regarding to the problem of evil, I found shortcomings in every Christian explanation (discussed in the next chapter) for why a good God would allow evil and suffering.

However, after analyzing the evidence and arguments on each side of the challenges over a span of many years, one by one the greater weight of persuasive power was found to fall to a greater probability of the credibility of the Bible and the existence of God. During the years of study, the atheist view seemed less likely. Then, later on, I was agnostic for a long time, still uncertain as to which side of the debate the evidence was pointing, but having a little inclination to believe in God. I eventually came to have the opinion of a high probability of God's existence. Then one day I made up my mind to choose faith in God's existence and will for me, and to live my life according to my faith.

Atheists might think me a pushover. But a few things are worth noting. First, I didn't let metaphysical naturalism or scientism[29] dictate my investigative study. Scientism holds a dogmatic commitment to a materialistic philosophy that dismisses the *possibility* of supernatural occurrence, a priori, because science cannot detect the supernatural, and whatever is undetectable by science does not exist. But scientism is invalid because it assumes that science can detect anything that exists, which is not necessarily true. Therefore, even though most atheists won't bother, an investigation into the claims of the supernatural is warranted.

Perhaps a reason for a priori dismissal of the supernatural is because it is often thought that such claims cannot be investigated by any historical or scientific methodology. However, the reality is that, to at least a small extent, they actually can. I touch on this in chapter 3.3 (and its notes) and in chapter 5.4.

Although to be sure, the evidence collected by scientists and investigators is not of the sort that would provide anything close to undeniable proof. But I found enough[30] to persuade me that, more likely than not, events do occur that defy known natural law, although the numbers and frequency are relatively low. I realize that while such events are suggestive of life beyond this terrestrial dimension, and thus supportive of the truth of Christianity, many of them could just as easily point to deism, or a non-Christian religion. But, unlike non-Christian religions, they make up only one part of a body of evidence and arguments for God's existence, including:

a. The proposition broadly agreed upon by physicists and cosmologists, and also by some scientists in other disciplines, that there is a nearly zero chance that a multitude of certain physical conditions and events necessary for human life to exist in the universe would all occur with just the right timing in accord with known natural laws because: (a) it is believed that out of a vast possible number of values of the universal fundamental physical constants and qualities of the universe, there is an extremely narrow range of values (balanced on a razor's edge) that would make life anywhere in the universe possible, so the chance that the universe would have life-permitting values is extremely low, if not inconceivably low;[31] and (b) there are a large number of galactic,[32] solar, planetary,[33] and biological conditions and events of just the right kind and timing that would need to occur on a planet in order for life on it to possibly originate, or survive for any significant length of time;

b. Anecdotal reports with third party verification of supernatural occurrences involving veridical near-death experiences, out-of-body experiences, extrasensory perception experiences, sightings of ethereal beings (i.e., angels or ghosts) (see chapter 3.3), and prayers (see chapter 5.4);

c. A low probability that mammals and humans would result purely from atheistic-naturalistic evolution within a span of roughly 3.8 billion years;

d. The Kalam cosmological argument for a creator of the universe;

e. The historical-documentary evidence of the New Testament supportable by: (a) ancient extrabiblical documents that mention the historical person of Jesus and his death; (b) the death of Jesus confirmed by advanced medical knowledge and knowledge of a Roman crucifixion; (c) the eye-witness testimony of Jesus' disciples of his teachings, supernatural performances and supernaturally-empowered post-resurrection body; (d) the eye-witness testimony of more than five hundred of the disciples' contemporaries who reportedly all saw Jesus' supernaturally-empowered post-resurrection body at the same time (1 Cor. 15:6), and (e) archaeologically discovered artifacts;

f. The ontological argument for a maximally great being;

g. Moral argument (axiological argument) for an ultimate, personally-embodied Good, and;

h. Apologist William Lane Craig's noölogical argument for an ultimate mind.[34]

Another reason why atheists shouldn't think me a pushover is because, unlike the vast majority of atheists, for my study I acquired considerable knowledge of the Bible, biblical exegesis, and the science behind interpretation (hermeneutics), studying the methodologies. Biblical exegesis is critical interpretation of a Bible text by systematic processes of analyses, including: literary, cultural-historical, and theological analyses (very briefly discussed in chapter 10.2). "Inspiration does not eliminate the need for the hard work of interpretation."[35] During a span of many years I studied and compared the views on creation, the Trinity, hell, salvation, the nature of Christ, et cetera, and the inerrancy and inspiration of Scripture (the subjects of inspiration and inerrancy are very briefly discussed in chapter 11.7).

So while it might seem that I was an atheist pushover, easily persuaded by arguments for Christianity, bear in mind that the vast majority of attempts by opponents of Christianity to enlighten me on what the Bible teaches appeared nothing short of pathetic. A few such attempts are found in some of the works of Michael Martin, David Mills, Richard Dawkins, Peter Singer, Christopher Hitchens, and Sam Harris. In fact, I would venture to say that one of the biggest obstacles to belief in God's existence is a lack of education in the Bible, biblical exegesis, and the inspiration and inerrancy of Scripture.

But perhaps the single greatest obstacle to belief is the challenge that God's nonexistence is demonstrated by the existence of evil (o). For many, it is so very difficult to believe that a God who abhors evil, and who is powerful enough to keep it from happening, keeps silent while many are victims of devastating illness, violence, pain and suffering. We seem to be alone against life's predators, or the pitiless and indifferent forces of nature. Even Christians struggling with evil and suffering can feel as though there is no God. The next chapter introduces my investigative study of this challenge, and my discovery of an explanation for why God would allow all of the kinds of evil and suffering that occur.

NOTES to Chapter 1

1. I maintain a broad definition of a Christian as one who by faith is in a positive relationship with God and holds to the tenets of the Trinitarian God who created the cosmos and living beings, authority of Scripture, and God's salvation for an eternally lasting afterlife in communion with God and his heavenly community that is made possible by the gracious ministries of Jesus Christ and the Holy Spirit.

2. A paraphrase of Phil. 4:13.

3. Bart D. Ehrman, *Misquoting Jesus: The Story Behind Who Changed the Bible and Why* (San Francisco: HarperSanFrancisco, 2005). Ehrman earned his M.Div. and Ph.D. from Princeton Theological Seminary, where he studied under Bruce Metzger. He has written and edited over twenty-five books, including: *God's Problem*; *Jesus Interrupted*; *Forged*; and *How Jesus Became God*. He is the James A. Gray Distinguished Professor of Religious Studies at the University of North Carolina at Chapel Hill.

4. Timothy Freke and Peter Gandy, *The Jesus Mysteries: Was the "Original Jesus" a Pagan God?* (New York: Three Rivers Press, 1999), 109; *The Laughing Jesus: Religious Lies and Gnostic Wisdom* (New York: Three Rivers Press, 2005), 55–56.

5. See www.tektonics.org/copycat.mithra.php. Assessed on April 20, 2014.

6. This view of creation is commonly referred to as young earth creationism (YEC). Theologians of this view believe Gen. 1:1–2:3 relays a divinely revealed phenomenological and literal account of the formation of all physical entities inside of six sequential twenty-four-hour days. They also believe the author of Gen. 5 and 11 recorded complete (or nearly complete) chronologies that would enable the reader to calculate the number of years between the time of Adam and Christ and so determine that the number of years since Adam is roughly six thousand to twenty thousand.

7. The teaching that all disease and death are the result of sin comes from the Augustinian theodicy that seeks to explain why a good God would permit us to suffer from disease and death. The Augustinian theodicy is discussed in chapter 2.3.

8. Some of the works read that discuss the age of the universe and Earth include: Alan L. Titus and Mark A. Loewen, *At the Top of the Grand Staircase: The Late Cretaceous of Southern Utah* (Bloomington, IN: Indiana University Press, 2013; Mikael Fortelius, John Kappelmann, Sevket Sen, and Raymond L. Bernor, eds. *Geology and Paleontology of the Miocene Sinap Formation, Turkey* (New York: Columbia University Press, 2003); Kenneth Oakley, *Frameworks for Dating Fossil Man* (Piscataway, NJ: AldineTransaction, second paperback printing 2009); Davis A. Young and Ralph F. Stearley, *The Bible, Rocks and Time: Geological Evidence for the Age of the Earth* (Downers Grove, IL: InterVarsity Press, 2008); Ken Ham, *The Lie: Evolution* (Green Forest, AR: Master Books, revised ed. 2012); John F. Ashton, *Evolution Impossible: Twelve Reasons Why Evolution Cannot Explain the Origin of Life on Earth* (Green Forest, AR: Master Books, 2012); Don DeYoung, *Thousands . . . Not Billions* (Green Forest, AR: Master Books, revised ed. 2005).

9. Neil A. Campbell, *Biology*, third ed. (Redwood City, CA: The Benjamin/Cummings Publishing Company, Inc., 1993), 506. Sometime between 3.5 and 4.1 billion years ago.

10. Davis A. Young and Ralph F. Stearley, *The Bible, Rocks and Time: Geological Evidence for the Age of the Earth* (Downers Grove, IL: InterVarsity Press, 2008), 156. Using phylogeny, mathematics, and other computations, scientists since 1859 have never been able to find a single dinosaur fossil that is as young as a human fossil. Many tens of thousands of repeated cross testings of carbon-14 dates and radiometric dates confirm their validity and accuracy. Age estimates have been cross-tested (often

in rival labs) by using different isotope pairs, and the results of different techniques continually confirm each other within approximately 1–2% chance of error, which is highly accurate [http://www.oldearth.org/radiometricdating.htm].

11. Professor of geology Keith B. Miller succinctly summarizes evidence for common descent in "An Evolving Creation: Oxymoron or Fruitful Insight?", *Perspectives on an Evolving Creation*, ed. Keith B. Miller (Grand Rapids, MI: William B. Eerdman's Publishing Company, 2003), 10–14. The evidence includes: (a) a consistent sequence of fossil species in the geologic record on a worldwide basis; (b) "the order of appearance of higher taxa in the geologic record" that is "broadly consistent with the evolutionary sequence inferred from the anatomical data and from DNA;" (c) transitional anatomical features common in the fossil record that are considered to be characteristic of different groups (genera, orders, classes, etc.); (d) "the geographic distribution of fossil species" that is considered to be "consistent with common descent and with independent geological reconstructions of the Earth's changing geography over time. That is, common descent makes sense of the locations in which specific fossil (and living) species are found;" and (e) "the fossil record of changing species over time yields a comprehensive picture of ecological and environmental change" such that "species changes do not occur randomly but rather are part of the evolution of communities and entire ecosystems" (e.g., "predators evolve with their prey, parasites evolve with their hosts, herbivores evolve with the plant communities, and so forth"). For the relationship between species evolution and the evolution of their physical and biological environments, Miller references: Anna K. Behrensmeyer et al., eds., *Terrestrial Ecosystems through Time* (Chicago: University of Chicago Press, 1992). For "the ways in which various ecological relationships (predator/prey, plant/herbivore, etc.) have impacted the evolution of individual species and biological communities," Miller references: Geerat J. Vermeij, *Evolution and Escalation: An Ecological History of Life* (Princeton, NJ: Princeton University Press, 1987). Even so, a gradualist view of the fossil record must hurdle the evidence in the fossil record of a substantial degree of stasis (long periods of no fundamental change of species), and sudden appearances of species, brought to light by biologist Stephen Jay Gould and others [Stephen Jay Gould, "The Episodic Nature of Evolutionary Change," *The Panda's Thumb* (New York: W. W. Norton & Co., 1980), 181-182].

12. Davis A. Young and Ralph F. Stearley, *The Bible, Rocks and Time*, 243–287; Paul Copan, *That's Just Your Interpretation: Responding to Skeptics Who Challenge Your Faith* (Grand Rapids, MI: BakerBooks, 2001), 150. Copan received his B.A. in biblical studies from Columbia International University (Columbia, SC), his MDiv from Trinity International University (Deerfield, IL), and his PhD in philosophy, with emphasis on philosophy of religion, at Marquette University (Milwaukee, WI). He is the Pledger Family Chair of Philosophy and Ethics at Palm Beach Atlantic University in West Palm Beach, FL. He is author and editor of many books, including: *Did God Really Command Genocide?: Coming to Terms with the Justice of God* (with Matt Flannagan); *Is God a Moral Monster?: Making Sense of the Old Testament God*; *An Introduction to Biblical Ethics: Walking in the Way of Wisdom* (with Robertson McQuilkin); *Passionate Conviction: Contemporary Discourses on Christian Apologetics* (with William Lane Craig); *Creation Out of Nothing: A*

Biblical, Philosophical, and Scientific Exploration (with William Lane Craig); *The Gospel in the Marketplace of Ideas: Paul's Mars Hill Experience for Our Pluralistic World* (with Kenneth D. Litwak); and *When God Goes to Starbucks: A Guide to Everyday Apologetics*.

13. Douglas Futuyma, *Evolutionary Biology* (Sunderland, MA: Sinauer, 1986).

14. Some believe the Bible teaches that Jesus' mutilated body was simply healed and made alive again; however, Scripture is clear that the substance of Jesus' body was *radically* transformed. It could pass through solid walls (Luke 24:36–37; John 20:26), dematerialize and rematerialize (Luke 24:31), fly through the air (Mark 16:19; Luke 24:51; Acts 1:9-11), and exist eternally (1 Cor. 15:42, 44–47, 50, 53). It was not because of his divine nature, or interventional miracles by the Holy Spirit, that he did these things, but rather because his natural body had been transformed into a supernatural body, as the prime example of the transformation at the end of the world (1 Cor. 15:20, 23; 1 Thess. 4:13–17). This is why I refer to Jesus' resurrection as his "resurrection-translation." It is not merely a dead body brought back to life, but a radically transformed body that is supernatural and immortal, but which retains its former resemblance. The resurrection-translation at the end of the world is of both the dead and the living (1 Thess. 4:16–17) and the saved and the unsaved (Dan. 12:2; John 5:28–29; Acts 24:14); however, it can be reasonably inferred that the celestial body of the unsaved, while supernaturally powerful, will suffer limits on that power as a result of being banished to hell.

15. Such as those of: 4:120; 16:9; 17:105; 25:54; 30:42; 41:21; 42:30; 51:8; 55:20–21; 81:4–11.

16. For those familiar with Richard Dawkins' belief scale (levels 1–7), I was a 6, a "De facto atheist." I felt I could not know for certain, but I thought God's existence to be very improbable, and I lived my life according to the opinion that God didn't exist [Richard Dawkins, *The God Delusion* (New York: Houghton Mifflin Company, 2006), 50–51].

17. In the early 1980s, Ian Stevenson, a professor of psychiatry, found "the record of an actual person whose life corresponded with the child's memory" of a past life [David Chamberlain, *The Mind of Your Newborn Baby*, third ed. (Berkeley, CA: North Atlantic Books, 1998), 189].

18. There are several ways that a person could obtain "past life" information without reincarnation. One is from historical records or from a person with knowledge of historical events. Another way of receiving "past life" information could possibly occur by retrocognition (also called postcognition), an extrasensory perception (ESP) ability (that appears to be significantly more pronounced in some people) by which an experience of a person in the past is known. Hundreds of well-controlled experiments support the existence of ESP, making ESP a far more plausible explanation than reincarnation. (The subject of ESP as a biblically supportable God-created ability to fulfill his plans in the afterlife is discussed in chapter 3.3). An alternate-but-related possibility is that evil angels and/or departed souls telepathically cause one to experience another person's life experience as if he or she were there (examples of ESP ability of this kind are in chapter 3.3).

19. Even if any sense of longevity could be experienced in a string of "past life memories," ultimately it would cease to exist in Brahman, nirvana, or moksha, and thus reincarnation does not hold any promise of immortality of the individual conscious self.

20. David Mills, *Atheist Universe: The Thinking Person's Answer to Christian Fundamentalism* (Berkeley, CA: Ulysses Press, 2006), 32–33, 39.

21. Ibid., 40.

22. Nontheists reject belief in God, but they can be religious (e.g., Hindu), as well as nonreligious (e.g., the secular atheist who discounts existence of any deities or the supernatural).

23. John W. Loftus, *Why I Became an Atheist: A Former Preacher Rejects Christianity* (Amherst, NY: Prometheus Books, 2008). Loftus received his MA and MDiv degrees from Great Lakes Christian College and his ThM degree from Trinity Evangelical Divinity School. Loftus was a conservative Christian apologist who, after finding Christian apologetic defenses unpersuasive, eventually embraced atheism.

24. A theodicy is an explanation of the reason why God is justified in permitting evil and suffering to occur.

25. Biblical exegesis is critical interpretation of a Bible text by processes of analyses, including: literary analysis, cultural-historical analysis, and theological analysis, and is briefly discussed in chapter 10.2.

26. This is a reasonable standard of persuasion reflective of objective consideration of proposed evidence and arguments sufficient for rational belief in God (or atheism). To insist on a standard of proof as high as "clear and convincing" (75–90 percent likely so), or "beyond any reasonable doubt" (90–99 percent likely so), implies bias, and/or unawareness of the Christian philosophy of the necessity of a divine hiddenness that arguably requires God to abstain from preventing a substantial amount of evil and suffering in order to mitigate human awareness of God's existence and his will to reward or punish necessary to bring about a greater good (discussed in this book).

27. The synoptic gospels are the earliest written gospels: Mark, Matthew, and Luke. They include many of the same stories in similar wording, and they read quite differently from the gospel of John.

28. Appendix D discusses the logic, morality, and coherence of the atonement of Christ.

29. Adherents of metaphysical naturalism (belief that the natural sciences reveal all of the elements and principles that exist) and scientism (a sense of which holds that truth is discovered by science alone) tend to hold a dogmatic commitment to a materialistic philosophy that dismisses non-materialist or non-naturalist possibilities, a priori, leaving only naturalistic explanations as real possibilities, such as naturally occurring hallucination, psychopathology, deception, overactive imagination, or false positives of cameras and videos made by light reflections, lens flares, double exposure, or shadows from natural light sources.

30. The amount of evidence of the supernatural that I collected far exceeds that which is discussed and referenced in chapters 3.3 and 5.4.

31. To name only six of many examples, consider: (a) if the cosmological constant that drives the expansion rate of the universe had been different in value by as little as one part in 10^{120}, the universe would have either quickly collapsed back on itself or expanded too rapidly for life-sustaining stars to form, which in either case would make life impossible; (b) if the atomic weak force were altered by as little as one in 10^{100}, the universe would not have sustained life; (c) if the gravitational constant that determines the force of gravity varied by just one in 10^{60}, life-sustaining stars like our sun could not exist; (d) if the strong nuclear force that binds protons and neutrons together in an atom had been stronger or weaker by as little as 5 percent, life would be impossible; (e) if the electromagnetic force were slightly stronger or weaker, several resulting factors would make life impossible; (f) if the neutron were not about 1.001 times the mass of the proton, all protons would have decayed into neutrons or all neutrons would have decayed into protons, making life impossible. [Robin Collins, "A Scientific Argument for the Existence of God: The Fine-Tuning Design Argument," *Reason for the Hope Within*, ed. Michael J. Murray (Grand Rapids, MI: Wm. B. Eerdmans Publishing Co., 1999), 47–75; William Lane Craig in *God and Evil: The Case for God in a World Filled with Pain*, eds. Chad Meister and James K. Dew, Jr. (Downers Grove, IL: InterVarsity Press, 2013), 293–294; https://en.wikipedia.org/wiki/Fine-tuned_Universe, assessed on September 12, 2015; see also Paul Davies, *The Accidental Universe* (Cambridge: Cambridge University Press, 1982), 90–91; *Superforce: The Search for a Grand Unified Theory of Nature* (New York: Simon and Schuster, 1984), 242.] There are three viable possibilities for why the universe is the way it is: (1) physical necessity, (2) chance, or (3) creation by an intelligent and powerful being. The first possibility can be ruled out because there is no evidence or reason to suggest that the constants and qualities of the universe are determined by the laws of nature which would make the fine-tuning for life of physical necessity. "In fact, string theory predicts that there are 10^{500} different possible universes compatible with nature's laws" [William Lane Craig in *God and Evil*, 294]. Regarding the second possibility (chance), the probability that the universe would be life-sustaining is, as Craig says, "so ridiculously remote as to put the fine-tuning well beyond the reach of chance." To try to increase the probability, some scientists have speculated that if there are a vast number of universes (multiverse), the chance that one could sustain life would be substantially increased. Hypotheses for this invoke either a vacuum fluctuation model or an oscillating big bang model. However, there is no evidence of the existence of any other universe, and none of the proposed models adequately explain how the multiverse originated. Given the unlikelihood of physical necessity, and the implausibility of chance, and taking into consideration a cumulative case for the existence of God from other forms of evidence and arguments, it is more plausible that the universe was designed and created by a phenomenally intelligent and powerful being interested in creating life.

32. It is estimated that the universe contains one hundred billion galaxies. The main types are: elliptical, spiral, and irregular. Spiral galaxies are the only type capable of supporting human life. Approximately 65 percent of the galaxies closest to the Milky Way galaxy are spiral galaxies, but spiral galaxies are thought to make up only about 20 percent of the galaxies in the universe. That's only 20 percent of all galaxies, or twenty billion galaxies, that are capable of having a planet on which life could

be possible. The chance that a spiral galaxy would contain such a planet is greatly lowered by virtue of the fact that there are very few places within a spiral galaxy in which conditions on a planet would not be too harsh for life to either originate or survive for any significant length of time.

33. A planet capable of originating and sustaining human life would need to contain at least one hundred planetary conditions (per astrophysicist Hugh Ross) with just the right timing sustained for several billion years, all of which are continually in jeopardy from various kinds of dangers that could increase the rate of species extinction by a few percentage points to 100 percent (extinguishing all life on the planet before humans could appear). A few of the more well-known planetary conditions are: (1) whether a planet is located in the narrow habitable region of a spiral galaxy; (2) a home star around which to orbit that has the right temperature and mass; (3) a planetary magnetic field strong enough to deflect the sun's radiation; (4) an orbital path that is neither too close nor too far from the orbital star; (5) an orbiting moon large enough to stabilize the tilt of the planet's axis and the movements of its ocean tides; (6) an oxygen rich atmosphere; (7) liquid water; and (8) large continental land masses.

34. Discussed in William Lane Craig, ed., *Philosophy of Religion: A Reader and Guide* (Edinburgh, UK: Edinburgh University Press, 2002).

35. Mark L. Strauss, "The Inspiration of the Bible," *The Baker Illustrated Bible Handbook*, eds. J. Daniel Hays and J. Scott Duvall (Grand Rapids, MI: BakerBooks, 2011), 995–1005.

2
My Discovery of an Integrated Theodicy

There are two sides to the problem of evil, like the two sides of a coin. One side is the claimed existence of God who is so good, so powerful and knowledgeable that he could, and arguably would, ensure that little or no evil and suffering occurs. The other side is the existence of a vast amount of evil and suffering, some of which is intense and seemingly senseless, which appears to fly in the face of the claim that God exists.

The amount and intensity of all of the barbarism, cruelty, and horrors throughout human history are staggering. It is estimated that approximately three thousand wars have taken place in human history. If the bodies of all war fatalities could be placed side by side at the equator, the line of bodies would circle the planet several times. The bodies from all of the Chinese wars alone, lying side by side, would encircle the equator approximately one and a half times. The number of fatalities of World War II is roughly the same.

The violence and cruelty seem to be beyond comprehension. People pummeled, stabbed, drowned, starved, hacked up, shot up, burned up, or blown up. During World War II in Auschwitz there were children thrown alive into a blazing furnace, and the children's screams were heard throughout the camp. In Cambodia there were children maimed and killed from stepping on landmines. Many war survivors have been disfigured, dismembered, and disabled and are suffering from diseases for which there is no cure.

The brutality of human evil is sickening. Examples include eyes being cut out, bones broken, flaying of skin, boiling in oil, and being dragged over sharp rocks. In medieval times many terrible devices were used to inflict pain, suffering, and horror. *The Brothers Karamazov* by Fyodor Dostoyevsky tells of Turks in Bulgaria who murdered babies for amusement by tossing them up in the air and catching them on the points of their bayonets before their mothers' eyes. There are terrorist killings, kidnappings, rapes of elderly women, rapes of little children, molestations, and gang rapes of boys with baseball bats. The almost unimaginable and senseless cruelty makes it difficult to picture God allowing it.

While finishing my writing of this chapter, several hundred people were horrifically killed by Islamic State militants in the town of Abu Hamam, in Syria's eastern Deir al-Zour province. After three days of fighting, the militants rounded up the survivors. Men and boys older than fifteen were either shot, crucified, or beheaded. Scores of bound captives were lined up on a road and decapitated, one at a time. Executioners taunted the ones not yet killed by "swinging severed heads in front of their faces and telling them, 'It's your turn next.'"[1]

In 1986 the heinousness of human conduct was brought home to me in a powerful way by an incident that happened in a medical facility where I worked as a hospital corpsman in the US Navy. One morning I arrived on an inpatient ward and found a Navy buddy at the nurses' station doubled over as if having a lot of pain in his gut. I asked him what was wrong and he told me that a corpsman had just been caught in the act of raping a quadriplegic patient and taken away by authorities. It was particularly shocking because hospital corpsmen are trained concerning their sacred responsibility to the trust and dignity of the patient.

Such moral evil is bad enough, but perhaps even more difficult to reconcile with the existence of God is the suffering brought on by natural causes. Homes are demolished, bodies are crushed, people drown, and lives are devastated— devastated from earthquakes, tsunamis, tornados, hurricanes, droughts, fires, floods, and mudslides. One example that is particularly difficult to reconcile with the existence of a loving God is that of a tornado that struck a Christian church during a Palm Sunday pageant, killing several small children.[2]

And then there are the billions who have suffered from disease. Every day malaria causes thousands to suffer and die. Many hundreds of millions of people every day are suffering from other serious and sometimes fatal diseases: influenza, diabetes, heart disease, cancer, AIDS, lupus, Parkinson's disease, Alzheimer's disease, emphysema, COPD, and on and on.

My oldest sister suffers from polychondritis, complicated by also having HPA axis dysfunction since the age of eighteen. Polychondritis is a condition of inflammation and deterioration of cartilage. It is painful, and, because it affects her respiratory tract, it causes respiratory issues. She has all but lost her ability to walk and moves about with a power chair. Recently, an ultrasound exam found two malignant cancer tumors on her left thyroid gland. She was not a candidate for chemotherapy, and had to undergo surgery to remove the gland.

Other natural causes of suffering are birth defects. There are people born with deformities: blindness, deafness, cleft palate, deformed limbs, no limbs, spina bifida, and anencephaly (absence of a major portion of the brain, skull, and scalp). One of my brothers-in-law was born with a heart defect. In 1995 he suddenly died from massive heart failure.

Each of us encounters pain and sorrow. As a Navy corpsman, I witnessed the suffering of many people from illness and injury. I worked in the areas of general surgery, the intensive cardiac unit, and oncology. There were many amputees. One was a victim of a motorcycle accident. He was impaled through his abdomen and out his back by his bike's handlebar. One of his legs was badly mangled and had to be amputated. There were many abdominal surgery patients with open cavities packed with gauze that had to be changed periodically. Some patients had bedsores (decubitus ulcers). I recall one patient with a bedsore that was large enough for me to insert almost my whole forearm as I was pulling out packed-in gauze that came out with very foul smelling necrotic tissue.

Suffering from accidents is also apparent to me in my career as an accident-injury paralegal. Accidents involving motor vehicles result in an array of different kinds of injuries, including broken bones, torn ligaments and tendons, injuries of the spine, burns, lacerations, and concussions. Some of the injuries cause severe and unrelenting pain that can last several weeks, or months, and often the victim incurs disability and financial hardship. Some involve mutilation, disfigurement, the loss of a limb, or loss of life.

Some accidents have struck me close to home. Years ago my sister was killed in a car crash, leaving behind her two small children and her badly injured husband. I, myself, suffered injuries in my neck and back in three car accidents.

Perhaps the most difficult to reconcile with the existence of a loving God is suffering that appears to be pointless. Sometimes positive changes result from some instances of calamity and suffering (e.g., a positive change in attitude or conduct). But some seem to have no productive value whatsoever. They often seem random and strike anyone without rhyme or reason and lead to no perceivable good, no purpose.

The injuries and suffering that appear pointless seem to defy a Christian defense. Philosopher William L. Rowe argues that this is the case for some instances of intense suffering from heinous conduct. An example he refers to is the incident of a five-year-old girl from Flint, Michigan, who was severely beaten, raped, and then strangled to death on January 1, 1986.[3] Another of Rowe's examples is of natural evil suffered by a fawn that gets trapped by a forest fire that resulted from a lightning strike to a dead tree. The fawn gets badly burned and lies in agony alone for several days and dies. There's nobody around to know it happened.[4]

Atheist John W. Loftus argues that God could have "prevented the fawn's apparently pointless suffering" by intervening to stop the fire from starting, or keeping the fawn from being burned, or quickly ending its life. "But since God didn't do any of these things, such a God doesn't exist, for he would not allow this fawn to suffer if it doesn't serve some outweighing attainable good, and not even a theist can come up with a good reason why such a fawn suffered."[5]

Many people feel that apparently pointless animal suffering presents a huge challenge to the existence of a loving and good God. During the 3.8 billion years before the arrival of humankind, countless animals suffered from savage predators and disease. Many simply cannot see any divine purpose behind all of the suffering of innocent animals.

Not only is it difficult to make sense of the suffering on an intellectual level, but it is also difficult on an emotional level. When it happens to us, we can be stunned, disoriented, scared, angry, or depressed. In the swell of intense emotion, any attempt to rationalize it goes out the window. Sometimes this seems to ruin a person, crushing his spirit and causing depression, a stress disorder, insanity, or suicide.

One example is that of a Christian couple who watched their three children slowly deteriorate mentally over the course of many years from a rare and untreatable genetic disorder. Their prayers were unanswered. The emotional strain was unbearable. The mother suffered a nervous breakdown and completely lost her faith in God. They became heavy drinkers and eventually divorced. Several years later the father lost his faith and was eventually fired from a previously successful job.[6] There are many other such instances where the victims, or the victims' loved ones, are emotionally, mentally, and spiritually wrecked.

I know firsthand how suffering can slowly drain a person of hope and faith as I reflect back on my illness of many years ago (mentioned briefly in chapter 1.1). I could not see any redeeming value in it, or any good purpose behind it. I felt permanently crushed, ruined, and nearly drained of hope, and, a few times, of the will to live. I saw no point in it. I saw no way for God to bring any good out of it. It just made no sense. Every area of my life was difficult. I powerlessly watched my wife suffer because of it. I lost friends and I gained a mountain of debt. I went through bankruptcy, divorce,[7] and a complete abandonment of faith in God.

We all know too well that the evil in the world is a demonstrable fact, whereas evidence of God's existence is comparatively slim. Thus, often the weight of evidence of evil casts doubt about God's existence. Some find it so strong that belief in God and Christ is rejected.

2.1 Defining the Problem of Evil

The Kinds of Evil. To understand the problem, it is important to comprehend what is meant by "evil." The definition of evil can be inclusive of: (a) morally wrong or bad conduct; (b) suffering and misery of sentient beings due to bad conduct (moral evil); and (c) suffering and misery of sentient beings due to conditions or events of nature that do not involve bad conduct (natural evil) (e.g., earthquakes, storms, drought, many kinds of diseases, and animal attacks without intentional provocation). I find it helpful in the discussion to use a term that is inclusive of morally wrong conduct, as well as moral and natural evils, which is "evil and suffering."

Dividing the Problem into Two. The problem of evil and suffering is often subdivided to enhance understanding and discussion. The two main subdivisions are the logical problem and the probabilistic (or evidentiary) problem.

The logical problem refers to an argument that it is a logical contradiction for both God and evil and suffering to exist, just as it is logically inconsistent to say that an immovable object can exist while subjected to an irresistible force. The two are logically incompatible. If one exists, the other does not. Christians claim that both God and evil and suffering exist, yet considering God's mindboggling power and perfectly loving and good disposition, it would seem to some people that God would never do anything that would result in the occurrence of evil and suffering. But it occurs, which is argued to be logically impossible. Logically, then, it is argued, God must not exist.

In the probabilistic problem it may be conceded that it is *possible* for God and evil and suffering to coexist *if* it is necessary to bring about a greater good. However, to many people this appears highly unlikely because of the vast amount, severity and senselessness of the suffering in the world, which supports a very strong case against the existence of a "greater good" that could only be made to exist by allowing it. It seems that with all of God's knowledge and power, he could find a way to bring about good things without a world of evil and suffering. This seems especially so in light of moral and natural evils that seem to be without purpose—that strike without any sign that a good God is in charge.

2.2 Facets of the Problem

A facet of the problem of evil and suffering is the alleged evil of divine silence (or divine hiddenness). Many nontheists take the silence from heaven as evidence of God's nonexistence. This is because God's silence in the world is seen as uncharacteristic of a disposition of perfect love and goodness. Friedrich Nietzsche expressed it this way:

> A god who is all-knowing and all-powerful and who does not even make sure his creatures understand his intentions—could that be a god of goodness? Who allows countless doubts and dubieties to persist, for thousands of years, as though the salvation of mankind were unaffected by them, and who on the other hand holds out frightful consequences if any mistake is made as to the nature of truth? Would he not be a cruel god if he possessed the truth and could behold mankind miserably tormenting itself over the truth?[8]

Simply stated, it is believed that divine silence is not consistent with a loving and good God. If God cares for us, why not give us what we would expect from a loving Father? Why not make himself far more evident so that many more would believe and be blessed? Why not show himself to us and speak directly to us? Many people are under the impression that if God wants people to believe in him, he has done a poor job of providing evidence of his existence needed for reasonable belief. As such, it is argued, there most likely is no God.

Another facet of the problem of evil and suffering is what is called the soteriological[9] problem of evil. It is related to the previous facet and is the argument for God's nonexistence based on the fact that there are many millions of spiritual believers in non-Christian faiths and philosophies that have died without having the opportunity to learn of the gospel necessary to be saved. Anyone unfortunate enough to have never heard the gospel (and so be saved by believing in it) is bound for hell. So, for example, a Buddhist, who is a paragon of compassion for the disadvantaged and who sincerely seeks truth, and who dies unaware of the Christian message, suffers eternal torment in hell with the likes of Hitler and child rapists. To many this does not seem consistent with a God who executes perfect justice and who desires all to be saved.[10] This apparent inconsistency reinforces the argument for the improbability of God's existence.

Another facet of the problem of evil and suffering is the problem of hell. It is argued that it is highly unlikely that God and hell could coexist. This is based on an argument that the conception of hell is inconsistent with God's character because its punishment does not fit the crime, and because it is too harsh and final of a punishment to be consistent with God's perfectly loving and good disposition. This is especially apparent if God casts a person into hell even if his only crime is nonbelief because he never had the fortune of learning of the gospel of Christ. Many see that God could not be both so loving and so cruel. How is this anger coming out of love? How can God be loving and angry with us at the same time?

2.3 Christian Responses and Their Shortcomings

Christian responses to the problem come to us in the form of explanations of the reasons why God is justified in permitting evil and suffering. These are called theodicies. There are several for us to consider. I found some to help in a Christian defense, while others of little use at all. In the following, I first identify the ones that I found to be the least helpful, and then I discuss the more promising ones, and their pros and cons.

Among the least promising are: the punishment theodicy, the counterpart theodicy, the Augustinian theodicy, the higher-order goods theodicy, and the

Griffin theodicy. In the punishment theodicy, the reason why we suffer is that God punishes sinners. The problem, though, is that while it is arguably just (fair) to mete out a fitting punishment for crimes committed by morally responsible creatures, it is unquestionably wrong to punish amoral creatures, such as animals, small children, and mentally incapacitated humans. Moreover, "good" people and Christians often suffer worse than bad people and non-Christians. Thus, if suffering is our earthly punishment, God is unjust in carrying it out, which creates a doctrinal contradiction. God cannot be perfectly loving and good while meting out unjust punishment. As such, this theodicy is actually of no use to those seeking a solution to the problem of evil.

In the counterpart theodicy, it is argued that good conduct cannot exist without the existence of evil conduct. Good and evil are like counterparts. Thus, God would be justified in permitting evil because good cannot exist unless evil does.

The problem, though, is that a traditional Christian doctrine teaches that good conduct *can* exist without the existence of evil conduct. According to the teaching, prior to the origin of evil conduct (before the sin of the angel Lucifer), only good conduct existed, yet its existence did not require the occurrence of evil. Moreover, this theodicy does not explain why God would permit innocent animals to suffer. Therefore, this theodicy does not solve the problem of evil.

In the Augustinian theodicy, the world was created idyllic, or hedonistic, without any discomfort, but because of angelic, and then human, fall into sin (bad exercise of free will), humans and animals began to suffer as a result of moral and natural evils. This is because God lets the world reap the full individual, societal, and global consequences of sinful choices (i.e. because the dominion given to Adam was transferred to Satan). In the end, when God is victorious over evil, the world will be remade into its pre-fallen, idyllic glory.

This theodicy might appear promising until a major flaw is brought to light. In order for it to succeed, the Bible must support the concept that all of the evil in the world resulted from Adam and Eve's fall into sin. However, Bible passages indicate that natural evil existed in the pre-fall world that God created. For example, in Gen. 3:16, after Eve had sinned, God made a pronouncement to her that the anguish, strain, and pain of being pregnant and giving birth would henceforth be greatly worse.[11] Anguish, strain, and pain could not be worse after she had sinned if it didn't exist before she had sinned.[12] So, according to the verse, before there was human sin, life for the sinless pair could not have been idyllic and without some natural suffering (without some natural evil).

Moreover, elsewhere in the Bible God is given credit for creating animals of predation (Job 38:39–40; 39:28–29; 41:1, 10, 14; Ps. 104).[13, 14] In Psalm 104, for example, God gets the credit for creating the lion to prey upon other animals (vv. 20–21, 24, 27–28) and their prey killed for food is called "good" (*tob*) (v. 28), which, as explained later in the chapter, indicates a functioning order in creation as God intended without intimation as to the quality of animal life, animal diet, or animal immortality. The conception of animal suffering and death as the result of Adam's sin appears to be a mistaken interpretation that developed after the time of the writers of the book of Job and Psalm 104. While some believe the apostle Paul taught that animal suffering and death were a result of Adam's sin (Rom. 5:12), careful exegesis shows that sin resulted in human *spiritual death* in the world. The Bible writers would've considered the Greek word for "death" (*thanatos*) to mean a literal bodily death, but it was used metaphorically "as a symbol of final separation from God, which we might describe . . . as spiritual death."[15] (The use of the word "death" metaphorically as spiritual death is discussed briefly in chapter 10.6).[16]

Taking these Bible passages into account, the world God created and pronounced very good is a world with natural evil. Moreover, biblical affirmation of the existence of human and animal suffering prior to the fall into sin is consistent with the old earth creationism (OEC)[17] view of Gen. 1:1–2:3. The OEC view conforms to biblical inerrancy by inspiration[18] of the Holy Spirit, which is supportable by a convincing body of scientific evidence for the existence of life-death cycles, animal diseases and suffering, droughts, storms, earthquakes, floods, volcanic eruptions, asteroid impacts, harsh climates, etc., prior to Adam and Eve, which further substantiates the existence of natural evil in the world created by God. How, then, can the theodicist attribute all evil (suffering) to the fall of man? He really cannot. And so the Augustinian theodicy leaves us without an explanation for why God would design and manufacture a world in which natural evil *can* occur, or why God would permit the natural evil that *has* occurred—prior to human sin, and ever since.

In the higher-order goods theodicy, certain forms of loving and good conduct ("higher-order goods") are said to require the existence of moral and natural evils. Such expressions of love and goodness include generosity toward the less fortunate, forgiveness of offenders, compassion, courage, sacrifice, caring for the sick, or rescuing the injured or potential victims. Because conditions of suffering from moral and natural evils are necessarily required for the exercise of *these* aspects of love and goodness, moral and natural evils are necessary for these higher-order goods to exist. And because the higher-order goods are of great value, God is justified in permitting the moral and natural evils that occur in the world.[19]

While it is true that such kinds of expressions of love and goodness could not exist if not for the existence of certain kinds of moral and natural evils, some of these evils existed long before there existed a human to express the higher-order goods in response to it. A prime example is the suffering of animals for millions of years before the arrival of humans. This would mean that God allows pointless suffering, which, as discussed in later chapters, goes against God's disposition.

Moreover, it is difficult to believe that the higher-order purpose is *worth* the vast amount and intensity of the evil and suffering that occurs in the world. This is especially so in instances of heinous and intense suffering, such as the brutal atrocities of war or assaults on little children. Therefore, because the higher-order goods theodicy doesn't explain the reason for a great deal of the natural evil in the world (e.g., animal suffering) before the arrival of humankind, or intense human suffering, it is inadequate to explain why God would allow all of the forms of evil, and thus does not entirely solve the problem of evil.

Now we move on to the more promising theodicies. First up for discussion is the natural consequences theodicy. In this explanation, humankind withholds its love for God (the fall of man), and its relationship with God is then ruined. One consequence of this is the suffering of harm done by post-fall evil doers. The other consequence is a loss of intellectual powers (dependent upon their unspoiled union with God) that protected them from harm and suffering from natural evil (from storms, earthquakes, disease, animal attacks, etc.). For example, they could no longer predict where and when a volcano would erupt or a tsunami would strike. But God ministers to us in the hope that we freely return to God for salvation and regeneration. The divine ministry involves leaving us to our misery in this world in order that we realize and accept the fact that our condition of estrangement and separation from God is wretched and dissatisfying, and then turn to God. Thus, our misery is a necessary motivation (necessary evil) in order that we experience a free repentance toward God for reconciliation and regeneration.[20] Although, God must temper our misery to an extent, as permitting too much misery would be pointless and counterproductive (1 Cor. 10:13) and go against God's perfectly loving and good disposition. So God would intervene at times to mitigate our suffering.

This theodicy goes a long way toward providing an explanation for why God would be justified in permitting evil and suffering. Part of the reason for its explanatory power is its incorporation of elements of the freewill theodicy that is discussed next. Unfortunately, the natural consequences theodicy does not account for the suffering of animals. This is a significant problem for many, especially those who are aware of the scientific evidence of the many millions of animals that suffered before humankind's relationship with God was ruined. As such, this theodicy falls short of justifying God for permitting every form of suffering, and therefore, it does not entirely solve the problem of evil.

But even more promising are the theodicies of freewill, natural law, and John Hick. In the freewill theodicy God creates humans each with the free will to determine the kind of character he or she is to have—a character compatible with either heaven or hell. The character created plays a vital role in God's judgment for heaven or hell. But the degree of freedom necessary for this process is enough that people are capable of causing one another substantial harm and suffering. Thus, evil and suffering are an unfortunate but necessary consequence of having the great good of free will and the process of determining our eternal destination. The value of the free will is high enough to outweigh the world's evil and suffering. Thus, God is justified in permitting us to suffer at the hands of evil doers in order to bring about a greater good.

At first blush this might seem to fully solve the problem of evil, but there are two problems worth noting. The first and perhaps most obvious one is that it does not explain why God would permit suffering due to natural causes—natural evil (e.g., storms, disease, and animal attacks). Although, suffering natural evil is often suffering that is not entirely without human cause. Famine, for example, could result partly from an oppressive political organization or government. Also, suffering would be greatly compounded for victims of an earthquake if there is immoral refusal to participate in rescue and relief from the catastrophe. Nonetheless, a vast amount of suffering *does* result from natural causes without the involvement of any apparent moral evil.

Some Christians object to this, claiming that natural evil is actually caused by evil angels intent on ruining God's creation generally, and, more importantly, injuring people so they may blame God and reject him. And so Satan and his army fly around the world with great power to cause storms, droughts, earthquakes, volcanic eruptions, pathogens, and DNA-copying errors and to overthrow the minds of animals (Mark 5:1–11) to cause natural evil.

While this explanation might seem plausible in a prescientific age, it is too incredulous today, given our thorough understanding of the natural causes of storms, earthquakes, genetic mutations, pathogens, predation, and other natural evils. Moreover, in an old earth creationism (OEC) model, in which humans appear after about 3.8 billion years of divinely guided evolution and pedigree, evil angels would play a big role in the creation of humans, which would seem to contradict *God's* big role in the creation of humans (Gen. 1:26–28, 31; 2:15–25). For these reasons, it is difficult to believe natural evil is actually moral evil caused by evil angels. It is much less difficult to believe that natural evil is a result of humankind's fall into sin, resulting in Satan having dominion in the world, as in the context of the natural consequences theodicy briefly discussed earlier, but this idea is dependent on young earth creationism (YEC), which has become untenable.

In sum, the freewill theodicy might explain why God allows moral evil, but it would seem to leave the problem of natural evil unaddressed. It doesn't identify a greater good that God would bring about by allowing natural catastrophes, diseases, and, most notably, the suffering of animals. For this reason alone it appears that the freewill theodicy does not fully solve the problem of evil.

The second objection to the freewill theodicy is that the value of free will is not adequately explained. According to atheist Andrea M. Weisberger, the Christian who says human free will is of superior and outweighing value should explain why. But, she says, Christians argue from the presupposition that free will is an outweighing good and offer either no explanation for it, or paltry or unsatisfactory reasons for it. Therefore, she believes that it is reasonable to conclude that free will is not an outweighing good, and, if God exists, he is *not* morally justified in creating a world in which there is free will that results in evil and suffering.[21] This leads many to think that we'd be better off in a world without free will in which humankind does not suffer. If the theodicy cannot explain why free will has *outweighing* value, then it cannot explain how God is justified in permitting even *moral* evil, not to mention natural evil. (An explanation of the value of free will is discussed in chapter 7).

From the foregoing two problems, it appears that the freewill theodicy is inadequate to entirely solve the problem of evil and suffering. It does not account for human harm and suffering that result from natural evil without input by freewill beings (e.g., drought, natural loss of food supplies, disease, and violent storms). It also doesn't account for animal suffering. Additionally, the value of free will that is claimed by Christians to outweigh all of the evil and suffering in the world is not adequately explained.

In the natural law theodicy, or nomic regularity theodicy, God creates the natural laws of physics (e.g., classical mechanics, Boyle's law of gases, conservation laws, and the four laws of thermodynamics) that give our world nomic regularity. Nomic regularity is the general principle that the functioning of the world will tend to follow common rules or principles that make it orderly, regular, and predictable.

A result of the world's predictability is that we can form certain expectations necessary for us to have moral free will. A free moral choice is not much of one if we cannot make it in the context of certain expected results. This is because such order provides an environment in which relationships between actions and effects are always similar. This allows us to predict effects and gauge the probability of effects. Having the ability to predict effects is essential if we are to make free moral choices. Having the ability to make free moral choices is naturally essential to develop moral habits and form moral character. Thus, in a world without predictability, significant moral free will and moral responsibility would not be possible.

One reason a rock thrower can be held culpable for attacking another is the predictability that if he throws the rock with accuracy at a person that it will strike him, rather than *sometimes* flying off on a wild course until it hits an unintended target miles away, or dematerializing upon release, or immediately dropping to the ground upon release. Suppose also that he throws a rock to fend off an animal attack to protect his children, but most of the rocks thrown cause damage in another part of the world. The result is pretty much out of the rock thrower's control if he is to stand a chance of saving his family from the animal attack. And it would be very difficult to hold him responsible for hurting other people struck by rocks as a result of his attempt to defend his family. Thus, a nomically regular world is necessary if we are to possess significant moral free will, and moral free will is a great good.

The unfortunate byproduct of such an environment, though, is that people and animals can suffer natural evil. The same water that sustains life can be a causal factor for starvation (destroyed crops). The medicine that relieves pain might also lead to life-threatening illness. The light and heat from the sun can be a causal factor for drought. The same law of gravity that keeps us alive can also kill us. Thus, the sources of suffering in the world, such as accidents, birth defects, disease, and storms, are all the unfortunate consequence of a nomically regular world necessary if we are to possess the greater good of free will.

There are a few notable objections to the nomic regularity theodicy. The first is the argument that God could've created a world with a different set of natural laws that provide a stable environment in which we could predict the effects of our choices and have moral free will but not suffer from natural evil. Thus, God could have made a world of free will beings that do not suffer natural evil, in which case Christians could not say that God is justified in permitting such suffering for the sake of free will.

Another objection is that instead of creating a different set of laws, God could create the world's natural laws just as they are, but intervene to prevent a substantial amount of suffering from natural causes. Such intervention, it is argued, would not substantially weaken our ability to predict the consequences of our choices, and thus free will would be retained. It would seem that this objection is true with regard to a great deal of the suffering in the world. Certainly divine intervention to reduce to some extent disease, drought, famine, predation, etc., would not upset the world's nomic regularity to the extent that we could no longer predict the consequences of our choices, and thus free will would be retained.[22]

An additional objection is that the value of free will is insufficient (or explanation of its value is insufficient) to justify having it at the enormous price of all of the evil and suffering that occurs in the world. Thus, the nomic regularity theodicy by itself does not appear sufficient to justify God in permitting a vast amount of suffering.

In Hick's Irenaean theodicy,[23] two stages of creation are involved. In the first stage, humans are brought into existence as intelligent animals in a world set at an "epistemic distance" from God to attenuate awareness of

God's existence and will to reward or punish to some extent, so that they can exercise free choices without divine coercion. (In this theodicy there is no historical fall of man into sin.) Their reactions to life's challenges and suffering result in "person making" and character growth ("soul making") until eventually they become God's children. Perfection lies in the future of our existence through successive reincarnations. Hick introduces the concept of reincarnations because he's trying to come up with a theology that harmonizes the various religious views (he advocates pluralism). Ultimately, there is universal salvation for all (universalism).

While aspects of Hick's theodicy provide valuable insight, it requires abandoning clearly understood Bible doctrines. It is no surprise, then, that Hick's theodicy has been rejected by Christians on theological grounds. Moreover, Hick's theodicy does not adequately explain a need for the suffering of the animal kingdom, or intense suffering that crushes a spirit and ruins a soul. Some are driven to alcoholism, drug abuse, divorce, or even suicide. Where is the character growth in any of these destructive ends? Where is the character growth of small children who are badly abused and murdered? Given all of these problems, Hick's theodicy appears insufficient to explain why God is justified in allowing the evil and suffering that occurs in the world.

2.4 A Comprehensive Solution

Considering the shortcomings in each of the theodicies, I did not find any to be sufficient to entirely resolve the problem of evil. While even the most promising ones (freewill, nomic regularity, John Hick's, and natural consequences) are successful in explaining how God could be justified in permitting *some* forms of the evil and suffering in the world, none account for *all* of it.

But in the midst of my study, I saw that certain elements of the theodicies fit coherently into an integrated theodicy that I, even when a nonbeliever, felt acceptably answered *all* of the challenges from evil and suffering. Not long afterward I became a believer, and, during what turned out to be the next five years, worked on synthesizing and developing it into what it is as it appears in this manuscript.

The integrated theodicy explains why a God who is hidden and seemingly uninvolved in the world is consistent with perfect love and goodness (chapters 3 and 4). It answers the question: If there is free will in heaven, why wouldn't

God bypass this earthly life and create us in heaven? It proposes a logical explanation of how evil conduct could have arisen in the first place—how Lucifer in heaven could initially sin against God (chapter 4.4). It explains why God would not answer a multitude of prayers for healing (chapter 5).

It explains why there is no logical inconsistency between the existence of God and evil (thus showing why the logical problem is solved) (chapter 6). It also answers the question as to why God would be justified in creating freewill persons *at all*, foreknowing that they would misuse their free will which would bring evil into existence (chapter 6.2). It identifies and discusses a greater good that necessarily entails permitting evil and suffering, and it explains why it has outweighing value. It explains how God could be justified in permitting barbaric and heinous horrors, and intense suffering (chapter 8).

It also discusses how God could be justified in permitting the suffering of every animal, including the animals that suffered before the appearance of the first humans (chapter 9). It even explains why God would prefer to create a world in which natural selection and predation occur for millions of years. Ultimately, it resolves the evidentiary or probabilistic problem of evil and suffering (chapters 7, 8, and 9).

It also explains how a perfectly loving and good God could be justified in consigning anyone to hell. It discusses why the punishment in hell is not pointless, and why and how it fits the crime (chapters 10 and 11). Finally, it offers a biblical explanation as to how God could be justified in judging people for hell who've never had the fortune of learning of the gospel (thus solving the soteriological problem of evil) (chapter 12).

This is the only theodicy with this much scope and success. My thanks to some of the world's leading Christian apologists, theologians, and philosophers for their very insightful conceptions and defenses: William Lane Craig,[24] Peter J. Kreeft,[25] Michael J. Murray,[26] Ronald H. Nash (1936–2006),[27] John Hick (1922–2012),[28] Michael A. Corey (1957–2011),[29] and others.[30] But the theodicy wouldn't be successful if not for the inter-relatedness and cohesiveness of the apologetic conceptions of: divine hiddenness, a two-phase life, compatibility determination by free will, nomic regularity, repentance and faith facilitated by suffering, the Holy Spirit's ministry, and God's plan to bring about the greatest good through his heavenly community in a consummate relationship with him (introduced in chapter 3.1). As such, it holds the greatest explanatory power of all.

The material is complex and deep, but I've taken care to present it in such a way as to appeal to readers who lack advanced knowledge in Christian teachings, theology, and apologetics. Still, it would aid the reader quite a bit to have a fair amount of knowledge of at least the basic tenets of Christianity. Probably most readers will experience some degree of intellectual stretching. But there is a rich reward for the reader willing to stretch a little.

2.5 Who Benefits?

This book is for readers who are suffering and in doubt about the credibility of Christianity because of the problem of evil and suffering. They're having difficulty seeing how God could bring any good out of it, or how God could be justified in allowing it to happen. This book is for them. But it is in times when we are suffering from pain, stress, upheaval, unemployment, an abusive relationship, illness, etc., that the problem of evil calls for an emotional solution. The emotional problem of evil is essentially a mind filled with hurt, betrayal, or anger against someone, or God, or the idea of God. It is triggered by distress and suffering that can close the mind to a philosophical-theological explanation.

To these readers, I have two points to make. The first is that I know what it is like to be slowly crushed under the weight of suffering and despair to the point when either Christianity doesn't seem to make sense, or I don't care if it makes sense; or when the evidence on the issue seems to weigh heavily on the side of those who say, "It's time to get real; there's no God to help you." But I know by my experience that at certain times the theoretical component *does* play a role (if only indirectly) in alleviating enough of the despair to give hope and strength and faith in God's plan to work it out in us for our ultimate benefit.

Many times knowing why we are suffering a particular plight can give us a whole new perspective about what we are going through. A young man was hired to carry a sealed backpack as quickly as he could across a rugged and dangerous terrain to a village where he would hand it over to its leader. On his journey he fell down and sprained his elbow, slipped on a rock crossing a river and hurt his back, and fended off wolves with a spear. He was hurt, sore, and angry, and he grumbled as he continued. Not long before reaching his destination, he met an older man also carrying a sealed backpack who told him that they were bringing vitally needed medicine, without which many of the villagers would die. Suddenly the young man stopped grumbling about his aching arm and sore back and raced to the village. What changed? His injuries? Of course not; it was his attitude.

Likewise, the integrated theodicy has a big picture of God's plan with many mysteries solved that enables sufferers to gain a new perception or perspective of their plight. It is this insight which helps suffering people understand why evil is no reason to believe that God does not love them. In that, there is solace, encouragement, strength, and wisdom—perhaps enough to help a sufferer to hold fast to, or find faith in, God. This is clearly what Jesus and his disciples believed and taught (discussed in chapter 8.2).

The second point is that the emotional problem is not solved until the sufferer perceives God as a person who is present in the suffering. This comes by way of learning of the life and person of Jesus Christ. It is much easier to conceive of God as empathetic when what he suffered is contemplated: his tiredness, his cries, his tears, his gashed flesh, his blood and exhaustion and death.

The sufferer can see this best, I think, if Christians visit the sufferer, to listen to him, to help him find relief from his misery, hope in his despair, and joy in his sorrow (see appendix B). Christians are to mourn with those who mourn (Rom. 12:15; Heb. 13:3). This may help defuse anger toward God (or the idea of God) because of evil.

But it alone will not aid the sufferer to establish a deeply rooted faith that would stand the tests of time and tragedy. That requires a philosophical-theological foundation of who God is, how he has demonstrated his love for us, and why he should not be rejected because of evil—a foundation on which to cultivate a never-ending, saving relationship. This is where the integrated theodicy comes in.

This book is also for Christian readers who want to have a knowledgeable grasp of the issues that will allow them to share confidently with others, or successfully defend their faith. Christian readers will also gain insights on doctrinal subjects, such as salvation (chapter 12, appendices D and E), God's judgment, and hell (chapters 10 and 11).

This book is also for anyone, including nonbelievers, interested in philosophies of God and Christianity, and whether Christians can come to have a successful explanation for why God would allow the existence of a world filled with all forms of pain and suffering. As an atheist, I wasn't an ardent nonbeliver, but because I didn't believe in God's existence, I forced Christianity to address the most troublesome aspects of the problem, including millions of years of animal suffering, divine silence, and suffering in hell, particularly the persons in hell who never had a chance to learn of the gospel. Readers will see arguments brought by many of the most influential opponents of Christianity, including: Michael Martin, William L. Rowe, Paul Draper, J. L. Mackie, Graham Oppy, Quentin Smith, Richard R. La Croix, Hugh LaFollette, David Hume, Andrea M. Weisberger, John L. Schellenberg, and Bart D. Ehrman.

NOTES to Chapter 2

1. http:// www.washingtonpost.com/world/syria-tribal-revolt-against-islamic-state-ignored-fueling-resentment/2014/10/20/25401beb-8de8-49f2-8e64-c1cfbee45232_story.html. Assessed on October 21, 2014.

2. In March 1994 the Goshen Methodist Church near Piedmont, Alabama, was conducting a Palm Sunday pageant when a tornado hit. A brick wall toppled onto a pew of six children, ages two to twelve, who were dressed in their Easter clothes and waiting to sing in the pageant.

3. William L. Rowe, "Evil and Theodicy," *The Improbability of God*, eds. Michael Martin and Ricki Monnier (Amherst, NY: Prometheus Books, 2003), 263.

4. William L. Rowe, "The Problem of Evil and Some Varieties of Atheism," *The Improbability of God*, 253.

5. John W. Loftus, *Why I Became an Atheist: A Former Preacher Rejects Christianity*, (Amherst, NY: Prometheus Books, 2008), 234–235.

6. This example of spirit-crushing suffering is found in Gregory A. Boyd, *Satan and the Problem of Evil: Constructing a Trinitarian Warfare Theodicy* (Downers Grove, IL: InterVarsity Press, 2001), 260–261. I discuss the example in appendix B.

7. On my way back to trusting in God's existence and will for my life, my ex-wife and I remarried.

8. Friedrich Nietzsche, *Daybreak*, trans. R. J. Hollingdale (New York: Cambridge University Press, 1982), 89–90, as quoted in Daniel Howard-Snyder and Paul K. Moser, "Introduction," *Divine Hiddenness: New Essays*, eds. Daniel Howard-Snyder and Paul K. Moser (New York: Cambridge University Press, 2002), 3–4.

9. Soteriology is the study of religious doctrines of salvation.

10. Ezek. 18:23, 32; 33:11; John 12:32; 1 Tim. 2:4; 2 Pet. 3:9.

11. John H. Walton, *The NIV Application Commentary: Genesis* (Grand Rapids, MI: Zondervan, 2001), 226–227, 238.

12. A point concerning the text that Henry M. Morris (an advocate of the view of

an idyllic world before human sin) does not mention in his commentary on Gen. 3:16 [*The Genesis Record: A Scientific & Devotional Commentary on the Book of Beginnings* (Grand Rapids, MI: Baker Book House, 1976), 122–124].

13. Henri Blocher, *Evil and the Cross: An Analytical Look at the Problem of Pain* (Grand Rapids, MI: Kregel Publications, 1994), 58. Blocher is a professor of systematic theology at the Faculte Libre de Theologie Evangelique in Vaux-sur-Seine, France, and holds the newly endowed Gunther H. Knoedler Chair of Theology in the Biblical and Theological Studies PhD program at Wheaton College. Widely recognized as a leading theologian and an evangelical statesman, Blocher has lectured or taught in schools in Europe, Australia, Africa, Canada, and the United States. He has written many works in French and English, including: *In the Beginning*; S*ongs of the Servant*; and *Original Sin: Illuminating the Bible*.

14. Paul Copan, *That's Just Your Interpretation: Responding to Skeptics Who Challenge Your Faith* (Grand Rapids, MI: BakerBooks, 2001), 150–152.

15. Charles H. Dodd, *The Epistle of Paul to the Romans* (London: Hodder and Stoughton, 1932), 81.

16. See also Gary R. Habermas and J. P. Moreland, *Beyond Death: Exploring the Evidence for Immortality* (Eugene, OR: Wipf and Stock Publishers, 2004), 305–306.

17. Old earth creationism (OEC) is held by a growing population of Christians who have adjusted their view of Genesis chapters 1, 2, 5, and 11 in light of the evidence for an ancient universe, a 3.8 year span of life on Earth, and a recent advance in methodology for Bible exegesis which incorporates comparative studies of ancient Near Eastern literature. Biblical inspiration and inerrancy do not mandate that Gen. 1:1–2:3 be interpreted as a narrative description of the physical manner and timing of God's creative activity, and thus leave room for interpretations of the text that are consistent with OEC, such as interpretations that recognize its liturgical structure, its polemical and calendrical aims, and use of universally-understood ancient Near Eastern cosmological and cosmographical conceptions.

18. The plenary-verbal view of inspiration is the orthodox view. The word *plenary* means "complete" or "full," and *verbal* means "the words of Scripture." Thus, the Holy Spirit moves on the writer in the writing process to the extent that the meaning of every word scribed is scribed by God's approval (2 Tim. 3:16–17; 2 Pet. 1:21). However, while *all* Scripture is inspired, authoritative and useful for teaching right living, the knowledge of the writers was limited (as the Holy Spirit intended) to the contexts of literary genre and culture, to address immediate concerns that played a significant role in God's grand scheme for humankind, as well as the overriding need for progressive revelation. Thus, to properly interpret Scripture, we are to adapt to genres, literary styles and conventions, and cultural considerations and recognition that revelation is progressive. "Inspiration does not eliminate the need for the hard work of interpretation" [Mark L. Strauss, "The Inspiration of the Bible," *The Baker Illustrated Bible Handbook*, eds. J. Daniel Hays and J. Scott Duvall (Grand Rapids, MI: BakerBooks, 2011), 995–1005]. Biblical inerrancy and inspiration are briefly discussed in chapter 11.7.

19. Richard Swinburne, "Some Major Strands of Theodicy," *The Evidential Argument from Evil*, ed. Daniel Howard-Snyder (Bloomington: Indiana University Press, 1996);

and *Providence and the Problem of Evil* (Oxford: Oxford University Press, 1998). See also John Hick, *Evil and the God of Love*, second ed. reissued 2007 (New York: Palgrave MacMillan, 2007).

20. Peter van Inwagen, "The Magnitude, Duration and Distribution of Evil: A Theodicy," *Philosophical Topics* (1988), collected in his *God, Knowledge and Mystery: Essays in Philosophical Theology* (Ithaca, NY: Cornell University Press, 1995), 110.

21. Andrea M. Weisberger, *Suffering Belief: Evil and the Anglo-American Defense of Theism* (New York: Peter Lang Publishing, 1999), 164.

22. As pointed out by Christian philosopher Daniel Howard-Snyder in "God, Evil, and Suffering," *Reason for the Hope Within*, ed. Michael J. Murray (Grand Rapids, MI: Wm. B. Eerdmans Publishing Co., 1999), 96.

23. Introduced by John Hick, *Evil and the God of Love*, second ed. reissued 2007 (New York: Palgrave MacMillan, 2007).

24. William Lane Craig, *Hard Questions, Real Answers* (Wheaton, IL: Crossway Books, 2003), chapters 4 and 5; *On Guard: Defending Your Faith with Reason and Precision* (Colorado Springs, CO: David C. Cook, 2010), chapters 7 and 10; reasonablefaith.org.

25. Peter J. Kreeft and Ronald K. Tacelli, *Handbook of Christian Apologetics: Hundreds of Answers to Crucial Questions* (Downers Grove, IL: InterVarsity Press, 1993), 122–146; Peter J. Kreeft, *Making Sense Out of Suffering* (Ann Arbor, MI: Servant Books, 1986).

26. Michael J. Murray, "Deus Absconditus," *Divine Hiddenness: New Essays*, eds. Daniel Howard-Snyder and Paul K. Moser (New York: Cambridge University Press, 2002), 62–82; "Heaven and Hell," *Reason for the Hope Within*, ed. Michael J. Murray (Grand Rapids, MI: Wm. B. Eerdmans Publishing Co., 1999), 287–317; *Nature Red in Tooth and Claw: Theism and the Problem of Animal Suffering* (New York: Oxford University Press, 2008). Murray earned his BA in philosophy from Franklin and Marshall and his MA and PhD from the University of Notre Dame. He has authored (and coauthored) many books, including: *Philosophy of Religion: The Big Questions* (with Eleonore Stump); *The Believing Primate: Scientific, Philosophical, and Theological Reflections on the Origin of Religion* (with Jeffrey Schloss); *Divine Evil?: The Character of the God of the Hebrew Bible* (with Michael Rea and Michael Bergmann); and *On Predestination and Election*.

27. Ronald H. Nash, *Faith and Reason: Searching for a Rational Faith* (Grand Rapids, MI: Zondervan, 1988), chapters 13, 14, and 15.

28. John Hick, *Evil and the God of Love*.

29. Michael A. Corey, *Evolution and the Problem of Natural Evil* (Lanham, MD: University Press of America, 2000).

30. Such as: Alvin Plantinga; Peter van Inwagen; Frederick R. Tennant (1866–1957); Ravi Zacharias; Paul Copan; Gregory A. Boyd; Bruce Reichenbach; Richard G. Swinburne; R. William Hasker; C. S. Lewis; Stephen Wykstra; Daniel Howard-Snyder; William V. Crockett; and John Sanders.

Part 1
The Problem of Divine Hiddenness

3

Would a Loving God Hide from Anyone? Part 1

Synopsis

Critics of Christianity argue that the concept of a hidden deity is not in harmony with the concept of a God who is perfectly loving and good because divine hiddenness makes us suffer unnecessarily, as there is no greater good being accomplished by his hiddenness.

A Christian response is that divine hiddenness would be necessary to bring about a greater good if it is necessary to create a consummate relationship between him and his heavenly community that would generate a consummate quality and quantity of expressions of love and goodness by the community, versus a low quantity and quality of expressions that would result from a mediocre relationship if God were not a hidden deity. (Note: This covers chapters 3 and 4.)

Jill[1] grew up in a Christian home and was homeschooled through grade twelve and then enrolled in college. The new environment and courses were eye-opening. She began to see the world differently. Instead of a world created and controlled by God, it was the happenstance result of mindless molecules colliding in space. Life wasn't God's handiwork, but the accidental occurrence of nature—a nature in which only the strongest survive without divine guidance and without hope beyond whatever moments of peace and plenty might be obtained by those best skilled in self-preservation.

She became keenly aware of the lack of evidence of God's existence, and of the global problems that result. If God really existed, she thought, he's left a very large portion of the world's population in the dark about his existence, a sin problem, or our need for salvation. Many millions of people in search of truth have no opportunity to know of Christ and make a decision for salvation. Why would God not make his existence and will obvious enough that the millions believing in non-Christian religions could come out of their "darkness" and into God's "marvelous light"? So much war and bloodshed in the name of religion could've been prevented if only God had provided obvious evidence of his existence and commandments. Why would a good God who desires that people believe in him leave so many people in unbelief? Why wouldn't he speak to millions of prophets on every continent instead of only a tiny number in the ancient Near East?

Meanwhile, Jill's older brother, who had recently begun pastoring a church, was diagnosed with terminal cancer. Despite all the many fervent prayers of the saints that God would heal him, often with tears, her brother died. She then became acutely aware of the billions of unanswered prayers around the world for people dying of diseases, starvation, or natural disasters without a reason from God that would alleviate their distress or loss of hope. Why, she wondered, would God keep hidden when so many are crying out for an explanation? Why would so many prayers be met with silence?

Jill felt her Christian faith had been disproven. Her worldview had changed. The world no longer seemed created and watched over by God. She stopped praying, reading her Bible, and attending church. By the time she graduated, she no longer believed.

Like Jill, I too had come to see the world I knew as uncharacteristic of the God that Christians claimed to know. The God of the Bible is all-knowing and all-powerful,[2] and perfectly loving and good.[3] Thus, it seemed that he would be willing and capable of providing us with enough evidence of his existence and his morality that there'd be no reasonable doubt, and everyone would have the opportunity to make an educated choice for or against an explicit, reciprocal relationship with God.

In a world with substantially more evidence of God's existence and will, there would be less strife, less crime, fewer wars, little or no starvation, less sickness, less animal suffering, and less environmental damage. Moreover, it is likely that there never would've *been* a fall of Adam and Eve into sin. Obviously, such a world is far different than our present world. And so it appeared to me that it's likely God doesn't exist, but if he did, it is evident by the extraordinary extent of his hiddenness that he's not a caring God.

The apparent inconsistency between divine hiddenness and a loving and good God is a facet of the problem of evil. Divine hiddenness itself is seen as an evil, as so many in the world suffer in ignorance as to why we are here, how we are supposed to live, and what lies beyond death. Directly resulting from such ignorance is a lack of hope, lack of wisdom, lack of moral virtue, fear, persecution, and religious conflict. It is argued that since God is willing and capable of preventing all such evil by disclosing more evidence of his existence without the loss of some greater good or causing greater evil, it is more probable that God does not exist.

The Christian response, I think, should first acknowledge the Bible's claim that revealing himself to the world is consistent with God's love. After all, Jesus' ministry and miracles were to "show us the Father" (John 14:7–11). But, it does not necessarily follow that because God is loving and good that he should always reveal his existence and will to a large degree. There may exist a greater good that could only be brought about if God's disclosure of himself is substantially limited. If so, then suffering divine hiddenness would be a necessary evil to achieve a greater good, which would be consistent with a caring God.

While the skeptic might admit that this is *possible*, he would probably argue that it is *unlikely*, because none of the goods proposed by Christian theodicists are valuable enough to justify the level of hiddenness that exists in our world. As I discussed in the previous chapter, opponents of Christianity argue that neither free will, nor "soul making," is of sufficient value to justify all of the confusion, lack of direct guidance, and suffering caused by divine hiddenness. However, in addition to free will and "soul making," the following proposes that divine hiddenness is necessary for God to bring about something more valuable than either free will or "soul making" which undoubtedly outweighs the price of divine hiddenness.

3.1 The Consummate Relationship

It is God's objective as a perfectly loving and good being to bring into existence the greatest degree of good possible. The degree of good existing is determined (in part) by: (a) the measure of a morally good disposition(s) that exist; the measure (quantity and quality) of expressions of love and moral goodness existing; and (c) the number of existing persons that express love and moral goodness. While (a), (b), and (c) exist by virtue of God's existence alone, (c) *cannot* exist to the greatest possible degree while God alone exists. The reason is simple. The existence of the greatest possible degree of good would require the existence of the maximum possible number of persons expressing love and goodness. But God consists of only three persons. Of course the dispositions of the Trinity are as good as possible—even omnigood,[5] thus fulfilling (a). And of course being all-powerful, God could deliver the greatest possible quantity and quality of expressions of love and goodness, thus fulfilling (b). But God cannot by himself be any more than three persons expressing love and goodness, and therefore, prior to creation, the degree of good then existing was limited. Naturally, to advance the degree of existing good, God would create a community of persons to join the triune community (God) in generating expressions of love and goodness.[6] As the apostle Paul tells us, persons (angels and humans) were created to do good works (Eph. 2:10).

But whether the quantity and quality of expressions of love and goodness by created persons would add much good, if any good, depends on the characteristic properties that define the nature of their relationship with God. The human aspect of a fruitful relationship with God must include such things as: an appropriate perception of God's disposition and personality; love of and trust in God; an appropriate attitude against sin; and good psychospiritual health.

Psychospiritual health is probably unfamiliar to most. The term "psychospiritual" is a conjoining of the words "psychological" and "spiritual." It is the concept of the psychological aspect of the spiritual experience and relationship with God. Psychospiritual health entails a sturdy self-esteem, an appropriate attitude about oneself in relation to God and others in a community, emotional regulation, an individual's spiritual developmental processes, and love toward oneself. It comes from knowing that the essential core of the person is intrinsically valuable, fundamentally accepted, loved and respected by God, by others, and by oneself. Loving oneself is one essential key to having a fruitful and flourishing relationship with God and others (Luke 10:27).

Fruitful properties such as these are like machines in a factory that produce expressions of love and goodness. One such "machine," for example, is trust in God, which we are told produces good works.[7] But trust and good works do not happen if one lacks an appropriate perception of God's disposition and personality. If, for example, it is believed that God compromises justice for arbitrariness or is partial, indifferent, or dishonest, there would be little, if any, trust in God. Thus, an appropriate perception of God's disposition and personality is also essential to the production of expressions of love and goodness.

Likewise, a poor psychospirituality from lack of love toward oneself, lack of significant self-responsibility, a persistent sense that one has little value, or negative feelings of shame (e.g., distress from an overheightened awareness of unworthiness to be in God's kingdom) could make a relationship with God unravel. Because an attitude of love toward oneself makes one capable of loving and respecting others, a healthy psychospirituality is essential to one's ability to express love and goodness.[8]

Like factory machines, the better the quality of the properties of the relationship, the better and more abundant the production, and the greater the quality and quantity of expressions of love and goodness. Thus, a mediocre (moderate to inferior) quality of the properties would produce a low measure of expressions, while a consummate (completely perfect) quality of the properties would produce a consummate measure of expressions.

One of the properties of mediocre quality that was mentioned previously is a perception of God's disposition and personality mixed with a belief that God is arbitrary and capricious or indifferent in his judgment concerning eternity in heaven[9] and hell. Such a perception would spawn fear, distrust, and resentment—ingredients that would work their way through a person's personality and disposition, like a little yeast that works its way through a batch of dough (1 Cor. 5:6[10]). A relationship like this is mediocre, and the result would be loss of spontaneous expressions of love and goodness. But if the perception of God's disposition and personality is of consummate quality (as discussed in the following chapter), there can be the greatest trust in and love for God followed by the deepest knowing of God, resulting in a perfect relationship that generates only positive feelings for the fulfillment of love to its greatest extent and maximal spontaneous loving and good expressions.

The degree of existing good from a consummate relationship would be phenomenally greater than any good generated by a mediocre relationship. To get a measurable sense of how much more good would be produced, let's consider the different degrees of good produced on a scale of 1–10. One (1) stands for a low degree of good produced by a low measure of the quality and quantity of expressions of love and goodness generated by a mediocre relationship multiplied by seven days of time. Such a relationship would produce seven units of good (1 level of good x seven days = seven units of good produced). Ten (10) stands for the greatest degree of good produced by the highest measure of the quality and quantity of expressions of love and goodness generated by a consummate relationship multiplied by seven days of time. Such a relationship would produce seventy units of good (10 level of good x seven days = seventy units of good produced). With this simple calculation it is easy to see that a relationship with God of a consummate nature produces ten times more good than a mediocre relationship, and that over the course of time, the degree of good of the consummate relationship is exponentially far greater.

Time exists in some form in the next life in eternity. Otherwise, souls that love could not exist, although it may run differently. That being true, we can extend the simple calculation into eternity and see that any good produced by a mediocre relationship with God in eternity is not worth comparing to the astronomical degree of good produced by the consummate relationship, which is tenfold greater. After a million years, the mediocre relationship would produce 365 million units of good. But the consummate relationship would produce 3.65 billion, which would be 3.285 billion (3,285,000,000) more units of good after a million years alone. The exponential increase is illustrated as follows:

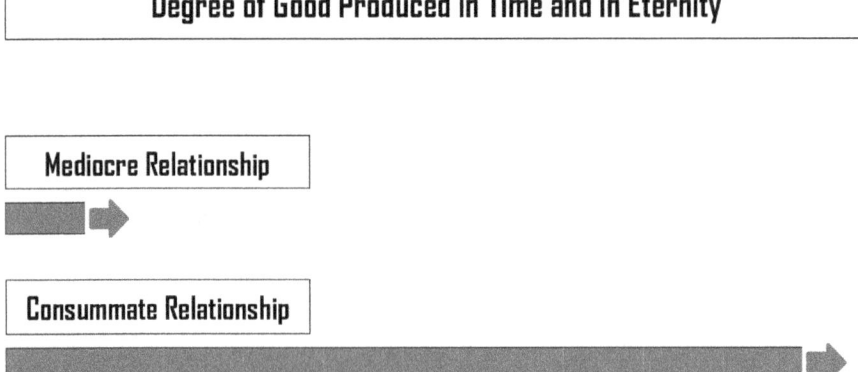

Certainly, when it comes to a relationship with God, the Bible is more concerned about a right relationship versus a wrong relationship, and not a mediocre relationship versus a consummate relationship. This is to be expected, since having a saving relationship with God versus not having one is of primary concern. But God's ministry to his people goes beyond merely getting them off of a sinking ship, so to speak. With eternity in view, God is working behind the scenes to bring about a relationship with him that in heaven is of consummate quality, a relationship that is perfect in every respect—a perfect perception of God, perfect psychospiritual health, perfect love and trust, etc. Bible commentators on John 15 note that "the relation of the believer to God is that of the vine to the owner of the vineyard. He tends it, waters it, and endeavors to protect it and cultivate it so that it will produce its maximum yield."[11]

Depicted metaphorically in John's visions in the book of Revelation is a prophetic glimpse of the consummate relationship in heaven. The number assigned to the saints is 144,000 (Rev. 7 and 14), which is a number symbolic of "completeness and perfection,"[12] because it is the sum of twelve times 12,000, and the number twelve in the Bible symbolizes completeness and perfection. The heavenly realm is also marked by numbers and dimensions symbolic of perfection. In Revelation 21, John describes a floating holy city of heaven (v. 2) with dimensions that form a perfect cube (v. 16), with twelve foundations (v. 14) and twelve open pearly gates (vv. 12-13, 21, 25) attended by twelve angels (v. 12).

Drawing upon teachings in the Bible, philosophy, and a little psychology,[13] it would appear that a consummate relationship with God would require the following properties of consummate quality (among others):

1. a perfect perception of God's disposition and personality (Ps. 63:2–5);
2. origination of the relationship with God from pure reciprocal love;
3. optimal psychospiritual health;
4. an appropriate attitude against sin;
5. an optimal feeling of meaning to life;
6. optimal trust in God;
7. having only positive feelings and emotions;
8. the fullest optimism of the future;
9. the fullest assurance of being in an eternally secure relationship with God; and
10. engagement in various forms of service to others.

Such are properties of the consummate relationship of the ultimate "glory that will be revealed" in each of God's people in heaven, with the greatest and most intimate knowing of God, which is "eternal life" (John 17:3), "the life that is truly life" (1 Tim. 6:19).

Certain Circumstances and Experiences of Life Are Necessary to Bring about a Consummate Relationship. It is a fact that circumstances and experiences of life play a role in establishing a relationship's properties. For example, whether there is a property of trust in the relationship depends on the circumstances that affect the existence and function of the relationship, as well as one's contact with and observation of the other person. Events and conduct leave an impression. If the impression is trustworthiness, then there can be an element of trust in the relationship.

Now with respect to a consummate relationship with God, let's consider an example of a necessary circumstance and experience if one is to have a perfect perception of God's disposition and personality—a property of the consummate relationship listed previously. This example is the person of Jesus Christ and his loving and selfless actions toward sinning humans. In addition to being a necessary circumstance if anyone is to be saved (see appendix D), it is also a necessary circumstance for a perfect perception of God—which is partially fulfilled in our earthly life, but completely and profoundly fulfilled in the afterlife.

Jesus said, "Just as Moses lifted up the snake in the desert, so the Son of Man must be lifted up."[14] Jesus was referring to the story in Num. 21:4–9 of the ancient Israelites who were plagued by deadly poisonous snakes. In a vision, Moses was instructed to make a bronze snake and put it on a pole so that anyone bitten could look at it and live. Jesus spoke of this metaphorically for the inspiration and disposition-transforming power experienced by the ones who would reflect on and meditate on Jesus' substitutionary act of being condemned to death by crucifixion ("the cross"). In what Jesus did we can see God's disposition from multiple significant angles. We see his compassion, his love of the sinner, his stance on upholding the principle of justice through accountability,[15] his righteousness, his position on sin, et cetera—all to an extraordinary extent.

The perception of God's disposition and personality profoundly influences the psyche and disposition such that there can be greater love and appreciation of God, greater trust in God, and a greater attitude toward God for a better relationship with God that generates greater expressions of love and goodness. Reflecting and meditating on Christ's doings is an experience that plays a role in the shaping of a perfect perception of God's disposition and personality.

Not only does this play a role in shaping an appropriate perception for the believer in her earthly life, but also in the heavenly life (Col. 1:20; Heb. 9:23–24[16]). The heavenly community is not eternally secure against a rise of sin without periodic meditation in eternity on "the cross." The angels never cease of taking moments to meditate intently on the events of the life and sacrifice of Christ (1 Pet. 1:12b).[17] This gives them a greater perception of God's disposition and personality, thereby establishing the greatest and most intimate knowing of God and even greater spontaneous expressions of love and goodness. As such, it is an experience resulting from a circumstance that is necessary for the consummate relationship and generating the greatest possible good.

While the existence of Jesus and his doings are a necessary circumstance for a consummate relationship with God, many other circumstances are also necessary. Long before God became the redeemer, he was the creator of a world designed with conditions for human experiences necessary to build consummate properties into humankind's relationship with the Trinity. Such circumstances include what I identify as a two-phase life, consisting of necessary circumstances and experiences of a terrestrial (earthly) life, followed by necessary circumstances and experiences of a celestial (heavenly) life. The terrestrial life's circumstances and experiences include a process of what I refer to as compatibility determination by moral free will in a world of divine hiddenness. These earthly life circumstances and experiences and their necessity for a consummate relationship with the Divine are discussed in the next chapter. The celestial life's circumstances and experiences involve the beatific vision and supernatural communication ability. These supernatural experiences and their necessity are discussed from the Bible and extrabiblical sources of evidence in section 3.3 of this chapter.

The following illustration gives a sneak peek overview of the necessary circumstances and experiences. Each element is a link in a chain of necessity for why divine hiddenness would be a necessary part of God's plan to bring about the greatest good.

3.2 The Circumstance of the Two-Phase Life

One of the circumstances designed by the Creator for a consummate relationship is the two-phase life, consisting of a preliminary, natural life followed by an eternal, supernatural life. The supernatural life begins when dissolution of the terrestrial (earthly) body releases its psyche or soul.[18] The soul is ultimately led from our spatial dimension into the celestial spatial

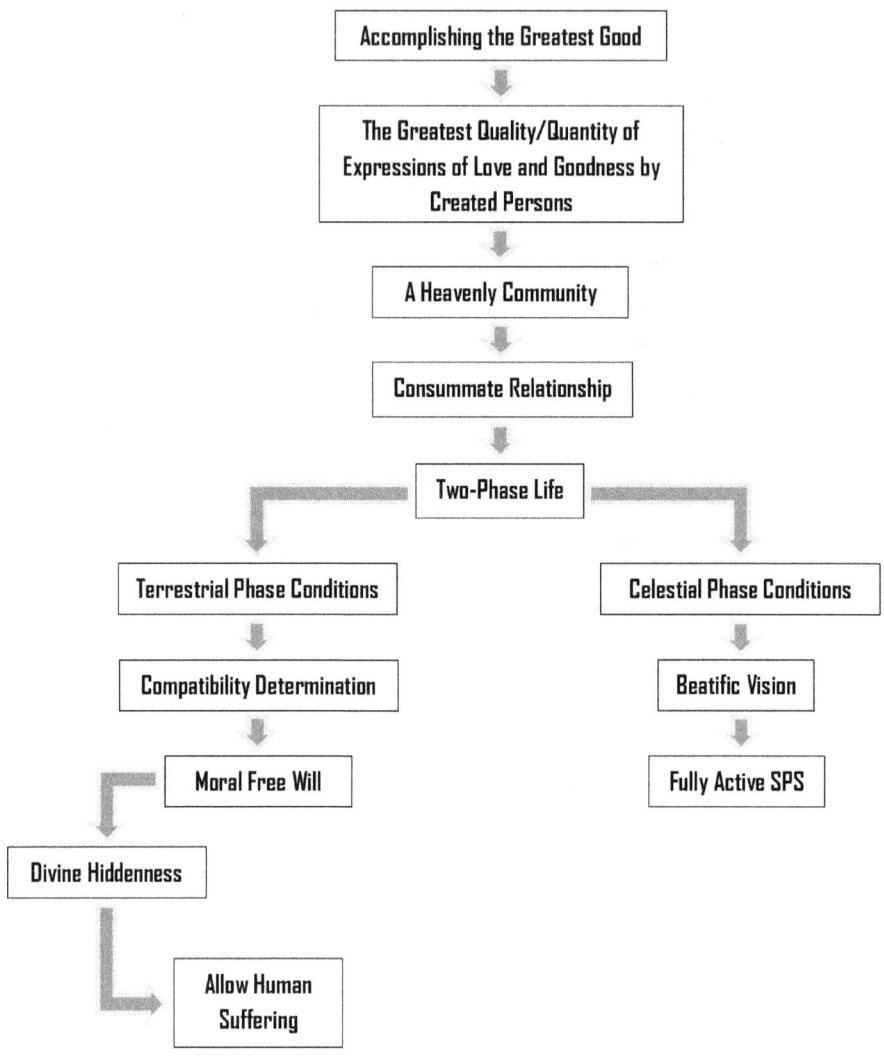

dimension(s) (the spirit realms)[19] where it remains in an intermediate state[20] until a future resurrection-translation. In the resurrection-translation, it receives an imperishable celestial body that manifests as a resurrected or translated body in our spatial dimension (the "resurrection of the dead").

With the exception of the intermediate state ("disembodied state"), which is a consequence of the fall of man, this appears to be God's design for humankind from the beginning. The Bible tells us that there is a resurrection to eternal conscious existence planned by God for all, irrespective of whether one is saved or lost. As the Old Testament prophet Daniel foretold, "Multitudes who sleep in the dust of the earth will awake: some to everlasting life, others to shame and everlasting contempt" (Dan. 12:2). Jesus elaborates on Daniel's prophecy: "For a time is coming when all who are in their graves will hear his voice and come out—those who have done good will rise to live, and those who have done evil will rise to be condemned" (John 5:28–29). ("Life" and "live" symbolize the eternal heavenly relationship with God.)[21] The apostle Paul also taught that "there will be a resurrection of both the righteous and the wicked" (Acts 24:15). See also John's book of Revelation (20:5).

Given that both the saved and unsaved receive immortal bodies, it would appear that there is a celestial afterlife planned and carried out as a matter of a providential order of creation. The only difference is where one exists in eternity (in heaven or hell). As Christian apologists Gary R. Habermas and J. P. Moreland put it: "The final states of the just and unjust are exactly analogous—both conscious, continuous modes of living—except for their respective destinations."[22]

There appears to be a hint of a two-phase life order for the redeemed and the unsaved in Paul's first letter to the Corinthian Christians (1 Cor. 15:35-58). Some Christians are adamant that the passage speaks only of a resurrection-translation of the saved without any hint of a resurrection-translation of the unsaved. However, close inspection indicates there is such an allusion.

Paul wrote the passage to address a mistaken idea held by some of the believers that God would resurrect the same mortal body we now have with its drives that tempt to sin, a body which obviously wouldn't be fit for eternal life (v. 35).[23] Paul has two objectives. The first is to clarify that the resurrection body would be immortal because it is supernatural. The second is to clarify that the supernatural body would no longer be a source of temptation to sin.

The second clarification relates to the life of the saved in heaven. Thus, this aspect of Paul's discussion of the supernatural body speaks only of a resurrection-translation body of the saved going to heaven (1 Cor. 15:43–44; 1 John 3:2; Phil. 3:21). But the first clarification—that the resurrection body would be immortal because it is supernatural—applies to the unsaved as well as the saved, as it relates to the previously cited Bible verses in Daniel, John, Acts, and Revelation of the resurrection of the righteous and the wicked. This suggests a providential order of creation of a temporal earthly life followed by an eternal celestial afterlife. Theologian Matthew Henry (1662–1714) appears to refer to it as God's "order of Providence."[24]

In this providential order, everyone initially has a body designed to be temporal (earthly) that is followed by a body that is immortal (celestial). The natural body, like that of the animal world, was not intended to last forever. God did not "plant the body that will be" (1 Cor. 15:37). Rather, he designed it as a "temporary" life (2 Cor. 4:18). It is thus "perishable" (1 Cor. 15:42, 50, 53) and ultimately will end in annihilation (1 Cor. 15:36). At death, the surviving soul leaves behind the body that is no longer useful to begin its second phase of life. The soul enters the celestial spatial dimension(s) (the spirit realms) and is led to either God's community or Satan's community. At the appointed time(s), the disembodied soul receives an "imperishable" celestial body (1 Cor. 15:42, 50, 53) in either the resurrection of the saved or the resurrection of the condemned. God's celestial people can manifest as a resurrected or translated body in our natural spatial dimension (1 Cor. 15:37–38)[25] and "inherit the new earth."[26] But Satan's celestial people are consigned to the dimension of hell. In one of Jesus' teachings, he mentions that the unsaved have a "body in hell" (Matt. 10:28b).[27]

The concept of two stages of life with two different kinds of bodies can be seen in nature. Consider the caterpillar that crawls until it becomes a butterfly and flies. The caterpillar (larva) "encases itself in a cocoon and becomes a pupa. Within the pupa, the larval tissues are broken down and the adult is built by the division and differentiation of cells that were quiescent in the larva. Finally, the adult emerges from the cocoon" and flies off.[28] This is a complete metamorphosis from a crawling creature into a flying creature. By this bodily transition, the caterpillar enters a remarkably different life with very different experiences. Likewise, God designed our natural body (caterpillar) to go through a kind of metamorphosis into a supernatural body (butterfly) for a supernatural life.

The Necessity of the Two-Phase Life. The reason God would create life with a terrestrial phase followed by a celestial phase is that each phase creates its own set of circumstances and experiences needed for the ones brought to heaven to be able to have a consummate relationship with God in eternity. Thus, if one were to come into existence in heaven (without an earthly life), she would be deprived of certain necessary circumstances and experiences (discussed in the next chapter) needed to be able to have a consummate relationship with God. Some atheists[29] and some Christians[30] ask why God didn't just create humans in heaven and bypass our earthly existence altogether. The answer is that if God had created humans in heaven and bypassed the earthly life, the heavenly community would forever be without certain circumstances and experiences needed to rise above a mediocre relationship, resulting in the substantial loss of good, discussed earlier (this is fleshed out in the next chapter). Conversely, if God had created his community to live only an earthly life, for eternity, the human community would miss out on circumstances and experiences inherent in the celestial life necessary in order to be able to have a consummate relationship with God. Both phases of life are needed—the terrestrial and the celestial—and the earthly must occur before the heavenly. As Paul says, the supernatural life does not come first, but the natural life, and after that the supernatural life (1 Cor. 15:46).

The types of circumstances and experiences of the earthly life and their necessity for a consummate relationship are discussed in the next chapter. But in order to fully appreciate the purpose, necessity, and value of the earthly life's circumstances and experiences, the ones inherent in the celestial life must first be discussed, as follows.

3.3 Celestial Phase Circumstances and Experiences

One of the celestial phase circumstances necessary for a consummate relationship with God is what some theologians refer to as the beatific vision—the ultimate communication by God to a member of the heavenly community, as the Bible indicates.[31] Often it is described as beholding God, and particularly Jesus Christ, in all his unimaginable glory. In John's vision of the holy city, the beatific vision is metaphorically represented by the absence of a temple (Rev. 21:22), as God's people then "will see his face, and his name will be on their foreheads" (Rev. 22:4). The circumstance is that of "face-to-face" and supernatural mind-to-mind interactive communication between members of the heavenly community and God (and between themselves).

We may have insight into how this supernatural and direct communication occurs. It appears from the Bible, and from certain scientific and anecdotal sources of evidence, that God may have innately equipped the soul itself with supernatural powers to engage in the beatific vision upon entering heaven. Such powers include mind-to-mind communication (telepathy), seeing things and events take place without the use of natural senses (clairvoyance), and foreknowledge of future events (precognition). Many refer to these supernatural powers of the soul (SPS) as extrasensory perception (ESP), "psychic" ability, or "psi" ability. This involves reception of information by the mind (soul or psyche) without the use of the five physical-biological senses.

This might seem strange to some Christian readers, if not heretical, and there certainly are heresies associated with ESP (SPS).[32] However, evangelical Christian apologists, such as the well-respected Gary Habermas and J. P. Moreland, recognize the plausibility of telepathy in the afterlife.[33] And there appears to be biblical support for innate, *but dormant*, SPS in our earthly life that at selected times is activated by the Holy Spirit.

For example, many times the Bible tells of experiences of certain people that receive transcendent information from the mind of God (telepathy). Some Bible figures are said to have gained information about events happening in places that are far out of the range of the natural senses (clairvoyance) (e.g., Acts 9:10–12). Prophets receive foreknowledge of events yet to happen when such events couldn't be predicted from knowledge of current conditions (precognition) (e.g., Dan. 2:19, 26–45; 7–8; 9:20-27; 10–12). Still others, filled with the Holy Spirit, directly influence matter by thoughts (psychokinesis) (Mark 11:12–14, 20–21; Acts 12:6–10). In silent prayer, the human mind conveys its petition by its thoughts which are heard, seen, and felt in God's mind (Gen. 24:45; 1 Sam. 1:12–13; Psalm 139:1–4, 23; Jer. 12:3; Matt. 12:24–26).

With fully active SPS in the celestial life in heaven, the angels and the redeemed can be in beatific vision and thus receive a phenomenal amount of information. Consciousness is greatly enhanced with intense and dynamic lucidness, alertness, memory, and emotion. Each picks up communications directly from God's mind (telepathy) and the minds of the angels and other redeemed humans. One is able to view an event in the mind's eye happening in a place that is far out of the range of natural sight (clairvoyance). The heavenly citizen can at times find herself having foreknowledge of events yet to happen (precognition), as well as events of the past (postcognition). An initial experience of the celestial life is a life-review of everything we've done—every loving act, and every unloving act (Matt. 10:26; 1 Cor. 4:5). All are able to move physical objects by mental effort alone (psychokinesis) (Acts 12:6–10), as well as heal creatures by thought (psychic healing). With SPS ability among the heavenly community, we should not have difficulty imagining the ultimate fulfillment of Jesus' prayer in John 17[34]—that all disciples of God be one with God in will, just as the three persons of God are one with each other in will (vv. 11, 21–22)—"I in them and you in me" (v. 23).

Of course it is possible for an all-powerful God to miraculously make people experience the beatific vision without innate SPS. But it makes more sense (by Ockham's razor[35]) for God, who has SPS, to have created the soul made in his image with SPS that is to be in an eternal and consummate relationship with him. Furthermore, thousands of controlled laboratory experiments (some of which have been published in peer-reviewed scientific journals) regarding SPS suggest that if humans have SPS, it would be an innate ability of all of humankind (in varying strengths), rather than the ability of only a few.[36] Some have reported having near-death, out-of-body experiences (NDEs/OBEs)[37] and recall being able to see through solid objects, or read the minds of people nearby.[38] Other sources also suggest that SPS is innate among humans, and even animals (e.g., horses, dogs, and cats).[39] SPS for animals would make sense if God brought forth humankind (Adam and Eve) from an evolutionary line in the animal kingdom in some form of biological "great chain of being" and intended that they have a celestial afterlife of bliss (see chapter 9.2).

Evidence That SPS and Other Supernatural Occurrences Are Real. In a 2002 CBS poll, 57 percent of Americans said "they believe in psychic phenomena such as ESP, . . . telepathy, or experiences that can't be explained by normal means."[40] According to a 2005 Gallup poll, about 41 percent of the residents of the United States claim belief in ESP (73 percent claim at least one paranormal belief).[41] The polls might tell us that probably roughly half of the world thinks SPS is hokum. However, SPS is supportable by thousands of controlled laboratory experiments that indicate that some kinds of SPS are repeatable. While the scientific community still labels SPS studies as pseudoscience, there is a small percentage of the scientific community that would like more work done in this field of study.

Nonetheless, many doubt it. This is probably due to a combination of several factors: the inability of the vast majority to engage in an observable SPS-like ability; a lack of a viable materialistic theory for why it would occur; a sparse amount of replicable data; a scientific culture; peer reviews of "straw man" cases; influence from metaphysical naturalism or scientism;[42] television shows like *The Big Bang Theory*[43] or *The Mentalist*;[44] and/or the evidently biased books of popular materialist atheists like Michael Shermer and Victor J. Stenger (1935–2014).

Readers of Shermer's recent book, *The Believing Brain*,[45] who are expecting an objective and comprehensive assessment of SPS (ESP) should be disappointed. He discusses a few straw man opinion points on meta-analysis and Ganzfeld techniques[46] that do not represent anything close to a complete and objective assessment of SPS. Shermer's book lacks discussion of the wide range of salient SPS data, analyses, and research, as are found in the books of scientists and researchers like Russell Targ,[47] Ian Stevenson (1918–2007), Dean Radin, and Charles Tart. As such, an astute investigator of SPS claims need not bother with Shermer's discussion.

What could Shermer say to explain away an incident in March 2015 in which three police officers and two fire fighters in Spanish Fork, Utah, each simultaneously heard a voice without any known materialistic origin? They responded to a call by a fisherman of a car found upside-down and partially submerged in the Spanish Fork River under a bridge. Many hours later the officers and fire fighters arrived at the scene to investigate. They did not expect to find anyone inside the car. They all reported that as they approached, they heard the voice of an adult coming from inside the car say, "Help me, help me." One of them responded, "We're trying. We're trying our best to get in there." The five men turned the car over and found an eighteen-month-old girl, Lily, alive, and her mother, Jennifer Groebeck, deceased for approximately thirteen hours. The police believed she most likely died upon impact from massive trauma.[48]

What could Shermer say to explain away a person who can go into a vision and see and describe things with 100 percent accuracy thousands of miles away that she never before knew existed that were verified by a third party, as well as confirmable past events and future events that later came to pass? I've known such a person as this during the past four decades. I'll call her Beth.[49]

In March 1987, Beth was twenty-eight years old and lived with her husband and two children in Brewer, Maine.[50] She drove to work using the same route at the same time of day. While driving along Wilson Street she began to pass by an auto repair and tire shop, and as she did so it appeared to explode into flames. It seemed very real until she continued past it and realized the explosion occurred only in her mind. The next day she drove to work and it happened again. It happened a third time the following day, and when she arrived at work she told her co-workers about her vision of the explosion. But the next day on her way to work she "spaced out" and missed her turn onto Wilson Street. The different route made her arrive at work five minutes late. When she arrived, all of her co-workers were talking about an explosion and fire at the auto repair and tire shop on Wilson Street and a passing car that was struck by flying debris and crashed. Knowing Beth's usual route to work, they were worried that it was her car that had crashed.

In the spring of 1990, Beth's younger sister, Pamela (younger by about two years), was living with her husband in Big Piney, Wyoming (about 2,300 miles away from where Beth lived). Pamela suspected that her husband was hiding money from her and knew of her older sister's SPS (ESP) ability to find lost items, so she called Beth and asked her for help to find out if her husband was hiding cash and where it could be found. Beth had never seen Pamela's house, but she sat quietly for a moment, cleared her mind, and instantly could see everything Pamela saw in the bedroom. She described the bedroom and Pamela confirmed that the description was accurate. Beth told Pamela to look in the left front pocket of her husband's blue jeans on the floor at the foot of the bed and she would find several coins and some other objects. Pamela checked and found all of them. Beth described some other articles of clothing on a chair and some objects on the bureau. Beth then saw Pamela's husband walking into their garage, opening the trunk of their car, and hiding cash in a hidden compartment that he had apparently made, as if she were having a memory of something that occurred earlier. After they ended their phone conversation, Pamela checked the trunk of the car and found the hidden compartment and cash money inside.

In December 1997, one of Beth's friends asked her if she could tell her where her husband went and who he saw when he left the house so often. Her friend knew Beth could have an SPS (ESP) vision from holding an object in her hands and brought one of her husband's T-shirts for Beth to hold.[51] Beth agreed to use her SPS ability[52] and held the T-shirt and could see everything her friend's husband could see, as if she were the husband driving along and stopping to visit some people at a house. Beth described the road, the house, the garage, and the people. Her friend knew exactly who they were and where her husband had been (and was glad that he wasn't cheating on her). Later, her friend told Beth that she had spoken with friends who confirmed that her husband had been there.

In addition to anecdotal evidence, there is evidence from thousands of well-controlled laboratory experiments with reproduced effects. Recently, research scientist Dean Radin conducted a double-blind study to measure a presentiment effect. Presentiment is the unconscious scanning of and biological response to future events. Volunteers were monitored for skin conductance (stress response) before, during, and after viewing a series of randomly generated images displayed at timed intervals. Some of the images were benign and calm, while others were shocking scenes of violence or sexuality. Radin's study was replicated in four separate experiments. Each one demonstrated an increase in skin conductance seconds before viewing the emotionally charged images, and no stress response prior to viewing the benign images. According to Radin, "The combined odds against chance for these four experiments was 125,000 to 1 in favor of a genuine presentiment effect. These studies suggest that when the average person *is about to see* an emotional picture, he or she will respond before that picture appears (under double-blind conditions)."[53]

Shermer's assessment of NDEs and OBEs, which, by the way, involve activation of the experiencer's SPS (ESP),[54] is no better than his assessment of ESP. He discusses scientific tests that invoke a feeling of floating or flying above the body, passing into a tunnel,[55] or seeing apparitions of loved ones.[56] Yet the tests and the hypotheses he discusses provide no materialistic-scientific explanation regarding veridical NDEs/OBEs, or corroborated reports by third parties of descriptions of things observed by the experiencers that defy any current scientific explanation and that make any future materialistic explanation unlikely.

For example, there is the report of a woman who was brain dead per electroencephalogram (EEG) for about three and one-half hours who regained consciousness while on the way to the morgue. "She precisely described not only the procedures used in her attempted rescue but also the number of persons who came into the hospital room, what they said (she even repeated a joke told to relieve the tension), and perhaps most interestingly, she described the designs on the doctors' ties."[57]

A popular example corroborated by others is a cardiac arrest victim brought to a hospital comatose and cyanotic. During the resuscitation procedures a nurse removed the man's dentures and placed them into a cart. After circulation was restored he remained in a coma and on artificial respiration in the intensive care unit. More than a week later he regained consciousness and was transferred back to the cardiac care unit. He immediately recognized the nurse who had removed his dentures. "He said further that he had watched from above the attempts of hospital staff to resuscitate him in the emergency room, and he described 'correctly and in detail' the room and the people working on him, including the cart in which the nurse had put his dentures.

The nurse corroborated and verified his account."[58]

Beth had a similar NDE/OBE in January 1981 at the James Taylor Osteopathic Hospital. She underwent an operation under general anesthesia to remove a perforated tumor on one of her ovaries that resulted in peritonitis. Beth recalls starting to go under the anesthesia and then being near the ceiling of the operating room and looking down at her body, seeing and hearing the medical staff. The surgeon, Dr. Ortiz, was on her right side dressed in white scrubs. A nurse was standing to his right dressed in blue scrubs. On the other side of the table stood a tall doctor in white scrubs and a nurse in blue scrubs to his left. The anesthesiologist was standing by her head. Beth heard the anesthesiologist say, "Her BP is 60 over 40 and dropping," and she heard Dr. Ortiz say, "We are losing her," and he gave instructions for medication. Three days later she awoke. Beth told Dr. Ortiz what she had seen and heard. He confirmed everything she saw and heard during the operation, but advised her not dwell on it and to focus on getting well.

There are many other such cases. Some involve patients whose souls appear to travel great distances (even miles) from the body, and after their souls return, the patients describe minute details of activities confirmed to have occurred. Some involve blind persons, including people blind from birth; still others involve deaf people who repeat exactly what was said; others are of comatose patients. Characteristics of NDEs/OBEs are similar regardless of age, culture, or worldview.[59] Some involve several people simultaneously experiencing NDEs/OBEs in which they see and speak with one another. One such case reportedly involved a twenty-man fire fighter crew known as the Hotshots, who after being revived from lack of oxygen in a fire were each investigated separately, before any of the other crew members had a chance to talk with one another and learn that the others had also reported having an NDE/OBE.[60]

One of the more well-known cases of a veridical NDE/OBE is that of Vicki Umipeg. Immediately following her premature birth, she was placed in an incubator where she became completely blind. In 1973 Vicki, then twenty-two years old, was riding in a van that crashed. She sustained very serious injuries, including a skull fracture, a concussion, and injuries to her neck, back, and one leg. Immediately following the accident, and while unconscious from the head injury, she found herself outside of her body and looking at the wrecked van. She then returned to her body, where she remained until after she had arrived by ambulance in the emergency room of Harborview

Medical Center, where she found herself near the ceiling watching medical staff work on her body and listening to their conversation. She had some difficulty recognizing her body because she had been blind all her life, but she was able to recognize a few identifying features such as her wedding ring. Then she found herself rising through the ceilings of the hospital to the roof, where she saw the surrounding terrain, and birds.[61] This is one of many cases of blind people experiencing a veridical NDE/OBE.

Similar veridical occurrences are said to have happened to people who experience an OBE that doesn't involve trauma, cardiopulmonary arrest, or a medical condition. One such case is that of my wife in the spring of 1981 in California (about five years before we first met). She fell asleep in the living room of her friend Stacy Wean's parents' house and then sat up and looked down at her body. Instantly, she went up to the roof. She felt incredible peace. She leaned against the chimney and felt a breeze move her hair. She saw the surrounding neighborhood and Stacy's car speedily heading home from work. She saw Stacy run a stop sign and park on the wrong side of the street (which Stacy had never done previously), where one of the tires of the car ran over the edge of a lawn and a sprinkler head. Immediately after her friend came in through the front door, my wife returned to her body and got up from the couch and questioned Stacy about running the stop sign and parking on the wrong side of the street. Stacy was astonished that my wife could know she had run the stop sign and where she had parked her car, because the street and lawn were not visible from the living room. My wife then walked out of the house and saw Stacy's car parked exactly where my wife had seen it while out of her body on the roof, and the broken sprinkler head! At that time my wife did not believe in the idea that a conscious soul could exist apart from the body. She didn't even know what an OBE was, and she wouldn't have thought it possible. To this day she still struggles to make sense of her experience.[62]

Another such example is of a woman who participated in a laboratory experiment conducted by the research scientist Charles Tart, whose background includes psychology and electrical engineering.[63] Prior to the study, she had reported having OBEs while sleeping, so Tart set up experiments to try to collect any evidence of her conscious mind leaving her body. She was set up in a sleep research laboratory where she was hooked up to an EEG to measure sleep states, and an optical plethysmograph to measure her heart rate and relative blood pressure. The room had an observational window, a bed beneath the window, and a small shelf high on a wall next to the observation window on which would be placed a small piece of paper. Tart randomly chose a five-digit number in his office down the hallway and wrote it on the piece of paper. When the woman was set up in the bed, Tart discreetly entered the room and placed the paper flat on the shelf while being careful not to let the woman see it. The number was visible to anyone whose eyes were located approximately six and a half feet or higher from the floor, so it was not visible to the woman. The woman slept while being watched from the observational window. Between about 5:50 and 6:00 a.m., there was a seven-minute period of stage-1 dreaming mixed with transitory periods of brief wakefulness, and then the woman "awakened and called out over the intercom that the target number was 25132," which Tart immediately wrote on the EEG recording. She reported leaving her body and ascending to where she could read the number on the piece of paper that was lying flat on the shelf (she reported that it was lying flat, contrary to her expectation prior to going to sleep that it would be propped up against the wall). "The number 25132 was indeed the correct target number near the ceiling above her bed." The odds of guessing the number by chance alone on one try is one hundred thousand to one.

Shermer presents no alternative materialistic-physiological hypothesis for such occurrences. He has no naturalistic explanation for how two or more people could simultaneously see (by SPS) a ghostly apparition;[64] how two humans and a dog could simultaneously see a ghostly apparition;[65] how several pets react simultaneously to an apparition that is also simultaneously observed by a human;[66] how multiple members of a family could hear their kitchen cabinets slam while they were watching television; or how rocking chairs that are positioned in the four corners of an upstairs room—a room that is locked to keep the children out—are repeatedly stacked together or moved into the adjacent room (possible examples of SPS by spirits[67] or angels).

Victor Stenger's assessment of SPS and NDEs/OBEs in his book *God and the Folly of Faith* is not much different than Shermer's, although Stenger offers the farfetched opinion that materialistically unexplainable reports of sensational veridical NDEs/OBEs must have been cooked up by dishonest people.[68] While it is true that there has been dishonesty by some, a comprehensive survey of veridical NDEs/OBEs makes the "dishonesty hypothesis" look like a conspiracy theory, especially in light of the fact that some NDE/OBE/SPS experiencers didn't believe in the supernatural.[69] What motive, then, would they have for making up a story contrary to their worldview?

Moreover, it is telling that Stenger mentions that the veridical NDE/OBE of "Sarah," who was blind from birth, had been dishonestly reported (brought out in the investigation by Kenneth Ring and Sharon Cooper),[70] but avoids discussion of other extraordinary veridical NDEs/OBEs discussed by Ring and Cooper (and others), similar in caliber to that of Vicki Umipeg mentioned earlier. If dishonesty is the naturalistic explanation for these experiences, why didn't Stenger discuss dishonesty issues regarding any of them? Perhaps the most sensational veridical NDE/OBE is that of Vicki. Why not discuss her case? All in all, it appears that Stenger's goal is not an objective and balanced discussion, but rather a biased one.

Skeptic Keith Augustine discusses blind from birth NDEs/OBEs in his online article, "Hallucinatory Near-Death Experiences."[71] I did not find in Augustine's article a viable, naturally occurring phenomena that would explain Vicki Umipeg's experience. The explanation that the brain of a blind person can "see light" doesn't work because Vicki didn't see mere masses or blobs of colored light—she saw vivid and detailed objects. Another proposed naturalistic explanation is that because it takes a long time for a blind person who gains sight to recognize and identify objects, Vicki didn't have enough time while out of her body to recognize the wrecked van, the emergency room, her body, the roof of the hospital, the terrain, or birds. But this doesn't work because, first, Vicki describes having difficulty recognizing and identifying these things, and second, if her soul was out of her body, she would have had fully active SPS that would have given her a supernaturally powerful mind and intelligence, and relatively instant knowing, as she describes. Her mental ability would have been far beyond the limitations of the normal brain and consciousness. According to leading researcher P. M. H. Atwater, NDE/OBErs blind since birth describe the shapes, sizes, colors, and patterns of objects, and even "people who had entered their hospital room—people they had never touched, heard, or had any knowledge of before . . . *as if they had once been sighted in a time previous to their birth.*"[72]

The Danger of SPS Activation in the Earthly Life without God. SPS is for the beatific vision in the celestial life, though, as previously discussed, there is a revelatory purpose for it in the earthly life when the Holy Spirit and his angels activate it in different ways in some people at appropriate times (discussed further in chapter 12). Such activation is sparse because of God's plan to remain divinely hidden in our stage of development (our earthly life), as discussed in the next chapter. As such, the innate SPS ability that sometimes manifests as telepathy, clairvoyance, precognition, or psychokinesis is part of God's good creation plan. (Such ability may have been a vital part of their pre-fall sinless life in the garden.) But like with so many of the good things that God created, the ability can, and often is, co-opted and misused for deviant purposes.

The activation of SPS in one of us involves some degree of coupling the psyche with the psyche of a supernatural being. If that supernatural being is the Holy Spirit, or one of his angels, the activation is good. Such would be the case in a person who is genuinely searching for God or surrendered in faith to God. But if the supernatural being is one of Satan's angels, the activation is not good. People who indulge the sinful nature, especially in combination with negative psychological issues (a situation any of us can find himself in at one time or another), extend an invitation to evil angels and spirits to come near, or to comingle, or to overtly harass. Other forms of invitation include practices that involve such things as mediumistic channeling, consulting the souls of the dead, séances, automatic writing, Ouija games, palm reading, psychic reading, astrology, spiritism, shamanism, Wicca,[73] and witchcraft rituals. Such things open a door to coupling with an evil angel who is capable of activating a person's SPS ability to see things (some true and some untrue) that ultimately lead away from God's salvation.[74]

Integrally related to SPS activation by the Holy Spirit in this life to communicate truth is the OBE and NDE. Given available evidence, there are apparently occasions of souls in celestial vision (NDEs) and temporary departure from the body (OBEs). Some Christians mistakenly interpret an NDE/OBE in which one travels to heaven and back as a soul's journey to heaven. But during an NDE/OBE, SPS is fully active, and thus a soul is able to be *shown* celestial realities, such as what it is like to travel to heaven, be in heaven, or even talk with God in heaven (2 Cor. 12:1–4). Therefore, NDEs/OBEs do not necessarily suggest that souls have traveled to heaven (or hell), as they could've been recipients of supernatural communication by fully activated SPS relative to things of a spirit realm.

Such communication could be of literal images, but perhaps more likely the images are metaphorical. Many of the images seen by the prophets in vision were metaphorical. For example, the prophet Daniel experiences visions where he sees strange looking animals, including a lion with wings, a bear with three ribs in its mouth, and a leopard with four wings (Dan. 7). It is later explained by an angel that the animals he saw are metaphorical for certain nations (Dan. 8:20–25). The lion is Babylonia, the bear is Medo-Persia, the leopard is Greece, and the terrifying and frightening beast is identified as Rome. Thus, God is known to show the future using metaphorical images. Another example of visions of metaphorical images is the vision of John in Revelation 21–22 (discussed in chapter 10).

The Necessity of the Beatific Vision and SPS for a Consummate Relationship. One of the properties of a consummate relationship is a perfect perception of God's disposition and personality. With a greatly enhanced consciousness, fully active SPS in beatific vision with direct mind-to-mind communication with God, the redeemed of heaven would receive a vast amount of information phenomenally. A multitude of images, sounds, and smells would most effectively convey information of God's plans, his loving actions, answers to any questions, and the understanding of anything a supernaturally empowered human mind could understand. Having received all of this information supernaturally, they would be able to acquire knowledge that would play a key role in having a perfect perception of God's disposition and personality in order to optimally know God, have the greatest love for God, have optimal psychospiritual health, etc. (taking into account other necessary circumstances of the earthly life discussed in the next chapter). In short, having innate and fully activated SPS in beatific vision is necessary to a consummate relationship with God that spontaneously emanates the greatest measure of expressions of love and goodness.

Conclusion

God's objective is to bring into existence the greatest possible good through a consummate relationship between God and his community of created persons. The consummate relationship must include certain necessary properties that require certain circumstances and experiences, such as a temporary terrestrial life followed by an everlasting celestial life (two-phase life) and the celestial experience of God-given SPS ability of the soul to experience the beatific vision. The next chapter discusses why the earthly life of divine hiddenness is also necessary if the redeemed are to have a consummate relationship with God in eternity.

NOTES to Chapter 3

1. Jill and her older brother are composites of several people I learned of during my investigative study of the credibility of Christianity.

2. Being all-powerful and all-knowing does not mean God can do anything. He cannot do that which is logically impossible. As Christian apologists (e.g., William Lane Craig) have said, God cannot defy the law of noncontradiction—he cannot create a married bachelor or a square circle. (God's ability is discussed in chapter 6.1.)

3. "Perfectly loving and good" sums up perfect wisdom, compassion, justice, responsibility, accountability, humility, honesty, meekness, mercy, care and respect for the well-being of others, faithfulness, and all of the relationship principles represented in God's Ten Commandments (Rom. 13:8–10), as well as in Jesus' teachings in the New Testament concerning having a right disposition.

4. My understanding of the problem of divine hiddenness results in large part from atheist John L. Schellenberg's discussion in *Divine Hiddenness and Human Reason* (Ithaca, NY: Cornell University Press, 1993), as well as his more recent writings on the same subject. Schellenberg received his doctorate degree in philosophy at Oxford in the late 1980s (studying with Richard Swinburne, David Brown, Maurice Wiles, and Anthony Kenny). *Divine Hiddenness and Human Reason* is Schellenberg's doctoral thesis at Oxford. Currently Schellenberg is professor of philosophy at Mount Saint Vincent University in Canada and adjunct professor in the faculty of graduate studies at Dalhousie University.

5. "Omni" is a Latin prefix meaning "all" or "every." The Bible depicts God's disposition as perfectly (flawlessly) good, or all good, or omnigood (Deut. 32:4; 2 Sam. 22:31; Ps. 19:7; Matt. 5:48), meaning that there could not be any better disposition. Sometimes Christians refer to God's disposition as "infinitely good," but this is only coherent with a definition of "infinite" that is synonymous with "perfect," which appears to be the definition implied in the writings of some theologians (e.g., Thomas Aquinas) [Frederick R. Tennant, *Philosophical Theology: Volume II: The World, the Soul, and God* (New York: Cambridge University Press, 1956), 140–141].

6. Thus, the atheist argument that God existing alone prior to creating anything constituted the greatest possible good, and therefore God need not have created, fails; for further discussion, see chapter 6.2.

7. Matt. 16:27; Rom. 1:5; 2:6; Phil. 2:17; 1 Thess. 1:3; 2 Thess. 1:11; Jam. 2:14–26; Rev. 18:6; 20:12–13; 22:12.

8. Nathaniel Branden, *The Power of Self-Esteem: An Inspiring Look at Our Most Important Psychological Resource* (Deerfield Beach, FL: Health Communications, Inc., 1992). Branden (1930–2014) received his MA in psychology from New York University and his PhD in psychology from California Graduate Institute. He authored over twenty books, including *The Psychology of Self-Esteem*, *The Six Pillars of Self-Esteem*, and *Taking Responsibility*.

9. Heaven is not a place up in the sky or anywhere in the universe that could be visited

using a spacecraft launched from Earth, but rather is a state of existence that involves a celestial spatial dimension(s) or plane(s) of existence. Consequently, a person present in heaven could be simultaneously present on earth, although undetectable by our physical senses (an extradimensional hypothesis is needed to understand heaven as a place). At death, Jesus' soul entered the celestial spatial dimension(s) and thus entered heaven (John 14:2–3). In Acts 1:9 the resurrected Jesus went to heaven by ascending into the sky, but he did not have to leave the ground to go to heaven. He ascended into the sky to provide a sign for his disciples concerning the manner of his return in power and glory (Acts 1:10–11), which would be distinct from the manner of any "antichrist" pretending to be the returning Jesus (Matt. 24:23–27).

10. See also Gal. 5:9 and Mark 8:15.

11. *Zondervan NIV Bible Commentary, Volume 2: New Testament*, consulting eds.: Kenneth L. Barker and John R. Kohlenberger III (Grand Rapids, MI: Zondervan Publishing House, 1994), 350.

12. Ibid., 1165.

13. Primarily from: Martin E. P. Seligman, *Flourish: A Visionary New Understanding of Happiness and Well-Being* (New York: Atria Paperback, 2011), 5–29; and Nathaniel Branden, *The Power of Self-Esteem*; and in lesser part from Benjamin B. Lahey in *Psychology: An Introduction*, eighth ed. (New York: McGraw-Hill, 2004).

14. John 3:14.

15. For a brief discussion of the principle (law) of justice through accountability see appendix D.

16. *Zondervan NIV Bible Commentary, Volume 2: New Testament*, 982.

17. The expression "long to look" in 1 Pet. 1:12 means "to stoop over to look," which implies "willingness to exert or inconvenience oneself to obtain a better perspective. The specific tense used means continuous regard rather than a quick look" [*Zondervan NIV Bible Commentary, Volume 2: New Testament*, 1044].

18. Matt. 14:26; Mark 6:49; Luke 16:19–31; 23:43; 2 Cor. 5:1–8; Phil. 1:23; Rev. 6:9–11. The biblical view of an immortal soul is corroborated by a large and growing body of scientific and anecdotal evidence, some of which is discussed in each of the following: Edward F. Kelly and Emily Williams Kelly, et al., *Irreducible Mind: Toward a Psychology for the 21st Century* (Lanham, MD: Rowman & Littlefield Publishers, Inc., 2010 paperback ed.); Pim van Lommel, *Consciousness Beyond Life: The Science of Near-Death Experience* (New York: HarperCollins Publishers, 2010); Gary R. Habermas and J. P. Moreland, *Beyond Death: Exploring the Evidence for Immortality* (Eugene, OR: Wipf and Stock Publishers, 2004); Charles T. Tart, *The End of Materialism: How Evidence of the Paranormal Is Bringing Science and Spirit Together* (Oakland, CA: New Harbinger Publications, Inc., 2009); Russell Targ, *The Reality of ESP: A Physicist's Proof of Psychic Abilities* (Wheaton, IL: Quest Books, 2012); Dean Radin, *Supernormal: Science, Yoga, and the Evidence for Extraordinary Psychic Abilities* (New York: Deepak Chopra Books, an imprint of the Crown Publishing Group, a division of Random House, Inc., 2013); *Entangled Minds: Extrasensory Experiences in a Quantum Reality* (New York: Paraview Pocket Books,

2006); *The Conscious Universe: The Scientific Truth of Psychic Phenomena* (New York: HarperCollins Publishers, 1997); P. M. H. Atwater, *Near-Death Experiences, the Rest of the Story: What They Teach Us about Living, Dying, and Our True Purpose* (New York: MJF Books, 2011); Jason Offutt, *Darkness Walks: The Shadow People Among Us* (San Antonio, TX: Anomalist Books, 2009); Brad Steiger, *Shadow World: True Encounters with Beings from the Dark Side* (San Antonio, TX: Anomalist Books, 2007; Scott S. Smith, *The Soul of Your Pet: Evidence for the Survival of Animals After Death* (Edmonds, WA: Holmes Publishing Group, 1998).

19. "The heavenly realms" of the angels of heaven (Eph. 3:10) and of the angels condemned to hell (Eph. 6:12).

20. The "intermediate state" is a term used by Christian theologians to denote the disembodied state of a soul from the time of bodily death until a resurrection body is received, which for most of humankind is at the end of the world (1 Cor. 15:50–52; 1 Thess. 4:13–17). It is a state of a soul that would not occur if not for humankind's fall into a sinful nature. Thus, as long as Adam, Eve, and their descendants continue in right relationship with God (continual obedience) they'd remain healthy, but eventually each body would expire from old age. At death, a resurrection-translation would immediately occur so that no intermediate state would be experienced. The natural body would instantly be transformed into a supernatural body and the soul would essentially jump from one to the other. Such a "death" (really a translation without experiencing death) would not create the fear and dread and mourning associated with death since sin entered the world at the fall. Such a "death" would not be our "enemy" (1 Cor. 15:25), as it would be without the "sting" or "victory" that death with an intermediate state has had (1 Cor. 15:55–56). This, of course, incorporates the belief that Adam was not made with an immortal body, which appears to be what Genesis teaches. Even a literal reading of the Eden narrative shows Adam and Eve had to "eat" from the "tree of life" or die like the animals (Gen. 2:17; 3:19; 3:23–24). According to Old Testament scholar John H. Walton: "The human body in and of itself was inclined to deterioration. . . . Thus, when the human pair was prevented from having access to the tree of life, death became an unavoidable reality. In this way, Paul's statements (Rom. 5:12-14) can be understood that with sin came death. That does not mean that the human body passed from immortal to mortal, but that the means by which mortality could be held at bay was taken away. This conclusion also suggests that death existed in the rest of the created world prior to the Fall" [*The NIV Application Commentary: Genesis* (Grand Rapids, MI: Zondervan, 2001), 183–184]. Scholar Tryggve N. D. Mettinger agrees: humans were created mortal and were destined for immortality (without a disembodied state), which was lost when they fell into sin [*The Eden Narrative: A Literary and Religio-historical Study of Genesis 2–3* (Winona Lake, IN: Eisenbrauns, 2007), 31, 59–60]. (See also Eccl. 3:18–20.) And according to Charles H. Dodd (1884–1973): "Obviously we cannot accept such a speculation as an account of the origin of death [that human beings began to experience bodily death because they had sinned], which is a natural process inseparable from organic existence in the world we know, and devoid of any moral significance. For the reason why the Jewish mind felt death to be unnatural and peculiarly horrible, we must probably go back to the state in which the Jewish

religion knew nothing of a life after death, so that death meant separation from God [Ps. 115:17]. This feeling, no doubt, Paul shared, and it is for him one of the greatest blessings of Christianity that bodily death no longer has this character, but to be 'absent from the body' is to be 'present with the Lord' (2 Cor. V. 8). But *he is speaking here of death apart from Christ, of bodily death as the symbol of final separation from God, which we might describe* (though Paul would not have used this language) *as spiritual death*. The death with which he is really concerned is the state of the man who is dead in trespasses and sins [Eph. 2:1; Rom. 7:9–10; 8:6]. . . . Thus 'the sting of death is sin' [1 Cor. 15:56]" [*The Epistle of Paul to the Romans* (London: Hodder and Stoughton, 1932), 81. Emphasis added]. All this is congruous with Paul's verse that says God did not "plant the body that will be" for eternity (1 Cor. 15:37). Therefore, we may understand Paul's statements that death is the result of sin (Rom. 5:12, 14, 21; 6:23; 8:10) as following the traditional rabbinic language of his time (Matt. 8:22; Luke 9:60), commonly used to mean "spiritual death" and not physical death. The "death" Adam and Eve were warned would follow disobedience (Gen. 2:17; 3:3–4) was what is referred to by the prophet John as the "second death" (Rev. 2:11; 20:6, 14; 21:8)—the ultimate "curse" and banishment from God and his community (Gen. 3:23; 2 Thess. 1:9) (the subject of hell is discussed in chapters 10 and 11).

21. John 17:3. See also John 10:10 and 1 Tim. 6:19.

22. Gary R. Habermas and J. P. Moreland, *Beyond Death: Exploring the Evidence for Immortality* (Eugene, OR: Wipf and Stock Publishers, 2004), 304. Habermas received his PhD in history and philosophy of religion at Michigan State University and his MA in philosophical theology from the University of Detroit. He chairs the department of philosophy and theology at Liberty University in Lynchburg, Virginia. He has written numerous books and articles on life-after-death issues. Moreland earned his PhD in philosophy from the University of Southern California. His dissertation advisor was the eminent Christian professor Dallas Willard. Moreland received a BS in chemistry from the University of Missouri. He is a distinguished professor of philosophy at Talbot School of Theology, Biola University, and director of The Center for Christian Worldview and Spiritual Formation. He has authored, edited, or contributed papers to more than thirty books and published over thirty magazine articles in such publications as *Christianity Today* and *Christian Research Journal*. He recently authored the books: *Consciousness and the Existence of God*, *The Recalcitrant Imago Dei*, and *The God Question: An Invitation to a Life of Meaning*.

23. *Zondervan NIV Bible Commentary, Volume 2: New Testament*, consulting eds.: Kenneth L. Barker and John R. Kohlenberger III (Grand Rapids, MI: Zondervan Publishing House, 1994), 653; John Phillips, *Exploring 1 Corinthians: An Expository Commentary* (Grand Rapids, MI: Kregel Publications, 2002), 369. Phillips received his DMin degree from Luther Rice Seminary. He served as assistant director of the Moody Correspondence School as well as director of the Emmaus Correspondence School, one of the world's largest Bible correspondence ministries. He also taught in the Moody Evening School and on Moody Broadcasting radio network.

24. *Matthew Henry's Commentary on the Whole Bible* (Peabody, MA: Hendrickson Publishers, 1991), 1821.

25. Both the angels and the resurrected and celestial Jesus can walk through walls,

disappear into thin air, fly through the air, etc., although they can also be handled, be hugged, and eat food as we can. Interdimensional travel from a celestial dimension to our spatial dimension would explain how this is possible.

26. Isa. 65:17; Matt. 5:5; 2 Pet. 3:13; Rev. 21:1.

27. Gary R. Habermas and J. P. Moreland, *Beyond Death: Exploring the Evidence for Immortality* (Eugene, OR: Wipf and Stock Publishers, 2004), 290.

28. Neil A. Campbell, *Biology*, third ed. (Redwood City, CA: The Benjamin/Cummings Publishing Company, Inc., 1993), 624–625. Campbell received his MA in zoology from UCLA, where he studied the control of protein synthesis during animal development, and went on to the University of California, Riverside, where he received his PhD in biology.

29. John W. Loftus, *Why I Became an Atheist: A Former Preacher Rejects Christianity* (Amherst, NY: Prometheus Books, 2008), 251.

30. Paul Copan, *That's Just Your Interpretation: Responding to Skeptics Who Challenge Your Faith* (Grand Rapids, MI: BakerBooks, 2001), 106.

31. Psalm 16:11; Isa. 35:10; Matt. 5:8; John 17:24; 1 Cor. 13:11–12; Rev. 7:9–17; 19:6–8; 21:3; 22:4.

32. My discussion of SPS (also known as ESP, psychic ability, or psi ability) is not intended to suggest that Christians be open to the concepts and practices of New Age, the occult, spiritism, astrology, psychic readings, and the like. On the contrary, later in this chapter I warn that the attempt to activate the supernatural powers of the soul (SPS) in this life, through means other than Divine enablement, is forbidden and invites members of the community of Satan into the home and life. Even some non-Christians know this to be true by their experience with such things as mediumistic channeling, consulting the souls of the dead, séances, automatic writing, Ouija games, palm reading, psychic reading, astrology, spiritism, shamanism, Wicca, and witchcraft [Jason Offutt, *Darkness Walks: The Shadow People Among Us* (San Antonio, TX: Anomalist Books, 2009), 151–162].

33. Gary Habermas and J. P. Moreland, *Beyond Death: Exploring the Evidence for Immortality,* 232, 235.

34. Matthew Henry (1662–1714) points out that "this prayer of Christ will not have its complete answer till all the saints come to heaven, for then, and not till then, they shall be *perfect in* one" [*Matthew Henry's Commentary on the Whole Bible* (Peabody, MA: Hendrickson Publishers, 1991), 1624, emphasis in the original].

35. A principle of parsimony, economy, or succinctness used in logic and problem solving that suggests that with two or more competing hypotheses, the simplest hypothesis with the fewest assumptions should be given the greater probability.

36. There is a growing body of empirical evidence that suggests that the human mind may have innate SPS that is not derived from chemical and electrical changes in our brains. The ability includes psychic phenomena such as telepathy, clairvoyance, precognition, psychokinesis, and psychic healing. Thousands of experimental findings show that "human beings can sometimes show mind-to-mind communication, clairvoyantly know about distant aspects of the physical world, precognize the

future, and affect both nonliving and living things by willing alone" [Charles T. Tart, *The End of Materialism: How Evidence of the Paranormal Is Bringing Science and Spirit Together* (Oakland, CA: New Harbinger Publications, Inc., 2009). Tart received his PhD in psychology at the University of North Carolina at Chapel Hill and studied electrical engineering at the Massachusetts Institute of Technology. He is known for his psychological work on the nature of consciousness, as one of the founders of the field of transpersonal psychology, and for his research in scientific Parapsychology]. See also Russell Targ, *The Reality of ESP: A Physicist's Proof of Psychic Abilities* (Wheaton, IL: Quest Books, 2012). Targ received his bachelor's degree in physics from Queens College and did graduate work in physics at Columbia University. He has received two National Aeronautics and Space Administration awards for inventions and contributions to lasers and laser communications and is a pioneer in the development of the laser and laser applications. See also Dean Radin, *Supernormal: Science, Yoga, and the Evidence for Extraordinary Psychic Abilities* (New York: Deepak Chopra Books, an imprint of the Crown Publishing Group, a division of Random House, Inc., 2013); *Entangled Minds: Extrasensory Experiences in a Quantum Reality* (New York: Paraview Pocket Books, 2006); and *The Conscious Universe: The Scientific Truth of Psychic Phenomena* (New York: HarperCollins Publishers, 1997). Dean Radin, PhD, is chief scientist at the Institute of Noetic Sciences (IONS) and adjunct faculty in the Department of Psychology at Sonoma State University.

37. While I believe NDEs (particularly the veridical kind) provide evidence of the supernatural and of God's existence, depicting details of God and the afterlife based on a synthesis of NDE reports is problematic. Reasons why include: (1) NDEs are fragmentary (notwithstanding similarities between NDEs that are categorized); (2) NDEs often involve a sensed "border" or limit to where the experiencer can go, which implies that knowledge gained of the afterlife is limited; and (3) NDEs involve ESP (SPS) activation by which the experiencer receives transcendent information specific to the needs of the experiencer, rather than a full disclosure of the afterlife, and sometimes with metaphorical sights, sounds, and feelings, which can be misinterpreted as literal. As such, it is not surprising that a researcher's synthesis of NDE reports could conflict with Bible doctrines on God, the judgment, Christ, heaven, or hell. On the other hand, it is interesting that much of the content of NDEs (even by the nonreligious) tell of a triune God who created everything and is all-powerful, all-knowing, and all-loving and good and just (consistent with some of God's attributes in the Bible).

38. One example is a man with an out-of-body experience caused by complications during surgery. He claimed to have never before heard of near-death experiences and to have had no interest in paranormal phenomena or anything of that nature. He suddenly became aware that he was hovering above his body near the ceiling. He heard everything said, including one of the operating staff say: "Hurry up, you bloody bastard." He could also "read the minds of everybody in the room" [Pim van Lommel, *Consciousness Beyond Life: The Science of Near-Death Experience* (New York: HarperCollins Publishers, 2010), 21–22. Van Lommel is a world-renowned cardiologist. Since his initial study of near-death experiences, which was published in

the prestigious medical journal *The Lancet*, Dr. van Lommel has resigned his post as a practicing cardiologist to devote his time to further research and lecturing on near-death experiences all over the world].

39. A great many NDErs report encountering animals that telepathically communicated [P. M. H. Atwater, *Near-Death Experiences, the Rest of the Story: What They Teach Us About Living, Dying, and Our True Purpose* (New York: MJF Books, 2011), 22]. Atwater received her Letters of the Humanities doctorate from International College of Spiritual and Psychic Studies, Montreal, Quebec, in 1992 and was awarded an honorary PhD in therapeutic counseling from Medicina Alternativa Institute, The Open International University for Complementary Medicines, Colombo, Sri Lanka, in 2005. Atwater has been conducting research in near-death studies since 1978. Activated SPS may be a reason why there are reported sightings of intangible or ethereal beings of various humanoid shapes, often referred to as "shadow people," and animal shapes [Jason Offutt, *Darkness Walks: The Shadow People Among Us* (San Antonio, TX: Anomalist Books, 2009); Brad Steiger, *Shadow World: True Encounters with Beings from the Dark Side* (San Antonio, TX: Anomalist Books, 2007); Scott S. Smith, *The Soul of Your Pet: Evidence for the Survival of Animals After Death* (Edmonds, WA: Holmes Publishing Group, 1998)]. These reports are indiscriminate of worldview, culture, religion, race, nationality, age, education, or career and span the entire record of human history. Some of the reports are made by scientists who are skeptical of the existence of God or the supernatural, and are leery of stories by people with overactive imaginations. Given the apparent verifiability of the reports, attempts to explain them away as naturally occurring physical phenomena fall substantially short. The descriptions of the sightings are remarkably similar in detail, even though many of the people reporting them had never heard of the sightings of others and lived on opposite sides of the planet. In some cases, two or more people see an apparition simultaneously [a few examples are reported by journalist Jason Offutt in his book *Darkness Walks: Shadow People Among Us*, 49, 56, 94–96, 124, 130–131, 139]. In others, it is apparent that the partially visible beings are seen simultaneously by people and their dogs or cats [Offutt reports on a few of these claims in *Darkness Walks: The Shadow People Among Us*, 39, 49, 56, 80-81, 130-131]. If a reason for the sightings by humans and animals is activated SPS, then it would appear that SPS is more likely an innate ability of humans and animals.

40. Bootie Cosgrove-Mather, "Poll: Most Believe in Psychic Phenomena," CBS News, April 29, 2002, http://www.cbsnews.com/news/poll-most-believe-in-psychic-phenomena, assessed on September 21, 2015.

41. Zak Bagans and Kelly Crigger, *Dark World: Into the Shadows with the Lead Investigator of the Ghost Adventures Crew* (Auberry, CA: Victory Belt Publishing, 2011), 232.

42. Adherents of metaphysical naturalism (a view that the natural sciences reveal all of the elements and principles that exist) and scientism (a sense of which holds that truth is discovered by science alone) tend to hold a dogmatic commitment to a materialistic philosophy that dismisses non-materialist or non-naturalist possibilities, a priori, leaving only naturalistic explanations, such as naturally occurring hallucination, psychopathology, deception, overactive imagination, or false positives of cameras

and videos made by light reflections, shadows from natural light sources, lens flares, double exposure, etc. (despite analyses by experts in video technology, physics, film editing, and staging that rule out false positives, video tampering, or staging) as real possibilities.

43. *The Big Bang Theory* is a sitcom in the United States. In the twelfth episode of the third season, entitled "The Psychic Vortex," Leonard argues with his girlfriend, Penny, who expresses her belief that psychic ability is real. Leonard is an experimental physicist at a university, while Penny is a waitress who had attended a community college and is trying to develop an acting career. I inferred from the episode a portrayal of a stereotype that people who believe in psychic or SPS ability are either uneducated in the sciences, irrational, and/or unintelligent. The reality, however, is that many intelligent, well-known physicists and other scientists, astronauts, business people, military leaders, and even former U.S. presidents, have expressed their belief in phenomena that science says do not exist. Examples include: physicists Albert Einstein (1879–1955) and Harold E. Puthoff, astrophysicist Peter Sturrock, neurologist Sigmund Freud (1856–1939), professor of psychiatry Ian Stevenson, Abraham Lincoln (1809–1865), and General George Patton (1885-1945), to name a few [Michael Schmicker, *Best Evidence*, second ed. (Lincoln, NE: iUniverse, 2002), 11–30].

44. *The Mentalist* is a television series in the United States (from 2008–2015) in which the lead character, Patrick Jane, formerly pretended to be a psychic using highly developed observational skills and is a consultant to the California Bureau of Investigation. Jane admits to having been a fraudulent psychic and often asserts that "there's no such thing as psychics."

45. Michael Shermer, *The Believing Brain: From Ghosts and Gods to Politics and Conspiracies—How We Construct Beliefs and Reinforce Them as Truths* (New York: St. Martin's Press, 2011).

46. Ibid., 149.

47. Russell Targ received a bachelor of science in physics from Queens College, followed by two years of graduate work in physics at Columbia University. He has worked in the Electronics and Bioengineering Laboratory at SRI as a senior research physicist in a program founded by Harold E. Puthoff. The two conducted research into psychic abilities and their operational use for the U.S. intelligence community, including NASA, the CIA, Defense Intelligence Agency, and Army Intelligence. In recent decades he worked in electro-optics as a senior staff scientist at the Lockheed Missiles and Space Company, where he contributed to aviation windshear sensing applications of Doppler heterodyne lidar technology.

48. http://abcnews.go.com/US/salt-lake-city-responders-heard-mystery-voice-rescuing/story?id=29531199, assessed on March 28, 2015. The police officers were Bryan Dewitt, Jared Warner, and Tyler Beddoes. The fire fighters were Paul Tomadakis and Lee Mecham.

49. The name "Beth" is made up by me. She gave me permission to discuss her SPS (ESP) experiences and her NDE/OBE on the condition that I do not disclose her real name or the real name of her younger sister. Even though I've known Beth for over

forty years, I did not learn of her ability until several years ago during my investigative study of the issues, evidence, and arguments for and against Christianity. I questioned witnesses who confirmed things Beth relayed to me.

50. Her first SPS vision happened when she was nine or ten years old in a family of seven in a house built in the late eighteen century in Winterport, Maine (1968–1969). She was on the staircase and saw herself walking down a winding staircase of a Southern mansion wearing an elegant dress. She heard the dress swish as she walked down the stairs and she smelled a sweet fragrance unknown to her at the time (almost thirty years later, after moving to North Carolina, she discovered that the fragrance was from magnolias in bloom). She saw young men and women in the foyer. The men were wearing uniforms and the women were wearing gowns. Years later, when she saw a picture of uniforms of the military forces of the Confederate States, she understood her vision to take place during the Civil War.

51. Having psychic visions while holding an object is called psychoscopy, token-object reading, or psychometry.

52. In March 1998, approximately twenty months after her conversion to Christ in July 1996, Beth came to believe that use of her ability invited evil angelic influences into her life, and since then has declined to use her ability. A significant SPS (ESP) event that played a role in her 1996 conversion occurred nearly three years earlier in September 1993, following the death of her younger sister as a result of an automobile accident. Beth asked to be taken to her deceased sister's bedroom. I was with Beth and went along with her. I did not then realize what she had planned to do. I observed as Beth looked in her sister's jewelry box to find a cross necklace that her sister often wore. Beth knew her sister wore it wherever she went, so she suspected that she might get a reading from it to find out how the accident happened and how her sister had been fatally injured. She clasped the necklace in her hand, sat on the bed, and immediately had a vision of what her sister had experienced in the car accident as if she were her sister, tumbling down a hill at night and feeling intense pain. In the vision, she was in and out of consciousness, in the ambulance, and in the hospital, and then very suddenly she felt that she was being quickly sucked upward and out of her body and seeing lights streak by as she headed toward greater and greater light. Just then she let go of the necklace and felt emotionally drained for a while. I was in disbelief (until over thirteen years later when my disbelief gradually and eventually gave way to belief). Even though Beth did not then have faith in God, her acquired understanding from the vision was that the light to which she was headed was heaven. This turned out nearly three years later to be a key factor in her belief in God.

53. Dean Radin, *Entangled Minds: Extrasensory Experiences in a Quantum Reality* (New York: Paraview Pocket Books, 2006), 164–168. Emphasis in the original. Radin received both his master's degree in electrical engineering and his doctorate degree in educational psychology from the University of Illinois at Urbana-Champaign. He has been senior scientist at the Institute of Noetic Sciences (IONS) in Petaluma, California, since 2001 and is on the adjunct faculty in the Department of Psychology at Sonoma State University, on the distinguished consulting faculty at Saybrook Graduate School and Research Center, and former president of the Parapsychological Association.

54. An inference drawn by researchers from studying NDE/OBE research results [Pim van Lommel, *Consciousness Beyond Life: The Science of Near-Death Experience* (New York: HarperCollins Publishers, 2010), 20, 60–62]. As researcher P. M. H. Atwater says: "If you weren't psychic before a near-death experience, you become psychic after. If you were psychic before, you become very psychic after." [*Near-Death Experiences, the Rest of the Story*, 78.] See also Edward F. Kelly and Emily Williams Kelly, et al., *Irreducible Mind: Toward a Psychology for the 21st Century* (Lanham, MD: Rowman & Littlefield Publishers, Inc., 2010 paperback ed.), 367–421, and footnote 26.

55. Contrary to popular opinion, a vast majority of NDE experiencers do *not* report having a "tunnel" experience [P. M. H. Atwater, *Near-Death Experiences, the Rest of the Story*, 20].

56. Michael Shermer, *The Believing Brain*, 152–162.

57. Gary R. Habermas and J. P. Moreland, *Beyond Death: Exploring the Evidence for Immortality* (Eugene, OR: Wipf and Stock Publications, 1998, paperback version pub. 2004), 161.

58. Edward F. Kelly and Emily Williams Kelly, et al., *Irreducible Mind: Toward a Psychology for the 21st Century* (Lanham, MD: Rowman & Littlefield Publishers, Inc., 2010 paperback ed.), 390.

59. Pim van Lommel, *Consciousness Beyond Life: The Science of Near-Death Experience* (New York: HarperCollins Publishers, 2010), 19–26; Gary Habermas and J. P. Moreland, *Beyond Death: Exploring the Evidence for Immortality*, 157–161.

60. P. M. H. Atwater, *Near-Death Experiences, the Rest of the Story*, 39.

61. Pim van Lommel, *Consciousness Beyond Life: The Science of the Near-Death Experience*, 24–25; Kenneth Ring and Sharon Cooper, "Near-Death and Out-of-Body Experiences in the Blind: A Study of Apparent Eyeless Vision," *Journal of Near-Death Studies*, 16(2), winter 1997, 108–112; Kenneth Ring and Sharon Cooper, *Mindsight: Near-Death and Out-of-Body Experiences in the Blind*, second ed. (Bloomington, IN: William James Center for Consciousness Studies at the Institute of Transpersonal Psychology/iUniverse, Inc., 2008), 14–17, 26–38, 101.

62. I understand now that what she described is referred to as a spontaneous out-of-body experience (OBE), which is said to happen to approximately 10 percent of the general population and nearly 25 percent of children and adolescents. Spontaneous OBEs usually occur on the threshold between waking and sleeping [Pim van Lommel, *Consciousness Beyond Life: The Science of the Near-Death Experience*, 77].

63. Charles T. Tart, *The End of Materialism: How Evidence of the Paranormal Is Bringing Science and Spirit Together* (Oakland, CA: New Harbinger Publications, Inc., 2009), 199–208. Tart earned his PhD in psychology at the University of North Carolina at Chapel Hill and studied electrical engineering at the Massachusetts Institute of Technology. He is known for his psychological work on the nature of consciousness, as one of the founders of the field of transpersonal psychology, and for his research in scientific parapsychology. There is mistaken information on the Internet that this woman ("Miss Z") had four guesses at the five-digit number, which

would lower the odds of a correct guess, but anyone who has actually read about the experiment in Tart's book can unmistakably see that during the four nights she had only one OBE and one instance of calling out a number that she claimed to have seen while out of her body (which Tart believes may have involved some form of ESP). Internet surfers also mistakenly think that Tart dozed off during the night that Miss Z had the OBE/ESP and called out the correct number, but nowhere in Tart's discussion of the study does he mention dozing off. Moreover, being hooked up to the electrodes allowed for very little movement; if Miss Z had stood up to see the number, the equipment would've clearly revealed it, as it would've caused the recording pens to leave a very distinctive trace on the polygraph record. One possible flaw in the experiment, however, was that "there was a remote possibility that she might subliminally have been able to see the target reflected in the glass surface of a clock," although "she called the five digits out in their correct left-right order" [Edward F. Kelly and Emily Williams Kelly, et al., *Irreducible Mind: Toward a Psychology for the 21st Century,* 401–402].

64. Edward F. Kelly and Emily Williams Kelly, et al., *Irreducible Mind: Toward a Psychology for the 21st Century,* 401–402; Jack Rourke, *The Rational Psychic: A Skeptic's Guide to Extraordinary Perception* (Boulder, CO: Sounds True, Inc., 2012), 38; Michael Schmicker, *Best Evidence: An Investigative Reporter's Three Year Quest to Uncover the Best Scientific Evidences for ESP, Psychokinesis, Mental Healing, Ghosts and Poltergeists, Dowsing, Mediums, Near Death Experiences, Reincarnation, and Other Impossible Phenomena That Refuse to Disappear*, second ed. (Lincoln, NE: iUniverse, Inc., 2002), 216–217, 220. Schmicker points out that researcher Ian Stevenson of the Division of Personality Studies discovered that approximately 40 percent of all claims of ghost sightings involve multiple witnesses.

65. Many such cases have been claimed. A few examples are in Jason Offutt, *Darkness Walks: The Shadow People Among Us* (San Antonio, TX: Anomalist Books, 2009), 39, 49, 56, 80–81, 94–96, 124, 130–131, 133–134, 139, 154. One instance is of two unbelievers in anything paranormal, Gary and Melissa Galka, who in 2004 simultaneously encountered a spirit [Zak Bagans and Kelly Crigger, *Dark World: Into the Shadows with the Lead Investigator of the Ghost Adventures Crew* (Auberry, CA: Victory Belt Publishing, 2011), 105–106].

66. Scott S. Smith, *The Soul of Your Pet: Evidence for the Survival of Animals After Death* (Edmonds, WA: Holmes Publishing Group, 1998), 47–51.

67. Some Christians are of the opinion that observed ghosts are inconsistent with the Bible, yet in the gospels of Matthew and Luke, Jesus is depicted on two different occasions to assuage the fear of the disciples by assuring them that he was not a ghost. When Jesus walked on the water of a lake at night the disciples were terrified because they believed they were seeing a "ghost" until Jesus identified himself to them (Matt. 24:26). After his crucifixion, Jesus appeared (out of thin air) before the disciples inside of a locked room (John 20:19). "They were startled and frightened, thinking they saw a ghost." To assure them that he was tangible, Jesus said, "Touch me and see; a ghost does not have flesh and bones, as you see I have" (Luke 24:37–39). The concept of souls in a celestial realm that are at times perceived or observed by people through SPS activation (whether activation by the Holy Spirit or activation

by evil angels) is not unbiblical. Condemned souls and evil angels awaiting final judgment to hell could work in concert to harass people; and saved souls could work in concert with the holy angels as ministering spirits in training. But the Bible warns that evil angels can masquerade as loved ones (2 Cor. 11:14). Thus we are warned not to consult the dead (Lev. 19:31; Deut. 18:9–11; Isa. 8:19).

68. Victor J. Stenger, *God and the Folly of Faith: The Incompatibility of Science and Religion* (Amherst, NY: Prometheus Books, 2012), 233–234.

69. From my experience as a paralegal in addition to what I've read about how to evaluate the reliability of witnesses, I feel I've acquired reasonable skill in spotting signs of dishonesty in anecdotal/testimonial evidence, and with regard to my wife's account of her OBE, I (including when I was an atheist) could find no hint whatsoever of dishonesty, embellishment, or lack of recollection of minute details, even after what has now been over three decades. Moreover, she had never believed in the possibility of OBEs, and to this day it is difficult for her to believe in the idea that a soul can exist outside the body. And before my investigative study of NDEs/OBEs/SPS (ESP) during the past several years I did not believe that SPS or OBEs were possible.

70. Victor J. Stenger, *God and the Folly of Faith*, 234.

71. Infidels.org/library/modern/keith_augustine/HNDEs.html. Assessed on June 12, 2015.

72. P. M. H. Atwater, *Near-Death Experiences, the Rest of the Story*, 35. Emphasis in the original.

73. My knowledge of Wicca is primarily from Scott Cunningham's book *Wicca: A Guide for the Solitary Practitioner* (Woodbury, MN: Llewellyn Publications, 2004), and secondarily from Wiccans of whom I've talked about Wicca.

74. Lev. 19:31; 20:6, 27; Deut. 18:9–12; 1 Sam. 15:23; 2 Kings 21:6; 2 Chron. 33:6; Isa. 8:19; 2 Cor. 11:14–15; Gal. 5:20–21; 2 Thess. 2:9–10; Jason Offutt, *Darkness Walks: The Shadow People Among Us* (San Antonio, TX: Anomalist Books, 2009), 151–162. It is interesting that the people who report having an encounter with a UFO also engage in these and other forbidden activities or are in relationships with people who do. UFO encounters are a perfect fit into the theory that by way of certain pursuits in the occult, or New Age rituals, invitation is extended to evil angels to activate otherwise dormant SPS (ESP) in humans so as to receive visions or hallucinations communicated directly from the mind of evil angels to the human mind [Hugh Ross, Kenneth Samples and Mark Clark, *Lights in the Sky & Little Green Men: A Rational Christian Look at UFOs and Extraterrestrials* (Colorado Springs, CO: NavPress, 2002), 116–125].

4

Would a Loving God Hide from Anyone? Part 2

Synopsis

Critics of Christianity argue that the concept of a hidden deity is not in harmony with the concept of a God who is perfectly loving and good because divine hiddenness makes us suffer unnecessarily, as there is no greater good being accomplished by his hiddenness.

A Christian response is that divine hiddenness would be necessary to bring about a greater good if it is necessary to create a consummate relationship between him and his heavenly community that would generate a consummate quality and quantity of expressions of love and goodness by the community, versus a low quantity and quality of expressions that would result from a mediocre relationship if God were not a hidden deity. (Note: This covers chapters 3 and 4.)

4.1 Compatibility Determination by Free Will

It was previously said that a consummate relationship with God in eternity must include certain necessary properties that require certain circumstances and life experiences in our present life. "Compatibility determination" is a term akin to the popular terms of "soul making," or "self-determination."[1] It is a life experience that involves having a particular kind of free will (made possible by the Holy Spirit) which forges the human disposition (whether a pre-fall disposition or a post-fall disposition) into either the kind that is compatible with God's community or the kind that is compatible with Satan's community.

There cannot be genuine compatibility for heaven without genuine love for God. Genuine love for God can only be born out of a maximal degree of free will. This is argued by at least the majority of theologians, but even the atheist philosopher John Schellenberg agrees that "freedom is *itself* essential to the explication of Divine love."[2] Thus, if people are to truly love God, they must have significant free will. But what kind of free will is required?

Genuine love for God requires a free will that is capable of choosing a (never-ending) relationship with God with respect to his personality and disposition separate from the coercive influence of significant awareness of his God-like status. (This concept, by the way, sheds light on one of the purposes of God's incarnation in Jesus Christ.) Genuine love is "having the freedom to love when you may choose not to love."[3] The only kind of free will that makes this possible is what some scholars call libertarian free will, or self-determining free will.[4] I refer to it as compatibility-determining free will. It is that which is capable of choosing to become either the kind of person suitable for heaven (though being undeserving of it) or the kind suitable for hell,[5] given the same set of circumstances. In other words, two identical people who are faced with the same circumstances could make different choices and end up in different eternal destinations. Thus, given any set of circumstances, both a good course and an evil course are real options, all past and present circumstances remaining the same.[6]

Moment by moment we make free moral choices, all of which play a role in shaping us into either the one kind of person or the other. C. S. Lewis (1898–1963) explains:

> Every time you make a choice you are turning the central part of you, the part of you that chooses, into something a little different from what it was before. And taking your life as a whole, with all your innumerable choices, all your life long you are slowly turning this central thing either into a heavenly creature or into a hellish creature: either into a creature that is in harmony with God, and with other creatures, and with itself, or else into one that is in a state of war and hatred with God, and with its fellow creatures, and with itself. To be the one kind of creature is heaven: that is, it is joy and peace and knowledge and power. To be the other means madness, horror, idiocy,

rage, impotence, and eternal loneliness. Each of us at each moment is progressing to the one state or the other.[7]

We absorb information and form beliefs and make innumerable choices. These are accompanied by contemplations and physical actions that influence future choices and actions by creating a tendency or disposition to cultivate similar choices and actions which form habits (in terms of good and bad conduct). The disposition, with its attendant beliefs,[8] constitutes an exercise of a determinative choice to become a certain sort of person suitable for either heaven's community or hell's community.

Of course, there are influential factors in every decision made. But these factors are not coercive to the point of replacing the *ultimate* cause, which is the free will. Every chain of humanly caused events can be traced back to free will. Our heredity, circumstances, experiences, and environment may influence and condition the choice of the action, but it is the free will that determines that the action occurs.

In this view we are the creators of different kinds of realities. We can make decisions that make things happen that otherwise would not occur. In this, *we* determine what shall be, in terms of the moral course of our life. If the freewill person determines the moral course, then she bears significant responsibility for the kind of person she becomes. As theologian Gregory Boyd says, "The buck must stop with [persons with free will] in terms of what ultimately produces and thus explains their behavior. They must be, to some extent, *self*-determining beings. The power to decide between alternatives, to turn possible courses of actions into actual courses of action, must ultimately lie within themselves."[9]

Thus, with compatibility-determining free will, *we* are the ultimate creators of our dispositions, our characters, and our moral beliefs (beliefs according to whatever light is given). And being the ultimate creators, we bear significant responsibility for the consequence of what we've created— the consequence of ending up in heaven or hell. As Paul says, "A man reaps what he sows. Whoever sows to please their flesh, from the flesh will reap destruction; whoever sows to please the Spirit, from the Spirit will reap eternal life" (Gal. 6:7–8; see also Mark 4:24 and Luke 6:38).

Three Observations. There are three observations from this worth noting. First, compatibility determination is not an experience in which humans are capable of positively responding to God on their own without divine aid. It is *not* consistent with Pelagianism or semi-Pelagianism.[10] On the contrary, the Bible is clear enough that each of us has an inherited, natural hostility toward God and a propensity to sin that leaves us with a will that is incapable *by itself* of choosing God. But God does not actually leave any of us completely alone as the Holy Spirit is continually orchestrating an overall balance of incentives in the life to make good and bad choices, thereby giving us a will that is significantly free to come to God. (This is referred to as prevenient grace and is discussed in chapter 12.)

The second observation is that it would appear that because our final destination is at stake, the disposition formed that would constitute a determinative choice for heaven or hell should be of a certain quality or strength. Some might suppose this would require a large amount of time and settlement in one's ways. However, such a disposition of sufficient quality or strength could be formed in a comparatively short amount of time if it is driven by a high degree of resolve or perseverance demonstrable by overt or radical conduct. For example, it might appear to us that a fifteen-year-old boy who persistently cultivates a great deal of hate and rash behavior and frequently gets into fights, and who one day bludgeons an innocent teenage girl to death to steal her jewelry, followed by little or no remorse, has determined which of the two kinds of people he is to be. (I say "might appear to us" because we are not in a position to judge.[11]) Thus, a determinative choice for heaven or hell could occur in a relatively short period of time.

The third observation is that a settlement in one's ways into the sort of person bound for hell does not preclude the possibility of a change in disposition (and a change in corresponding eternal destination) at any point in life. This is in accord with the Bible's teaching that a long-held disposition that is bound for hell can be transformed so as to constitute an exercise of a determinative choice for heaven (Matt. 5:24; John 3:3–8; Rom. 6:1–14; 12:2). However, genuine end-of-life conversions ("death-bed conversions") are very infrequent, or rare. There would need to suddenly be a very high resolve and perseverance to know God, real humility and appreciation for the principles of love and goodness, and radical change in conduct (Luke 3:8; Acts 26:20). (This is not to suggest that good deeds save anyone, but rather that a genuine, saving faith is evident by obedience to God.[12])

Some Christians might think death-bed conversions are more frequent because of the passage in Luke about the criminal crucified next to Jesus who asked if he might be saved for heaven (Luke 23:40–43). However, the text doesn't suggest a *sudden* conversion to trust in God (vv. 40–41). Perhaps he trusted and obeyed but fell away into a criminal activity followed by immediate remorse and repentance. The fact that he believed in Jesus as the Christ (v. 42) suggests that he had walked a life of faith in God at an earlier time, during which he could've cultivated a disposition compatible for heaven but lost his way, and found it again.

Not All Undergo Compatibility Determination. Some readers may be thinking that the process of compatibility determination creates a difficulty for the theodicist because not everyone is able to participate. It is limited to persons who possess the cognitive ability to be held accountable, such as persons who've reached the age of accountability (whatever that is)[13] and who are capable of sufficient moral thought to be justly held accountable.[14] As such, children under the age of accountability, and older children and adults who are mentally incapacitated, are unable to engage in the process of compatibility determination. If this experience is necessary in order for a person to receive the greatest blessing and for God to bring about the greatest possible good, then wouldn't God make sure that everyone be mentally capable of the experience?

As to children under the age of accountability, it arguably plays a role in the achievement of the greatest good that God create persons to cognitively develop in stages over the course of years. In the earlier years a person would not yet possess the capacity to participate in the process of compatibility determination. However, in an unfallen world, all young children could grow to the age of accountability and then participate. Thus, the creation design of creatures that spend years growing up to the age of accountability is not a design flaw. Although, in a world fallen into sin, many young children die prematurely. An unfortunate consequence of this is that their souls bypass the process of compatibility determination. *But this would not be so if not for human sin*. And the existence of sin is a consequence of having a world in which there is the free will necessary for compatibility determination. Thus, the bypass of some souls of the earthly process is a necessary evil for a greater good. The very young children who bypass it enjoy heavenly bliss, but sadly they'll never experience a consummate relationship with God that comes from having experienced compatibility determination in the earthly life.[15]

Regarding mentally incapacitated persons of the age of accountability, whether they participate in the process of compatibility determination depends on the nature of the incapacitation. If it resulted from drug abuse, an accident, or an acquired illness after reaching the age of accountability, then they would've participated in the process prior to their incapacitation. However, if it began prior to reaching the age of accountability (e.g., from a birth defect), then, similar to the situation of very young children under the age of accountability, they'll be among the special ones who bypass the process.

4.2 Compatibility Determination Requires Divine Hiddenness

Before discussing the necessity of the experience of compatibility determination in order to have a consummate relationship with God, it is helpful to understand the necessity of having our world of divine hiddenness in order to experience compatibility determination. As previously discussed, experiencing the process of compatibility determination requires that there be an overall balancing of incentives to choose between good conduct and bad conduct. If incentives to do good significantly outweigh incentives to do evil (or vice versa), then there would be significant coercion and no moral free will of the compatibility-determining kind.[16]

A situation that would upset this balancing would be a significantly high awareness of God's existence, presence, and will to reward or punish.[17] Therefore, our life and environment must be such that there is what is called epistemic distance between us and God. "Epistemic" refers to our awareness, and not to any spatial distance. So God need not be spatially distanced from us (which would be logically impossible, as God is present everywhere), but hidden from our awareness to a significant extent. This would arguably entail a life in which it is not obvious by empirical evidence that God exists, or how humankind came into existence, or if there is divine punishment and reward.

British philosopher and theologian John Hick (1922–2012) explains it this way:

> In creating finite persons to love and be loved by Him God must endow them with a certain relative autonomy over against Himself. But how can a finite creature, dependent upon the infinite Creator for its very existence and for every power and quality of its being, possess any significant autonomy in relation to that Creator? The only way we can conceive is that suggested by our actual situation. God must set man at a distance from Himself, from which he can then voluntarily

come to God [or go away from God]. But how can anything be set at a distance from One who is infinite and omnipresent? Clearly spatial distance between God and man that would make room for a degree of human autonomy is epistemic distance. In other words, the reality and presence of God must not be borne in upon men in the coercive way in which their natural environment forces itself upon their attention. The world must be to man, to some extent at least, *etsi deus non daretur*, "as if there were no God." God must be a hidden deity, veiled by His creation. He must be knowable, but only by a mode of knowledge that involves a free personal response on man's part, this response consisting in an uncompelled interpretative activity whereby we experience the world as mediating the divine presence.[18]

According to Hick and other scholars, our environment and bodily makeup affect our level of awareness of God's existence and will to reward or punish. They can be created so as to cause our level of awareness to be much higher than what it is in the world, or, alternatively, much less. If our environment and bodily makeup continually push up our level of awareness, significant free choices are lost to an extent that there would not be sufficient autonomy for the process of compatibility determination. Thus, God must create a people to live a life in which the awareness is mitigated. Observable evidence of God in the world must be hidden to a certain extent so that our awareness doesn't significantly deprive us of the possible choice against the Divine will. As Richard Swinburne says:

> The existence of God would be for [human beings] an item of evident common knowledge. Knowing that there was a God, men would know that their most secret thoughts and actions were known to God; and knowing that he was just, they would expect for their bad actions and thoughts whatever punishment was just. . . . In such a world men would have little temptation to do wrong—it would be the mark of both prudence and reason to do what was virtuous. Yet a man only has *a genuine choice of destiny* if he has reasons for pursuing either good or evil courses of action.[19]

Let's imagine such a world in which evidence of God's existence and will to reward or punish are dialed up significantly from what it is in our world. (We'll assume that despite this lesser degree of hiddenness of God, man still fell into sin.) Much more scientific data point to a strong hypothesis of God's handiwork in nature. There could be a few brief angelic visitations every year, or maybe several overt supernatural events caught on several cameras or witnessed by thousands. As a result there are far fewer skeptics, and no die-hard atheists. Skepticism is marginalized. Nearly the whole world believes in a personal God. Such evidence and religious worldviews cause the world environment to be much different than that of our world. All major human constructs reflect the universal belief in the existence of God—in governments, politics, businesses, science, medicine, literature, art, music, architecture, buildings, homes, means of transportation, theme parks, clothes, food, books, magazines, movies, television, advertising, technology, the Internet, and on and on. A result is virtually no ability to get away from a continual heightened awareness of God's existence and will to reward or punish. This would so condition and influence life choices that at least a great many people wouldn't have enough freedom to become the kind of person who is incompatible with heaven. Being compatible with heaven in this way would deprive us of significant responsibility for being there. Indeed, it would be difficult to say that the characters we would bear would be "our" characters. We'd be somewhat autonomic.

The Christian philosopher Michael Murray explains:

By doing this, God would have removed the ability for character-determination since there are no longer good and evil courses of action between which creatures could freely and deliberately choose. Thus we would all be compelled to choose in accordance with the divine will and would all thereby become conformed to the divine image. However, a character wrought in this fashion would not be one for which we are responsible since it does not derive from morally significant choosing. It has instead been forced upon us.[20]

Assuming for the sake of discussion that God exists, critics object to the idea that the level or degree of hiddenness in our world is necessary. They may concede that some degree of hiddenness would be necessary in order to mitigate coercion and preserve significant free will. But they would argue that God does not need to be hidden as much as is claimed. This, it is argued, is because our awareness of his existence and will would not actually be significantly affected if God were to show more evidence of his existence and will. In other words, it's okay for God to be hidden, just nowhere near as much as he is.

The argument is valid, but not successful. Three aspects of the argument are discussed in appendix A. Each has a fatal flaw, leaving us with the conclusion that God could *not* make his existence more known without a significant increase in the world's awareness of his existence and will that would deprive the world of significant compatibility-determining free will.

4.3 The Necessity of Compatibility Determination for a Consummate Relationship

Among the many good things created by the experience of compatibility determination in our world of divine hiddenness are the properties of a consummate relationship with God that were introduced in the previous chapter. The properties are: (1) origination of the relationship with God from reciprocal love; and (2) a perfect perception of God's disposition and personality. The remainder of the properties, to a great extent, result from the existence of these two. Why the properties are necessary for a consummate relationship and how they result from compatibility determination are discussed in the following.

How Origination of a Relationship with God from Pure Reciprocal Love Results from Compatibility Determination and Why It Is Necessary for a Consummate Relationship. When it comes to a relationship between God and a human, the origin of the relationship determines the fundamental reason for the existence of the relationship between the two beings. An origin from love requires a choice by each of the persons to be in a relationship with the other, out of love, without significant coercion. As said previously, love cannot abide in an atmosphere of coercion. Love cannot be reciprocated if there is significant coercive influence.[21]

For reasons that are rather obvious, God is under no coercive influence to enter into a relationship with a human that he created where there would be conversation, companionship, and quality time spent. God's aseity, immutability, glory, and phenomenally greater power mean that God is obviously under absolutely no compulsion, influence, or intimidation to act to initiate a relationship with a human. As such, entering into a relationship could occur from pure love.

But this would certainly not be the case for the origin of the relationship if the human is created in the unmitigated presence of God. Suppose for the sake of this discussion that God had not created humans with a preliminary life of divine hiddenness followed by a life in which God is not hidden (i.e., had not created us to have a two-phase life), but instead created celestial humans in heaven where they would fully know of his phenomenal power, his holiness and his will to reward or punish. The completely dependent humans would feel God's overwhelming love and know the full extent of the punishment for choosing autonomy from the creator (i.e., in hell) and thus be under profound coercion to respond affirmatively to a relationship of obedience. There might be a little love of God's personality, but it would be overshadowed by coercive feelings which would make coercion the fundamental reason for the relationship—not love.

A relationship based in love on the part of both parties is more meaningful and valuable than a relationship in which one party is lacking in love for the other party. This is true ontologically. Consider for example the difference between the relationship that a human has with a dog and a relationship between a human and an artificially intelligent robot dog (e.g., one of the robot dogs designed and manufactured by Sony). The robot dog is not capable of reciprocating the love it receives from its owner. This is why most people prefer the human-dog relationship over the human-robot dog relationship despite having to clean up messes and care for a sick pet. The human-dog relationship has far more value and meaning because a dog is apparently capable of reciprocating some of the love it receives from its owner.

Of course God is fully aware of the lesser meaning and value of a nonreciprocal-love relationship as compared to the phenomenally greater meaning and value of a reciprocal-love relationship. But the celestial human in heaven would also be aware of the difference in the types of relationships. Celestial humans have supernatural mentation with lucid consciousness, intense emotion, expanded mental faculties, and perfect eidetic memory—all amplified by fully active SPS. As such, celestial humans would understand that their relationship with God could've originated in an environment without coercion. They would also understand the concept of the purest love from maximal free will, and that it was not an experience given them. Such a realization would probably yield a mediocre or poor psychospiritual condition. There could be issues such as a lack of personal dignity, lack of a sense of intrinsic value, and low self-esteem.[22] Contrary to what some Christians think, the willingness, inspiration, and motivation to express love and goodness do not come exclusively in response to God's forgiveness of sin. The psychospiritual condition is an important factor, and if it is less than consummate, so too would be the expressions of the one with it.

The view of oneself with a mediocre or poor psychospiritual condition could include a feeling of being unworthy of respect from others, of little value, unlovable, unacceptable, or fundamentally unworthy of being in a relationship with God, even if one had never sinned (i.e., pre-fall Adam). A sinner saved by grace would inherit a poor psychospiritual condition if he could not say he genuinely chose God. He could only say that *if* he had maximal and significant free will to do so. Of course it is the Holy Spirit who imparts such free will, so he would not be in heaven if not for the Holy Spirit (and Christ and the Father). But that misses the point that without the freewill experience of compatibility determination, none could make a genuine choice for God. It is known in psychology that such a circumstance of the relationship with God would attenuate a feeling of self-love and value. Thus, without the life experience of compatibility determination, a consummately healthy psychospirituality would not likely be possible—not for a celestial person with a supernatural mind. It would negatively affect a person's perceptions, beliefs, and feelings about himself, God, and his relationship with God. Such a negative perception might lead to withdrawal from opportunities, withdrawal from God, distrust, poor decision-making, and, ultimately, a less than optimal psychospiritual condition. Such a condition would generate a mediocre quality and quantity of expressions of love and goodness (expressions such as ministering "angels" to people of other worlds, perhaps).

The poor psychospiritual condition of even one person in heaven would adversely affect the rest, bringing the heavenly community at large into a state that would further diminish the degree of expressions of love and goodness. In heaven, communication is on a whole new level, as mentioned previously. The thoughts of one person are telepathically felt and understood by another. Thus, there are no poker faces in heaven. What you feel about another person (or God) is known by that person. Thus, a person's perceptions, beliefs, and feelings about himself, God, and his relationship with God are communicated to others in the community and spread throughout. What you feel about someone would permeate every aspect of your eternal life and relationships in heaven (like a little yeast that works its way through a batch of dough). At a minimum, it would be a less than optimal situation, resulting in an imperfect heaven, less glory to God, and a lesser degree of good brought about. Therefore, if God is to accomplish the greatest good possible, he must level the playing field, so to speak, by mitigating our awareness of his God status so that a relationship originates out of pure love, versus significant fear. Accomplishing this involves an epistemic[23] distance between us and God to attenuate our awareness of God's existence and will to reward or punish.

One might think that God could fix any psychospiritual problem in heaven (that is logically possible to fix). However, God could not then undo the manner that the human came to be introduced to God or the manner of the origination of the relationship. The phrase "You will never get a second chance to make a first impression"[24] is much more certainly true in the celestial life. Thus, the origin and early history of the relationship could not be undone, and the condition then needing to be fixed and the resultant loss of good would be irreversible.

In summary, an origination and early history of a human relationship with God based on coercion would create a mediocre relationship, because its meaning and value would be mediocre to the human and to God, which would result in a poor human psychospiritual condition that would be irreversible. Because of the poor psychospiritual condition, human expressions of love and goodness would be substantially less than if God had created humans with a two-phase life, beginning with life in our world of divine hiddenness, where we would have the free will to experience compatibility determination. Therefore, compatibility determination is necessary for a consummate relationship in God's plan to bring about the greatest possible good through a heavenly community.

How a Perfect Perception of God's Disposition and Personality Results from Compatibility Determination and Why It Is Necessary for a Consummate Relationship. All celestial beings reflect on and learn from history. One of the most prominent object lessons in history is the person of Jesus Christ. Having fully active SPS in beatific vision with the celestial Jesus will accomplish a great deal toward bringing about a perfect perception of God's disposition and personality. But all of the benefit that a one-on-one with Jesus would bring about would be insufficient for a perfect perception if there is any lingering doubt that God's adjudication (decision making for his judgment) wasn't perfectly just in accord with perfect love and goodness. It is clear from the Bible that this is an issue that God anticipates and works to resolve (Rom. 3:25–26; Eph. 3:10;[25] Col. 1:20;[26] Heb. 9:23–24;[27] 1 Pet. 1:12[28]), as all of heaven will observe the judgement and study it (Dan. 7:9–10; 1 Cor. 6:2–3; Rev. 20:11–15).[29] Thus, in addition to "the cross," the judgment scene will be another one of the most prominent circumstances of history from which to learn.

In the judgment, God determines the eternal destination of everyone. At the end of the world, his judgment will be complete (Rev. 22:11–12) and Christ will appear in full disclosure in the sky (Acts 1:9–11; Rev. 1:7). "He will separate the people one from another as a shepherd separates the sheep from the goats" (Matt. 25:32). Then each will go to his or her respective eternal destination. The unsaved go to the regrettable realm referred to as hell, and the saved go to the glorious realm of heaven.

Because the judgment entails personal decisions, it is an unavoidable reflection of God's disposition and personality. And so the study of the judgment is a study of God. The heavenly community desires to understand why some were saved and some not. It examines the adjudication and naturally forms a perception of God over his decisions. This is fundamental to our psyche. According to psychology, "We have a tendency to evaluate other people both on the basis of what they do and *why* we think they do it."[30] The minds of the community search the motives of God to fully understand them, to come to know God better, and then to make adjustments of their perceptions of God's disposition and personality.

This, of course, is part of God's plan for the study of his decisions in the judgment to play a vital role in gaining a perfect perception of his disposition and personality for a greater and more intimate knowing and loving of God. In this we can see one reason for the necessity of the person, life, and substitutionary sacrifice by Jesus on "the cross" (Rom. 3:25–26) and his God-man role in the judgment.[31] If not for Christ's relevance to the judgment, there could not be a consummate relationship with God to fulfill his plan to accomplish the greatest good. (Skeptics of Christianity who argue that Christ's sacrificial death was unnecessary miss *this* important point about its necessity, as well as its necessity for salvation.[32])

However, an eternally secure and consummate relationship for the greatest good would not occur where there is lingering suspicion that God's judgment was at all unjust or unfair, because God either decided arbitrarily, or with favoritism, or allowed unjust circumstances in life that coerced some people into sin and disbelief, and others into faith and obedience. According to at least twelve Bible passages,[33] showing favoritism goes against a principle (law) of love and goodness with respect to treatment of persons, and is therefore a sin. "God does not show favoritism," especially with regard to the judgment (Rom. 2:11). It's just not consistent with a God "who loves so indiscriminately that he sends sun and rain on both the righteous and the unrighteous."[34]

While it might seem that being in beatific vision with the celestial Jesus would clear up any lingering suspicion (or accusation by Satan) that God's judgment was unfair, we should keep in mind that we are looking at this with natural minds from the earthly life perspective. Persons of the celestial life have supernaturally empowered minds in an everlasting and ineffable celestial realm. Mental capacities are phenomenally enhanced. Evidence of celestial mental expansion comes to us from people who have had a near-death experience (NDE) who report having "IQ enhancements" and "expanded faculties; thinking becomes more spacial, non-verbal, sensory-dynamic; creative problem solving emerges with a more active sense of what memory is; sensing multiples can open up new worlds of time and space; the higher mind develops in league with greater concerns for social justice and moral integrity."[35] Moreover, in the judgment there is likely to be telepathic exchange of opinion—even between the condemned (e.g., evil angels and lost humans) and the saved. Thus, our ability to fully grasp the situation is probably quite limited.

We may gain a little insight of our limitation from NDEs that entail an intense life review, a viewing of life's actions and their consequences as God sees them. According to people who have had NDEs, many of the actions reviewed that had been previously thought to be trivial or mundane turned out to be profoundly important.[36] If the life reviews of NDEs are an experience in the afterlife,[37] then it seems likely that in eternity there could be a phenomenally high potential or innate capacity as a celestial being for scrutiny concerning the judgment. (Of course such would be part of God's plan to create beings capable of maximal expressions of love and goodness to bring about the greatest possible good.)

Foreknowing that there would be such a potential for suspicion and insecurity in the relationship, God creates circumstances and experiences in both the earthly and celestial life that make his judgment transparent. Some Christians imagine God flashing a panorama of images of human decisions made in the earthly life to the mind's eye, to demonstrate the fairness of his judgment. Fully active SPS would play an important and necessary role in this. However, despite the beatific vision with the celestial Jesus, flashing images, and "open books" in the judgment scene (Dan. 7:10c; Rev. 20:12), the supernatural minds of the afterlife would still not be entirely secure from feelings of suspicion and distrust concerning the judgment unless they underwent a personal experience of compatibility determination by free will in a life of divine hiddenness.

By the process of compatibility determination, each will know experientially that he or she had the freedom and responsibility in charting a life course to an eternal destination. As such, God's judgment would merely reflect the genuine determinative choice each had made. It will be clearly demonstrated, internally and externally, and beyond any conceivable doubt, that the motivation behind God's adjudication is perfect justice, mercy, wisdom, rightness, and love. As theologian Ronald Nash tells us, "None will be able to complain that they were treated unfairly."[38] This, combined with being in beatific vision with the celestial Jesus with fully active SPS, will leave nothing with which to question the justice of God, which would prevent a potential impediment to having an eternally lasting and completely secure and perfect perception of God's disposition and personality.

Having a perfect perception of God's disposition and personality opens a door to the greatest possible knowing of God (John 17:3). The apostle Paul's prayer for the Ephesian Christians was that they would have the ability to grasp the full depth and breadth of God's love for them and would know this love that surpasses knowledge—that they be filled to the measure of all the fullness of God (Eph. 3:16–19). A person can know this only if she knows she has been perfectly respected as a person of intrinsic value. She can know this by personal experience by having gone through the process of compatibility determination by free will in a world of divine hiddenness, in which a genuine choice for who she is to become is fully respected. This will be fully realized in retrospective reflection by the heavenly community. As such, God's perfectly loving and good disposition and personality could be perfectly known, and the community with that perception would experience a phenomenal and as of yet inconceivable knowing of God—the ultimate fulfillment of Jesus' prayer in John 17[39] that all disciples of God be one with God in will, just as the three persons of God are one with each other in will (verses 11 and 21–22)—"I in them and you in me" (v. 23). Along with the greater knowing of God through having a perfect perception of God's disposition and personality will flow greater expressions of love and goodness in fulfillment of God's plan to bring about the greatest good.

Also along with the greatest knowing of God will flow the greatest psychospiritual health. As discussed previously, because compatibility determination is a way God can perfectly respect the individual, a person in the afterlife who can then look back with supernatural mentation on her life will know, in a profound way, that she has been treated as a being with intrinsic value. Consequently, she is able to have the greatest psychospiritual health in heaven. And a consummate psychospirituality is a necessary component of God's plan to bring about the greatest expressions of love and goodness.

In summary, compatibility determination is necessary for members of the heavenly community to gain a perfect perception of God's disposition and personality and know God perfectly. Because they know God perfectly, they are able to have the greatest possible psychospiritual well-being. Being in perfect psychospiritual health and knowing God perfectly are two of the necessary elements of God's plan for maximal expressions of love and goodness to bring about the greatest possible good.

What has been discussed so far is the necessity of divine hiddenness in God's plan to bring about the greatest good of a consummate degree of expressions of love and goodness by the heavenly community. An illustration for an overview of this appeared in the previous chapter, which is shown for review as follows.

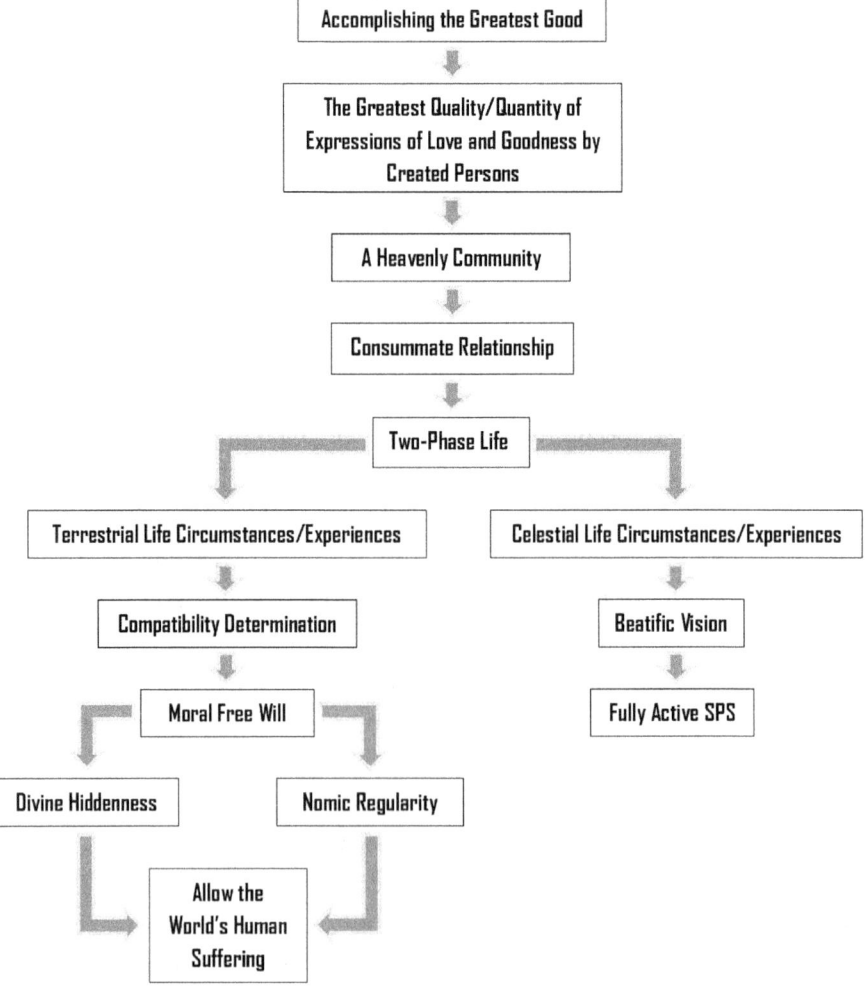

4.4 What about the Angels?

By now it may become apparent to some readers that if a natural life like ours is needed in order to have a consummate relationship with God to generate the greatest good in eternity, what about the angels? Didn't God create the angels in heaven to immediately experience the beatific vision? If so, their relationship would be mediocre and inconsistent with God's plan to bring about the greatest possible good (and the whole theodicy would fall apart).

The Christian response can be that, first of all, the Bible does not tell us how the angels were created. Bible verses said to shed light on the creation of angels include Ezek. 28:11–19 and Isa. 14:12–17. It is thought by some that the Ezekiel passage talks about the angel Lucifer, but it really pertains to the king of Tyre. Nonetheless, even a "dual" application of the message (about the king and about Lucifer) would tell us nothing about the manner of the creation of the angels or whether Lucifer was created with fully active SPS in beatific vision that would preclude compatibility determination. In fact, in a dual application interpretation, it could be argued from verse 13 that Lucifer was not created in beatific vision as he was created in "Eden, the garden of God," which could metaphorically reflect a preliminary life of divine hiddenness comparable to that of Adam and Eve (a garden *adjoining* the palace of the King).[40] Verse 14 says he was "on the holy mount of God," but this phrase is symbolic of the Garden of Eden motif just discussed concerning verse 13.

Isa. 14:12–17 also pertains to the king of Babylon, and not Lucifer, but, again, a dual application of the passage still does not indicate the angels were created in beatific vision. Verse 12 says the king (or Lucifer) was cast from "heaven" and fell to "earth." These are metaphorical terms, but even taken literally, they do not say Lucifer was created in beatific vision. The phrase "fallen from heaven" is used in Scripture to indicate a fallen condition of the heart and not a spatial depiction. But even in a dual application view, it could indicate Lucifer's fallen condition that occurred while in a celestial realm of divine hiddenness, a kind of preliminary heaven. He then would've lost out on entering into a beatific face-to-face communion with God in the eternal heaven (see Rev. 18:2-3 and Gen. 3:22b).

Because the Bible is silent on the manner of the creation of the angels, God has left Christians with room for Spirit-guided philosophical speculation. And given the providential two-stage life design for humans for a consummate relationship for the greatest good (discussed previously), it appears very probable that this is the paradigm for all beings of higher intelligence made with the capacity to love God. Thus, it may very likely be that the angels were created with a preliminary life experience where God is set at an epistemic distance so that they would have compatibility-determining free will (and could either remain faithful or rebel), followed by a second phase of life in beatific vision in heaven (or in condemnation if any choose to rebel).

To accomplish this, God could create the angels in a preliminary developmental state with limited abilities. This could be accomplished by many possible ways. God could create them as natural, carbon-based life forms not much different than humans. Or God could bring them into being in a temporary supernatural state in a kind of preliminary "heaven" with substantially limited powers. In such a life their SPS would be suppressed, or dormant, and they wouldn't move across spatial dimensions. Whatever the makeup of the preliminary life, it would be a life of divine hiddenness in which God is at an epistemic distance so that the beings (angels) could experience compatibility determination by moral (libertarian) free will.

In such a life they (the angels) would have the freedom to sin. They would either self-determine a disposition compatible with God or a disposition incompatible with God. When the preliminary life would run its course, the compatible ones would enter into God's unmediated presence in beatific vision. Once there, it would be virtually impossible to ever succumb to temptation to sin. As Matthew Henry (1662–1714) says:

> The happiness of heaven consists in the vision of God seeing him face to face as he is, beholding his beauty; this the angels have without interruption; when they are ministering to us on earth, yet even then by contemplation they behold the face of God, for they are *full of eyes within*.[41]

The angel Gabriel, for example, when speaking to Zacharias, experiences the beatific vision that overwhelms any notion of sin (Luke 1:19; Rev. 4:8). Henry's phrase "full of eyes within" appears consistent with the view of having fully active SPS to experience the beatific vision. Such would be the life of the holy angels. But any angels that sin in a preliminary life (of divine hiddenness) would, at the end of the preliminary life, enter an afterlife condemned.

Tradition has it that the angel Lucifer rebelled (and became Satan). His rebellion was followed by the rebellion of many other angels against God.

Under the view of a two-phase life for the angels, when the preliminary lives of Satan and the others had each run their course, they lost their chance to enter into heaven's beatific vision with God (2 Pet. 2:4; Jude 6[42]). They "did not keep their positions of authority but abandoned their proper dwelling" (Jude 6)—"positions of authority" that they could've held in a preliminary life, just as Adam did. "For God did not spare angels when they sinned, but sent them to hell [*Tartaroō*[43]] putting them in chains of darkness to be held for judgment" (2 Pet. 2:4).

Assuming that the angels were created with advantages in knowledge and ability over humans, an angel who rebels against God would receive less mercy than a human would. As Henry says,

> If the angels, who excel us vastly in strength and knowledge, violate the law of God, the sentence which that law awards shall be executed upon them, and that without mercy or mitigation, for God did not spare them. Hence . . . by how much the more excellent the offender, by so much the more severe the punishment. The angels, who had the advantage of men as to the dignity of their nature, are immediately punished. There is no sparing them for a few days, no favour at all shown them.[44]

Thus, for anyone questioning if God had a salvation plan for the angels that would have been anything like the plan he has for humans, the answer is "no" (Heb. 1:5).

4.5 The Evil of Divine Hiddenness is Outweighed by the Good of God's Heavenly Community in Consummate Relationship with Him

I discussed that our world of divine hiddenness is necessary for God to harvest a heavenly community in a consummate relationship with him in eternity. But, and supposing for the sake of discussion that this is God's plan, is the degree of humankind's suffering from divine hiddenness too much of a price to pay for the greater good brought about?

This is certainly an answerable question, but not without difficulty, for two reasons. First of all, on this side of the afterlife we cannot know the full extent of the good that would result from the beatific community. But we can conceptualize enough to come to a reasonable conclusion that it is so exceptionally good that it outweighs the price of divine hiddenness. We have valuable insight about it from the writings of Paul the apostle, of whom it is said received visions that may include snapshots of the afterlife in the beatific relationship with God (2 Cor. 12:1-4). Paul was sure of its outweighing value. He considered that even the worst forms of suffering in this life were without doubt outweighed by the glory that will be revealed in the ones in the beatific relationship (Rom. 8:18–22; 2 Cor. 4:17). Likewise, Jesus was just as sure (Matt. 5:12; Luke 12:33). Thus, considering the previous discussion, and the claims of Jesus and Paul, it's not difficult to imagine that the good that results from divine hiddenness has outweighing value.

The second reason we may have difficulty answering the question is the challenge of imagining suffering from divine hiddenness separate from suffering from other causes. It's not easy to make this distinction when so much of what happens to hurt us seems to result partly from the fact that God's existence is not obvious to everyone and isn't perceived by our natural senses. For example, some tribal conflicts, military attacks, and murders surround disagreements over which religion is true. But if people would love peace (Matt. 5:9) and cultivate a loving heart (1 Cor. 13:1–8), such disagreements need not lead to hostility. So I think one can navigate around the difficulty by seeing suffering from divine hiddenness as primarily one's emotional distress from living a life without any way to see, hear, or touch God, or feel fully confident from empirical evidence that the world exists by divine creation.

For example, emotionally we may suffer fear and distress about what happens at death. A person can get some relief from this distress by holding tightly to belief in God, but much of the world does not believe; and even believers can struggle with unbelief (Mark 9:24). Taking the preceding into account, suffering from divine hiddenness can be seen as separate from suffering from moral or natural evils, which can give us a more accurate comparison of the price of suffering from divine hiddenness to the good of the beatific community.

An even more accurate perception can be gained from also recognizing that some of the emotional distress non-Christians might attribute to divine hiddenness is actually from willful ignorance—that of refusing to expend effort to seek truth, study world religions and the Bible, or do a reasonable investigation of the claims of Christianity. While it is true that there are spiritual seekers in non-Christian religions who've sought truth and still suffer from ignorance and uncertainty, according to the Bible everyone, regardless of faith or nationality, is given a guiding light that would lead along a path to the truth (of God), but many deep down inside really do not appreciate the partial light given and shut the door on opportunities to receive greater light (this concept is discussed in chapter 12). Therefore, according to the Bible, a substantial amount of suffering from divine hiddenness isn't God's doing. Again, recognizing this enables us to gain a more accurate comparison of the price of divine hiddenness to the good produced by the heavenly community in consummate relationship with God.

The bottom line is that after dividing out the suffering that results from sources other than divine hiddenness, suffering from divine hiddenness alone is actually relatively minimal. Given this degree of this kind of suffering, one can imagine that the suffering from divine hiddenness is outweighed by the greater good.

Conclusion

I discussed why God would be a (partially) hidden deity and thus have us live a life in a world in which there is little evidence of God's existence and will to reward or punish. His hiddenness is part of his objective to bring into existence the greatest possible good through a consummate relationship between God and his community. The consummate relationship must include certain necessary properties that require certain circumstances and experiences. The circumstances and experiences include a temporary terrestrial or earthly life of compatibility determination by free will, and an everlasting celestial life and experiences of God-given SPS to experience the beatific vision.

In our earthly life, our experience of compatibility determination gives us significant responsibility that makes us the ultimate creators of our celestial destination (heaven or hell). As such, the properties for a consummate relationship with God are made to exist. Compatibility determination requires maximal moral free will. Having that free will requires a life in our world of divine hiddenness.

Divine hiddenness entails emotionally suffering from ignorance and uncertainty as to what to believe about the existence of the universe and our lives, and how to conduct ourselves, apart from suffering from moral evil and natural evils. But, considering the biblical picture of the degree of good of the consummate relationship, it is conceivable that the good brought about through having our world of divine hiddenness is so phenomenally great that it outweighs the price of divine hiddenness. As such, one could reasonably conclude that the problem of divine hiddenness is not a problem for Christianity. It can be explained, and it can be considered resolved.

NOTES to Chapter 4

1. "Soul making" is a phrase coined by philosopher John Hick (1922–2012). It is a process in which a person develops in personality and character in a challenging world to be more like God. "Self-determination" is a term used by philosophers Daniel Howard-Snyder and Michael J. Murray, and by theologian Gregory A. Boyd.

2. John L. Schellenberg, *Divine Hiddenness and Human Reason* (Ithaca, NY: Cornell University Press, 1993), 27. Emphasis in the original.

3. Ravi Zacharias, *Beyond Opinion: Living the Faith We Defend* (Nashville, TN: Thomas Nelson, 2007), 191; Gary D. Chapman, *The Five Love Languages: The Secret to Love That Lasts* (Chicago: Northfield Publishing, 1992), 96, 100.

4. Gregory A. Boyd, *Satan & the Problem of Evil: Constructing a Trinitarian Warfare Theodicy* (Downers Grove, IL: InterVarsity Press, 2001), 53–55, 57; Michael A. Corey, *Evolution and the Problem of Natural Evil* (Lanham, MD: University Press of America, 2000), 210. Corey (1957–2011) received two PhDs: a PhD in philosophy of science and religion from The Union Institute and a PhD in the psychology of religion from Columbia Pacific University. He also received an MA in philosophy of religion and theology from Claremont Graduate School. He has authored many books, including: *The God Hypothesis: Discovering Design in a Just-Right Goldilocks Universe*; *God and the New Cosmology*; and *Job, Jonah, and the Unconscious: A Psychological Interpretation of Evil and Spiritual Growth in the Old Testament*.

5. A biblical hell is not the torture chamber that some good-intentioned theologians of centuries past mistakenly made it out to be (see chapters 10 and 11).

6. Alvin Plantinga, *The Nature of Necessity* (Oxford: Oxford University Press, 1974), 165–166; Gregory A. Boyd, *Satan & the Problem of Evil*, 56–57; Ronald H. Nash, *Faith and Reason: Searching for a Rational Faith* (Grand Rapids, MI: Zondervan, 1988), 189–190; Peter J. Kreeft and Richard K. Tacelli, *Handbook of Christian Apologetics*, 136–137; William Lane Craig, *On Guard: Defending Your Faith with Reason and Precision* (Colorado Springs, CO: David C. Cook, 2010), 156; Michael A. Corey, *Evolution and the Problem of Natural Evil*, 253. I believe that compatibility-determining free will (also called libertarian free will or self-determining free will) is indicated in the Bible (Jos. 24:15; Prov. 1:29; Isa. 7:15–16; 56:4; Phil. 1:22).

7. C. S. Lewis, *Mere Christianity* (New York: HarperCollins Publishers, 1980), 92. Lewis was an atheist who converted to theism and then eventually to Christianity. He became a lay theologian and Christian apologist.

8. An array of beliefs formed in response to whatever light is given by God.

9. Gregory A. Boyd, *Satan & the Problem of Evil*, 60. Emphasis in the original.

10. Pelagianism teaches that one is capable of having the free will and ability to

transform the disposition to obey God by faith, unaided by the Holy Spirit. Semi-Pelagianism teaches that the free will for initial conversion to God is without divine aid, but the Holy Spirit aids in the transformation of the disposition in the relationship with God (sanctification). Such views are different from compatibility determination in that the workings of the Holy Spirit are needed to have the free will (by balancing incentives to choose to do good or bad things) to initially respond in a positive manner to God for conversion and for transformation of the disposition in a growing relationship with God (see chapter 12).

11. The Christian is to *lovingly* and *humbly* exercise tentative judgment about the spiritual condition of others while doing self-examination to find and root out personal hypocrisy, pride, malice, prejudicial discrimination, or selfishness (Matt. 7:1–6; 15:21–27; John 7:24; 1 Cor. 2:15; 5:1–13; 2 Cor. 6:14–16; James 4:11–12).

12. Matt. 16:27; Rom. 1:5; 2:6; Phil. 2:17; 1 Thess. 1:3; 2 Thess. 1:11; Jam. 2:14–26; Rev. 18:6; 20:12–13; 22:12.

13. Many see the age of accountability as early as nine years old; however, it seems to vary among children, and it is arguably younger than nine for at least some children. Thus, there may be some souls of particularly bad children who've gone to the mediocre afterlife in the community of fallen angels. While is it true Jesus said heaven is for "little children" (Matt. 19:13–14; Mark 10:13–14), we are not sure of the ages of the children he was referring to, especially in light of Luke 18:15–16 which indicates the young children were "babies."

14. The Christian view holds that very young children have souls—even before birth—with personal identity, self-consciousness, desires, learning, dreaming, and the forming of preferences regarding things heard and felt, all of which is verified by science [David Chamberlain, *The Mind of Your Newborn Baby* (Berkeley, CA: North Atlantic Books, third ed., 1998), 186]. However, the ability of such souls to discern good from bad may be too underdeveloped to form a disposition of sufficient quality to constitute an exercise of a determinative choice for either of the two final destinations. Chamberlain (1928–2014) received his PhD in psychology from Boston University; he was president of the Association for Prenatal and Perinatal Psychology and Health (APPPAH), editor of birthpsychology.com, and author of over thirty scholarly publications.

15. Some may argue that: (a) every soul in heaven must experience genuine love for God in this life to be admitted into heaven; and (b) every human soul in heaven must have a consummate relationship with God or else God could not be justified in permitting suffering from divine hiddenness, as well as suffering from moral and natural evils. However, neither argument is valid because: (1) God is not morally precluded from bringing cognitively underdeveloped souls that exist because of sin into the heavenly community; and (2) God need not have only as many souls in consummate relationship with him in heaven as are needed to generate enough good to outweigh and justify permitting the evil of divine hiddenness (and arguably other kinds of evil), which does not necessarily mandate that 100 percent of heaven's inhabitants be in consummate relationship with God.

16. Michael J. Murray, "Deus Absconditus," in *Divine Hiddenness: New Essays*, eds.

Daniel Howard-Snyder and Paul K. Moser (New York: Cambridge University Press, 2002), 65, 68.

17. The two things that potentially can overpower our moral free will are: (1) too much awareness of God's existence, and (2) too much awareness of God's will to reward or punish [Michael J. Murray, "Deus Absconditus," in *Divine Hiddenness*, 76].

18. John Hick, *Evil and the God of Love*, second ed. reissued 2007 (New York: Palgrave MacMillan, 2007), 281.

19. Richard G. Swinburne, as quoted in J. L. Schellenberg, *Divine Hiddenness and Human Reason* (Ithaca, NY: Cornell University Press, 1993), 117–118. Emphasis added. Swinburne graduated from Exeter College, Oxford, with a first class BA in politics, philosophy, and economics. He's held various professorships, lectured at universities, and authored many books, including *Faith and Reason, Is There a God?* (translated into 22 languages) and *Providence and the Problem of Evil*. He is considered to be one of the foremost Christian apologists.

20. Michael J. Murray, as quoted in J. L. Schellenberg, *Divine Hiddenness and Human Reason*, 68.

21. Ravi Zacharias, *Beyond Opinion: Living the Faith We Defend* (Nashville, TN: Thomas Nelson, 2007), 191; Michael A. Corey, *Evolution and the Problem of Natural Evil*, 196–197; Gary D. Chapman, *The Five Love Languages*, 96, 100.

22. Psychologist Nathaniel Branden tells us that being "the chief causal agent in our lives and behavior" for significant "self-responsibility is clearly indispensable to good self-esteem" and "a nontragic sense of life" [*The Power of Self-Esteem: An Inspiring Look at Our Most Important Psychological Resource* (Deerfield Beach, FL: Health Communications, Inc., 1992), 71].

23. The term "epistemic" is an adjective relating to knowledge.

24. The source of the phrase is unclear. Some attribute it to author and humorist Mark Twain (1835–1910); others to poet, playwright, and novelist Oscar Wilde (1854–1900); and others to newspaper columnist, social commentator, and humorist William "Will" Rogers (1879–1935).

25. *Zondervan NIV Bible Commentary, Volume 2: New Testament*, consulting eds. Kenneth L. Barker and John R. Kohlenberger III (Grand Rapids, MI: Zondervan Publishing House, 1994), 764.

26. Ibid., 821.

27. Ibid., 982.

28. The expression "long to look" in 1 Pet. 1:12 means "to stoop over to look," which implies "willingness to exert or inconvenience oneself to obtain a better perspective. The specific tense used means continuous regard rather than a quick look" [*Zondervan NIV Bible Commentary, Volume 2: New Testament*, 1044].

29. *Zondervan NIV Bible Commentary, Volume 2: New Testament*, 623.

30. Benjamin B. Lahey, *Psychology: An Introduction*, eighth ed. (New York: McGraw-Hill, 2004), 630. Emphasis in the original.

31. Matt. 25:31–46; John 5:24; Rom. 2:16; 2 Tim. 4:1; James 5:9.

32. The necessary role of the Son of God for human salvation is discussed in appendix D.

33. Lev. 19:15; Deut. 10:17; 2 Chr. 19:7; Matt. 22:16; Acts 10:34; Rom. 2:11; Gal. 2:6; Eph. 6:9; Col. 3:25; 1 Tim. 5:21; James 2:1, 9; 1 Pet. 1:17.

34. *Zondervan NIV Bible Commentary, Volume 2: New Testament*, 29.

35. P. M. H. Atwater, *Dying to Know You: Proof of God in the Near-Death Experience* (Faber, VA: Rainbow Ridge Books, 2014), 82. See also Edward F. Kelly and Emily Williams Kelly, et al., *Irreducible Mind: Toward a Psychology for the 21st Century* (Lanham, MD: Rowman & Littlefield Publishers, Inc., 2010 paperback ed.), 386–387.

36. An example is a particular incidence of compassion in which a war soldier, out of sympathy and compassion, gave a fatally wounded soldier a puff on his cigarette moments before he died. "One of the great puzzles in all of this [life reviews by NDErs] is why almost mundane incidents tend to be highlighted in the life review over seemingly more important ones. The life review actually highlights the little things in life—how we treat each other, lies we told, what we did about our promises and goals, how willing we were to 'walk that extra mile' to get a job done or lend a helping hand" [P. M. H. Atwater, *Near-Death Experiences, the Rest of the Story*, 22].

37. While I believe NDEs (particularly the veridical kind) provide evidence of the supernatural and of God's existence, depicting details of God and the afterlife based on a synthesis of NDE reports is problematic because: (1) NDEs are fragmentary (notwithstanding similarities between NDEs that are categorized); (2) NDEs often involve a sensed "border" or limit to where the experiencer can go, which implies that knowledge gained of the afterlife is limited; and (3) NDEs involve ESP (SPS) activation by which the experiencer receives transcendent information specific to the needs of the experiencer, rather than a full disclosure of the afterlife, and sometimes with metaphorical sights, sounds, and feelings, which can be misinterpreted as literal. As such, it is not surprising that a researcher's synthesis of NDE reports could conflict with Bible doctrines on God, the judgment, Christ, heaven, or hell. On the other hand, it is interesting that much of the content of NDEs (even by the nonreligious) tell of a triune God who created everything and is all-powerful, all-knowing, and all-loving and good and just (consistent with some of God's attributes in the Bible).

38. Ronald H. Nash, *Is Jesus the Only Savior?* (Grand Rapids, MI: Zondervan, 1994), 165.

39. Matthew Henry (1662–1714) points out that "this prayer of Christ will not have its complete answer till all the saints come to heaven, for then, and not till then, they shall be *perfect in* one" [*Matthew Henry's Commentary on the Whole Bible* (Peabody, MA: Hendrickson Publishers, 1991), 1624, emphasis in the original].

40. As Henri Blocher says, "Holy Scripture shows the Lord entrusting to mankind's care an estate of his own, situated 'at a distance' from heaven where God dwells in glory [*Evil and the Cross: An Analytical Look at the Problem of Pain* (Grand Rapids, MI: Kregel Publications, 1994), 56]. See also John H. Walton, *The NIV Application Commentary: Genesis* (Grand Rapids, MI: Zondervan, 2001), 168.

41. *Matthew Henry's Commentary on the Whole Bible*, 1355. Emphasis in the original.

42. See also Luke 10:18 and 1 Tim. 3:6. Some Christians ascribe other texts to Lucifer's fall into rebellion: Isa. 14:12–17; Ezek. 28:12–19; and Rev. 12:7–9. While some of the verses in these passages convey the truth of Lucifer's fall into rebellion and exile, the exegetical conclusions are that Lucifer's fall is not the intended message of these prophets (*Matthew Henry's Commentary on the Whole Bible*, 877, 1104; *The Zondervan NIV Bible Commentary, Volume 2: New Testament*, 1184).

43. The author of 2 Peter wanted to depict the most awful state of existence and chose to characterize this hell with the term *Tartaroō*. It "referred in classical Greek to a subterranean region, doleful and dark, regarded by the ancient Greeks as the abode of the wicked dead, a place of punishment" [*Holman Concise Bible Dictionary* (Nashville, TN: Broadman & Holman Publishers, 1997), 309].

44. *Matthew Henry's Commentary on the Whole Bible*, 1957.

5

Divine Hiddenness and Unanswered Prayer

Synopsis

Critics of Christianity argue that Jesus' promise to answer prayer is empty, as there is no evidence prayers are answered, which harmonizes with atheism.

A Christian response is that the Bible tells us Jesus promised God would grant prayer petitions if certain qualifications are met, one of which is that God's plan of divine hiddenness not get derailed. Moreover, contrary to what the critics claim, evidence of answered prayer that corresponds to the qualifications actually exists.

Jesus promises that whatever the believer asks of God in prayer, in his name, will be granted (Matt. 7:7a; John 14:13a; 15:16b; 16:23b). Recall in chapter 3 that a great many Christians prayed for Jill's brother who had terminal cancer. During a span of a few months, several pastors and church leaders, as well as a whole congregation, prayed that God would heal him. They claimed the promise in James 5:14–15a that, if a believer is sick, the pastors should be brought to pray over him and anoint him with oil in the name of the Lord and "the prayer offered in faith will make the sick person well."

But despite many fervent prayers and anointing with oil (and the latest advances in medicine), Jill's brother died. The faith of some in the congregation was deeply shaken. Why, Jill wondered, would an all-loving God not be true to his promise to answer their prayers? Perhaps, she thought, Jesus' promise was not true after all. If so, then perhaps the Christian faith was not true.

Opponents of Christianity typically refer to situations like Jill's in their argument that because so many of the prayers of believers are not answered, God's promise is either empty or there is no God. For further support they draw upon data of prayer experiments, such as the Great Prayer Experiment (discussed in section 5.4), which arguably provide no verifiable evidence that prayer has any supernatural effect at all. The conclusion drawn is Jesus is a fraud, and God does not exist.

When I was an atheist I felt that the problem of unanswered prayer was just one more reason to reject belief in God's existence. However, I studied the biblical promise, and I reviewed data of prayer experiments. In light of my conclusions concerning divine hiddenness discussed previously, I concluded that Jesus' promise is not empty, and unanswered prayer is actually no problem for Christianity at all.

5.1 The Prayer Promise Has Conditions

I've heard some Christians say God always answers prayers, but sometimes his answer is "no." However, this misunderstands the issue. An "unanswered prayer" is an "ungranted petition." If God's answer is "no," then he declines to grant the petition. Thus, the title of this chapter could be "Divine Hiddenness and Ungranted Prayer Petitions."

Nevertheless, the real problem is not ungranted petitions. It is actually a misconception of the prayer promise that God will grant whatever a believer asks for in Jesus' name with few or no conditions.

The reason for this misconception is twofold. It results from improper Bible study and lack of appreciation for, or understanding of, God's plan for divine hiddenness.

Regarding improper Bible study, consider, for example, John 14:13a: "I will do whatever you ask in my name." Trying to understand this verse without reading the preceding (and following) verses is likely to lead one to think that, regardless of what a believer asks for, God will make it happen. But the neighboring verses imply conditions to the promise.

There is the condition that whatever is asked of God is consistent with God's purpose of glorifying the Father in the Son (v. 13b). There is also the condition that the petition is made "in Jesus' name" (vv. 13, 14) and by a believer truly cultivating obedience to God's commandments (v. 15).

Essentially, the promise is conditioned upon cultivating a right relationship with God through Jesus and asking for things that mesh with God's plans, character, and glorification (2 Cor. 12:9–10). According to theologians:

> The phrase "in my name" . . . is not a magic charm like an Aladdin's lamp. It was both a guarantee, like the endorsement on a check, and *a limitation on the petition; for he would grant only such petitions as could be presented in a manner consistent with his character and purpose*. In prayer we call on him to work out his purpose, not simply to gratify our whims.[1]

Thus, a brief acknowledgement of the immediate context shows that the prayer promise is not meant as a kind of blanket promise without condition or qualification. The same is true for the promise as stated in John 15:16 and 16:23.

But we should not think John's list of conditions is complete. His aim was not to record a comprehensive list of conditions, but rather to provide enough essential information about Jesus to inspire a relationship with God in Christ for salvation (John 20:31). Most likely he presupposed the believer's awareness of a full array of conditions of the promise mentioned elsewhere in Scripture, such as in the writings by Paul and the other apostles (that were circulating in the middle and late first century to churches around the then known world[2]).

Perhaps the most popular Bible passage of God's promise to grant prayers for the sick is in James 5:14–16:

> Is anyone among you sick? Let them call the elders of the church to pray over them and anoint them with oil in the name of the Lord. And the prayer offered in faith will make the sick person well; the Lord will raise them up. If they have sinned, they will be forgiven.

In this passage, the apostle James gives detailed instruction concerning the sick, that they should be visited by the pastors, whose ministry for the sick included prayer and anointment with oil. Probably the purpose of the oil was medicinal rather than sacramental. Of the two choices of Greek words that James could have used, he chose not to use the usual word for sacramental or ritualistic anointing (*chriō*), but instead chose a word (*aleiphō*) that means to daub or smear. This suggests that James had in mind giving the sick person medicine along with prayer, especially in light of the fact that in the first century oil was one of the most common medicines (Luke 10:34; see also

Isa. 1:6). Jewish historian Josephus reported that Herod the Great was given a bath in oil in hopes of being cured of his last illness. Other ancient sources refer to the use of oil as medicine, such as Philo of Alexandria, Pliny, and the physician Galen of Pergamon, who described it as "the best of all remedies for paralysis" (*De Simplicium Medicamentorum Temperamentis* 2.10ff).[3]

Nonetheless, while the pastors were to medically treat the sick, James' emphasis and assurance is that God will intervene in response to the *prayer* prayed in faith that God make the sick person well. Exegetical commentators on James 5:14–16 tell us that if the person gets well, it is because of such conditions as the faith of the believers praying, the confession of sin, and the faith of the sick person, as well as God's use of the medicine to cure the sickness.[4] "If he be a person capable and fit for deliverance, and if God have any thing further for such a person to do in the world," he will get well.[5]

Like John, James mentions only a few of the conditions to Jesus' prayer promise. Most likely James also presupposed the believer's awareness of a full array of conditions of the promise mentioned elsewhere in Scripture. This is affirmed by the fact that James spent much time with Paul in prayer and official discussion of matters of faith and doctrine (Gal. 1:17–19; 2:9–12; see also Acts 9:19, 26–28; 15:1–35; 21:18–25). And of all of the New Testament writers, it is Paul who writes the most about Jesus' prayer promise and its conditions, including the conditions concerning prayer for the sick.

Paul prayed fervently and persistently for God to intervene to take away what he called "a thorn in my flesh, a messenger of Satan, to torment me," which he believed made him weak in some way (2 Cor. 12:7, 9). Most Christians believe it was a health issue of some kind (there is textual evidence that he suffered from one or more maladies, one of which may have been poor eyesight). God did not grant his petition. But Paul believed the malady was useful to help keep him humble and meek and concluded that his prayer went against the work that God was doing to improve his faith, disposition, and character. Sometimes God sends the sickness as a disciplinary agent (1 Cor. 11:30). Thus, he could not claim the promise of answered prayer because his prayer did not meet the conditions of the promise. Realizing this, Paul's faith was strengthened and he went on boasting all the more gladly about his weakness (2 Cor. 12:9).

Christians who have thought that the prayer promise has few or no conditions may find the previous discussion a bit distressing. However, there are two things that should be kept in mind. First, many of God's other promises recorded in Scripture can only be claimed upon meeting certain conditions. One prime example is God's promise of salvation. While his promise to forgive is a free gift offered to all, it is received only when certain conditions are met, such as a faith-based relationship with God.

Second, a conditional promise is a *responsible* promise. While there are responsible promises made by God which are fulfilled for a believer without the believer having to meet conditions (e.g., God's promises to minister to the world by his Son and the Holy Spirit), other kinds of promises made by God without conditions would clearly be irresponsible. As William Lane Craig points out to fellow believers:

> When you reflect on it, it would be a recipe for disaster for God to simply give us whatever we ask. For we would always pray to be delivered from any suffering or trial, and yet we know from Scripture that suffering builds character and trials perfect our faith. If God gave us whatever we asked, we would be immature, spoiled children, not men and women of God.[6]

5.2 Conditions of the Prayer Promise

Conditions or qualifiers to God's promise to grant prayer petitions include:

1. The person praying must be cultivating a faith and disposition that are compatible with an eternal relationship with God (the person must actually be saved versus merely profess to be saved);
2. The prayer must be offered in earnestness and perseverance;
3. The person praying must have a significantly right motive for the prayer;
4. The person praying for God to intervene to remove obstacles standing in the way of significant spiritual progress must trust that God will answer the petition and be willing to forgive others;
5. The prayer petition must be within God's power to grant (be logically possible to grant);
6. The prayer must be according to God's timetable; and
7. The prayer must be according to God's purposes and will.

Condition one is probably the most prevalent obstacle to the granting of prayer requests. God does not answer the prayers of those cultivating a selfish and malevolent disposition and beliefs (Psalm. 66:18; Prov. 28:9; Isaiah 59:1–2; John 15:15–16; James 5:16; 1 Pet. 3:7; 1 John 3:21–22). There are professed believers in God who are not really walking with God. They are unwilling to either forgive others (Mark 11:22–25; James 1:6-8; 5:14–16) or give up a significant habit or way of life that cultivates a character unbefitting of the people God saves for eternal glory.

Due to known sins that are cherished and an unwillingness to trust God, their petitions are not in the name of Jesus. Their only right in approaching God is in Jesus' name. But Jesus would not profess to know such people. Jesus said:

> Not everyone who calls out to me, "Lord! Lord!" will enter the Kingdom of Heaven. Only those who actually do the will of my Father in heaven will enter. On judgment day many will say to me, "Lord! Lord! We prophesied *in your name* and cast out demons *in your name* and performed many miracles *in your name*." But I will reply, "I never knew you. Get away from me, you who break God's laws." (Matt. 7:21–23 NLT, emphasis added; see also 2 Tim. 2:19 and Heb. 10:26–27).

The people who most clearly fall within this camp are those who are playing church. God does not call his people into a social club. Such people may attend church and volunteer at soup kitchens, but they cultivate a heart that is not redeemable for eternal life in the heavenly community.

Condition two (that prayer must be offered in earnestness and perseverance) is really a two-part condition. The person praying must be serious about the intervention he is asking of God and be persistent with his petition. Jesus prayed with seriousness. We know of one occasion in which he prayed throughout the entire night (Matt. 26:36–45). Hannah's prayer is another example (1 Sam. 1). She went to the tabernacle to pray for God's intervention so that she could have a son. She prayed in deep anguish and intensity. Her lips were moving but she was not making a sound. The priest noticed her praying and thought she was intoxicated. This is the kind of prayer for which God dispatches celestial aid. It is with seriousness and sincere feeling of dependency upon God, from the gut—with an all or nothing attitude—not letting God go until intervention is seen.

But so many believers today pray casually with little care that God would intervene to grant the thing prayed for. Most of the prayers are prayed in the worship service or prayer meeting and then forgotten about. Prayers may go ungranted because the believer doesn't care all that much whether God grants the thing requested.

Some believers like to pray once about something and leave it up to God to take care of it. However, Jesus taught his disciples to be persistent in prayer. The words translated as "ask," "seek," and "knock" are symmetrically repeated and in present tense in Matt. 7:7–8 to stress the importance of being persistent in prayer.[7] Jesus told the story of the widow who petitioned the judge persistently as a lesson to his disciples "that they should always pray and not give up" (Luke 18:1). Jesus told the story of a man who persistently asked his friend for three loaves of bread in the middle of the night to illustrate persistence in prayer (Luke 11:5–8). Paul admonished the believers to not give up on a petitionary prayer (Rom. 1:9; 1 Thess. 5:17; 2 Tim. 1:3). The persistence is to break us of self-dependency and to facilitate transformation of the disposition toward the feeling of dependency upon God. God promises to grant the petition of a heart of true dependency upon him, all other conditions of his promise being met.

Regarding condition three, the person praying must have right motives. This is mentioned in James' epistle: "When you ask, you do not receive, because you ask with wrong motives" (James 4:3). Believers will not claim the promise of answered prayer with selfish motives for personal gain.

Atheist John W. Loftus objects to this, arguing that since all human motives are at least a little selfish, most all believers, including pastors, probably will never claim the promise of granted prayer. According to Loftus:

> There is nothing a human can do or say that is completely free of selfish motives. *Psychological egoism*, for instance, is the theory that everything we do, even if in some small degree, benefits us the most. Even if we don't take that extreme stance, and I don't, most all of our prayers contain some selfish motives. Even the preacher who prays that his church mature and grow can also want a bigger paycheck, more power, some recognized fame, and fewer problem people as they mature in their Christian faith. So which prayers qualify to be answered when many, if not most of them, are prayed from selfish motives?[8]

It might appear that Loftus makes a good point. However, the context of the passage is clear enough that the believers James writes about are lost in worldly pleasures (James 1:27; 2:5; 4:4). The motives and goals behind their prayers were to obtain money to pay for things to cultivate their selfish pleasure. "They wanted to gratify themselves rather than help others and please God."[9] Their prayers are not answered because, as the NLT reads, "Your motives are all wrong—you want only what will give you pleasure. You adulterers! Don't you realize that friendship with the world makes you an enemy of God?" (James 4:3–4). Notice that James says their motives were *all* wrong—not with a trace amount of selfishness, but fundamentally off the path set by Jesus for them to follow. Thus, James is not saying that prayers are not answered if the motive is not completely free of any trace of selfishness. That won't happen for a believer until he enters the beatific vision (discussed in the previous chapters). Rather, they are not answered if the motive is predominantly or fundamentally selfish. In other words, this condition for answered prayer is akin to condition one, that prayers are not answered if the one making the petition is (despite profession) cultivating a disposition and beliefs contrary to eternal life in heaven. These are the believers today who are praying for a giant flat-screen color television and singing, "O Lord won't you buy me a Mercedes Benz. My friends all drive Porsches, I must make amends."[10]

Loftus' example of the preacher who can have motives tainted with a little personal gain does not appear to fall within the bounds of the condition of James 4:3. A bigger paycheck is a motive that can meet this condition for answered prayer if it is intended that more money be given to the less fortunate or to evangelism programs. Motives for more power or fame are not necessarily precluding motives for granted prayers, because these things can help advance God's kingdom (e.g., the fame of Billy Graham or Martin Luther King Jr.). On the other hand, if the preacher's primary motive includes amassing wealth, expensive personal luxuries, power, or fame for self-glorification and worldly pleasures, then the preacher could not claim Jesus' promise of answered prayer (although Satan might be happy to oblige).

Condition four concerns faith in divine power to remove sin and temptation and other obstacles standing in the way of advancement in a relationship with God. If a person who prays does not trust that God will answer the petition, he or she cannot claim the promise of answered prayer. "Truly I tell you, if anyone says to this mountain, 'Go, throw yourself into the sea,' and does not doubt in their heart but believes that what they say will happen, it will be done for them. Therefore I tell you, whatever you ask for in prayer, believe that you have received it, and it will be yours" (Mark 11:23–24).

Jesus was speaking figuratively of "mountains" that stand in the way of fellowship with God. Such things are cherished sinful habits, or even sinful addictions. The petitioner must trust in God and his interventional work to remove such mountains. Theologians tell us that "the greatest possible difficulties can be removed when a person has faith."[11] But a particular kind of faith is called for. It must be a faith followed by action that corresponds to belief that the thing prayed for will happen or is happening despite no observable evidence initially. We are told it does not take a lot of faith to move mountains (Luke 17:6). But what is required is constancy in trust in God's leading in the life that perseveres. As James says, "When you ask, you must believe and not doubt" (James 1:6). According to theologians:

> Faith must be more than mere acceptance of a creed. To believe is to be confident that God will give what is requested. The extent of the faith that God looks for is emphasized by the words "not doubt." ... "Doubt" describes one who is divided in the mind and who wavers between two opinions. One moment he voices the yes of faith; the next moment it is the no of disbelief. Such an attitude is graphically illustrated by "a wave of the sea." Completely lacking in stability, it is "blown and tossed by the wind." First there is the crest, then the trough. Instead, prayer that moves God to respond must be marked by the constancy of unwavering faith.[12]

Such believers, who oscillate between belief and unbelief in God's power to intervene to remove sin and temptation and other spiritual obstacles, cannot claim God's promise to grant prayer. Consequently, they do not receive divine aid to overcome a sinful habit. They lack trust in God's advice for course correction. "There is a way that appears to be right, but in the end it leads to death" (Prov. 14:12). Over and over they fall prey to temptation and end up cultivating a sin-laden disposition. But believers are to "watch and pray" so that they will not "fall into temptation (Matt. 26:41). Like condition three, this condition is also akin to condition one.

Regarding condition five, the prayer must be within God's power to grant the petition. Sometimes believers pray for contradictory things. If two believers pray to receive the same object, the prayers of both believers cannot be granted. William Lane Craig gives the example of two young men who were both in love with the same young lady. "Each one was praying that God would turn her affections toward him so that he might marry her. Now clearly the prayers of at least one of those young men was going to be unanswered.

God couldn't answer them both because their prayers were contradictory."[13]

Regarding condition six, believers are told to have patience because of God's timetable. The Bible tells us that God's timetable is often very different from that of humans. For many years the Hebrews cried out to God in prayer for deliverance (Exod. 2:23–25). For decades the Israelites prayed for deliverance from Babylonian captivity (Lamentations 1–5). Jews prayed for centuries for the advent of the Messiah. And for nearly two thousand years Christians have been praying for Jesus' second advent—his return in power and glory. There are numerous other examples that illustrate that unanswered prayers include the ones that are not in line with God's timetable.

Regarding condition seven, prayer must be according to God's purposes and will. "If we ask anything according to his will, he hears us. And if we know that he hears us—whatever we ask—we know that we have what we asked of him" (1 John 5:14–15; see also Matt. 27:39–43; Luke 22:42; John 14:13–14; 15:16; 16:23).

The Bible reveals much of God's purposes and will that would otherwise be hidden from us.[14] But, in our world of divine hiddenness there is still much that the Christian does not know, or cannot be sure of, especially with respect to any given situation. As discussed previously (and in chapters 7 and 8), God intervenes to curtail free actions, but he must limit his intervention so that people retain significant compatibility-determining free will. The level of intervention God would employ is of course something the believer would not know. Consequently, many prayers are likely to ask for levels of intervention that are outside of God's will.

Thus, a man who prays for his wife's protection as she walks home from a store may find that all, or none, or some of his prayer is answered. The free will of a mugger may be curtailed enough to divert him away from the woman entirely, or to an extent that she is robbed but not physically harmed, or to a lesser extent that she is bruised and scraped. The believer, in his limited perspective, would of course pray for the woman to be spared *any* harm. But in a world of divine hiddenness and free compatibility determination, having the entire prayer answered may not be best. And this is something the praying believer could not know.

Some Christians find this discouraging. They don't feel that they know what to pray for and give up. The apostle Paul assures them that there's really no need to feel discouraged. He tells his fellow Christians in Rome: "We don't know what God wants us to pray for. But the Holy Spirit prays for us" and "the Spirit pleads for us believers in harmony with God's will" (Rom. 8:26–27 NLT). The Holy Spirit takes the prayers and modifies them so that they are in accord with God's will and then presents them to the Father who grants each and every one. This is why Christians often include the closing phrase in prayer: "not my will but God's will be done."

With the Holy Spirit as the believer's prayer intercessor, she is encouraged to pray, and to pray often and persistently. As mentioned earlier, the words translated as "ask," "seek," and "knock" are symmetrically repeated and in present tense in Matt. 7:7–8 to stress the importance of being persistent in prayer. Jesus told the story of the widow who petitioned the judge persistently as a lesson to his disciples "that they should always pray and not give up" (Luke 18:1). Jesus reinforced this teaching with the story of a man who persistently asked his friend for three loaves of bread in the middle of the night until his friend got up out of bed to give him the bread (Luke 11:5–8). Paul elsewhere encourages believers to keep on asking God (Rom. 1:9; 1 Thess. 5:17; 2 Tim. 1:3).

5.3 The Death of a Thousand Qualifications

After covering all of the conditions previously discussed, the skeptic could argue that it is a wonder that God (if he exists) would answer any prayers at all. What meaning, then, is there in Jesus' promise that whatever the believer asks of God in his name will be granted? As Loftus says: "[The] question here is whether the biblical promise of answered prayer 'dies the death of a thousand qualifications,' so to speak."[15]

I think the Christian response should first of all acknowledge a misnomer. There is a prayer promise that dies the death of a thousand qualifications, but it is not the biblical one. Rather, it is the unbiblical conception of a promise with few or no conditions that some assume to be taught in Scripture. Such a conception is dying in the light of what the Bible actually teaches about prayer. And so it should. But the biblical promise lives on, qualifications notwithstanding.

It lives on because genuine believers feel sure enough by experience and faith that while many petitions are not granted, some are. By faith they believe there are divine answers to prayers being carried out beyond our senses by the Holy Spirit and his angels. Sometimes the intervention is not observed, including intervention to prevent harm due to a disease or accident. Perhaps the most popular unobservable divine response to prayer is God's response to the one that asks for God's forgiveness. The true believer can be confident that God grants that one. The confidence comes from having Bible knowledge, faith, and a serious and persevering commitment to fellowship with God (1 John 5:14–15).

Christians can also feel sure that there are prayers that are answered by their observations of occurrences that appear to be supernatural responses to prayer. When all known natural explanations are ruled out, it can appear more likely than not that a prayer was answered. (Observable evidence of answered prayer is discussed in the next section.)

Still, because some prayers are unanswered, believers may be discouraged in their prayer life and maybe doubt the reality of God. But there are a few things for the believer to keep in mind. First, having petitions granted is not the primary purpose of prayer. Believers are not to pray to get stuff. Rather, *it is to foster the development of an intimate relationship with God*. The admonitions to pray fervently, persistently, and seriously are about striving for a deeper, stronger, and thus more rewarding, relationship. That a particular petition is granted, for healing, or a job, is icing on the cake.

Second, the believer should acknowledge the reality that the "flesh" crucified is not yet dead, and that some of the battles in the "good fight" are lost. Finally, the believer should be aware that we live in a world of divine hiddenness, as discussed. Consequently, many petitions are not granted. But believers should feel comforted that it's best that they aren't, as God would have the best reasons for not granting them, which would be fully explained in the afterlife.

5.4 No Evidence That Prayer Is Answered?

Skeptics may concede that God's promise to grant prayer requests is multiconditional, and therefore believers should expect some (if not many) prayers to go unanswered. But, they argue, while believers can validly argue that God is keeping his prayer promise, Christians are left with no evidence that any prayer request is granted.

To shore up their case, some skeptics[16] draw upon the Great Prayer Experiment published in the *American Heart Journal* (151, No. 4 [2006]: 934–942). Patients at six hospitals who had heart bypass surgery were separated into three groups. Believers prayed for the rapid healing of group one, and those of group one did not know they were being prayed for. None of the believers prayed for the rapid recovery of anyone in group two, and they did not know that they were not prayed for (the control group). Believers prayed for the patients in group three, and the patients were informed that they were being prayed for. The believers who prayed were among three groups: two were Roman Catholic (one in Massachusetts and the other in Minnesota) and one was a Protestant group (Silent Unity in Lee's Summit, Missouri). The result was that there was no difference between the patients who were prayed for and the patients who were not prayed for. Additionally, the patients of group three, who knew they were being prayed for, suffered significantly more complications than the patients in groups one and two, who did not know whether they were being prayed for. The experimenters commented that the patients in group three may have suffered additional stress from anxiety brought on by the thought that their condition was so bad that a prayer team was called in and/or perhaps by a kind of performance anxiety.

Does this experiment provide evidence that prayers are not answered? Atheists like Richard Dawkins would have us think so. But the reality is that the experiment is flawed. The believers' petitions did not meet the conditions for the kinds of prayers that God would answer. In order to standardize the prayers, the believers were given scripts to read for their prayers. The problem here is that at least some of the people could not pray from the heart as they were led by the Holy Spirit. This appears to go against at least one of the prayer conditions that must be met before a believer can claim the promise of granted prayer (Matt. 6:7). Moreover, if the motive of the believers was predominantly to generate evidence of God's existence, rather than the welfare of the patients, God may not have responded to such prayers. Wanting group two to not be prayed for just to prove God exists does not appear to be in the spirit of love. Furthermore, there may be other conditions that were not met to claim the promise of answered prayer that were beyond the control or fault of the believers who prayed. Therefore, the results of the experiment do not provide evidence that prayer does not work. At least some negative results *should* be expected. The only verification, from the results of the experiment, is that God will not grant petitions that fail to meet the conditions of the biblical promise.

However, the skeptic argues, while the Great Prayer Experiment provides no evidence that prayer doesn't work, it doesn't provide evidence that prayer *does* work. Thus, they argue, Christians would seem to be left with no verifiable evidence that any prayer is answered. However, they fail to recognize that there are other prayer experiments with positive results that lower the probability of chance or coincidence to such a low degree that answered prayer appears to be the more likely explanation.

For example, there is the double-blind prayer experiment published in the *Southern Medical Journal*.[17] Cardiac patients from the San Francisco General Medical Center were randomly divided (using a computer-generated list) into two groups. A group of Christians were given the names of the patients in one group to pray for while the patients were in the hospital. All of the Christians chosen for the experiment professed to be "born again" believers according to John 3:3 and to have the habit of praying daily and being in fellowship in a Christian church. The believers praying in the study did not pray for the patients of the other group (the control group). None of the patients knew if they were being prayed for (there was no "placebo" group in this study). The hospital staff did not know which patients were being prayed for. Prior to initiation of the prayers, there were no statistical differences in the conditions of the patients in the groups. However, following the prayers, the conditions of the patients in the group prayed for were substantially better than the conditions of the patients not prayed for. "The prayed-for patients were five times less likely to require antibiotics and three times less likely to develop pulmonary edema. None of the prayed-for group required endotracheal intubation, and fewer patients in the prayed-for group died."[18] Statistics demonstrated that the likelihood of these outcomes being due to chance or coincidence is one in one hundred (1 in 100). Multivariate analysis of all the parameters measured demonstrated that the likelihood that the outcomes were due to chance or coincidence is one in ten thousand (1 in 10,000).[19]

The skeptic could argue that it should have been one in a billion. However, there are at least a few reasons why the results of the experiment were not more dramatic. First, when the conditions for claiming the promise of answered prayer are taken into account, the results of this experiment are actually congruous with the Bible's promise. Second, the experiment did not control (prevent) anyone outside the study from praying for the patients. It is likely that Christians outside of the study prayed for many of the patients in the control group. Third, a possible flaw in the experiment was that no one verified that the people in the prayer groups actually prayed as they were supposed to.

Moreover, when it comes to evidence of answered prayer, the skeptic should keep in mind that no other religion has succeeded in scientifically demonstrating that prayer to their god has any efficacy in healing. In fact, studies that have used prayer groups from multiple religious backgrounds have failed to provide significant evidence of answered prayer.[20]

In addition to the evidence of this prayer experiment, there is a multitude of testimonials by Christians of occurrences following prayer that seem very unlikely to have occurred by chance or coincidence. In his book, *Atheist Universe*, atheist David Mills objects to counting such testimonials as evidence because a few prayers that ambiguously appear to have been answered are emphasized while many prayers with no apparent answer are conveniently forgotten, and the few that appear answered can easily be explained away as coincidence (i.e., the doctor lowballed the odds of the patient's recovery).[21] Therefore, talk of answered prayer is just the hype of wishful thinkers deluded by the illusion of selective observation. Such testimonials really provide no evidence.

But Mills' conception of the prayer promise overlooks the biblical conditions, including divine hiddenness. With regard to the ambiguity, it was discussed in the previous chapters that this would accord with a world of divine hiddenness (a concept that atheists do not mention when trying to debunk evidence of answered prayer). In a modern world of mass communication, where hundreds of millions of people can learn of an event in an instant, even one profoundly and undeniably granted prayer request for an injured or sick person (e.g., an amputee waking up with a newly grown limb) would likely cause changes in our world environment that would further cause a significant reduction of God's hiddenness that could deprive people of a significant degree of compatibility-determining free will. It might be difficult for some to imagine such a miracle having a significant impact, but then it is difficult to imagine how the fluttering of a butterfly on a twig in West Africa may set in motion forces that eventually issue in a hurricane over the Atlantic Ocean.[22] Therefore, it is reasonable to expect ambiguous answers to prayer, as well as secrecy[23] of miraculous responses to prayer that would cause significant interruption of divine hiddenness.

While many answers to prayer can be difficult to discern, sometimes answers to prayer are not so ambiguous. The prayer experiment previously discussed regarding the cardiac patients from the San Francisco General Medical Center is one example. Other examples of unambiguous answers to prayer in everyday life may include prayers that are followed by the kinds of occurrences that make a God hypothesis more likely than a random coincidence hypothesis. Factors that increase the probability include evidence of the supernatural (discussed in chapter 3) and apparent synchronicity between the time when a petition is made and the time when a seemingly corresponding event occurs.

Conclusion

People who try to debunk Christianity argue that there is no God to answer prayer evidenced by the apparent disparity between Jesus' promise to grant whatever the believer asks of God in his name and the undeniable observation that some prayer requests are not granted. Moreover, they argue that there is no evidence that *any* prayer request is granted. Therefore, real life experience tells us that the God of the Bible probably doesn't exist, which might appear to be a problem for belief in the Christian God.

However, what they are calling a problem is really no problem at all. This is because their argument is based on a misunderstanding of the biblical promise. The Bible defines several conditions that must be met to claim the promise. Some of the conditions are within the believer's control (e.g., a heart of true repentance from sin), and some conditions are outside of the believer's control (e.g., God's purposes related to preserving compatibility-determining free will with divine hiddenness).

The critic's claim that there is no evidence that *any* prayer request is granted is an overstatement. While the Great Prayer Experiment provided negative results, the study was flawed. Moreover, there are other prayer experiments (with fewer flaws) with positive results. Additionally, there are the testimonials of believers of answered prayers surrounded by factors that make it unlikely that the claimed answers occurred due to chance or coincidence. The evidence of answered prayer is not glaring, but in light of God's plan for divine hiddenness, the degree of observable evidence appears to be just what Christians should expect.

NOTES to Chapter 5

1. *Zondervan NIV Bible Commentary, Volume 2: New Testament*, consul. eds. Kenneth L. Barker and John R. Kohlenberger III (Grand Rapids, MI: Zondervan Publishing House, 1994), 346. Emphasis added. By praying "in Jesus' name" the believer acknowledges that his prayer would not be heard if not for God's promise of

the messiah and its fulfillment in the person and work of Jesus Christ.

2. Col. 4:16; Rev. 1:11. See also 1 Cor. 1:1–2; Gal. 1:1–2, 21–23; Eph. 1:1; 1 Thess. 5:27.

3. *The Expositor's Bible Commentary*, gen. ed. Frank E. Gaebelein, consul. eds. James Montgomery Boice and Merrill C. Tenney, Vol. 12 (Grand Rapids, MI: Zondervan Publishing House, 1976), 203–204; *Zondervan NIV Bible Commentary, Volume 2: New Testament*, 1038.

4. Ibid.

5. *Matthew Henry's Commentary on the Whole Bible* (Peabody, MA: Hendrickson Publishers, 1991), 1942.

6. William Lane Craig, *Hard Questions, Real Answers* (Wheaton, IL: Crossway Books, 2003), 56. Craig received his PhD at the University of Birmingham, England, and his DTheol at the University of Munich, Germany. He is currently research professor of philosophy at Talbot School of Theology in La Mirada, California. He is also the founder of Reasonable Faith (www.reasonablefaith.org), a web-based apologetics ministry. Craig has authored numerous books, including: *Reasonable Faith*, *Time and Eternity*, and *On Guard*.

7. *Zondervan NIV Bible Commentary, Volume 2: New Testament*, 36.

8. John W. Loftus, *Why I Became an Atheist: A Former Preacher Rejects Christianity* (Amherst, NY: Prometheus Books, 2008), 222. Emphasis in the original.

9. *Zondervan NIV Bible Commentary, Volume 2: New Testament*, 1032–1033.

10. "Mercedes Benz" was written by Janis Joplin (1943–1970) and recorded on October 1, 1970, three days before she died of a drug overdose.

11. *Zondervan NIV Bible Commentary, Volume 2: New Testament*, 181.

12. Ibid., 1020.

13. William Lane Craig, *Hard Questions, Real Answers*, 43.

14. God keeps some of his plans and blessings secret from us (e.g., Matt. 24:36; Rom. 16:25–26; 1 Cor. 2:6–8; Eph. 3:4–5, 9; Col. 1:26–27).

15. John W. Loftus, *Why I Became an Atheist: A Former Preacher Rejects Christianity*, 221.

16. A few of them include: Victor J. Stenger in *Has Science Found God? The Latest Results in the Search for Purpose in the Universe* (Amherst, NY: Prometheus Books, 2003), chapter 9; Richard Dawkins in *The God Delusion* (New York: Houghton Mifflin Company, 2006), 61–66; and John W. Loftus in *Why I Became an Atheist*, 225–227.

17. Randolph C. Byrd, "Positive Therapeutic Effects of Intercessory Prayer in a Coronary Care Unit Population," 81 [1988]: 826–829. Other prayer experiments include a 1999 experiment: W. C. Harris, M. Gowda, J. W. Kolb, C. P. Strychacz, J. L. Vacek, P. G. Jones, A. Forker, J. H. O'Keefe and B. D. McAllister, "Randomized, Controlled Trial of the Effects of Remote, Intercessory Prayer on Outcomes in Patients Admitted to the Coronary Care Unit," *Archives of Internal Medicine (JAMA*

Internal Medicine), Vol. 159, 2273–2278; and a 2001 experiment: L. Leibovici, "Effects of Remote, Retroactive Intercessory Prayer on Outcomes in Patients with Bloodstream Infection: Randomized Controlled Trial," *British Medical Journal*, Vol. 323, 1450–1451. All three prayer experiments are discussed by Richard L. Deem, "Scientific Evidence for Answered Prayer and the Existence of God," http://www.godandscience.org/apologetics/prayer.html (accessed on November 11, 2014). Deem received his master of science degree in microbiology from California State University, Los Angeles, and has been working in basic science research since 1976. He has authored and co-authored studies in molecular biology and genetics, immunology, inflammatory bowel disease, natural killer cells, and infectious diseases. He is employed as senior researcher/specialist in the Inflammatory Bowel Disease Center at Cedars-Sinai Medical Center in California.

18. Dean Radin, *The Conscious Universe: The Scientific Truth of Psychic Phenomena* (New York: HarperCollins Publishers, 1997), 163.

19. Richard L. Deem, "Scientific Evidence for Answered Prayer and the Existence of God," http://www.godandscience.org/apologetics/prayer.html. Accessed on November 11, 2014.

20. M. W. Krucoff, et al., 2005, "Music, Imagery, Touch, and Prayer as Adjuncts to Interventional Cardiac Care: The Monitoring and Actualisation of Noetic Trainings (MANTRA) II Randomized Study," *The Lancet*, Vol. 366, Issue 9481, 211–217.

21. David Mills, *Atheist Universe: The Thinking Person's Answer to Christian Fundamentalism* (Berkeley, CA: Ulysses Press, 2006), 158–161.

22. William Lane Craig, *On Guard* (Colorado Springs, CO: David C. Cook, 2010), 158. Craig mentions this illustration in *Hard Questions, Real Answers* (Wheaton, IL: Crossway, 2003), 92. There is an expanded use of this illustration in chapter 8.1.

23. Matt. 6:4, 6.

Part 2
The Problem of Evil and Suffering

6
Would God Even Allow Evil and Suffering?

Synopsis

Critics of Christianity argue that it is a logical impossibility for God and evil and suffering to coexist.

A Christian response is that it is actually logically possible because it is possible that God has a plan to achieve a greater good which necessarily entails the permitting of evil and suffering, which renders the critics' argument invalid. Attempts are made to try to revalidate it using variations of the argument, but all such attempts contain logical fallacies and/or doctrinal errors and consequently fail.

Christians claim this world is the creation and providential object of God's care. God is perfectly loving and good and possesses phenomenal and incomprehensible power, knowledge, wisdom, and intelligence. It would seem, then, that because he is perfectly loving and good, and has unfathomable ability, God could and would keep evil and suffering from occurring. Yet there is evil and suffering in the world—and in no small quantity or severity.

Indeed, we have difficulty trying to get our minds around the vast amount, intensity, and extent of the cruelty, calamity, and pain and suffering that spans the existence of all complex life. Chapter 2.2 gave the reader some idea of the vast brutality. There have been thousands of wars in which many hundreds of millions are pummeled, stabbed, drowned, starved, hacked up, shot up, burned up, or blown up. Methods of torture seem to stretch the limits of our imaginings of the horrors and cruelty. But even in times of peace, billions of children have suffered from beatings, rape, molestation, confinement, or abandonment. Today, thousands of such crimes occur daily in the world.[1] In the United States alone, approximately five children a day die from child abuse.[2]

Further injury and suffering result from violent storms, droughts, fires, floods, mudslides, accidents, birth defects, and thousands of various kinds of diseases. Every day thousands are suffering and dying from malaria. Many suffer from heart disease, cancer, Alzheimer's disease, respiratory infections, Lyme disease, botulism, hepatitis, etc.

All too many times the sufferers feel that it would be pointless for God to allow it. Calamity strikes without known rhyme or reason, and often it leaves its victims dehumanized, depressed, or suicidal.

Even the people who enjoy life in good health, and comfortable living conditions, still suffer from not having direct guidance and undeniable evidence of God's existence, as discussed in chapter 4.5. As a result, there is distress, disagreement, and frustration over what happens at death, why we exist, whether there is a God, or how we are to live.

But, Christianity's opponents argue, a perfectly loving and good God would always prefer a world without evil and suffering. And since God is also powerful enough and knowledgeable enough to make it so, there shouldn't be any evil and suffering. Thus, it appears logically impossible for both God and evil to exist, just as it is logically inconsistent to say that an immovable object can exist while subjected to an irresistible force. The two are logically incompatible. If one exists, the other does not. Therefore, it is argued, Christians face a problem that God cannot logically exist.

6.1 Is It Contradictory for God to Prefer a World in Which Evil and Suffering Occur?

Philosophers have long argued that it is logically impossible for God to prefer to create a universe in which there exists evil and suffering. The argument is based on two assumptions: (1) an all-powerful/all-knowing God can create a world with creatures (made in his image) that have compatibility-determining free will and that cannot commit evil and cause suffering; and (2) a perfectly loving and good God would always prefer to create a world in which there is no evil and suffering over a world in which there is evil and suffering. Both of these assumptions must be true for this argument to succeed. If they are true, then it would be logically impossible for God to exist. The question is: Are these assumptions necessarily true?

The first assumption says God can create beings with compatibility-determining free will that cannot choose evil and cause suffering. After all, the Bible says "all things are possible with God" (Mark 10:27). In response to this, first of all, the "all things" are all *logically possible* things—things not self-contradictory—things that do not defy the law of noncontradiction. Examples of logically impossible things are: a married bachelor, a colorless color, and a square circle. It is logically impossible for such things to exist. Therefore, God's power is limited to what is logically possible.

Second, the critic's assumption is that God is capable of creating a being with compatibility-determining free will that cannot choose evil. But such an act is a logical impossibility. The very definition of such free will includes having the ability to choose evil. This sets a logical limitation on God's power to create freewill beings (made in his image). As philosopher Michael A. Corey (1957–2011) says,

> In order for this form of creaturely freedom to be valid . . . God necessarily had to have enacted a voluntary self-limitation of His own all-power. For insofar as humans are going to be capable of possessing significant behavioral freedom, then God *cannot* concurrently have the power to coerce them into doing His bidding, at least not to the extent that they are intended to be simultaneously free.[3]

And as philosopher Peter Kreeft says, "Creating a world where there's free will and no possibility of sin is a self-contradiction—and that opens the door to people choosing evil over God, with suffering being the result."[4] Any creature incapable of committing a moral evil does not have moral free will. Having such free will without the ability to commit evil defies the law of noncontradiction. Therefore, the first assumption is not logically possible and not necessarily true.

Now, having said that, it *is* possible for God to create beings with compatibility-determining free will who never actually commit evil. This was the *possible* course of humankind. But God cannot ensure that possibility. "To put it another way, even Omnipotence himself could not have created a world in which there was genuine human freedom and yet no possibility of sin, for our freedom includes the possibility of sin within its own meaning."[5] God could not fix it so that evil could never happen. The only way to do this is to create us *without* compatibility-determining free will.

In sum, it is not logically possible for God to create freewill beings who cannot commit evil. The possibility to choose evil must exist. The first assumption, then, that God can create freewill beings that are incapable of choosing evil is not true, necessarily or otherwise. Since it is not necessarily true, the argument that God and evil (and suffering) logically cannot coexist is fallacious (has a failure in reasoning which makes it invalid). (Remember both of the two assumptions must be true for the argument to succeed.)

But what about the second assumption, that a perfectly loving and good God would never prefer a world in which there is evil and suffering? Is the assumption necessarily true? Many assume that a perfectly loving and good God is never unkind and therefore would never prefer any instance of suffering in his world. He would design a world and intervene in it so that everyone would always be loving, good, smiling, content, and comfortable.

A problem, however, is that the second assumption is based on a misunderstanding of love and goodness. Many conflate love and goodness with kindness. To be kind is to prevent or alleviate pain and suffering, but to be loving and good involves acting to achieve the highest good for a person, whether by acting kindly or unkindly, depending on what any given situation calls for.[6] Therefore, to be loving and good can sometimes entail allowing suffering.

This is illustrated in the *Star Trek* episode "The City on the Edge of Forever," where McCoy accidentally injects himself with an overdose of cordrazine and, in his delirious state, enters a vortex that transports him to Earth in 1930. Kirk and Spock go after him through the vortex but can only approximate the date when McCoy arrives on Earth. Following their arrival, Kirk and Spock are given lodging by Edith Keeler. While searching for McCoy, Kirk falls deeply in love with Edith, only to learn she must die in an accident in order for time to return to normal and prevent a change in the course of history that would result in the Nazis winning World War II. In the closing scene of the episode, Kirk finds McCoy on the side of a street. McCoy, of course, is unaware that Edith must die for the world to be saved. McCoy then sees Edith about to step into the path of a truck and instinctively begins to try to stop her, but McCoy is held back by Kirk, and Edith steps in front of the truck and is killed.

If McCoy had stood by and watched Edith get killed, he would have been needlessly unkind and morally wrong (sadistic). This is because he had no vision of the greater good coming from Edith's death. However, because Kirk knew of the greater good, his unkindness in letting her get killed was not morally wrong.

Healthcare professionals, legal professionals, police officers, athletic trainers, teachers, and parents all know there are times when being loving and good means being unkind. Having our teeth cleaned is unpleasant, but needful. Suffering detox from drug addiction is painful, but needed. Having a gangrenous limb amputated is horrific, but it needs to be done to save the life. Similarly, God could be allowing evil and suffering and depriving us of the lesser good of pleasure in order that greater goods can be made to exist.

Some critics of Christianity object to this on the grounds that God would appear to be a cruel monster. A parent would be seen to be a cruel monster if he were to let his child thrash about in the cold sea crying for help until she became exhausted and drowned. Wouldn't God be a cruel monster for doing essentially the same thing? Despite cries for help, God lets countless numbers of children starve to death, or die of malaria. He lets girls be abducted, raped, and murdered. Looking at it this way, if God preferred a world with evil and suffering, he would seem to be sadistic.

A Christian response should first point out that the analogy of the human parent-child relationship (used in many arguments by atheists) is based on fallacious reasoning by the use of what students of logical thinking call "false analogy." A false analogy assumes that because two things are alike in some ways, they must be alike in other ways. The strength of the analogy depends on the amount of shared characteristics of two things being compared. A parent-daughter relationship shares enough characteristics with a parent-son relationship that such an analogy could be effectively used to argue that permitting a boy's suffering is just as wrong or right as permitting a girl's suffering. But the problem with using the parent-child relationship in an argument concerning the God-human relationship is that there are too few characteristics shared to make a valid argument.

A quick Bible study of God's characteristics helps make this abundantly clear. Unlike humans, God is uncreated,[7] all-knowing,[8] sovereign,[9] and responsible for bringing about the greatest possible good in created beings, which is the more salient difference given that it is arguably necessary for the greatest good that humans are created to experience two developmental stages. As discussed in chapters 3 and 4, we are made to experience a natural life in which the creator is hidden, followed by a supernatural life in which the creator is no longer hidden. Thus, the God-man relationship is one in which God is to be hidden temporarily, unlike the situation generally in the human parent-child relationship.

Moreover, God takes no pleasure in our pain (Ezek. 18:23). God is sorrowful and angry about all of the evil and suffering that goes on. He is angry and sorrowful when children are victimized (discussed in chapter 8). But, as the Christian asserts, God sometimes (many times) does not intervene (despite his sorrow and anger) in order that good things, that outweigh the price of the evil, come to fruition. Thus, we might be deceived into thinking God is cruel when he allows evil and suffering, just as a small child could mistakenly think her father is cruel because he let the "evil" doctor remove a gangrenous limb to save her life.

To us it may *seem* unlikely that there could be greater goods that could not be made to exist without the existence of such evil and suffering, or that there could be things that are so valuable that they would be worth permitting the world's evil and suffering. But it is not necessary to demonstrate the likelihood of such greater goods to refute the logical version of the problem of evil. As long as it is *possible* that God allows evil and suffering for a greater good—even horrible and heinous evils and suffering—then the second assumption cannot be necessarily true.

Therefore, given that being loving and good does not always entail being kind enough to stop evil or suffering, the second assumption is not necessarily true. It is not necessarily true that a perfectly loving and good God would never prefer a world in which there is evil and suffering. This is because it is possible that God permits it in order to bring about a greater good or prevent the occurrence of a greater evil (like a parent taking his child to a doctor for a penicillin shot).

To summarize, both assumptions must be necessarily true for the argument that God and evil and suffering cannot coexist to succeed. Both turn out to be *not* necessarily true. Therefore, the argument fails and it *is* logically possible that God could prefer to create a world in which there occurs evil and suffering for a period of time.

6.2 Attempts to Resurrect a Dead Argument

Today, most of the critics of Christianity that are familiar with the logical argument realize that it does not stand up to scrutiny.[10] But there are a few holding onto a recent notion that it has been revalidated based on a few variations of the argument.

Two such variations worth discussing are presented by philosophers Hugh LaFollette[11] and Richard R. La Croix.[12] LaFollette argues that God and evil cannot coexist on the basis of two propositions. The first is that humans have a kind of free will such that they cannot act morally good without also acting morally evil. The second is that both God and creatures made in his image share the same kind of free will and thus share a capacity to act morally evil. If these propositions are true, then God could not act morally good without also acting morally evil, which, of course, is logically inconsistent, as the Bible is emphatic that there is not a scintilla of moral evil in God's disposition (1 John 1:5).

However, LaFollette's propositions are neither necessarily true, nor indicated in the Bible. As discussed in chapters 3 and 4, in order that we possess a kind of free will needed to experience compatibility determination, God needed to create us in our first phase of life (earthly life) in a world of divine hiddenness—outside of the beatific vision. Having such free will, humans have the capacity to commit moral evil. But while we have a capacity to sin, as long as the pre-fallen condition is maintained (Gen. 2), moral evil need not occur. Thus, LaFollette's first proposition that humans *cannot* act morally good without also acting morally evil is not true.

Although, even if it were true that God created humans with an inability to act morally good without also acting morally evil, God does not share the same kind of free will that he bestows on humans in our world. Each of the three persons[13] of God is in beatific vision with the other two, and thus have a sort of free will that lacks the capacity to commit moral evil.[14] Thus, LaFollette's second proposition is also not true. Because both propositions are untrue, his argument fails to resurrect the logical argument.

La Croix's attempt to resurrect the logical argument is not so easily defeated. His argument consists of the following seven paraphrased propositions: (1) God is sovereign and can choose whether to create something other than himself, including beings with free will; (2) if God is all-knowing, he would know in advance that there would be disobedience by billions of beings created with compatibility-determining free will; (3) being perfectly loving and good, God prefers to achieve the greatest degree of good possible; (4) creating a universe in which evil exists is morally justified if an outweighing good is thereby attained; (5) prior to creation, only God existed, therefore the degree of the overall good then existing was the greatest ever possible, presumably because the degree of good attributable to God is the greatest ever possible; (6) because the greatest degree of good existed prior to creation: (a) no greater good could have been brought into existence by creating; and (b) no greater good would be prevented by not creating; (7) since there is no greater good to be attained (or lost) by creating a universe of freewill beings, some of which choose evil, God is morally precluded from creating [see proposition (4) above]. Therefore, the existence of God is logically inconsistent with the existence of a universe in which there is evil.

If all of these propositions are true (particularly proposition 5), then God would have freely chosen *not* to create a world at all because creating a world, especially one with evil, could not possibly have resulted in a greater degree of good than the greatest possible degree of good already in existence.

At first it may seem that La Croix has successfully argued a logical inconsistency between the existence of God and the existence of evil and suffering. However, closer inspection reveals that this is not the case. The survival of La Croix's argument appears to depend on whether the degree of good attributable to God is the greatest overall degree that could ever possibly exist. La Croix believes that this proposition is essential to Christian theism. However, after taking account of what constitutes what is good, it would appear that this proposition is not essential to Christian theism.

As discussed in chapter 3.1, the degree of good existing is determined (in part) by: (a) the measure of a morally good disposition(s) that exist; (b) the measure (quantity and quality) of expressions of love and moral goodness existing; and (c) the number of existing persons that express love and moral goodness. While (a), (b), and (c) exist by virtue of God's existence alone, (c) *cannot* exist to the greatest possible degree while God alone exists. The reason is simple. The existence of the greatest possible degree of good would require the existence of the maximum possible number of persons expressing love and goodness. But God consists of only three persons. Of course the dispositions of the Trinity are as good as possible—even omni-good,[15] thus fulfilling (a). And of course being all-powerful, God could deliver the greatest possible quantity and quality of expressions of love and goodness, thus fulfilling (b). But God cannot by himself be any more than three persons expressing love and goodness. Therefore, prior to creation, the degree of good then existing was limited, and thus could not have constituted the greatest overall degree that could possibly exist.

This is where La Croix's argument falls apart. It is not true that no greater good could have been brought into existence by creating and that no greater good would be prevented by not creating. On the contrary, the addition of good persons by which more expressions of love and moral goodness occur *adds* to the overall degree of goodness in existence. Thus, prior to creation there was a good reason for God to create beings in his image—namely, to advance the degree of overall goodness that existed prior to creation. Therefore, God is not morally precluded from creating, and the existence of evil and suffering remains logically consistent with the existence of God.

It is at this point that the critic might argue that the above response to La Croix's argument creates a contradiction of Christian teachings because it suggests that God needed something or desired something that could not be fulfilled in himself. The premises for such an argument are that: (1) the perfect being has all of his needs and desires fulfilled in himself; and (2) God is the perfect being. Therefore, there is no cause for God to create. As such, the account of creation would contradict the biblical definition of God.

However, there is no contradiction here at all because the first premise is not necessarily true. Prior to creating, God could imagine, foresee, and know all that could be known about what it would feel like to be in a love relationship with created beings. But he wouldn't actually be in such a relationship. Thus, a desire to experience this could not possibly be fulfilled if God did not create. When God alone existed, he wished to fulfill this desire, and so he created. Therefore, the critic's argument is fallacious, and the previously discussed response to La Croix's argument does not create a contradiction of Christian teachings.

And fulfilling his wish by creating is not morally wrong as long as it does not cause the existence of a degree of evil that outweighs whatever good results from creating. As the creator, God is responsible for designing, planning, and intervening into the course of history as necessary to ensure that his creation goal stays on track. Biblical history tells us of various interventions (and there would be interventions not recorded in the Bible), such as his numerous revelations to his prophets. "In the past God spoke to our ancestors through the prophets at many times and in various ways" (Heb. 1:1). Other kinds of interventions include various miraculous, and nonmiraculous, events that altered the course of history (e.g., the destruction of Sodom and Gomorrah, the destruction of the Amalekites, the origination of the Israelites, the fall of the Babylonian Empire, and the advent of Jesus the messiah).

The final intervention necessary to ensure that God's creation goal stays on track is the return (second advent) of Jesus Christ in power and glory to carry out judgment in the world. Jesus prophesied that evil would grow worse before the end. It appears that evil will rise to a degree that might threaten God's creation plan by bringing into existence an outweighing degree of evil and suffering (Matt. 24:3, 10, 12). But, at the appropriate time (the harvest metaphor[16]), Christ will bring this world to a close (Matt. 24:37–39), which will forever cease proliferation of evil so as to prevent it from advancing to a degree that would make creating this universe unjustifiable.

It is here that a critic might object that the degree of evil and suffering that now exists in the world already outweighs the good. Thus, it might seem that the degree of evil in the world has already risen to a level that has morally precluded God from creating. But the problem with the objection is that it does not account for good and evil that exists outside of our world. A proper judgment is based on an accurate assessment of the total degree of evil and the total degree of good, everywhere. We can take account of the evil and good that occurs in the terrestrial world, but in our life phase in a world of divine hiddenness the scope of any of our comparisons would be too limited for us to accurately judge.

For example, we do not know the population of the holy angels. A glimpse of the angelic population in Dan. 7:10 suggests an innumerable multitude: "thousands upon thousands and ten thousand times ten thousand" (which should not be interpreted as a literal counting). For all we know there could be one hundred billion or more. We also do not know the fraction of the population of angels in rebellion against God. Some theologians suggest that it is one third.[17] If this is true, then with regard to the angelic population alone, the current degree of good is far greater than the current degree of evil. Moreover, for all we know Satan's angels could make up *less* than one third of the angelic population, perhaps a lot less. We also don't know how many humans will be saved and how many will be lost. Some theologians suggest that most are lost, but even the population of the lost is doing some good things (by the aid of the Holy Spirit). There is obviously much evil in the world, but to many people it appears that there is a lot more good in the world than evil.

We also do not know the distant future. We do not know all of the good that is to come from the ministries of Jesus Christ and the Holy Spirit. It may be that on judgment day there will be more loving and good persons (angels and humans) in God's community (heaven) than in Satan's community (hell). Even if there ends up being more evil persons in Satan's community than good persons in God's community, the intensity of goodness in God's community could exceed the intensity of evilness in Satan's community by virtue of heaven being in direct relationship and mind-to-mind communication with God.

Taking account of all these unknowns, we are incapable of accurately judging whether the amount of evil outweighs the amount of good. But the believer can trust that God ensures that the degree of good will always be greater than any degree of evil.

Critics still unwilling to concede to the death of the logical argument could argue that by creating freewill beings, some of which God foreknew would choose evil, God intentionally created evil. Doesn't this make a logical problem for Christianity?

It doesn't, because God did not create evil. God created the *possibility* of evil (which he foreknew would be realized). But the beings created would have the free will to be ultimately responsible for choosing to obey or disobey God's commandments. Whether disobedience would exist would be up to them. As apologist Peter Kreeft says, "The blame, ultimately, lies with us. He did his part perfectly; we're the ones who messed up."[18]

Some critics object to this, arguing that if God knew that the beings he would create would cause a lot of evil and suffering, shouldn't he have refrained from creating? That depends. God is not morally precluded from creating beings he foreknows would turn the possibility of evil into a reality, as long as the ultimate degree of good achieved by creating outweighs any degree of evil that results from creating.

On this point some critics feel that God is still not off the hook. Atheist John W. Loftus, for example, argues that if God gave us more free will than we can be responsible for, as is evidenced by the horrible deeds humans do, then God is blameworthy for those horrible deeds.[19] In other words, God should limit free will to the extent necessary to ensure that humans never choose evil and cause people to suffer. Otherwise, God is blameworthy because God (if he exists) would never give a creature a free will that could be used to choose evil. Thus, he argues, the giving of compatibility-determining free will to creatures is not logically consistent with God's loving and good disposition.

However, this is not a valid argument, as it is based on a premise that God would never prefer to create in such a way that evil might arise. But as already discussed, this is not necessarily so; as long as God is bringing about a greater degree of good, he is not acting inconsistent with his loving and good disposition. Loftus may believe there is a contradiction, but he is yet to lay out an argument for why this is necessarily so.

But still the critic could argue that it is not logically consistent for a good God to give humans the ability to cause *so much* harm. Why give humans that much ability? Why couldn't God have given us less ability to harm each other than we have?

The answer is because the power to cause harm is directly proportionate to the power to do good. To the extent that God limits our ability to do evil, he would also limit our ability to do good. As theologian Gregory Boyd says, "When people who have the capacity and moral responsibility to bless many fail to do so, their extraordinary potential to bless becomes an extraordinary capacity to harm."[20] Likewise, according to David Griffin: "Every increase in the capacity for good means a similar increase in the capacity for evil"[21] The principle is evident in nature, as C. S. Lewis (1898–1963) points out:

> The better stuff a creature is made of—the cleverer and stronger and freer it is—then the better it will be if it goes right, but also the worse it will be if it goes wrong. A cow cannot be very good or very bad; a dog can be both better and worse; a child better and worse still; an ordinary man, still more so; a man of genius, still more so; a superhuman spirit best—or worst—of all.[22]

Again from Boyd:

> The fact that certain humans and fallen angels behave in grotesquely evil ways testifies to the enormous potential for love and moral goodness they have, or at least had, in their original created natures. A mother's potential to benefit her children is proportionate to her potential to harm them. The same charisma a leader can use to help thousands can also be used to hurt them. The same creativity and genius that can be used to cure diseases can also be used to invent biological weapons of mass destruction. The potential for a diabolical evil in someone like Adolf Hitler is the inverse of the potential for Christ-like love revealed in Mother Teresa.[23]

The same hands that are strong enough to save a child from drowning are also strong enough to strangle that same child to death. God has given us a considerable degree of ability to do good. But this is balanced by a considerable degree of ability or power to cause harm. Therefore, God is not culpable for giving us a lot of power to harm. He has simply given us a lot of power that we can choose to use for either good or evil. The fact that humans use it for evil does not make God culpable for the evil, since those people could also use it for good. Moreover, having power to do good (which necessitates having equal power to do evil) is necessary to fulfill God's creation plan of increasing the degree of overall good in existence to the greatest possible degree.

Notwithstanding, the critic could also argue that it is not logically consistent for an all wise and knowing God to create us without enough intelligence that we would not sin by causing harm to others. Agnostic Bart D. Ehrman asks the question: Why didn't God make us with enough intelligence to know better than to hurt each other and live together peaceably?[24]

The critic assumes that increasing a being's intelligence would prevent it from misusing its power. Ehrman and others think Christianity has no answer to this. The assumption is that all God had to do was create beings with enough intelligence and there'd be no sin and all would live happily ever after. The reality is that we know from traditional Christian thought concerning the angels, as well as from our own experience, that a lack of intelligence is not the reason we hurt each other. The angels are commonly thought to be more intelligent and knowledgeable than humans,[25] yet some of them cause an almost indescribable amount of harm by their sins.

The fact that higher intelligence would not prevent evil is also affirmed by our experience. A police detective, for example, is required to have a certain degree of intelligence above most officers on the force and knows full well the various kinds of harm he would cause if he were to kidnap a child for ransom money. But despite his intelligence, experience, and knowledge of the consequences of kidnapping a child for ransom money, he could become obsessed with getting a bigger piece of the pie. This example is portrayed in the movie *Ransom*, starring Mel Gibson and Gary Sinise. Thus, both Christian teaching and our experience affirm that no increase in intelligence per se would prevent evil and suffering.

Conclusion

Philosophers have argued that the existence of God is not logically consistent with the existence of evil and suffering. However, the logical problem of evil turns out to be invalid because it is possible that God's allowance of evil conduct and suffering is necessary in order to bring about a greater degree of overall existing good. As long as this is possible, there is no contradiction between the existence of evil and suffering and the existence of God.

In recent decades, attempts have been made to resurrect the logical problem with variant arguments. The most promising ones are presented by Hugh LaFollette and Richard R. La Croix. However, all such attempts contain logical fallacies and/or doctrinal errors and consequently fail.

While the logical problem does not hold up under scrutiny, there is another form of the problem of evil and suffering: the probabilistic (or evidentiary) version. While it may be conceded that it is *possible* that God and evil and suffering coexist, it is insisted that such coexistence is highly *unlikely*. This is because it seems very doubtful that God would have justifying reasons for permitting a vast amount of evil and suffering, including the apparently pointless suffering of innocent children and animals. The evidentiary (probabilistic) argument is discussed in the following three chapters.

NOTES to Chapter 6

1. See chapter 8.1 and its footnotes.

2. According to statistics posted by Childhelp at www.childhelp.org.pages/statistics and by Tennyson Center for Children at www.childabuse.org/facts, both accessed on July 10, 2014.

3. Michael A. Corey, *Evolution and the Problem of Natural Evil* (Lanham, MD: University Press of America, 2000), 253. Emphasis in the original.

4. Peter J. Kreeft, as quoted in Lee Strobel, *The Case for Faith: A Journalist Investigates the Toughest Objections to Christianity* (Grand Rapids, MI: Zondervan, 2000), 38. Kreeft received his AB from Calvin College and his MA and PhD from Fordham University. He did postgraduate work briefly at Yale University. He has been a philosophy professor at Boston College, Villanova University (in Pennsylvania), and King's College (in New York City). He is the author of over sixty-seven books, including: *Handbook of Christian Apologetics* (with Ronald K. Tacelli), *Christianity for Modern Pagans*, and *Fundamentals of the Faith: Essays in Christian Apologetics*.

5. Peter J. Kreeft and Ronald K. Tacellli, *Handbook of Christian Apologetics: Hundreds of Answers to Crucial Questions* (Downers Grove, IL: InterVarsity Press, 1994), 138.

6. This concept is supported by Bible depictions of Jesus as always perfectly loving and good, but on some occasions unkind, such as when he: (a) drove the money changers from the temple with a whip and tipped over their tables (Matt. 21:12–13; Mark 11:15–17; John 2:13–17); (b) insulted and harshly scorned the Pharisees and Scribes, calling them snakes, hypocrites, and blind fools (Matt. 23:13–33; Luke 11:37–53); (c) glared at a crowd of people in anger (Mark 3:1–6); and (d) returns in power to execute judgment in the world (Rev. 19:11–16).

7. Ps. 90:2; Isa. 43:10; Col. 1:16.

8. Job 37:16; Ps. 134:4; 147:5; Isa. 46:9; 55:9; Matt. 10:30; Heb. 4:13; 1 John 3:19–20.

9. Ps. 115:3; Job 42:2; Isa. 46:9–10; Rom. 9:19–21; 1 Tim. 6:15.

10. Atheist philosophers John L. Mackie (1917–1981) and William L. Rowe have conceded to its defeat [Ronald H. Nash, *Faith & Reason: Searching for a Rational Faith* (Grand Rapids, MI: Zondervan, 1988), 193–194].

11. Hugh LaFollette, "Plantinga on the Free Will Defense," in *The Impossibility of God*, ed. Michael Martin and Ricki Monnier (Amherst, NY: Prometheus Books, 2003), 97–105.

12. Richard R. La Croix, "Unjustified Evil and God's Choice," in *The Impossibility of God*, ed. Michael Martin and Ricki Monnier (Amherst, NY: Prometheus Books, 2003), 116–124. La Croix is a philosopher of religion. La Croix's variation of the logical argument from evil is discussed briefly by John W. Loftus in his book, *Why I Became an Atheist: A Former Preacher Rejects Christianity* (Amherst, NY: Prometheus Books, 2008), 233–234.

13. See appendix D for illumination on the coherence of the doctrine of the trinity.

14. Heb. 6:18. See also Num. 23:19 and Tit. 1:2.

15. "Omni" is a Latin prefix meaning "all" or "every." The Bible depicts God's disposition as perfectly (flawlessly) good, or all-good, or omni-good (Deut. 32:4; 2 Sam. 22:31; Ps. 19:7; Matt. 5:48), meaning that there could not be any better disposition. Sometimes Christians refer to God's disposition as "infinitely good," but this is only coherent with a definition of "infinite" that is synonymous with "perfect," which appears to be the definition implied in the writings of some theologians (e.g., Thomas Aquinas) [Frederick R. Tennant, *Philosophical Theology: Volume II: The World, the Soul, and God* (New York: Cambridge University Press, 1956), 140–141].

16. Hos. 6:11; Joel 3:13; Matt. 13:30, 39; Rev. 14:15.

17. This might be due to an interpretation of Rev. 12:4 which says that Satan swept away a third of the stars ("stars" sometimes symbolize angels in Scripture) and flung them to the earth, but more likely it refers to a third of the saints of God [*Zondervan NIV Bible Commentary, Volume 2: New Testament*, consul. eds. Kenneth L. Barker and John R. Kohlenberger III (Grand Rapids, MI: Zondervan Publishing House,

1994), 1183].

18. Peter J. Kreeft, as quoted by Lee Strobel, *The Case for Faith*, 38.

19. John W. Loftus, *Why I Became an Atheist: A Former Preacher Rejects Christianity* (Amherst, NY: Prometheus Books, 2008), 237, 249.

20. Gregory A. Boyd, *Satan and the Problem of Evil: Constructing a Trinitarian Warfare Theodicy* (Downers Grove, IL: InterVarsity Press, 2001), 170.

21. David Griffin, as quoted in Gregory A. Boyd, *Satan and the Problem of Evil*, 170.

22. C. S. Lewis, *Mere Christianity* (New York: HarperCollins Publishers, 1952. Renewed 1980), 49.

23. Gregory A. Boyd, *Satan and the Problem of Evil*, 171.

24. Bart D. Ehrman, *God's Problem: How the Bible Fails to Answer Our Most Important Question—Why We Suffer* (New York: HarperCollins Publishers, 2008), 13. Ehrman received his PhD from Princeton Theological Seminary, where he studied under Bruce Metzger. He has written and edited over twenty-five books, including *Misquoting Jesus* and *Forged*.

25. Biblical support for angels having intelligence superior to humans is arguable from Ps. 8:5 and Heb. 2:5–9.

7

Solving the Probabilistic Problem of Evil and Suffering: Part 1

Synopsis

Critics of Christianity argue that it's doubtful God (if he exists) would have a justifying reason for permitting a vast amount of evil and suffering, including the apparently pointless suffering of innocent children and animals.

Christians commonly respond that God is justified in permitting the vast amount and severe intensity of evil and suffering in the world because: (a) having the greater good of moral free will necessarily entails God's allowance of moral and natural evils; and (b) moral free will is of sufficient value to outweigh or justify all the evil and suffering God allows to occur.

The critics argue back that: (a) moral free will is not valuable enough to be a greater good, thus God is not justified in allowing the evil and suffering that occurs in the world; and (b) while having moral free will might necessarily entail allowing some forms of moral and natural evil, it would not be necessary for God to allow the vast amount that is in the world, or the intense, horrific, or apparently pointless moral and natural evils, or animal suffering.

A Christian reply is that: (a) the greatest good is not moral free will, but rather the expressions of love and goodness by an ever-growing heavenly community in consummate relationship that constitutes a good that is valuable enough to outweigh or justify God's allowance of all of the evil and suffering that occurs in the world; and (b) such a greater good necessarily

entails the existence of compatibility-determining free will, a two-phase life, divine hiddenness, and nomic regularity, all of which necessarily limit God's intervention in the world to an extent that corresponds to every occurrence of evil and suffering in the world. (Note: This covers chapters 7 and 8.)

The conclusion of the previous chapter was that it is possible for both God, and evil and suffering to exist. It is possible because there could be a greater good that God could not bring into existence if he did not allow evil and suffering to occur. There would have to be no better way for God to bring it about, and it would have to be of such high value that God would be justified for letting people suffer harm, bloodshed, and catastrophe.

However, critics of Christianity argue that while it is possible that God allows the world's suffering in order to bring about a greater good and so be justified, it is unlikely. Indeed, it seems very doubtful God would have a justifying reason, considering the vast amount of suffering, and the intense, horrific, and pointless moral and natural evils, particularly the suffering of innocent children, and animals.

7.1 Free Will, Divine Hiddenness, and Nomic Regularity

Regarding a justifying reason for the world's evil and suffering, perhaps the best known among the most promising theodicies is that it is necessary for the existence of the greater good of moral (libertarian) free will. Moral free will by definition means that there is a real chance that evil might be chosen. As discussed in chapters 3 and 4, moral free will (of the compatibility-determining kind) is not possible unless God is to us a hidden deity. This substantially limits God's intervention in the world to the extent that some evil and suffering must be allowed to occur.

Moreover, God's intervention is further limited because having moral free will would not be possible if not for our world's predictability by natural laws. Philosopher Michael J. Murray refers to the predictability as "nomic regularity."[1] Nomic regularity is the general principle that the functioning of the world will tend to follow common rules or principles that make it orderly, regular, and predictable.

A result of the world's predictability is that we can form certain expectations necessary for us to have moral free will. A free moral choice is not much of one if we cannot make it in the context of certain expected results. According to some of the most prominent Christian philosophers and theologians, like Frederick R. Tennant (1866–1957),[2] Michael Peterson,[3] Peter van Inwagen,[4] Michael J. Murray,[5] Richard G. Swinburne,[6] and Ronald H. Nash (1936–2006),[7] a world of physical order is required for moral choices and character formation. This is because such order provides an environment in which relationships between actions and effects are always similar. This allows us to predict effects and outcomes, and gauge their probability, which is essential if we are to bear significant responsibility for our conduct.

One reason a motorist can be held accountable for causing injury while impaired by consumption of an intoxicating liquor is the predictability of causing an accident after getting extremely drunk and driving (as opposed to drinking the same liquor and sometimes remaining sober). One reason a shooter can be held accountable for killing a store clerk is the predictability of fatal injury when he squeezes the trigger of a loaded 9 mm pistol aimed at the clerk's head (as opposed to the round sometimes leaving the barrel and slipping into another spatial dimension).

Because a cause-and-effect world of predictability (nomic regularity) is a condition necessary if we are to have moral free will, the world that God would create would need to be the world that exists by natural laws that God must not inhibit (for the most part). Examples of such natural laws are our world's laws of physics (e.g., classical mechanics, Boyle's law of gases, conservation laws, and the four laws of thermodynamics).

An unfortunate downside of nomic regularity is the possibility of undesired consequences—namely suffering hardship, injury or pain. As Peterson notes, "The same water which sustains and refreshes can also drown; the same drug which relieves suffering can cause crippling psychological addiction; the same sun which gives light and life can parch fields and bring famine; the same neural arrangements which transmit intense pleasure and ecstasy can also bring extreme pain and agony."[8] The same law of gravity that keeps us alive can also kill us. The same planet that provides a tropical paradise also has places that are inhospitably cold. The fire that keeps people comfortable and alive can burn a house down and cause injury and death.

Of course one could argue that God should intervene to prevent or alleviate any evil and suffering that would occur from the downside of a nomically regular world. But such intervention would disrupt the world's nomic regularity to an extent that would significantly deprive humankind of moral free will (and divine hiddenness). Consider how the world would be affected if God were to intervene to prevent most murders. Sometimes people would have the ability to kill with a gun and other times they wouldn't. Guns would either malfunction without a scientific explanation, or events would be altered so that murders could not be carried out. Consequently, it would be difficult to convict killers of murder.

Moreover, there'd be far less doubt about the existence of a good, supernatural intelligence acting in the world. Such evidence of God's existence would profoundly transform the world's landscape, making our environment coercive. Elements that comprise our world environment include: governments, laws, the practice of medicine, businesses, transportation, education, books, entertainment, movies, advertising, television commercials and shows, games, sports, architecture, arts, décor, family traditions, and on and on. Probably most or all of these would be dramatically altered in ways that would flood the mind with continual heightened awareness of God's existence and will to reward or punish. This would narrow the epistemic gap (reduce divine hiddenness in the world), causing a significant loss of compatibility-determining free will. This becomes obvious when we consider the consequences if such an interventional force prevented other kinds of crimes from being committed. Therefore, God must let the world's natural causes and effects (nomic regularity) occur without much of any interference.

I say "much" rather than "any" because there is room for some divine intervention without significant loss of nomic regularity, divine hiddenness, or moral free will. Some unpredictability here and there would not significantly disrupt them. There is enough room for some overt intervention—more in ancient times because a few overt miracles then (e.g., the parting of the Red Sea) wouldn't alter world cultures enough to deprive humankind of significant compatibility-determining free will. Today, however, most all intervention must be undetectable. For example, a slight adjustment in the wind current in the Atlantic Ocean that appears perfectly natural could prevent a hurricane from entering the Gulf of Mexico and making landfall where it would devastate the lives of millions of people. Given instances of such *hidden* intervention,[9] we should expect that if the world was created by God it would appear indifferent to our needs and desires.

Critics of Christianity, however, argue that nature's indifference is more consistent with an atheist universe. As atheist David Mills says:

Nature is obviously a mixture of order and disorder, the appealing and the loathsome, the purposeful and the arbitrary. Such an undeniably mixed bag would lead an objective observer to conclude that Nature is governed neither by benevolent gods nor by evil demons. Nature simply exists and, irrespective of our desires or best interests, operates through natural law, rather than through mystical or purposeful legerdemain.[10]

After recalling the devastating 9.0–9.3 Sumatra-Andaman earthquake and resultant tsunami on December 26, 2004, which killed over 230,000 people in fourteen countries and maimed or left homeless countless others, Mills says, "To any rational observer, this catastrophic tsunami—and other earthquakes, hurricanes, tornados, floods, droughts, fires, famines, and epidemics—are evidence not of a loving God, but of Nature's indifference to humanity."[11]

Mills no doubt thinks that a world created by God would *not* appear so indifferent to our needs and desires because God would intervene to ensure that all people are protected against any (or at least most) natural evil. But, like so many critics of Christianity, Mills appears unfamiliar with a Christian theodicy that includes the concepts of nomic regularity and divine hiddenness, so he wouldn't imagine an "objective observer" viewing our world as a creation of God. He wouldn't imagine the best of all possible worlds[12] being a world like the present world with its apparent indifference to human well-being. But through the lenses of nomic regularity and divine hiddenness, maintained by God for a greater good, it is quite rational to see God as its creator.

Mills and other critics leave out another important factor in their discussions. While many people suffer horribly from hurricanes, earthquakes, tsunamis, and other harmful events in nature, it is a fact that a great deal of the suffering is not as much from "acts of God" as from the sinful conduct. This is because much of the suffering of victims of catastrophes is intertwined with, and compounded by, human conduct.

William Lane Craig brings up this fact in his book *Hard Questions, Real Answers*. According to Craig, if everybody lived in accordance with the teachings of Jesus Christ most all would be well fed and cared for. Following a drought in Ethiopia, for example, the world would rush to the hungry people with aid and supplies. The caring and generous world would see to it that the world's wealth would be largely applied to educating, training, housing, clothing, feeding, and medically caring for the poorest peoples. As a result, there would be a lot less sickness, and people would either live in buildings that could withstand natural catastrophes or be relocated to places that do not suffer major natural catastrophes. Of course, natural disasters, accidents, and some diseases would still occur. But there would be substantially less suffering, if not an absence of any significant suffering, solely because of the abundance of people committed to being loving, respectful, faithful, pure, honest, and humble.[13]

Perhaps the most prevalent objection to the nomic regularity theodicy is the one based on the notion that God has enough intelligence, knowledge, power, and ability to have created different laws of nature that would not entail as much (or any) evil and suffering, and in which he would also have morally free creatures. The problem with this objection, however, is that it is naïve, as it is not humanly possible to know if the existence of such a world is actually possible. Michael Peterson gives us a sense of the impossibility of the task:

> It is not obvious that God could have created a significantly better world than this one with different natural laws, laws whose regular operation produces the good and approvable effects of the present system without the ostensibly evil consequences. . . . Natural laws are simply descriptive statements about how natural objects act and react under certain conditions, which means that a change in our present natural laws entails a change in the natures of the relevant natural objects. Since almost all natural objects are capable of producing harmful as well as beneficial results, virtually all of them would have to be modified to suit the critic. And even a small change in the objects in the present system may bring about manifold and intricate differences in the effects they produce. Such changes end up being so vast and complicated that it becomes unclear what the new system would be.[14]

Most people have no clue of the vast and complex ramifications of even the slightest change in the nature of the universe. As mentioned in chapter 1.5, it is a fact almost beyond question that almost everything about the basic structure of the universe—for example, the fundamental laws and parameters of physics and the initial distribution of matter and energy—is balanced on a razor's edge for life to occur.[15] Scientists refer to this as the "fine-tuning of the cosmos." One of many examples of the fine-tuning is if gravity had been stronger or weaker by one part in 10^{40}, then life-sustaining stars like the sun could not exist, which would most likely make animal/human life impossible.[16]

A popular illustration for each independent instance of fine-tuning is a radio dial. Unless the dial is set exactly right, animal/human life would be impossible. And there are many such radio dials that would all have to be set exactly right for life to be possible. That each and every one is exactly on the right setting by chance is enormously improbable.

Astrophysicist Hugh Ross enumerates thirty-eight characteristics that must take on specific values for life to be possible in the universe. A few of these include: the ratio of electromagnetic force constant to gravitational force constant; the carbon-12 to oxygen-16 nuclear energy level ratio; and the mass of the neutrino.[17] Moreover, Ross has a list of seventy-seven planetary conditions necessary for life to be possible.[18] If Earth's axial tilt were slightly greater or lesser, surface temperature differences would be too great to support animal/human life. If seismic (earthquake) activity were less, nutrients on the ocean floors from river runoff would not be recycled to continents through tectonics and an insufficient amount of carbon dioxide would be released from carbonates. A planet with fewer earthquakes could not support animal/human life. If volcanic activity were less, insufficient amounts of carbon dioxide and water vapor would be returned to the atmosphere to support animal/human life. This is especially so since soil mineralization would become too degraded for life.

If the quantity and extent of forest and grass fires were less, growth inhibitors in the soils would accumulate and soil nitrification would be insufficient. Also, there would be insufficient charcoal production for adequate soil water retention and absorption of certain growth inhibitors. Alternatively, a greater number of forest fires would destroy too many plant and animal life forms for human life to exist. And yet if a physical law is slightly different, or if matter is slightly different, the quantity and extent of forest and grass fires would be too great or too little for human life to exist. And a result of these alterations would be a multitude of alterations in other characteristics of the universe, which further adds to the impossibility of the existence of human life if a multitude of factors were not fine-tuned by a powerful superintelligence.

But the critic could argue that God could've created alternate creatures with moral free will and therefore didn't need to create humans. He could propose that God could've created a more robust creature whose existence need not depend on such a fine-tuning of matter, energy, and physical laws and that has significant moral free will but is not capable of causing as much evil and suffering. Perhaps such a creature would not be made up of carbon, hydrogen, nitrogen, oxygen, phosphorus, and sulfur. Or perhaps its existence would depend on only a few of these elements in combination with some other element (like arsenic instead of phosphorus, as in the case of a silicon-based life form).

However, as previously said, such conjecture is naïve, as it cannot hope to provide enough detail of the vast and complex array of modifications that would be necessary to the physical laws, matter, and energy of the universe in order to know if such a life form is possible, or if it is possible, that it would contribute to God's plan to accomplish the greatest possible good (through an optimum balance of good and evil). Here is where the critic often quips: "God can do anything, can't he? If so, he could successfully make all the needed modifications to have a life form that is far more robust than humans, allowing for a reduction of the fine-tuning and an increase of possible modifications to the universe so that the creatures still have moral free will, express love and goodness, and commit less evil and suffering."

This may sound like a good argument until a few things are realized. God's objective to advance the goodness in existence to the greatest possible degree limits his options as to what sort of creature he can make. This is especially so when we consider that a mind-blowing multitude of good or evil actions and outcomes could occur as a result of the existence of any one sort of creature made. Even the actions of one small creature like a butterfly would've been significant in God's creation plan to create the best of all possible worlds. William Lane Craig explains:

> In so-called chaos theory scientists have discovered that certain large-scale systems, for example, the weather or insect populations, are extraordinarily sensitive to the smallest disturbances. A butterfly fluttering on a twig in West Africa may set in motion forces that will eventually issue in a hurricane over the Atlantic Ocean. Yet it's impossible for anyone [of us] observing that butterfly fluttering on that branch to predict such an outcome. We have no way of knowing how the alteration of some seemingly insignificant event can radically alter the world.[19]

Thus, there may be an instance of a hurricane that causes thousands of people to suffer from destruction and severe injury that would not have occurred if not for the existence and movement of a few flying insects. Consequently, we could never speculate with any certainty that it is possible for God to create alternate beings that are capable of advancing the goodness in existence to the greatest possible degree and that do not cause a substantial amount or intensity of evil and suffering. The human mind doesn't have the ability to even rationally assess its probability. Therefore, for all we know, the human being is a creature necessary to advance existing good to the greatest possible degree.

Of course the critic could respond by saying, "Naturally *we* cannot come up with a different world, or a different race of creatures, that would produce just as much good without the evil and suffering, but a being with God's intelligence, knowledge, and power could." Atheist John W. Loftus believes "it would seem that he could" because he "can indeed criticize [God's] so-called creative handiwork," just as he can criticize poor workmanship in a house, even though he doesn't know how to build one himself.[20]

But a problem with Loftus' layman's-ability-to-recognize-poor-construction analogy is that it is based on fallacious reasoning by the use of what students of logical thinking call false analogy. A false analogy assumes that because two things are alike in some ways, they must be alike in other ways. The strength of the analogy depends on the amount of shared characteristics of two things being compared. With regard to Loftus' analogy, the intelligence and knowledge needed to criticize the design and construction of a house are wildly disproportionate to the intelligence and knowledge needed to criticize the design and construction of the world that serves to bring about the greatest possible good (through an optimum balance of good and evil). His analogy is tantamount to arguing that because ants can construct a nest, they can recognize whether a spaceship is designed and built well enough to get them safely to Mars. All of the human intelligence/knowledge on the planet *combined* is obviously inadequate to realistically criticize the "handiwork" involved in creating the best of all possible worlds (even with the greatest computer humans could build).

In sum, Christian responses to the probabilistic problem of evil and suffering typically involve a plan of God for us to have moral (libertarian) free will (for compatibility determination). Such free will requires an environment and life of divine hiddenness and nomic regularity. Sustaining these conditions requires a substantial limitation on supernatural intervention to prevent moral and natural evils. God must (with sadness) allow some amount of suffering from such things as evil conduct, earthquakes, tsunamis, droughts, floods, animal attacks, birth defects, and diseases.

Some critics of the nomic regularity theodicy argue that God could've created a better world. However, trying to imagine a different world with different natural laws that would accomplish greater good than the degree of good purported to come out of the present world is futile. It is humanly impossible to conceive of such a world, or even judge whether it would be probable.

7.2 Critics Argue Free Will Lacks Value, and Not All Evil Allowed Is Necessary

While the foregoing theodicy would seem to provide a persuasive explanation for why God would allow evil and suffering, critics of Christianity argue that it fails to do so for two reasons. The first reason is that even if having moral free will would necessarily entail allowing all forms of evil and suffering, it is not valuable enough to justify God in letting them occur. In other words, the price of all of the evil and suffering that occurs in the world is too high a price to pay just so that we may have moral free will. Moral free will in and of itself does not have outweighing value.

The second reason why the theodicy is said to lack persuasive power is that while one could concede that having moral free will by way of divine hiddenness and nomic regularity would necessarily entail allowing *some* occurrences of evil and suffering, it would not require God to allow the vast amount that is in the world, or the intense horrific suffering, or the animal suffering. If it is true that some occurrences *could* be prevented and still preserve human free will, then God's allowance of such occurrences would be pointless.

The glaring problem of the existence of pointless evil and suffering is that it does nothing to bring about a greater good (or prevent a greater evil) and thus is not logically consistent with the existence of God. Most all Christian philosophers, theologians, and apologists are of this belief, including William Lane Craig,[21] Terence Penelhum,[22] Michael J. Murray,[23] and Richard L. Purtill[24] (although some theists disagree[25]). Thus atheist John W. Loftus is correct in saying that "to admit the existence of an evil which demonstrably cannot have this function [of bringing about a greater good or preventing greater evil] would be to admit a proposition inconsistent with Christian theism. For such an evil would be pointless. It is logically inconsistent for a theist to admit the existence of a pointless evil."[26] Therefore, if pointless evil and suffering exist, God could not exist.

The First Reason: Free Will Lacks Value. Regarding free will's purported lack of outweighing value, according to Andrea M. Weisberger, the Christian who says human free will is of superior and outweighing value should explain why. But, she says, Christians argue from the presupposition that free will is an outweighing good and offer either no explanation for its value or paltry or unsatisfactory reasons for it. Therefore, she believes that it is reasonable to conclude that free will is not an outweighing good, and that a response with a freewill theodicy to the probabilistic problem fails.[27]

Atheist John W. Loftus appears to agree. In his book *Why I Became an Atheist*, he argues that if having moral free will necessarily entail allowing evil and suffering, God would not create beings with moral free will. Like Weisberger, he also argues that Christians cannot adequately explain why living with moral free will is so much greater than living without it. The absence of such an explanation strongly suggests to Loftus that Christian theodicists really have no defined *greater* good.[28]

The Second Reason: Not All Evil Allowed Is Necessary. The critics' argument regarding apparently pointless evil and suffering can be broken down into three issues. The first is that there is so much suffering among people that it is difficult to believe that *all* of it must be allowed to preserve our moral free will. This takes into account the evil and suffering of billions of people since the dawn of humankind from harsh environmental conditions, starvation, disease, accidents, animal attacks, sexual abuse, physical abuse, and wars. Given the vast amount, it seems easier to believe that some of it is unnecessary.

The second issue does not concern the amount of evil and suffering in the world, but rather the situations of intense, horrific suffering. As mentioned in chapter 2.2, William L. Rowe argues that there are situations of evil and suffering in the world that defy an explanation as to what greater good could possibly be achieved by allowing them. He argues that such situations could be prevented by God without losing some greater good or causing some evil to occur that would be equally bad or worse. Rowe argues from the example of a little girl in Michigan who was severely beaten, raped, and then strangled to death in 1986 (this example is specifically addressed in the next chapter). Other examples of apparently gratuitous moral evil could be cited, such as: the little children during World War II in Auschwitz that were thrown alive into a blazing furnace; the murdering of babies by Turk soldiers while the babies were held by their mothers; or people in Medieval times convicted of homosexuality and other "crimes" that were hung upside down by their feet and sawed in half.[29] While it might be *possible* that such instances must be allowed so that free will among humankind is preserved, many feel an intuitive sense that they need not be allowed. If such a perception is correct, then some occurrences of evil and suffering would be pointless.

The third issue regarding apparently pointless suffering is of the countless intelligent animals capable of feeling great pain that have suffered during the course of millions of years from savage predators, harsh environmental conditions, disease, and natural disasters. Many simply cannot see any divine purpose behind all of the suffering of innocent animals. Rowe argues for this from an example of a situation in which a forest fire occurs from a lightning strike to a tree and a fawn gets trapped and badly burned. The fawn lies alone in agony for several days and dies. The argument is that God would not be morally justified in permitting the fawn to suffer since God could have intervened without causing a greater good to be lost or preventing a greater evil to occur.[30] (The example of the fawn is specifically addressed in chapter 9.)

7.3 The Outweighing Value of the Greatest Greater Good

Regarding the critics' argument that free will lacks outweighing value, according to Weisberger and Loftus, Christians assume human free will is of superior and outweighing value, and provide little or no explanation as to why. Consequently, they are not persuaded that the good of moral free will is greater than the price of evil and suffering. According to Loftus, because free will appears to be of little worth, "The value of having moral free agents cannot outweigh the pain and suffering caused by these free moral agents to others and to themselves."[31] They conclude that because Christians haven't made an adequate case for the value of free will, a free will theodicy concerning the probabilistic problem fails. They propose that given God's foreknowledge of the evil and suffering that *would* occur as a result of misuse of human free will, God would prefer to create a world *without* human free will in which everyone's conduct does no harm and causes no suffering. Weisberger poses her question: "Which is more desirable, a world in which there is no free will but where humans always do what is right and in which there is no suffering, or a world such as the present? It seems many of us would opt for the former world."[32]

However, their argument collapses when it is realized that human free will's value is derived *not* so much from its intrinsic goodness, but rather from its instrumental purpose in making possible the existence of the *greatest* greater good—the growing heavenly community of persons with perfect psychospiritual well-being in consummate relationship with God, which generates the greatest quality and quantity of expressions of love and goodness (*summum bonum*). Other than God, this is the thing of supreme value. It is the "apple of God's eye" (Jer. 2:8).[33] In a growing, good-producing community such as this, God is accomplishing his plan to bring about the greatest possible good. Therefore, the greater good at which the critics should aim their argument is not human free will, but rather the good-producing heavenly community in consummate relationship with God.

But none of the opponents of Christianity who speak on the problem of evil and suffering argue against the value of the heavenly community in consummate relationship with God. Search as you may the writings of William L. Rowe, Paul Draper, Michael Martin, Graham Oppy, and others[34]—none argue against the value of it as a greater good that necessarily entails God allowing the evil and suffering that occurs in the world. In light of this, and assuming for the sake of this discussion that having the community in consummate relationship necessarily entails allowing *all* kinds of evil and suffering (argued in section 7.4 and chapters 8 and 9), the salient question is: Does the consummate community have outweighing value?

In order to answer the question "yes," the degree of good generated by the community would have to be perceived as being phenomenal. It would have to be seen to be so phenomenal as to outweigh the sum of all occurrences of evil and suffering in the world.

Such a value conception is evident in the way Jesus lived and died in order to make it possible for the community to exist. He suffered while remaining sinless in a harsh first century world. He surrendered himself to being flogged half to death, to being crucified, and to suffering divine condemnation and death. He felt the horror and the most intense loneliness of severance (for a time) of his relationship-connection-interaction with God the Father (see appendix D for discussion of the coherence of this separation). All this he suffered so that a community of persons in consummate relationship would be possible.[35] Jesus, "who for the joy set before him endured the cross" (Heb. 12:2). The "joy set before him" was the satisfaction he felt in doing his part to make it possible for a multitude of humans to be among the heavenly community in consummate relationship. His great love for humankind climaxed at the cross (John 3:16) is arguably the most persuasive evidence of the outweighing value of the consummate community.

Moreover, Jesus' value conception is made clearer by what he said about the glory of the community despite all he knew of the evil and suffering in the world. He understood suffering. It was all around him during his life. He saw the sick, the dying, the blind, the crippled, the hungry, and the oppressed. The amount of the suffering in the crowds around him was at times overwhelming—many pleaded with him to heal people with various kinds of serious diseases and disabilities. Jesus knew of the brutal wars, tortures, and killings of the history of the ancient Near East. Multitudes were mutilated with swords and spears. There were beheadings and impalements. Eyes and tongues were cut out. Hands were chopped off. Some were burned to death. Jesus even foreknew of atrocities that would take place in the first Jewish-Roman war (66–73 AD) (Mark 13:1–2, 12–17). Historian Josephus (37–ca. 100 AD) tells us of its horrors, including mass starvation, thousands of crucifixions, brutal killings, and even cannibalism.[36] Jesus had been around Jerusalem when convicted criminals were flogged or crucified by Roman soldiers. He listened to the cries of mothers who had lost their sons. He wept for them. He knew of prophets of old who had been tortured and savagely killed. Jeremiah had been put in stocks, put in prison (Jer. 32:2), and lowered into a mucky dungeon (Jer. 38:6). According to Jewish tradition,[37] King Manasseh had the prophet Isaiah pushed into a hollow log and sawed in half. Jesus' cousin John the Baptist was beheaded in prison.[38]

Yet, despite all that he knew of the amount and extent of evil and suffering in human history, he still taught his disciples to "rejoice and be glad, because great is your reward in heaven, for in the same way they persecuted the prophets who were before you" (Matt. 5:12). If God exists and Jesus really was God's greatest prophet, then the revelation from God through Jesus is that the good generated by the community is so phenomenal that it outweighs all instances of the evil and suffering in the world—even intense, horrific instances, and the suffering of animals.

Solving the Probabilistic Problem of Evil and Suffering: Part 1

Jesus' value conception of the heavenly community in consummate relationship with God is underscored by Paul's writings. Paul was acquainted with the atrocities of war and of the grotesque punishments of criminals. His contemporaries suffered brutal punishments and torturous deaths. Paul saw Stephen get dragged out of Jerusalem and stoned to death (Acts 7:55–60; 8:1[39]). Paul's friend James, who was the elder brother of the apostle John, was beheaded (Acts 12:2). Peter was imprisoned (Acts 12:3–5). According to church tradition: Peter was crucified upside down; Andrew was crucified on an X-shaped cross; Mark was dragged to death; Matthew was nailed to the ground and beheaded with an ax; James, the brother of Jesus, was stoned to death; Jude was crucified; Bartholomew was cruelly beaten and crucified; and Thomas was stabbed through with spears and thrown into a fiery oven.[40]

Paul himself suffered terribly. In Philippi he was arrested, stripped, flogged (which was sometimes fatal), and chained to a wall in a dark dungeon.[41] In the town of Lystra Paul was stoned, dragged out of town, and left for dead (Acts 14:19). Fortunately his friends medically cared for him and he survived. He also suffered a hurricane at sea while crossing the Gulf of Messara (Acts 27:13–44). He suffered from three shipwrecks, beatings, hunger, illness, distress, and persecution (2 Cor. 11:23–27; 12:7, 10).

By AD 57, about nine years before his execution,[42] Paul had weighed the evil and suffering in this life against the phenomenal degree of good of the perfect heavenly community, and he counted even the worst kinds of torture as a very small price. Paul relays this valuation to his fellow believers in Rome: "I consider that our present sufferings are not worth comparing with the glory that will be revealed in us" (Rom. 8:18). He counted these as "light and momentary troubles" (2 Cor. 4:17) compared to the phenomenal degree of good of the consummate community.

Critics of Christianity suggest that Paul's perception is irrational because he was a religious fanatic. However, if Paul actually received revelation from God of the afterlife and the good of the consummate community, then chances are he is making a rational comparison. Paul claimed to have had many visions.[43] In the autumn of AD 56, he mentioned to the Corinthian church a vision he had of the consummate community ("paradise") (2 Cor. 12:1–4). Perhaps he obtained a glimpse of the beatific vision in supernatural mind-to-mind communication with citizens of heaven, and with God, of the phenomenal good that was being accomplished through the community. According to theologians, "What Paul heard (and saw?), human words were inadequate to relate (v.4b)."[44] But in his earlier letter to the church he may have tried:

> We do, however, speak a message of wisdom among the mature, but not the wisdom of this age or of the rulers of this age, who are coming to nothing. No, we speak of God's secret wisdom, a wisdom that has been hidden and that God destined for our glory before time began. None of the rulers of this age understood it, for if they had, they would not have crucified the Lord of glory. However, as it is written: 'No eye has seen, no ear has heard, no mind has conceived what God has prepared for those who love him'—but God has revealed it to us by his Spirit (1 Cor. 2:6–10).

Whether or not he could find the words to describe it, it is apparent that Paul "was not permitted to try to share the content of the revelation, perhaps because it had been designed for him alone, to fortify him for future service and suffering" (Acts 9:16).[45] God reveals only enough information of the coming glory to strengthen loyalty to God or promote cultivation of love and goodness; his plan in a world of divine hiddenness does not include satisfying our curiosity.[46]

It appears that Paul's friend Peter had a similar concept of the phenomenal value of the coming glory. This comes through in places in Peter's epistle (1 Pet. 1:3–9; 5:10–11) as he affirms the outweighing value of the eternal life in the consummate community as compared to this life's sufferings from evil men.

This is also the opinion of Christian philosophers. According to Peter J. Kreeft:

> Compared with knowing God eternally, compared to the intimacy with God that Scripture calls a spiritual marriage, nothing else counts. If the way to that is through torture, well torture is nothing compared with that. Yes, it's enormous in itself, but compared to that, it's nothing.... On the one side of the scale, this torture or all the tortures of the world; on the other side of the scale, the face of God.... The good of God, the joy of God, is going to infinitely outweigh all of the sufferings—and even the joys—of this world.[47]

Michael A. Corey (1957–2011) adds: "The future good that awaits [the redeemed] in the eschaton will be so transcendently glorious that it will end up outweighing—and therefore morally justifying—all of the evils that led up to it," for "no matter how large the sum total of the world's evil happens to be . . . it will always be infinitely outweighed by the limitless glory that presumably awaits [the redeemed] in the eschaton."[48]

An additional Bible teaching, supportive of this value conception, is that the population of the heavenly community in consummate relationship with God is enormous, and it continues to grow; and it may continue to grow eternally. Before the creation of humans, the community consisted of an enormous population of the angels.[49] Since the death of the first redeemed human, the population has grown. It is said to continue to do so until at the end of the world it becomes "a great multitude that no one could count, from every nation, tribe, people, and language."[50]

The size of its population is directly proportionate to the degree of good it generates. If, as suggested in chapter 6, the degree of good in existence is determined in part by the quality and quantity of expressions of love and goodness, then the larger the population, the greater the degree of love and goodness generated. The Bible's phrase that the population will be "a great multitude that no one could count" may be an indicator that there will be a phenomenal population that will generate a phenomenal degree of good. The size of the population makes for a strong argument that the value of the greater good is more than enough to outweigh each and every instance of evil and suffering in the world—even intense and horrific suffering of small children, and the suffering of the whole animal kingdom.

But long after the end of the world, the population of the community may continue to grow—possibly for eternity. God may continue to create other Earth-like worlds of beings that go through a preliminary phase of life (see chapters 3 and 4) to determine compatibility with God. If so, then even after the end of this world, the community would continue to grow. If God never stops creating worlds, his community would be an ever-growing community in consummate relationship with God.

And if God creates future worlds (even possibly future universes), most of which, or all of which, do not fall into sin, then any evil and suffering that might arise would be infinitesimal by comparison. If so, then the degree of good generated by the consummate community in the consummate relationship would be so high and so great that it may be humanly unimaginable. Without a doubt, any and all of the evil and suffering in existence would be outweighed by the seemingly limitless degree of the good of the community. All of the evil and suffering would indeed be "not worth comparing with the glory" of the consummate community.

Additionally, the value of the consummate community is enhanced by the many instances of suffering in this world that lead to a decision for salvation and eventual inclusion into the community, or facilitation of the building of good character for believers (discussed in appendix B). This takes *some* (if even only a small fraction) of the evilness out of some our suffering, which changes our perception of the price of the world's evil and suffering as compared to the high value of the community.

In sum, opponents of Christianity challenge Christians to present an adequate case for an outweighing value of the so-called greater good said to necessarily entail God's allowance of all of the instances of evil and suffering that take place in the world. Given that the *greatest* greater good is not free will, but rather the celestial community in consummate relationship with God in eternity made possible by compatibility-determining free will, Christians indeed have an adequate case for a greater good, the value of which can reasonably be perceived to outweigh all of the evil and suffering in the world (and even arguably also all occurrences of evil and suffering in hell).

7.4 The Necessity of Allowing All Instances of Evil and Suffering

Critics of Christianity might concede that the greatest greater good previously discussed is valuable enough to justify God's allowance of the majority of evil and suffering in the world, but God would not be justified if the greater good did not *necessarily* entail allowing *every instance* of the world's evil and suffering. This brings us to the critics' second reason for finding the theodicy of free will in a world of divine hiddenness and nomic regularity unpersuasive. While they might imagine our world of divine hiddenness and nomic regularity requiring God to permit the majority of the world's evil and suffering, it is difficult for them to see how it is necessary for God to allow every instance of intense suffering, particularly the heinous abuses against children, or the horrors in wars and natural catastrophes that brutally destroy people (sometimes on a massive scale), or the suffering of innocent animals. Is all of this apparently gratuitous suffering necessary to fulfill God's plan?

Thus far it has been discussed that God's plan to accomplish the greatest good includes having the consummate community which necessarily requires creating humankind to experience a two-phase life, the first of which enables people to experience compatibility determination by moral free will. Free will of this kind necessarily requires our world of divine hiddenness and nomic regularity. Unfortunately, as discussed, having such conditions makes it necessary that God limits his preventative intervention, and the extent of the limitation is determinable by the extent of evil and suffering that occurs in the world (what occurs is what is allowed to occur). The above chain of necessary links in God's plan is illustrated as follows:

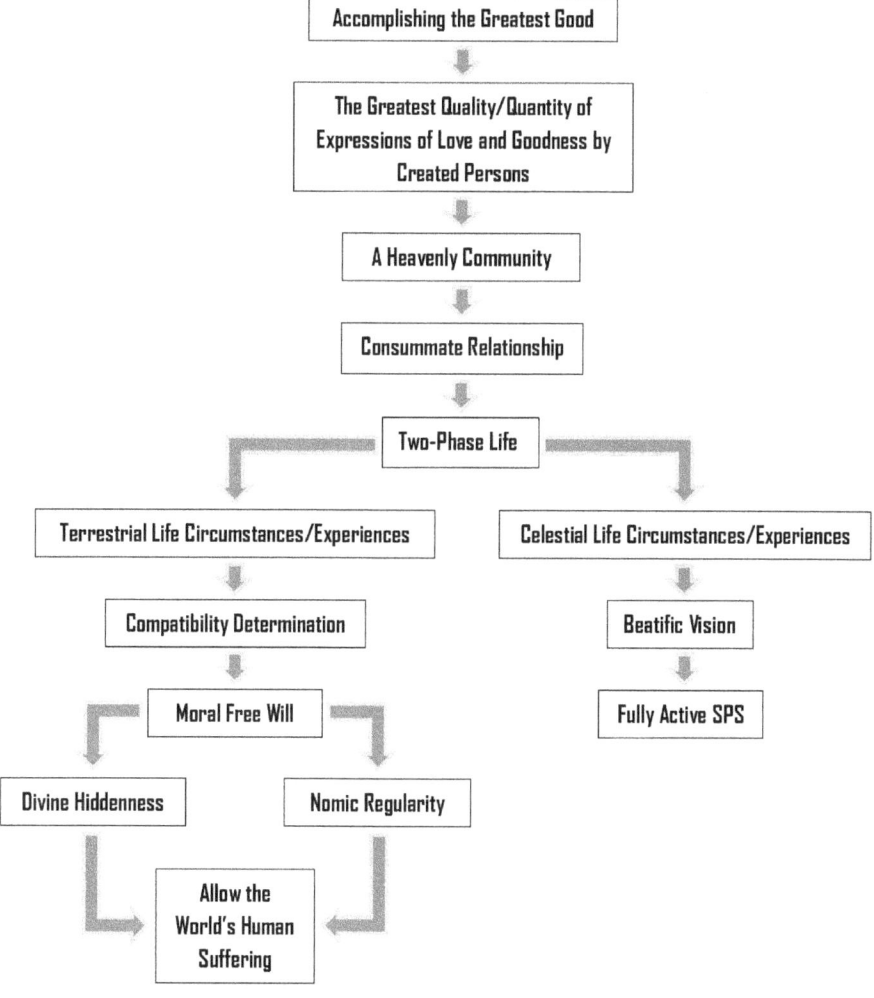

The theodicist's explanation for the necessity of intense suffering and animal suffering begins by arguing that the extent of the limitation on God's interventional activity corresponds to the number, intensity, circumstances, and duration of occurrences of evil and suffering in the world. In other words, God and his angels are involved behind the scenes (and to a very small extent in the scenes) to prevent and alleviate a great deal of evil and suffering that otherwise would occur, as the Bible tells us.[51] Unseen angels are servants to protect our free will and opportunity to be in a saving relationship with God.[52] But preserving that free will necessarily entails having a threshold to God's interventional activity, thus instances of evil and suffering must be permitted to occur.

Opponents of Christianity argue against this because they do not perceive how a significant amount of divine hiddenness or nomic regularity would be lost if some instances of evil and suffering were prevented, or mitigated. The instances they have in mind include heinous acts against children, or some situations of animal suffering. Examples include the five-year-old Michigan girl who was severely beaten, raped, and strangled to death and the fawn that suffers for several days from fatal burn wounds alone in a forest. Argument may be made that instances such as these do not significantly deteriorate divine hiddenness or nomic regularity to an extent that significant compatibility-determining free will is lost, which would deprive many of the good-generating consummate relationship with God. Moreover, if what they argue is true, God would be allowing pointless occurrences of evil and suffering, which goes against God's nature. The issues and instances of intense and apparently pointless evil and suffering (including animal suffering) are discussed in the next two chapters.

Conclusion

The probabilistic problem of evil and suffering is that it appears doubtful that God would have a justifying reason for permitting a vast amount of evil and suffering, including the apparently pointless suffering of innocent children, and animals. The common Christian response is that: (a) having the greater good of moral free will necessarily entails God's allowance of moral and natural evils; and (b) moral free will is of sufficient value to outweigh or justify all the evil and suffering God allows to occur.

Some critics of Christianity are willing to admit that having moral free will would necessarily entail allowing some occurrences of moral and natural evils. However, they argue, it would not be necessary for God to allow the vast number of occurrences in the world, or many of the intense, horrific incidents of evil and suffering, or animal suffering. Moreover, even if having moral free will would necessarily entail allowing all forms of evil and suffering, it would not be valuable enough to justify it. Therefore, if God exists, he would create a world without moral free will in which humans always do what is right and in which there is no evil and suffering. Such a world would actually be the best of all possible worlds, and it would be a world that a perfectly loving and good God would more likely create.

A Christian reply is that the greatest good is not moral free will, but rather the expressions of love and goodness by an ever-growing heavenly community in consummate relationship with God. It is a vital part of God's plan to bring into existence the greatest possible good. Its population is immense and growing (possibly for eternity). Therefore, it is quite perceivable that the good of the consummate community outweighs the price of all of the evil and suffering that God allows to occur in the world (and in hell).

The consummate relationship between God and his people with their optimal psychospiritual well-being necessarily entails the existence of a two-phase life, compatibility-determining free will, divine hiddenness, and nomic regularity—all of which necessarily limits God's intervention in the world to prevent or alleviate evil and suffering. Moreover, God's interventional activity is also limited for the reason that at least some occurrences of evil and suffering facilitate a decision for salvation and eventual inclusion into the community, or facilitation of the building of good character for believers. Consequently, if God is to bring into existence the greatest possible good, he must necessarily allow a great deal of instances of suffering caused by natural events and bad conduct. The edge of his limitation is seen in the occurrences that take place in the world.

But critics object that there are some instances that appear to cause no detrimental loss of divine hiddenness, nomic regularity, or compatibility-determining free will that would depopulate, reduce, or eliminate the consummate community. Such are the most intense, cruel, and horrific occurrences that involve small children, or innocent animals. If so, then pointless occurrences of evil and suffering exist, and it is logically impossible for pointless occurrences to exist if God exists. The issue of the intense suffering of children is discussed in chapter 8; and animal suffering is discussed in chapter 9.

NOTES to Chapter 7

1. Michael J. Murray, *Nature Red in Tooth and Claw* (New York: Oxford University Press, 2008), 134. Murray is the senior visiting scholar in philosophy at Franklin and Marshall College.

2. Frederick R. Tennant, *Philosophical Theology: Volume II: The World, the Soul, and God* (New York: Cambridge University Press, 1956), 199–200.

3. Michael Peterson, *Evil and the Christian God* (Grand Rapids, MI: Baker, 1982), 108. Peterson earned his PhD in philosophy of religion at State University of New York at Buffalo. His published works include: *Reason and Religious Belief*; *God and Evil: An Introduction to the Issues*; *Philosophy of Education: Issues and Options*; and *With All Your Mind*.

4. Peter van Inwagen, "The Problem of Evil, the Problem of Air, and the Problem of Silence," in *The Evidential Argument from Evil*, ed. Daniel Howard-Snyder (Bloomington: Indiana University Press, 2008), 160.

5. Michael J. Murray, *Nature Red in Tooth and Claw*, 105, 135–143.

6. Richard Swinburne, "Natural Evil," in *American Philosophical Quarterly* 15 (1978): 298. Swinburne graduated from Exeter College, Oxford, with a first class BA in politics, philosophy, and economics. He's held various professorships, lectured at universities, and authored many books, including: *Faith and Reason*, *Is There a God?* (translated into twenty-two languages); and *Providence and the Problem of Evil*. He is considered to be one of the foremost Christian apologists.

7. Ronald H. Nash, *Faith & Reason: Searching for a Rational Faith* (Grand Rapids, MI: Zondervan, 1988), 200–204.

8. Michael Peterson, *Evil and the Christian God*, 111.

9. Atheists argue that there's no evidence of God intervening in the world. However, if most of the supernatural or miraculous interventional activity is intentionally hidden from us for a greater good, we should not expect to find much overt or undeniable evidence of God's existence. Notwithstanding, infrequent or rare occurrences of miracles would not cause a significant loss of divine hiddenness. Evidence of God's existence was discussed in chapters 1.5, 3.3, and 5.4.

10. David Mills, *Atheist Universe: The Thinking Person's Answer to Christian Fundamentalism* (Berkeley, CA: Ulysses Press, 2006), 162–163.

11. Ibid., 243.

12. German mathematician and philosopher Gottfried W. Leibnitz (1646–1716) taught that God is capable of creating any (logically) possible world and, being perfectly loving and good, would create the best possible world.

13. William Lane Craig, *Hard Questions, Real Answers* (Wheaton, IL: Crossway, 2003), 104.

14. Michael Peterson, "Recent Work on the Problem of Evil," in *American Philosophical Quarterly* 20 (1983):330, as quoted in Ronald Nash, *Faith & Reason*, 203.

15. Robin Collins, "A Scientific Argument for the Existence of God: The Fine-Tuning Design Argument," in *Reason for the Hope Within*, ed. Michael J. Murray (Grand Rapids, MI: Wm. B. Eerdmans Publishing Co., 1999), 48.

16. Paul Davies, *Superforce: The Search for a Grand Unified Theory of Nature* (New York: Simon and Schuster, 1984), 242.

17. Hugh Ross, Kenneth Samples and Mark Clark, *Lights in the Sky & Little Green Men: A Rational Christian Look at UFOs and Extraterrestrials* (Colorado Springs, CO: NavPress, 2002), 191–192.

18. Ibid., 171–184.

19. William Lane Craig, *On Guard* (Colorado Springs, CO: David C. Cook, 2010), 158. Craig mentions this illustration in *Hard Questions, Real Answers* (Wheaton, IL: Crossway, 2003), 92.

20. John W. Loftus, "The Darwinian Problem of Evil," in *The Christian Delusion: Why Faith Fails*, ed. John W. Loftus (Amherst, NY: Prometheus Books, 2010), 261–262.

21. William Lane Craig, *Hard Questions, Real Answers*, 101–103.

22. Terence Penelhum, "Divine Goodness and the Problem of Evil," *Readings in the Philosophy of Religion*, ed. Baruch Brody (Englewood Cliffs, NJ: Prentice-Hall, 1974), 214–226, as quoted in John W. Loftus, *Why I Became an Atheist*, 235.

23. Michael J. Murray, *Nature Red in Tooth and Claw*, 14, footnote 5.

24. Richard L. Purtill, *Reason to Believe* (Grand Rapids, MI: Eerdmans, 1974), 57.

25. Such as Peter van Inwagen [*Proceedings of the American Catholic Philosophical Association*, 74 (2000), 65–80] and William Hasker [*Providence, Evil, and the Openness of God* (London: Routledge, 2004), chapters 4 and 5].

26. John W. Loftus, *Why I Became an Atheist: A Former Preacher Rejects Christianity* (Amherst, NY: Prometheus Books, 2008), 235.

27. Andrea M. Weisberger, *Suffering Belief: Evil and the Anglo-American Defense of Theism* (New York: Peter Lang Publishing, 1999), 164.

28. John W. Loftus, *Why I Became an Atheist*, 248–255.

29. Dominique Busnot, *Das Leben des Blutdürstigen Tyrannen Muley-Ismael, jetztregierenden Kaysers von Marocco* (Hamburg: von Wiering, 1717), 167–170; Robert Held, *Inquisition. A Bilingual Guide to the Exhibition of Torture Instruments from the Middle Ages* (Qua d'Arno, 1985).

30. John W. Loftus, *Why I Became an Atheist*, 234–235.

31. Ibid., 252.

32. Andrea M. Weisberger, *Suffering Belief*, 164.

33. The phrase "apple of my eye" refers to something or someone that one cherishes above all others.

34. Such as John L. Mackie (1917–1981), Hugh LaFollette, Quentin P. Smith, Richard R. La Croix, Thomas Metcalf, Andrea M. Weisberger, and John W. Loftus.

35. The indispensable role of Jesus Christ in the salvation of humankind is discussed in appendix D.

36. Recorded in Josephus' *War of the Jews*.

37. It is believed that the Old Testament prophet who was "sawed in two" (Heb. 11:37) is Isaiah.

38. Matt. 14:1–2; Mark 6:14–29; Luke 9:7–9.

39. At that time Paul was known as Saul.

40. *Foxe's Book of Martyrs* (Gainsville, FL: Bridge-Logos, 2001), 4–8.

41. Acts 16:22–24, 37; 24:27; 26:10; 28:16, 30; Rom. 16:7; 2 Cor. 11:23, 25; Heb. 11:36.

42. Paul was imprisoned in Rome from AD 61–64 (Acts 28:30). Then there was a fire in Rome. Nero blamed Christians and had them killed by various heinous methods. "Covered with the skins of beasts, they were torn by dogs and perished, or were nailed to crosses, or were doomed to the flames and burnt, to serve as a nightly illumination, when daylight had expired" [Tacitus, *Annals* 15.44 in *Complete Works of Tacitus*, translated from Latin by Alfred John Church and William Jackson Brodribb (New York: McGraw-Hill, Inc.), 381]. In AD 66 Paul was arrested and put back into prison. Church tradition has it that he was judged guilty of crimes against the emperor and taken to the execution block and beheaded [*Foxe's Book of Martyrs* (Gainsville, FL: Bridge-Logos, 2001), 8].

43. Acts 9:12; 16:9–10; 18;9–10; 22:17–21; 23:11.

44. *Zondervan NIV Bible Commentary, Volume 2: New Testament*, consul. eds: Kenneth L. Barker and John R. Kohlenberger III (Grand Rapids, MI: Zondervan Publishing House, 1994), 697.

45. Ibid.

46. 1 Thess. 4:15–18; 2 Pet. 3:10–14; 1 John 3:2–3.

47. Peter J. Kreeft, as quoted in Lee Strobel, *The Case for Faith: A Journalist Investigates the Toughest Objections to Christianity* (Grand Rapids, MI: Zondervan, 2000), 48.

48. Michael A. Corey, *Evolution and the Problem of Natural Evil* (Lanham, MD: University Press of America, 2000), 209–210.

49. Job 38:4–7; Dan. 7:9–10.

50. Rev. 7:9–15. See also Rev. 19:1–8.

51. 2 Kings 6:14–17; Job 1:6–12; see also James 4:7–8.

52. Matt. 4:11; 18:10; Acts 15:15; Heb. 1:14.

8

Solving the Probabilistic Problem of Evil and Suffering: Part 2 (Intense and Horrific Human Suffering)

Synopsis

Critics of Christianity argue that it's doubtful God (if he exists) would have a justifying reason for permitting a vast amount of evil and suffering, including the apparently pointless suffering of innocent children and animals.

Christians commonly respond that God is justified in permitting the vast amount and severe intensity of evil and suffering in the world because: (a) having the greater good of moral free will necessarily entails God's allowance of moral and natural evils; and (b) moral free will is of sufficient value to outweigh or justify all the evil and suffering God allows to occur.

The critics argue back that: (a) moral free will is not valuable enough to be a greater good, thus God is not justified in allowing the evil and suffering that occurs in the world; and (b) while having moral free will might necessarily entail allowing some forms of moral and natural evil, it would not be necessary for God to allow the vast amount that is in the world, or the intense, horrific, or apparently pointless moral and natural evils, or animal suffering.

A Christian reply is that: (a) the greatest good is not moral free will, but rather the expressions of love and goodness by an ever-growing heavenly community in consummate relationship that constitutes a good that is valuable enough to outweigh or justify God's allowance of all of the evil and suffering that occurs in the world; and (b) such a greater good necessarily entails the existence of compatibility-determining free will, a two-phase life,

divine hiddenness, and nomic regularity, all of which necessarily limit God's intervention in the world to an extent that corresponds to every occurrence of evil and suffering in the world. (Note: This covers chapters 7 and 8.)

I discussed a divine plan to accomplish the greatest possible good through the heavenly community in a consummate relationship. The existence of the community necessarily depends on the existence of a world (or worlds) with agents of compatibility-determining free will, divine hiddenness, and nomic regularity (discussed in chapters 3, 4, and 7). Moreover, some occurrences of evil and suffering facilitate a decision for salvation and eventual inclusion into the community, or the building of good character for believers (see appendix B). An unfortunate downside is that God's interventional activity to prevent or alleviate the evil and suffering in the world must be limited. Thus, occurrences, that would thwart God's plan if prevented, must be allowed to occur. Given that the population of the consummate community would exhibit a maximal quality and quantity of expressions of love and goodness, and be highly populated and growing (possibly for eternity), it is quite believable that the price of all of the evil and suffering that God allows in the world is outweighed by the greater good.

However, while opponents of Christianity might concede that such an explanation is possible, they may object to its believability. This is because it is especially difficult to imagine that securing the greater good would necessarily entail such a limit on God's intervention that it would be necessary to allow intense or horrific instances.

It strains the imagination to see God permitting the intense suffering of the little children that were thrown alive into a blazing furnace in Auschwitz during World War II; or the shock and grief of the mothers whose babies were shot or stabbed before their eyes by Turkish soldiers; or the pain and horror of those in Medieval times that were hung upside down by their feet and sawed in half, from crotch to torso.

It is counterintuitive to think God cares for the children that he watches suffer. A popular example is the abuse of a five-year-old Russian girl as described in *The Brothers Karamazov*. The girl's parents are said to have beaten her, thrashed her, and kicked her until her body was completely covered with bruises. One night, because she did not ask to go to the outhouse and soiled herself, she was punished by smearing her face and filling her mouth with excrement and shutting her up all night in a cold, dark outhouse while her parents slept in their warm bed.[1]

Another example happened in November 1985 in Colombia, when a volcano erupted, causing a mudslide. Rescuers found a thirteen-year-old girl, Omayra, who was pinned up to her shoulders in muddy water, concrete, and other debris from collapsed houses. The rescue workers could not free her or remove her from the watery mud. Red Cross rescue workers had apparently repeatedly appealed to the government for a pump to lower the water level and for other help to free the girl. Finally rescuers gave up and spent their remaining time with her, comforting her and praying with her. She drifted in and out of consciousness and appeared to be mentally confused at times. After about sixty hours she died of exposure.[2]

But perhaps the most popularly discussed occurrence of intense, horrific suffering is the one in William L. Rowe's evidentiary argument of a five-year-old girl in Flint, Michigan, who was severely beaten, raped, and then strangled to death on January 3, 1986.[3] The girl and her two siblings lived with their mother and her boyfriend. An unemployed man was staying there also. The mother and the two men got drunk that night at a nearby bar. The boyfriend had been taking drugs and drinking heavily and was asked to leave the bar. Eventually he left. The woman and the unemployed man remained at the bar for about another four and a half hours until the woman went home and the man went to a party at a neighbor's house. When the woman got home, the boyfriend, perhaps out of jealousy, attacked her, but the woman's brother was there and broke up the fight. When her brother left, the boyfriend was passed out and slumped over a table. Later the boyfriend attacked the woman again, but this time she knocked him unconscious. After checking the children, she went to bed. Shortly afterward, the five-year-old girl went downstairs to go to the bathroom. Then, allegedly either the boyfriend or the unemployed man, who had returned to the house from the neighbor's party, severely beat the girl over most of her body and raped her before strangling her to death. The window of time in which this instance occurred appears to have been roughly an hour.

Rowe argues that it is unreasonable to believe that God needed to permit this to happen to attain an outweighing good.[4] Considering all similarly intense, horrific instances of human suffering, in addition to seemingly unnecessary animal suffering (which is discussed in the next chapter), Rowe, and other critics of Christianity feel certain that the idea that they must necessarily be permitted by God for a greater good is absurd. As Rowe explains:

> We must then ask whether it is reasonable to believe that all the instances of profound, seemingly pointless human and animal suffering lead to greater goods. And, if they should somehow all lead to greater goods, is it reasonable to believe that an omnipotent, omniscient being could not have brought about any of those goods without permitting the instances of suffering which supposedly lead to them? When we consider these more general questions in the light of our experience and knowledge of the variety and profusion of human and animal suffering occurring daily in our world, it seems that the answer must be no. It seems quite unlikely that all the instances of intense human and animal suffering occurring daily in our world lead to greater goods, and even more unlikely that if they all do, an omnipotent, omniscient being could not have achieved at least some of those goods without permitting the instances of suffering that lead to them. In the light of our experience and knowledge of the variety and scale of human and animal suffering in our world, the idea that none of these instances of suffering could have been prevented by an omnipotent being without the loss of a greater good seems an extraordinary, absurd idea, quite beyond our belief.[5]

Rowe's reason for his belief lies not only in "our experience and knowledge" of the variety and extent of suffering in the world, but also apparently in the belief of many skeptics that Christian theists haven't adequately explained how such instances as that of the Michigan girl are necessary to bring about a greater good, or prevent a greater evil. As Jane Mary Trau (1951–2008) says:

> It seems that unless it can be shown that all cases of apparently gratuitous suffering are in fact not purposeless, it is most reasonable to believe that they are as they appear to be; and since it cannot be shown that they are in fact not purposeless, it is reasonable to believe that they are as they appear to be; since there appear to be such cases it is more reasonable to believe that God does not exist.[6]

Trau's argument for God's nonexistence boils down to a logical inconsistency between the existence of overly intense and apparently unnecessary evil and suffering, and the existence of God. As discussed in the previous chapter, it is logically impossible that if God exists there would be pointless or gratuitous evil and suffering because: (a) God is perfectly loving and good and thus would do all that he could do to prevent unnecessary occurrences of evil and suffering; and (b) God is fully able to intervene to prevent any injurious action or event that would cause such suffering.

R. William Hasker explains:

> God exercises ... a meticulous providence—that is, a providence in which all events are carefully controlled and manipulated in such a way that no evils are permitted to occur except as they are necessary for the production of a greater good. ... God determines in each particular case that the good involved in allowing the creature to make that particular choice outweighs the evil that results from the choice that is made.[7]

Therefore, if God exists, unnecessary occurrences of evil and suffering cannot.

In sum, because of our experience and knowledge of intense, horrific suffering in the world, and the belief that theists haven't come up with an adequately believable explanation for why God would allow it, occurrences like that of the Michigan girl can seem to defy an argument that would justify God in allowing them. Many feel that God *could* intervene to stop them without losing the existence of a greater good (or permitting the existence of some equally bad or worse evil). Consequently, opponents of Christianity argue that it is very probable that especially intense, horrific instances are pointless. And if there is no good and justifying purpose behind allowing them to occur, God could not exist.

8.1 Why the Intense, Horrific Evil and Suffering in the World Is Not Pointless

Two frequently proposed ways for God to prevent intense, horrific instances of evil and suffering are: (a) create a different kind of world in which they are not possible; or (b) intervene in the present kind of world to prevent them from occurring. Regarding proposition (a), as discussed previously, the best of all possible worlds[8] from which God brings about the greatest possible degree of overall good could not be one in which it is not *possible* for intense, horrific instances to occur because such a world would lack conditions necessary for God to bring about the greatest possible good (through an optimum balance of good and evil). The creatures in such a world would either: (1) lack significant compatibility-determining free will (which would exclude humans from being among the consummate community);[9] or (2) have the free will but be severely limited physically to do good (reducing the ability to harm reduces the ability to do good[10]); or (3) both. With any of these possible kinds of worlds, it does not appear likely that God could advance the degree of good in existence to a level that is equal to, or greater than, that which will come about as a result of the creation of the present kind of world. This is because God would need to bring out of such a world some other form of good that does not require compatibility-determining free will or a maximal degree of expressions of love and goodness by the heavenly community that is in a consummate relationship with God. But, as of yet, there is no such good proposed by thinkers on either side of the issue. Therefore, it appears unlikely that God could accomplish his plan by creating a different kind of world in which it is not possible for intense, horrific suffering to occur.

Nevertheless, some opponents of Christianity continue to flail about the notion that an all-knowing and all-powerful God could. They sketch out conceptions of a better kind of world to argue that it is reasonable to believe that it is likely that God could have done it, from which they infer that the present world is most likely not a creation of God. And, of course, if God didn't create the world he could not exist because the Bible is emphatic that God created the world.

But, as discussed in the previous chapter, such conceptions are naïve. Even if all of the most intelligent and knowledgeable people were to work together on the task of designing a different world using the greatest human technology, they would never be able to map out a world that would demonstrate that God could've created a better kind of world. It wouldn't even provide enough information to reasonably determine the *likelihood* that God could've done it (see chapter 7.1). Therefore, for all we know, the present world is the best of all possible worlds necessary to bring about the greatest possible good.

Our first conclusion, then, should be that the proposed option of creating a world from which God could bring about the greatest possible degree of good, and in which there never is intense, horrific evil and suffering [option (a)] cannot be validly argued. This leaves us with the probability that the present world, with its natural laws, freewill humans, divine hiddenness, and nomic regularity, is the best of all possible worlds. The critic is thus left to argue for option (b): divine intervention in the present kind of world to prevent instances of intense, horrific evil and suffering, including ones like the brutal assault on the five-year-old girl in Flint, Michigan.

Atheist philosopher Bruce Russell tells us that every day there are many thousands of occurrences of little girls being severely beaten, raped, and strangled.[11] I have no idea where he would have obtained such information because government statistics indicate a substantially lower amount. According to a United Nations report made from government sources, more than 685 cases of rape or attempted rape were recorded by police daily in the world.[12] According to an FBI report, in the United States only 32 percent of rape occurrences are reported to police.[13] This percentage worldwide may be lower due to the fact that in many countries raped women fear being disowned by their families, or being subject to violence, including honor killings, or prosecution in countries in which premarital or adulterous sex is illegal. Supposing, then, that the percentage of reported rape/sexual assault cases in the world is something like 25 percent, there would be approximately 2,740 occurrences of rape or attempted rape in the world every day.

According to the United States Department of Justice, 15 percent of sexual assault and rape victims in the United States are under the age of twelve.[14] That would be about 410 incidents of rape or attempted rape of children under the age of twelve occurring every day in the world. Now, if we suppose that approximately 12 percent of the 410 incidents of children involve a degree of suffering that is close to that of the Michigan girl, there would be roughly eighty occurrences every day of girls younger than twelve years old being substantially beaten and raped with the perpetrator's hand pressing against the mouth or throat. The number is higher if a comparable level of intensity of suffering is also felt by other children from natural causes, such as: storms, violent illness, animal attacks, earthquakes, tsunamis, and tornadoes. Perhaps, then, we're talking about maybe one hundred occurrences of intense suffering of little children every day in the world that, according to the critics, a good God would prevent.

If God were to intervene to prevent one hundred occurrences of this type daily (36,500 prevented every year), humankind would figure out that any attempt to commit violent rape against a young child would be impossible, due to a repeatable and reproducible phenomenon that would be unexplainable by nature or science. Given sinful man's scientific curiosity of the phenomenon, God would not be able to conceal such interventions and open miracles would be commonly witnessed. This would strongly suggest to the human population that the world is a world of perpetual miracles performed by a good and all-powerful being.

Atheist John W. Loftus sees "nothing in the world that could not be bettered by God through perpetual miracles."[15] He wonders "if Christian theists have really thought through the implications of a God who prefers this present set of natural laws with its sufferings over constant divine, miraculous maintenance."

However, perpetual intervention by God (that would defy naturalistic theory) to prevent one hundred occurrences of intense evil and suffering daily would substantially disclose God's existence and will to reward or punish, and a substantial degree of divine hiddenness would be lost.

This is because a disclosure of God due to this many miraculous interventions daily would most likely make the world environment into a coercive one, as discussed in the previous chapter. Elements of our world environment, such as governments, laws, information exchange, advertising, art, and family life, would probably be dramatically altered in ways that would flood the mind with continual heightened awareness of God's existence and will to reward or punish. This would narrow the epistemic gap (reduce divine hiddenness in the world), causing a significant loss of compatibility-determining free will. (The necessity of divine hiddenness for compatibility-determining free will was discussed in chapter 4.2.)

The loss of free will would be compounded by a significant loss of nomic regularity (discussed in the previous chapter), as there would be uncertainty as to which evil actions attempted would be stopped by an unseen supernatural force or entity, and which would be allowed to be carried out. Although, probably people would eventually figure out that actions miraculously prevented correspond to a level of evil and suffering, and they would anticipate which evil actions or harmful events would be miraculously prevented (which would further diminish the degree of divine hiddenness). All in all, there would be a substantial loss of divine hiddenness and compatibility-determining free will in the world, resulting in loss of the greatest good by way of the consummate community in an everlasting state of consummate psychospiritual well-being.

Therefore, it is most probable that the proposed option (b) of divine intervention to prevent occurrences of intense, horrific evil and suffering would hinder God's plan to bring about the greatest possible good through the consummate community that would be harvested from the world. As such, it appears most likely that occurrences of intense, horrific evil and suffering (including the ones equal to, or worse than, that of the Michigan girl) are *not* pointless. Rather, allowing them is an unfortunate necessity in God's plan to ultimately bring about the greatest overall degree of good.

8.2 Counterarguments by Critics

There is, however, an objection by some critics of Christianity that is worthy of discussion. If God exists and is intervening in the world, it seems plausible that he could disallow more occurrences of intense, horrific evil and suffering than he presently does without the loss of significant nomic regularity, divine hiddenness, or free will. It seems believable, they argue, that decreasing the number of occurrences by only a few thousand daily would not be detrimental. (A few thousand is a proposed guesstimate, inclusive of people of all ages and all types of intense, horrific suffering.) And if disallowing only a few thousand daily *wouldn't* thwart God's plan, why not prevent the assault on the Michigan girl? How would preventing this one instance have fouled up his plan? To the critics, it seems plausible that God didn't have to permit her suffering, so it appears likely to them that her suffering was pointless and a contradiction to Christian theism.

A Christian response may be that while we want to know exactly how many and which occurrences of evil and suffering are necessary to bring about a greater good, this theodicy tells us that having such knowledge is not the privilege of those in the first stage of human development in a life of divine hiddenness. For reasons discussed in chapters 3 and 4, such knowledge is reserved for persons in the second stage of life, in which many things (past and future) are explained by direct mind-to-mind communication by SPS[16] with God and angels. The afterlife mind is capable of learning in minutes what would take us years to learn in this life. And since God is outside of time (as well as inside of time) and knows the future, or any possible future given the existence of any possible event, he is able to convey what would result from the existence of any given event. Thus, it is easy to imagine how a person in the supernatural life could understand the necessity of any instance of evil or suffering.

Theologians compare the difference between the natural and supernatural stages of life to the difference between being in a train station's master control room (afterlife) and being in the train yard next to the tracks (earthly life). James I. Packer illustrates the difference with what he calls the "York signal box mistake,"[17] which is explained by William Lane Craig:

In the train yards of the city of York is a master control room containing an electronic panel showing in lights the position of every train in the yard. Someone in the control tower, who sees the whole panel, can understand just why a particular train was put on hold at one spot or why another was shunted into a siding somewhere else, even though to someone down on the tracks the movements of the trains may appear to be inexplicable.... So we may never know why God permits any particular evil in our lives.... Since we're not in the control tower, we shouldn't expect to be able to know why *every* evil is permitted by God or how it fits into His plan.[18]

Likewise, in our life of divine hiddenness, we observe inexplicable occurrences of intense, horrific evil and suffering, or we experience them ourselves and fail to see their necessity. Some surmise that it is reasonable that if a necessity exists, we should be able to see it. Because no necessity is seen, it is inferred that most likely none exists.

William L. Rowe applies this reasoning in his argument against God's existence on account of the existence of intense, horrific evil and suffering. Daniel Howard-Snyder calls it "Rowe's Noseeum Inference."[19] "We don't see 'um, so they ain't there!"

Sometimes it is reasonable to make such an inference, and sometimes it's not. It depends on the situation. It is reasonable for me to infer that my Boston terrier, Daisy, is not in my small home library where I am sitting and writing this chapter. It is reasonable because a dog is a thing I would expect to see or hear if it were in the room. But it would be unreasonable for me to argue that "there are no bacteria on my desk just because I can't see them since bacteria are not visible to the naked eye."[20]

Likewise, our limited knowledge prevents us from being able to fathom a multitude of events that would result from any given event in order to ascertain whether any given instance of evil and suffering would be necessary to occur to bring about a greater overall degree of good. The following illustration by Craig may help us see the extent of our limitation:

The movie *Sliding Doors*, starring Gwyneth Paltrow, tells the story of a young woman who is rushing down the stairs to the subway to catch a train. As she nears the train, the movie splits into two paths her life might take. In the one life the doors to the train slide shut just before she can board. In the other life she makes it through the doors just before they close. Based on this seemingly trivial event, the two paths of her life increasingly diverge. In the one she's enormously successful, prosperous, and happy. In the other life she encounters failure, misery, and unhappiness. And all because of a split-second difference in getting through the subway doors!

Moreover, that difference is due to whether a little girl playing with her dolly on the stair railing is snatched away by her father or momentarily blocks the young woman's path as she hurries down the stairs to catch the train. We can't help but wonder about the innumerable other trivialities that led up to that event: whether the father and his daughter were delayed leaving the house that morning because she didn't like the cereal her mother gave her for breakfast, whether the man had been inattentive to his daughter because his thoughts were preoccupied with something he had read in the paper, and so on.

But the most interesting part is the film's ending: In the happy, successful life the young woman is suddenly killed in an accident, while the other life turns around, and the life of hardship and suffering turns out to be the truly good life after all![21]

Given that merely one event that seems trivial could lead to a multitude of events and life-path alterations, it is not difficult to imagine that deleting one occurrence of intense evil and suffering (e.g., the assault on the Michigan girl) could alter the course of millions of lives, which could, in turn, alter the course of history and consequently make the world environment coercive. A consequence of a coercive environment could be the deprivation of enough moral free will that a multitude of people would be unable to experience compatibility determination and be among the consummate community. As argued in previous chapters, the loss of such a human contribution to the population of the consummate community would indeed substantially lower the degree of good brought about in God's plan.

Thus, perhaps if God *had* prevented the awful tragedy of the brutal rape and strangulation of the Michigan girl his plan to bring about the greatest good *would've* been thwarted. Perhaps a long chain of certain unpreventable[22] events would've occurred over the course of decades or centuries that would've led to making the world environment coercive. But in a life of divine hiddenness and predominantly dormant SPS communication ability, "we don't see 'um"—we don't see the necessity of allowing it for a greater good.

Given the likelihood that the prevention of one occurrence of evil and suffering could end up transforming the world's environment into a coercive one, an argument is believable that God's allowance of all of the intense, horrific occurrences is necessary. It is believable and persuasive because it is a reasonable explanation in light of God's plan discussed herein.

Atheist John W. Loftus might object to the foregoing on the grounds that it is punting to ignorance, which decreases the plausibility of a theodicy, as it "presupposes what needs to be shown."[23] However, while this might be true of some theodicies, it is *not* so with this one, for a few reasons.

First, this theodicy's recognition of our position of ignorance is not to explain away most or all instances of evil and suffering in the world, which would clearly presuppose what needs to be explained, thereby decreasing the plausibility of a theodicy. On the contrary, its recognition of our ignorance pertains to a very limited set of occurrences of human suffering, such as a few thousand a day, or one hundred a day, or even one occurrence, such as that of the Michigan girl. All other instances of evil and suffering, including that of animals (see chapter 9), are explained by appealing to what we *can* know and not to what we cannot know.

Second, other theodicies simply appeal to God's phenomenally superior knowledge and intelligence as the reason why we cannot fathom a greater good that would necessarily entail allowing intense, horrific evil and suffering. According to them, God is able to fathom the vast complex interconnectedness of events, both present and future, and sort out which events are necessary to be allowed for a greater good. But, since our knowledge and intelligence is so vastly beneath God's, we should just trust that he knows what he's doing.

I agree that our mental ability will always be vastly less than God's, and that this difference renders us incapable of understanding why some instances of intense evil and suffering would be allowed to occur. But the present theodicy explains that our ignorance concerning evil and suffering is commensurate with our temporary stage of development in God's plan for divine hiddenness. Given that there is this purpose behind our temporary ignorance, rather than merely a circumstance of different natures and knowledge as the reason for our ignorance, this theodicy is more plausible and thus more persuasive.

Third, other theodicies that appeal to ignorance may consequently leave a lot of questions unanswered about why God would allow evil and suffering. However, because this theodicy's appeal to ignorance is so limited, it retains its ability to answer many and the most significant questions. While it is true that a question about a detail of any given incident many not be answered, not having an answer to such a question need not and should not nullify the plausibility of the theodicy. In this regard, it retains its explanatory power, its plausibility, and its persuasiveness. Therefore, Loftus' objection does not apply to this theodicy, as the foregoing appeal to ignorance does not presuppose what needs to be shown.

Although, there is another objection raised by some opponents of Christianity. It is that if we know so little in this world because of divine hiddenness, no one could persuasively argue for God's existence. But this also does not apply to this theodicy, because even in a world of divine hiddenness, sufficient clues are left to perceive the existence of evidence for God and construct several different persuasive arguments. Examples were listed in chapter 1.5.

Still, while this theodicy may give us perspective to help us see why a loving and good God would allow the assailant to severely beat, rape, and strangle the Michigan girl, we are often still beset with difficulty seeing it this way. We imagine the scene taking place and find ourselves shocked, angry, and sad, and wanting so badly for it to stop. We instantly think of how we'd stop it (with force!). And, unless faced with a situation like that of Captain Kirk in the *Star Trek* episode discussed in chapter 6, a human person able to lawfully stop it *should* try to stop it, given our human makeup, circumstances, and knowledge. But this is not necessarily also a moral imperative for God, given *his* makeup, *his* circumstances, and *his* knowledge.

What God would foreknow would be that of all of the brutal and disgusting acts that evil people choose to commit, it was necessary to let this act against the little girl (and similar other instances) occur to keep a multitude of various kinds of events on a track toward the culmination of the fruition of the existence of the greatest possible good by way of the consummate community in an everlasting state of consummate psychospiritual well-being. Foreknowing that, God would have to let it occur to be consistent with his makeup, circumstances, and knowledge. But we should not think that by allowing it, God had any scintilla of indifference to what the girl was suffering. Being able to telepathically experience what she saw, heard, felt, and thought, and being all-knowing, God understood the abuse from every conceivable human perspective, including the child's. It is thus not reasonable to picture God as indifferent or cruel when such evil occurs. Instead we should picture God as suffering along with the victim — as if he is the victim (Matt. 25:41–46). Even though he allowed it to occur, he felt complete disapproval, indignation, and anger (and he knew of the reward that the perpetrator would receive in eternity).

But God also would foreknow that while the girl's (earthly) life would be brutally cut short, she would move into her second (celestial) life, into the company of God's angels, where she would begin to feel love, acceptance, and emotional healing of such a degree that is hard for us to imagine. She would enter into the beatific vision — a whole new experience and supernatural life of wonder and knowledge and comfort and lucid beauty, which would swallow up all of her hurts. In direct, telepathic communication with God, she would be taken into the "master control room" and shown how her suffering and short earthly life played a necessary role in bringing about the greatest possible overall degree of good. Because she would be of the disposition to want God's plan to be fulfilled, she would be completely and forever at peace with the price she paid.

8.3 Problem Solved?

Atheist William L. Rowe, the so-called leading proponent of this evidential argument,[24] argues that there is no plausible, rational, Christian explanation for why intense, horrific instances of evil and suffering, such as the brutal assault on the Michigan girl, could *not* be prevented by God without the loss of a greater good. He argues that there is no good that he can think of that would necessarily entail God allowing it to happen. And, he argues, even if such a good could be thought of, it would not be valuable enough to outweigh or justify allowing the little girl to suffer as she did.[25] Rowe even goes so far as to say that such an assertion would be "absurd" and "quite beyond belief."[26]

Yet nowhere in Rowe's published evidentiary argument does he discuss the key concepts of the preceding discussion. He apparently hasn't thought of the outweighing good generated by a community of an ever-growing number of persons in consummate relationship with God in heaven, which, if it is to generate the greatest possible degree of good, must be joined with a new species (e.g., human race) that experiences compatibility determination by free will in a first phase of life followed by a supernatural phase. He also does not discuss the explanation that such a free will necessarily requires

Solving the Probabilistic Problem of Evil and Suffering: Part 2

an environment of divine hiddenness and nomic regularity—both of which necessarily limit God's intervention in the world to prevent or alleviate occurrences of evil and suffering, including, as discussed in this chapter, some intense, horrific instances such as that of the little girl. Moreover, Rowe also does not discuss the explanation that God's interventional activity is also limited for the reason that at least some occurrences of intense, horrific evil and suffering facilitate a decision for salvation and eventual inclusion into the consummate community, or facilitate the building of good character for believers. When these concepts are apprehended, a Christian theodicy is hardly absurd or beyond belief. Rather, it appears persuasive that intense, horrific instances of evil and suffering, such as the brutal assault on the Michigan girl, could *not* be prevented by God without the loss of a greater good.

Because no published atheist or critic of Christianity discusses these integrated concepts of theodicy, the evidentiary argument against God's existence with respect to human suffering appears to be lost. This was my conclusion while a nonbeliever studying the subject. I felt that a rational evaluator of both sides could reasonably feel that the probabilistic argument is defeated, exclusive of the evidentiary problem of animal suffering (addressed in the next chapter). The ball, so to speak, seemed to be returned back over the net into the critic's side of the court.

But, of course, when I say "defeated," I mean defeated on an intellectual or philosophical level. Understanding the big picture might be of little comfort to someone who is suffering intensely from cruel and evil people, or from a natural catastrophe. Many severe sufferers who are rejecting God are often not willing to listen to a big-picture lecture about why they should trust God despite their pain and suffering. I know what that is like—as a result of both moral and natural evils. I know they just want the evil and the suffering to go away. They are in a state of impatience, anger, or depression. They don't care about the philosophical solution; they are hurting and bitter. This is because for them it is not an intellectual problem—it is an *emotional* problem.

This is something Jesus and his disciples understood. They acknowledge the reality that no suffering is comfortable while it is happening—it's painful (Heb. 12:11)! But they press beyond merely acknowledging the aggravation of suffering to a picture of a God who cares, who feels the sufferings going on in our minds as we feel them (God's SPS), and who in the person of Jesus suffered intense, horrific evil and suffering. We are not to equate the suffering of innocent children with an uncaring God, or a God who is indifferent to our pain.

Rather, we are to picture God as a super person who has the best intentions, who loves us and suffers with us, but who is working out a big plan across dimensions of space, time, and eternity to accomplish the greatest ultimate good that lasts eternally. That, unfortunately, entails a degree of noninterference, and consequently sometimes bad things must be allowed to occur.

The big plan of this theodicy offers hope so that sufferers may have strength to hold on and hold up under the pain, and not let evil and suffering be an obstacle that hinders a choice to believe in God. Seeing the big picture has been a source of strength for me in the midst of some of my suffering. And for me the obstacle in the way of my faith was removed. If I had continued to reject belief in God, it would have been on other grounds.

Notwithstanding, sometimes resolving the emotional problem calls for more than prayer, supportive friends or family, or this theodicy. Sometimes it calls for the assistance of a qualified Christian counselor.

Conclusion

Chapter 6 concluded that it is not logically impossible for God to create a world in which evil and suffering occur because it is possible (and arguably plausible) that such a world would be a necessary part of a plan to advance the degree of overall good in existence. Such could be the case if God is bringing into existence an ever growing and eternal community in a consummate relationship with God that requires the world's creatures to experience compatibility determination by moral free will. Such free will necessarily entails living a life of divine hiddenness in a nomically regular world. These conditions necessarily limit God's interventional activity in the world to an extent that events of evil and suffering must be permitted to occur. The edge of the limitation is observable by the occurrences of evil and suffering in the world. The vast amount of evil and suffering, then, is arguably a necessary amount.

But to many people it seems that intense, horrific instances could be prevented without significant loss of compatibility-determining free will, or any other so-called greater good. If so, then there exists pointless evil and suffering, and such would be inconsistent with God's existence.

This problem, however, is solved by taking into account that a single event could cause a chain of events that could ultimately transform the world's environment, making it coercive. We will remain unable to fathom how a single event could create a coercive world until we enter our second state of life, where we will have the supernatural ability to understand it. Thus, we have a plausible explanation as to why in this life some occurrences of evil and suffering seem pointless, and how, with the aid of this theodicy, such occurrences can be seen to plausibly fulfill a necessary purpose in God's plan.

However, animal suffering has not been explained. As long as this subject area is not addressed, the evidentiary argument is not fully resolved. The next chapter takes up this discussion.

NOTES to Chapter 8

1. William Lane Craig, *Hard Questions, Real Answers* (Wheaton, IL: Crossway, 2003), 77, 106. While there would be children her age that endure such suffering and grow up resenting God, in this case the child did not blame God for not intervening.

2. Ibid. While some children her age might've remained fearful or frantic until death, in this case a witness said Omayra faced death with courage and dignity.

3. William L. Rowe, "Evil and Theodicy," in *The Improbability of God*, eds. Michael Martin and Ricki Monnier (Amherst, NY: Prometheus Books, 2003), 263.

4. Ibid., 263–264.

5. William L. Rowe, *Philosophy of Religion: An Introduction* (Encino, CA: Dickerson, 1978), 89, as quoted in Ronald H. Nash, *Faith & Reason: Searching for a Rational Faith* (Grand Rapids, MI: Zondervan, 1988), 210.

6. Mary Jane Trau, "Fallacies in the Argument," 487–488, as quoted in Ronald H. Nash, *Faith & Reason: Searching for a Rational Faith*, 211. Trau was a scholar in ethics, philosophy, and religion who taught at the University of Miami's philosophy department. She passed away in 2008.

7. R. William Hasker, "Must God Do His Best?" in *International Journal for Philosophy of Religion*, 16 (1984): 216–217, as quoted in Ronald H. Nash, *Faith & Reason*, 216. Hasker received his PhD in theology and philosophy of religion from the University of Edinburgh. He is distinguished professor emeritus of philosophy at Huntington University. He has published many journal articles and books dealing with issues such as theodicy, divine omniscience, and the mind-body problem.

8. German mathematician and philosopher Gottfried W. Leibnitz (1646–1716) proposed that God is capable of creating any (logically) possible world, and, being perfectly loving and good, would create the best possible world.

9. See discussion in chapter 4.

10. See discussion in chapter 6.2.

11. "Why Doesn't God Intervene to Prevent Evil?," an article originally published in *Philosophy: The Quest for Truth* (third ed., ed. Louis P. Pojman, Belmont: Wadsworth,

1996), 74–80, at http://www.infidels.org/library/modern/bruce_russell/intervene.html, accessed on December 6, 2013. Russell received his PhD from the University of California, Davis. He is professor and chair of the philosophy department at Wayne State University. He has published several articles in philosophy of religion and moral philosophy.

12. "Eighth United Nations Survey on Crime Trends and the Operations of Criminal Justice Systems," at http://unodc.org/unodc/en/data-and-analysis/Eighth-United-Nations-Survey-on-Crime-Trends-and-the-Operation-of-Criminal-Justice-Systems.html, accessed on December 4, 2013.

13. FBI, *Uniform Crime Reports, Arrest Data: 2006-2010*, at https://www.rainn.org/get-information/statistics/reporting-rates, accessed on December 14, 2013.

14. U.S. Department of Justice. *2003 National Crime Victimization Survey*.

15. John W. Loftus, "The Darwinian Problem of Evil," in *The Christian Delusion: Why Faith Fails*, ed. John W. Loftus (Amherst, NY: Prometheus Books, 2010), 262.

16. The God-given, supernatural communication power of the soul that includes such abilities as telepathy, clairvoyance, and precognition to experience the beatific vision (see chapter 3.3).

17. James I. Packer, *Knowing God* (London: Hodder & Stoughton, 1973), 314. Packer received his DPhil from Corpus Christi College in the University of Oxford. He currently serves as the Board of Governors' Professor of Theology at Regent College in Vancouver, British Columbia. He is considered one of the most influential evangelicals in North America. He has authored over forty books, including: *Divine Sovereignty and Human Responsibility* and *Weakness Is the Way*.

18. William Lane Craig, *Hard Questions, Real Answers*, 70, 103. Emphasis added.

19. Daniel Howard-Snyder, "God, Evil, and Suffering," in *Reason for the Hope Within*, ed. Michael J. Murray (Grand Rapids, MI: Wm. B. Eerdmans Publishing Co., 1999), 103–105.

20. My thanks to John Danaher for his examples of reasonable and unreasonable "noseeum" inferences at http://philosophicaldisquisitions.blogspot.com/2010/09/end-of-skeptical-theism-part-5-wykstra.html, accessed on January 11, 2015.

21. William Lane Craig, *On Guard* (Colorado Springs, CO: David C. Cook, 2010), 159–160. Craig mentions this illustration in *Hard Questions, Real Answers*, 92–93.

22. Unpreventable in God's plan to bring about the greatest ultimate good through the consummate community from a race of creatures that experience compatibility determination by free will.

23. John W. Loftus, *Why I Became an Atheist*, 256–258.

24. Ibid., 234.

25. William L. Rowe, "Evil and Theodicy," in *The Improbability of God*, 262–273.

26. William L. Rowe, *Philosophy of Religion: An Introduction*, 89, as quoted in Ronald H. Nash, *Faith & Reason*, 210.

9
Solving the Probabilistic Problem of Evil and Suffering: Part 3 (Animal Suffering)

Synopsis

Critics of Christianity argue that it would not be necessary for God to bring about a greater good using a world in which he allows animals to suffer. Because God would never allow unnecessary suffering to occur, it is probable that God does not exist.

A Christian response is that it is possible and quite believable that God is achieving an outweighing good by allowing animal suffering to occur in the world, because the creation of an animal kingdom that suffers plays a necessary role in the creation of humans who would be part of the consummate community in an everlasting state of consummate psychospiritual well-being as part of God's plan for a maximal advancement of the degree of overall good in existence. The amount of good produced outweighs the price of animal suffering, especially since each animal that suffers is compensated with an immortal life of celestial bliss.

The preceding chapters offered a plausible explanation as to why God would allow evil and suffering, including intense and apparently pointless instances of human suffering. But a question about animal suffering remains: What greater good is being achieved by the suffering of millions of animals from savage predation, starvation, thirst, harsh climate, or natural catastrophe?

Typical of opponents of Christianity are colorfully depicted caricatures of animals that suffer severe injury. Popular examples include: caterpillars that are eaten alive from within by wasp larvae; rodents and other small animals that are squeezed by boa constrictors, crushing organs and bones before being swallowed; mice are eaten alive by cats; and large mammals that are torn apart by lions, crocodiles, or wolves. Atheist John W. Loftus provides us with such a depiction from Gary Paulsen's book *Woodsong*:

> Two wolves held the doe by the nose, held her head down to the ice, and the other wolves took turns tearing at her rear end, pulling and jerking and tearing, until they were inside of her, pulling out parts of her and all this time she was still on her feet, still alive. . . . She was still on her feet though they had the guts out of her now, pulled back on the ice, eating and pulling, and I wanted it to end, wanted it to be over for her.[1]

With our stomachs queasy from such a reading, atheists ask: Why would God create such an inherently violent, frightening, and painful animal world? Why would he design nature to be filled with creatures preying on one another for food? Why a world where only the strong survive, a world that is "red in tooth and claw?"[2]

They argue that the world does not seem to be a world that God would create or allow. If God is perfectly loving and good, it's inconceivable that he would not care about his animals. And if he is all-powerful and all-knowing, he would be aware of their suffering and be able to prevent it. But because there are many millions of animals suffering in the world, it would appear that God does not exist. In the book *The Christian Delusion*, atheist John W. Loftus calls this the "Darwinian Problem of Evil."[3]

A Christian response consistent with the previous discussion and theodicy could be that God permits animal suffering because it is necessary in order for God to bring about a greater good (or prevent a greater evil). But, the critic argues, there is no such greater good perceivable that could come from the suffering of many millions of innocent animals. If the greater good is, as proposed previously, bringing about the eternal community in a consummate relationship with God for the greatest expressions of love and goodness, what role could animal suffering play? How could animal suffering be necessary for human life conditions, such as divine hiddenness, nomic regularity, or human free will? Even if it would be needed to bring about these conditions, how could it be so in a prehistoric world millions of years before a human had yet arrived?

Solving the Probabilistic Problem of Evil and Suffering: Part 3

To try to underscore the apparent absence of any Christian answers to these questions, William L. Rowe presents an instance of one suffering animal that seems to defy a good explanation:

> Suppose in some distant forest lightning strikes a dead tree, resulting in a forest fire. In the fire a fawn is trapped, horribly burned, and lies in terrible agony for several days before death relieves its suffering. So far as we can see, the fawn's intense suffering is pointless. For there does not appear to be any greater good such that the prevention of the fawn's suffering would require either the loss of that good or the occurrence of an evil equally bad or worse. Nor does there seem to be any equally bad or worse evil so connected to the fawn's suffering that it would have had to occur had the fawn's suffering been prevented. Could an omnipotent, omniscient being have prevented the fawn's apparently pointless suffering? The answer is obvious, as even the theist will insist. An omnipotent, omniscient being could have easily prevented the fawn from being horribly burned, or, given the burning, could have spared the fawn the intense suffering by quickly ending its life, rather than allowing the fawn to lie in terrible agony for several days.[4]

Loftus agrees with Rowe that God could have prevented the fawn's suffering by intervening to stop the fire from starting, or keeping the fawn from being burned by the fire, or quickly ending its life after it had sustained the fatal burn wound(s). "But since God didn't do any of these things, such a God doesn't exist, for he would not allow this fawn to suffer if it doesn't serve some outweighing attainable good, and not even a theist can come up with a good reason why such a fawn suffered."[5]

According to these and other opponents of Christianity, God would only allow the suffering of innocent animals if doing so was necessary to bring about a greater good (or prevent the occurrence of evil that would be equally bad or worse). But, they argue, "so far as we can see," there is no such greater good that necessarily entails God permitting many millions of animals to suffer from pain and distress. Such a claim, therefore, would be absurd.

9.1 Why God Would Permit Animal Suffering

A Christian response should begin by looking at the two main views of creation. One of the views holds that God created the universe in which each species of creature is instantaneously brought into being in a recent past. Each materializes into physical existence as an adult and then mates and propagates within its own kind. In this view, none of the species in the world evolved from an ancestral species. This view is called young earth creationism (YEC). Theologians of this view believe Genesis 1 is a literal description of the manner by which the universe, Earth, animals, and humans all came into being approximately six thousand to twenty thousand years ago.[6] A few notable Christian figures holding to this view include: George McCready Price (1870–1963), Henry M. Morris (1918–2006), John C. Whitcomb Jr., John Baumgardner, Duane Gish (1921–2013), Jerry Falwell (1933–2007), and Ken Ham.

The other view of creation suggests that God created an undeveloped universe that, over a vast amount of time, gave birth to stars, which later produced planets. At least one planet (Earth) was fit for life, and life began in its simplest forms—prokaryotic cells, eukaryotic cells, bilaterians, fish, etc. By means of a divinely guided evolutionary process involving reproduction, mutation, and natural selection, the simple species evolved into increasingly more complex species: fish and proto-amphibians to amphibians, to reptiles, to mammals, to primates, to human predecessors, and finally to humans capable of moral reasoning (and being among the consummate community). This divinely orchestrated evolution and emergence of new species was either completely gradual (theistic evolution)[7] or occurred by sudden and miraculous macrochanges that appeared in newborn (or newly created) animals, followed by long periods of stasis[8] in which there were micro-evolutionary adaptive changes (progressive creation),[9] or perhaps something in between. Bible verses cited for this view of creation indicate that animal predation, disease, and death were part of God's design from the beginning (Job 38:39–40; 39:28–29; 41:1, 10, 14; Ps. 104). (These Bible verses are actually in harmony with the best understanding of the few verses in the New Testament that tell us "death entered the world through Adam.")[10]

This view is referred to as old earth creationism (OEC).[11] A few notable Christian figures either espousing OEC, or being open to it, include: Charles Hodge (1797–1878), C. I. Scofield (1843–1921), B. B. Warfield (1851–1921), William Jennings Bryan (1860–1925), C. S. Lewis (1898–1963), Francis Schaeffer (1912–1984), Bernard Ramm (1916–1992), Gleason Archer (1916–2004), Chuck Colson (1931–2012), Norman Geisler, Robert C. Newman, Walter Kaiser, Hank Hannergraff, Bruce Waltke, N. T. Wright,

Tremper Longman III, Robert Godfrey, J. P. Moreland, William Lane Craig, Francis Collins, Paul Copan, Lee Strobel, Davis Young, and David Snoke.[12]

In OEC, Genesis 1 is interpreted differently than in YEC. Opinions of OEC theologians on Genesis 1 may be divided into two camps: concordist and nonconcordist. The concordist theologians, believing that the text is entirely God's revelation of the manner by which the universe came into physical being, interpret the six "days" of creation as six epochs of vast amounts of time (the day-age view of Genesis). The Hebrew word translated "day" (*yom*) is taken to mean an indefinite period of time. Thus, the six epochs, or eras, are believed to concord with the origination of the universe, galaxies, Earth, and life on Earth during a span of time that is consistent with that of mainstream modern science.

Nonconcordist theologians, however, interpret Genesis 1 (actually Gen. 1:1–2:3/4a) in a way consistent with either a framework view,[13] the view of Genesis 1 by Conrad Hyers (1933-2013),[14] John H. Walton's view,[15] the protohistorical view of Gordon J. Wenham,[16] or any other nonconcordist view of the text that suggests its primary purposes are either polemical, theological, liturgical, protohistorical, calendrical, and/or literary, rather than a divinely revealed account of when and how God created the world. Thus, how and when God created may be understood by either a theistic evolution model or a progressive creation model, as a result in part from scientific observations and theories.

Opponents of Christianity, however, argue that God would *not* create according to OEC, but rather according to YEC, because a YEC world would potentially involve far less animal suffering (and human suffering). With only six thousand to twenty thousand years in which animals could live and reproduce, there would be vastly fewer animals that could suffer. Moreover, they could argue that in the YEC world God could still fulfill his plan to bring about a maximal degree of good by way of the conditions of divine hiddenness, nomic regularity, and compatibility determination by free will— all necessary to have the consummate relationship with God in heaven.

Given the proposition that if God existed he would create the YEC world, they argue against God's existence by pointing out that an overwhelming body of scientific evidence affirms that the present universe is not young, but rather very, very ancient. Multiple dating analyses corroborate to show Earth's age to be around 4.55 billion years[17] and the origin of life to have occurred roughly 3.8 billion years ago.[18] Moreover, examinations of the fossil record show that millions of years ago animals died from predation, harsh climate conditions, natural catastrophe, and disease.[19] Therefore, they argue, because the YEC world is very different from the present world, and because if God exists he would likely create the YEC world, it is most likely that there is no creator God.

In response, the Christian theodicist should agree that by creating the YEC world God could bring about a degree of good with some freewill humans that could join the consummate community of angels, and in which comparatively far fewer animals would suffer. However, it does not appear that creating the YEC world would result in a greater degree of good on balance than that which would result from creating the OEC world, because the YEC world would likely result in a substantially coercive environment that would deprive some, or most, of the human population of the free will needed to have an optimal psychospiritual well-being and consummate relationship with God (versus an eternally mediocre relationship).

According to Christian philosophers John Hick (1922–2012)[20] and Michael A. Corey (1957–2011),[21] as well as biologist Kenneth R. Miller,[22] the YEC world in the modern era would likely cause awareness of God's existence and will to reward or punish to be so prevalent and heightened that God's hiddenness (epistemic distance) would be diminished to an extent that significant compatibility-determining free will would be lost. As Corey explains:

> If God had acted to bring about the living world instantaneously by miraculous fiat—that is, without the use of a protracted evolutionary process dominated by cause and effect—then this fact would have surely been visible to virtually all human beings, especially those who have been trained in the physical sciences, and this, in turn, would have significantly jeopardized the freedom of human beings by reducing or even eliminating the necessary epistemic distance between God and the human race. As it stands now, the evolutionary process itself is *already* highly suggestive of an Intelligent Designer, so it stands to reason that the sudden creation of all life forms by miraculous fiat would have probably made the creatorship of God that much *more* obvious to everyone, because it would have removed any hint of a naturalistic origin of life.[23]

Consequently, with the YEC world and the resulting loss of compatibility-determining free will, the overall number of people in consummate relationship with God would be far fewer (than in the OEC world). This would entail a substantial loss of good discussed in chapters 3 and 4. Such a loss would be morally objectionable because of the small gain of a reduction in the number of animals that suffer. In other words, the good obtained by having fewer animals that suffer in a YEC world wouldn't be anywhere near enough to justify the resulting phenomenal loss of a multitude of souls that could've had a consummate relationship with God. This is especially apparent when it is realized that the consummate community continues to generate a higher degree of existing good eternally, while the good of fewer suffering animals is capped off by a finite number of animals, and a finite duration of animal suffering.

Given the net degree of good resulting from the OEC world (even with more animals that suffer), Corey argues that it appears more likely that God would create the OEC world, given the two options:

> The only legitimate alternative appears to be the gradual creation of the entire living world by natural processes alone (via the process of evolution by natural selection), because this is the only possibility that would have enabled God to remain substantially hidden from the world, so that human freedom could be preserved as a result. Far from constituting evidence against God, then, we see that the evolutionary process paradoxically ends up *serving* the divine purpose in the end, through the indirect facilitation of human freedom.[24]

Two Objections. Theist philosopher Michael J. Murray discusses two objections to this. One of the objections is that it seems unbelievable that human belief in the YEC world would diminish God's hiddenness and deprive us of significant compatibility-determining free will.[25] Murray supports this with the fact that ever since the first century up until about 1859 a vast number of people in the West believed they were living in the YEC world, yet God's hiddenness was not significantly diminished, and significant compatibility-determining free will was not lost. Since this is so, Murray says, it appears that belief in YEC would not actually deprive humankind of the greater good of souls in the eternal consummate relationship with God, and God could create the YEC world without loss of good.

Murray is correct that prior to the mid-nineteenth century a vast number of people in the West believed they were living in the YEC world and yet were able to retain compatibility-determining free will. However, and with all due respect to Murray, while belief in YEC before the mid-1800s was not coercive, a YEC belief since then very likely would be. This is because the twentieth century saw the beginning of the postscientific-industrial-technological-information age. This age has had a profound effect on the world environment. It has dramatically affected religions, philosophies, cultures, governments, laws, wars, schools, businesses, sciences, architecture, arts, family life, etc. Now if God had created a (scientifically verifiable) young universe, by the time of the postscientific-industrial-technological-information age, YEC would no longer be a matter of belief, but a matter of *fact*.

An established fact of YEC would be substantiated by scientific data collected in the fields of physics, thermodynamics, cosmology, astronomy, geology, petrology, biology, anthropology, et cetera. There would not be a God hypothesis proposed by Christians, but a God fact supported by science and taught in public schools around the world. And in an age of high technology, radio, television, and the Internet, God's creatorship by now would be well known and believed throughout the world.

After a few centuries of living with YEC as a scientific fact, nearly every aspect of the lives of people throughout the world would reflect biblical creationism—in law, business, media, information exchange, education, architecture, entertainment, careers, and on and on. Virtually every household on every continent would be acquainted with Judeo-Christian doctrines (and probably also Islamic teachings) and would feel continually and coercively aware of God's existence. Noncreationist faiths and philosophies would be marginalized by educational institutions, governments, and community leaders. Multitudes who would otherwise be Hindu, Buddhist, Taoist, pantheist, atheist, et cetera would adhere to a creationism consistent with the YEC view. There would be virtually no competing faiths or theories concerning origins or God's existence.[26]

Such a modern, scientific world majority of young earth creationists would very likely influence so many environmental constructs that nearly every aspect of human life would cause significant coercive awareness of God's existence and will to reward or punish. In a substantial portion of the human population, that would narrow the epistemic gap (reduce divine hiddenness), causing significant free will to be lost. Everywhere one would turn, there would be continual and forceful influence to have faith in God and obey his commandments. Such a relationship with God would not be significantly free. As previously discussed, such a loss of free will would substantially reduce the population of the consummate community in an everlasting state of consummate psychospiritual well-being and thwart God's plan to bring about the greatest possible good. Therefore, this objection discussed by Murray does not appear to hold up under scrutiny.

The other objection is that God *could* create the YEC world (roughly six thousand to twenty thousand years ago) in which life is brought into being relatively instantaneously as long as it *appears* to human observers to be very ancient and with biological evolution and millions of years of prehistoric animal suffering.[27] This is sometimes referred to as the Omphalos hypothesis, or apparent age concept.[28] Even though the universe would be very young, the empirical data, hypotheses, and theories of every scientific field would all point to an ancient universe (i.e., a universe that is 13.7 billion years old) and an Earth with a few billion years of geological and biological evolution. God would create Earth is such a way as to appear as if its surface, with its mountains, volcanoes, glaciers, valleys, oceans, lakes, and rivers, all formed and changed shape across the span of approximately 4.55 billion years. Mountains would appear as if they had been pushed up by incredibly slow tectonic plate movement over the course of many hundreds of millions of years. Yet God would have done it inside of a day (without producing such an enormous amount of heat from rapid plate movement that would destroy the planet). The fossil layers of increasingly more complex species would be an elaborate deception to make us believe that there were a few billion years of animal prehistory when in reality animal death and fossilization would've occurred inside of only several thousand years. God would provide evidence on every continent of a rock cycle that appears to occur over hundreds of millions of years, even though he would've formed and moved them all that way in a day.

Murray says that such a deception would be consistent with God's perfectly loving and good disposition as long as there is an outweighing good that would be brought about which necessarily requires the deception. In other words, if the deception ensures a degree of divine hiddenness and free will for the greatest good, then it would seem that God would not be morally precluded from carrying out such an extraordinarily elaborate deception.

The problem, though, is that such a deception would *not* likely bring about the greatest good through the consummate relationship. It is true that it would help God maintain a degree of hiddenness, just as the OEC world would. But, in the afterlife, such an extraordinarily elaborate deception, then unveiled, would probably permanently damage a relationship with God to an extent that optimal psychospiritual well-being would be lost, along with the consummate relationship with God.

Our understanding of our world has a huge impact on so much of the lives of many hundreds of millions of people in a postmodern age. It is a big part of our life experience. So to discover that God didn't actually allow the previously-believed long prehistory of animal suffering, and that so much of what we thought we understood about the life we lived was a divine hoax, would likely make us question God's word and whether his judgment, heaven, or hell are hoaxes as well.

The likely result of such a situation would be an eternal life in a problematic relationship with God and a resultant less than optimal psychospiritual well-being, if not psychospiritual ill-being. As discussed in chapters 3 and 4, such a situation would result in a multitude in a mediocre relationship with God and a substantial loss of expressions of love and goodness. The reason for such a psychospiritual decline would be because God's conduct surveyed in the afterlife wouldn't inspire sufficient trust in God. Whatever a person does inspires a perception, attitude, and beliefs in others. That is God's law of accountability. God is not above his law. He takes account of what he creates and he holds himself fully accountable for all he creates in a relationship. Obviously some degree of deception would not pose a problem, otherwise God could not be a hidden deity. He deceives us into thinking the angels are not among us because their presence is generally imperceptible to the senses. But if there is a mindboggling amount of deceptive work by God about the natural world and life, reality in the afterlife could be questioned to an extent that trust in God is significantly damaged (and permanently so). If so, this would go against God's plan to bring about the greatest degree of good. Therefore, it appears unlikely that God would create the YEC world and deceive us about its age, development, and the manner by which life originated. And since an OEC world is arguably necessary for the proper degree of divine hiddenness, it appears more probable that God would create the OEC world with its long prehistory of animals capable of suffering.

The OEC Universe Is More Consistent with God's Knowledge and Power. Another reason believers may expect God to create the OEC world over the YEC world is that the OEC universe reflects to a far greater extent the ability, intelligence, and wisdom of God. This is because, as Murray points out, the OEC universe is like a machine designed to make new kinds of machines, whereas the YEC universe is only a machine that does not make new kinds of machines.[29] To explain this, let's first consider a few things manufactured in the YEC universe. In the created YEC universe no additional stars are born and there are no new galaxies, thus there are no additional planets. There are no new species that would appear on Earth—only procreation of the kinds of animals that were instantaneously created.

By contrast, the OEC universe's origin (i.e., big bang) gives birth to the first stars that eventually produce elements that, billions of years later, form into planets, one of which (Earth) has the right conditions to generate simple life forms. The life forms are able to reproduce, undergo transitional mutations, and evolve (by divine design and guidance). As a result, new species, and new body plans, come about; and more and more complex creatures come into existence over the course of a vast amount of time. Eventually the OEC world's "machines" "manufacture" humans that have the capacity to join the consummate community.

Creating such a universe takes an incredible degree of intelligence, knowledge, wisdom, and ability—far above that needed to create the YEC universe. Clergyman Henry W. Beecher (1813–1887) illustrates this by reflection on the manufacturing process of the Waltham watch factory:

> Suppose, then, that someone should take [a man] to Waltham and introduce him into that vast watch-factory, where watches are created in hundreds and thousands by machinery; and suppose the question be put to him: "What then do you think about the man who created this machinery, which of itself goes on cutting out wheels, springs, and pinions, and everything that belongs to making a watch? . . . If it be evidence of design in creation that God adapted one single flower to its place and functions, is it not greater evidence if there is a system of such adaptations going on from eternity to eternity?"[30]

The YEC universe would be a marvelous display of God's ability, but creating the YEC universe is far beneath what we should expect of God, given his intelligence, knowledge (including foreknowledge), and power. It takes far more intelligence, knowledge, ability, and wisdom to create a universe designed to manufacture new things that subsequently manufacture other new things (as the OEC universe does) than a universe that does not manufacture any new systems, worlds, or creatures (i.e., the YEC universe).

Biblical Exegesis Is Supportive of Old Earth Creationism. Another reason for Christians to believe God created the OEC world is that the exegetical analyses of reputable theologians suggest that "creation and chronology" Bible passages like Gen. 1:1–2:3; 5, 11 and Ex. 20:11 were not meant to depict the YEC world. Moreover, other Bible passages suggest animals were created mortal and suffered predation, disease, and death before the fall of the first humans into sin in the garden.[31]

In Psalm 104, for example, God gets the credit for creating the lion to prey upon other animals (vv. 20–21, 24, 27–28) and their prey killed for food is called "good" (*tob*) (v. 28). This arguably sheds light on the Genesis creation narrative in which it is declared that the animal kingdom that God created was "good" (Gen. 1:25). Contrary to the view that a "good" animal kingdom does not suffer pain and death, the Hebrew word translated as "good" (*tob*) actually indicates that the animal kingdom functions in an orderly manner in creation as God intended, without intimation as to the quality of animal life, animal diet, or animal immortality.[32]

While some claim that Gen. 1:30 affirms that all animals were originally herbivores, exegesis tells us that diet is not the point of the text, but rather that God is the great provider in that he has blessed humans with the privilege (option, not an obligation) of wild vegetation for food (Gen. 1:29), as he had for the animals.[33] Thus, wild vegetation was intended as the animal kingdom's privilege, not its restriction. This corresponds to the fact that some meat-eating animals will sometimes munch on vegetation when prey is not available.

Therefore, it is argued, the conception of animal suffering and death as the result of Adam's sin is a mistaken interpretation that developed after the Old Testament writers. While some believe the apostle Paul taught that animal suffering and death were a result of Adam's sin (Rom. 5:12), careful exegesis shows that sin resulted in *human spiritual death* in the world. For Bible writers, the Greek word for death (*thanatos*) literally meant bodily death, but was used metaphorically "as a symbol of final separation from God, which we might describe . . . as spiritual death."[34] The metaphorical use of the Greek word translated as "death" to mean "spiritual death" in the Bible is discussed briefly in chapter 10.6.[35]

Space is far too limited for further discussion on this topic. Suffice it to say that a legitimate biblical case has been made for God's creation of the OEC world.

In summary, it appears likely that given the two creation options, and a plan of God to bring about the greatest degree of good possible by way of the consummate community in an everlasting state of consummate psychospiritual well-being, God would create the OEC universe. Moreover, the OEC universe is a superior reflection of God's intelligence, knowledge, ability, and wisdom. These two arguments, plus a biblical case for OEC, and the overwhelming amount of scientific evidence for an ancient Earth and universe, combine to form a strong Christian argument for the view that God created the OEC universe.

The OEC World Necessarily Requires Animal Suffering. A highly essential goal of the OEC world is the creation of creatures (humans) with the mental complexity necessary for the capacity to be in a consummate relationship with God. Such is the crowning act of God's creation on Earth. In the OEC world, the process involves a long prehuman animal pedigree. The pedigree originates with creatures that have very simple mental states that, over a vast amount of time, evolve (by divine design and guidance) into more and more complex species. The vertex of this biological "great chain of being"[36] is the human species.

The earliest animals in the chain are creatures with simpler mental states, such as those with only first-order awareness. A necessary byproduct of these mental states is the capacity to suffer pain. The degree of pain and suffering would be proportionate to the level of mental complexity. Thus, the most primitive animal forms would experience comparatively less pain and suffering than other animals with higher complexity, such as those with second-order awareness of first-order mental states (primates). In addition to a higher level of suffering from pain, they would also suffer from distress, loneliness, and bereavement. A little further along the chain would be a hominid catalyst from which would emerge humans with the highest mental complexity that would include abstract thinking, moral reasoning, the ability to love, and the capacity for compatibility-determining free will. As a result, we would expect to find a great variety of animals that bear varying degrees of mental and physical capacities similar to humans, including varying capacities to experience pain and suffering.[37]

The Necessity of Animal Suffering for a Greater Good. In summary of this section of the chapter, God's best option to bring about the greatest possible good by way of the consummate relationship with God is the OEC world. The OEC world allows for divine hiddenness and nomic regularity necessary for compatibility determination by humans necessary to be among the ones in consummate relationship with God in heaven. Intrinsic of such a world is a long prehuman pedigree by way of a divinely orchestrated evolutionary process that ultimately creates humans. A necessary driver of the evolution is an aspect of the world that only the fittest survive. An unfortunate byproduct of creating in this manner is an increasing capacity of animals to suffer. But, given that such a situation is necessary to bring about a phenomenal good—the greatest possible good—through the consummate community, animal suffering would appear to be a necessary evil for the greater good.

The necessity of animal suffering in God's plan is illustrated as follows:

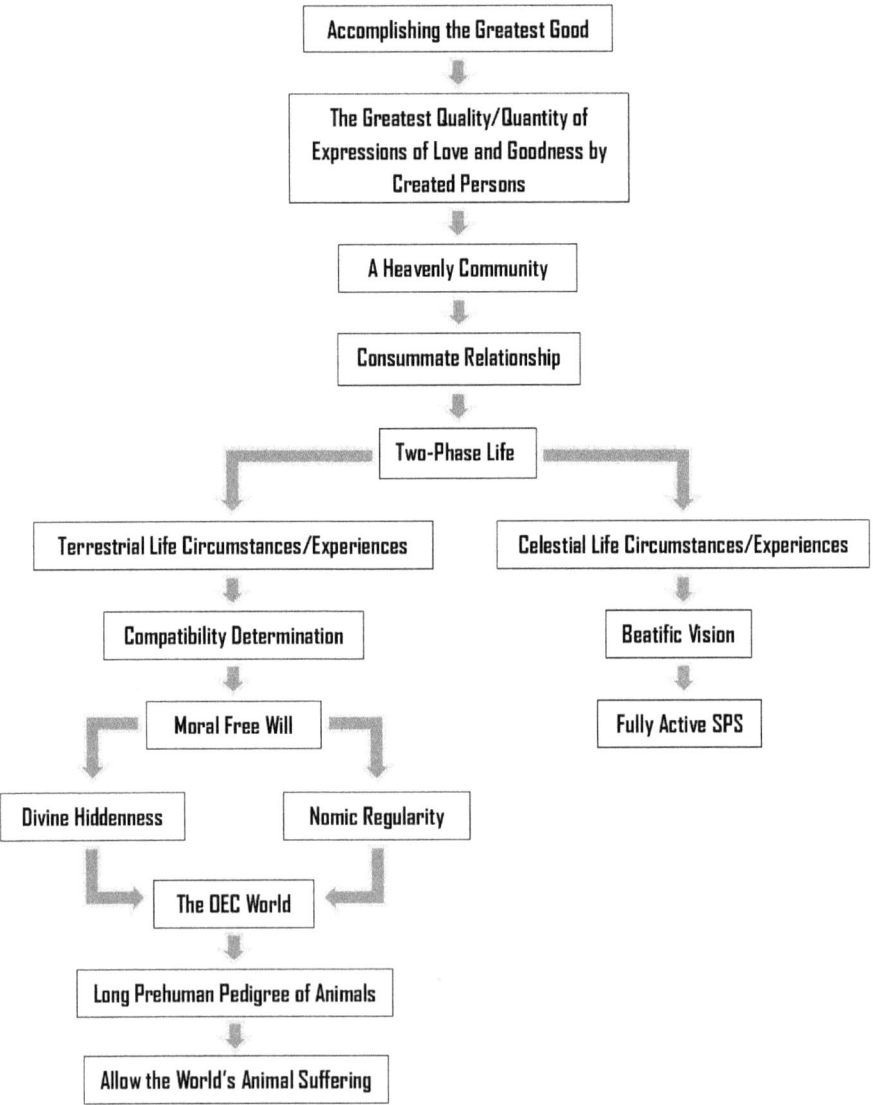

The foregoing explains the necessity of creating animals. It explains why God would have animals suffering and dying during a span of many millions of years prior to the arrival of humans. It explains why God would have an apparently wasteful extinction of 95–99 percent of all species in a world in which the fittest survive. It even lays the groundwork for an explanation of the necessity of creating carnivorous predators.[38] And it explains why such a creation would be in harmony with the character of a perfectly loving and good God.

9.2 Compensation to Animals

"Not so fast," some critics fire back. "If animals serve as a necessary means for the creation of humans, and themselves receive no compensation for their pain and suffering, God would be treating animals purely as a means to an end, without regard for their intrinsic value, which is *not* consistent with a perfectly loving and good God." As atheist John W. Loftus says, if animals "only have instrumental value and no intrinsic value," and "[t]heir intense suffering doesn't matter to God so long as they have been used by him to produce human beings who can be made into his children," then God is not "perfectly good and caring to all of his creatures."[39]

Loftus and other critics are correct on this point, but the point is resolved by the fact that there is theological and indirect biblical indication of an eternal, celestial life of bliss in store to compensate the animals. While most pre-Reformation Christian thinkers (e.g., Thomas Aquinas [1225–1274]) rejected the conception of animal immortality, many Reformation and post-Reformation theologians endorsed it. One theologian okay with animal immortality is the premier reformer of the sixteenth century, Martin Luther (1483–1546), who believed that the community of heaven will have celestial animals as companions. Luther is reported as saying:

> Peter said that the last day would be the restitution of all things. God will create a new heaven and a new earth and new Tölpels [the name of Luther's pet dog] with hide of gold and silver. God will be all in all; and snakes, now poisonous . . . will then be so harmless that we shall be able to play with them.[40]

The passage in the Bible so often cited in support of animal immortality is Romans 8:19–23:

> For all creation is waiting eagerly for that future day when God

will reveal who his children are. For the creation was subjected to frustration, not by its own choice, but by the will of the one who subjected it. But with eager hope, *the creation looks forward to the day when it will join God's children in glorious freedom from death and decay*. For we know that all creation has been groaning as in the pains of childbirth right up to the present time. And we believers also groan, even though we have the Holy Spirit within us as a foretaste of future glory, for we long for our bodies to be released from sin and suffering. We, too, wait with eager hope for the day when God will give us our full rights as his adopted children, including the new bodies he has promised us.[41]

Notice that the personified "creation" (*ktisis*) that is waiting to be delivered from death, decay, groaning, and suffering is distinguished from "we believers also" who are waiting to be delivered from death, decay, groaning, and suffering. If Paul's distinction is between humans and animals (and vegetation) and not between Jews and Gentiles, as some Bible commentators believe, then as with humans, animals too await deliverance from a body of pain and suffering. Thus, all in the biological "great chain of being" will be made new (2 Pet. 3:13; Rev. 21:1). But the eternal bliss of animals would have to be different from that of humans. Remarking on Romans 8:19–23, John Calvin (1509–1564) wrote: "Paul does not mean that all creatures will be partakers of the same glory with the sons of God, but they will all share in their own manner in the better state."[42]

It would appear, then, from the Bible, and from prominent Christian thinkers, that animals may also experience a postmortem, supernatural existence, albeit inferior in glory to the glory of humans. Yet, the animals each would have their eternal bliss, the blessedness of which would be proportionate to the animal soul's mental complexity. As Matthew Henry (1662–1714) says, "There shall be a glory conferred upon all the creatures, which shall be (in the proportion of their natures) as suitable and as great an advancement as the glory of the children of God shall be to them."[43] The glory of a lizard's "heaven" is far inferior to the glory of a chimpanzee's "heaven," which is far inferior to the heaven of humans.

It might not be a stretch to suggest that Paul indirectly alluded to animal immortality in 1 Cor. 15:37–39, which reads: "God gives it [an eternal and supernatural] body as he has determined, and to each kind of seed he gives its own body. All flesh is not the same: Men have one kind of flesh, animals have another, birds another and fish another." (Obviously Paul does not directly answer the question of animal immortality in this text, but in light of Rom. 8:19–23 it seems possible that he might have drawn upon an analogy he had used in a separate discussion on the question of an animal afterlife.)

John Wesley (1703–1791) argued that Rom. 8:21 implies that at the end of the world the animals will be compensated for their pain and suffering by transformation into a supernatural state to live in immortal bliss. The verse says, "With eager hope, the creation looks forward to the day when it will join God's children in glorious freedom from death and decay." But an annihilation and recreation of animals in the eschaton, Wesley argues, would not be consistent with the language of the passage, since "annihilation is not deliverance." God would not grant animals "freedom from death and decay" by annihilating them. Thus, according to Wesley, the animals that suffer in this life are to be compensated in the next, "A recompense for what they once suffered, while under the 'bondage of corruption,' when God has 'renewed the face of the earth,' and their corruptible body has put on incorruption, they shall enjoy happiness suited to their state, without alloy, without corruption, and without end."[44]

Modern theologians also endorse the conception of an afterlife for animals. Keith Ward argues for a second phase of animal life in never-ending bliss in the divine presence as compensation for their pain and suffering, and even emphasizes that animal immortality is a vital ingredient in a Christian theodicy. As Ward says:

> Theism would be falsified if physical death was the end, for then there could be no justification for the existence of this world. However, if one supposes that every sentient being has an endless existence, which offers the prospect of supreme happiness, it is surely true that the sorrows and troubles of this life will seem very small by comparison. Immortality, for animals as well as humans, is a necessary condition of any acceptable theodicy; that necessity, together with all the other arguments for God, is one of the main reasons for believing in immortality.[45]

Christian philosopher Peter Kreeft argues in favor of animal immortality, including that of the same pets we owned on Earth. "Why not?" he asks in his book *Everything You Ever Wanted to Know about Heaven*. "It seems likely that the right relationship with animals will be a part of Heaven."[46] C. S.

Lewis (1898–1963) seems to leave it as an open issue. Lewis was open to the possibility of an animal afterlife.[47]

In addition to Luther, Calvin, Henry, Wesley, Lewis, Ward, and Kreeft, there are other notable Christian thinkers with belief in an animal afterlife: Irenaeus (second century), Athanasius of Alexandria (ca. AD 296–373), John of the Cross (1542–1591), Jürgen Moltmann, Robert N. Wennberg (1935–2010), Christopher Southgate, John F. Haught, and Jay McDaniel.

9.3 Theological Objection to Animal Immortality and Its Problems

While many Christian scholars are in favor of an afterlife for animals, it is worth noting that some theologians argue against it. Most notable is Thomas Aquinas (1225–1274), who argues that in order for a soul to be capable of existing without a body, it must be capable of the kind of thought needed to exist outside of a body, which includes: contemplation of one's existence, causation, or truth. But because animals cannot contemplate such things, their thoughts, being so tied to bodily sensations, are not able to survive the death of the animal body.[48]

It is clearly true that the cognitive capacity of even the higher animals is less than that of humans, but it does not follow from this (non sequitur) that the animal soul is dependent on the body for its existence while the human soul is not. None of us knows how, precisely, a conscious soul could exist after the death of the body. Without this knowledge, how could one know which thoughts are necessary for a soul's disembodied existence?

The theologian's source for transcendent truth is, of course, the Bible. One may wonder if the reason for the distinction between human and animal souls came about in part from the Bible's teaching that human souls are made in "God's image" (Gen. 1:26–27) and animal souls are not. But as theologians tell us, to make humans in God's image only means that they are equipped for two roles: a kingly role and a priestly role. God endowed humans with the mental ability to share in ruling the part of creation placed under them—the animal kingdom (Gen. 1:26). Their priestly endowment included having the mental ability to think rationally, make moral decisions, be loving and good, and be creative. As such, humans have the capacity to relate to ("walk with") God and orient their lives around him.[49] While animals don't have the mental ability to walk with God, it cannot be theologically (or logically) inferred from this that there is no afterlife for animal souls.

The Bible is fairly silent about an animal afterlife. Studies in Genesis, Numbers, Psalms, and Ecclesiastes provide nothing definitive. Romans 8:19–23 seems to be the only text that might indirectly address this issue, and it is somewhat unclear, although Calvin, Henry, Wesley, and others believe Paul intimates an afterlife for animals.

The bottom line is that theologically speaking, the matter should at least remain open, as we do not have clear biblical revelation on the subject. As such, Christian leaders should refrain from expressing a dogmatic position against animal immortality.

Moreover, while the Bible doesn't provide much insight on the issue, a significant amount of anecdotal evidence does. Regardless of culture, education, social status, religion, or historical period, there are many reports by people who claim to have seen, heard, or felt apparitions of animals. The animal apparitions reported are not always pets or domestic; sometimes they are the wild variety, such as a gorilla or a giraffe.[50] While it is likely many of the reports result from a naturally occurring hallucination, overactive imagination, or dishonesty, some of them have features that make explaining them away difficult.

In many cases, there is no emotional attachment to the animal encountered (often the witness did not even know the animal once existed). Many of the reporters did not know that the ghost animal observed was of an animal that had died. Sometimes there are multiple witnesses; sometimes two or more human witnesses; and sometimes a human witness and one or several pets that simultaneously observe an apparition.

One of the more seemingly credible stories involves Dina Andrews, DVM, a faculty member at the Purdue University School of Veterinary Medicine, who, in 1992, made a house call regarding an ill horse in Hidden Hills, California. Dr. Andrews arrived at dusk. After treating the horse, she instructed the owners to separate the ill horse from its companion to prevent it from becoming infected from the fecal matter. "The owners looked at Dr. Andrews in bewilderment: they did not have another horse, they informed her. The vet looked back where she had seen another white horse, but it had disappeared. As she described it, however, the owners recognized the horse as one which had recently died."[51] This account has credible marks because of Dr. Andrews' credentials and the fact that she had no idea that the owners had another horse or that it had recently died, and clearly had no emotional attachment to the deceased animal.

Karen B. of San Diego, California, tells of a strange experience that occurred on October 14, 1987. Karen owned a black-and-white terrier dog named Sluggo and a tabby cat named Juniper. She saw Juniper at her bedroom door looking at something in the hallway; he had his mouth wide open, hissing and spitting; his ears were drawn back close to his head. She went to the doorway to see what was bothering Juniper. The only thing in the hallway was her dog Sluggo; he was just standing there, cocking his head from side to side. This seemed strange to Karen because they had always gotten along together fine. Just then the doorbell rang, and Karen went to answer it. She opened the door to see her next-door neighbor, who was carrying the limp body of a black-and-white terrier in his arms. "I'm so sorry, Karen," he told her. "This van came roaring down the street and hit Sluggo. Didn't even stop. I saw it all happen. Sluggo died right away, though. Thank God, he didn't suffer." Instantly Karen thought it couldn't be Sluggo because she had just left him in the hallway where her cat was still hissing. She looked at the lifeless dog. She recognized his collar, his dog tag, and his familiar rumpled fur. She took him into her arms and returned to the hallway. Her cat was still frozen in a posture of fear, but there was no longer any image of Sluggo. She laid Sluggo's body in his doggy bed, and then her cat suddenly ran into her bedroom behind the dresser, where he remained for the rest of the evening. The cat avoided the hallway for several days thereafter.[52]

In this instance a human and (apparently) a cat saw an apparition that looked exactly like the dog that had died moments earlier. If Karen was honest in her telling of the occurrence, it would be very difficult to dismiss it as a naturally occurring hallucination.

There are many reports of pets reacting to ghost animals. Sometimes several pets react simultaneously to an animal apparition that is also simultaneously observed by a human.[53]

These are just a few of the hundreds of such anecdotes. Of course they could all be made up by dishonest people. And if there were no third-party verifiable cases of supernatural events such as near-death experiences (NDEs), out-of-body experiences (OBEs), or ghosts (see chapter 3.3), it would be easy to dismiss stories of animal apparitions as such. But, the great amount and caliber of evidence of an afterlife appears sufficient for reasonable belief in an immortal soul. If humans are the vertex of a biological "great chain of being," then it would not be a stretch to think that the souls of animal predecessors also continue after death.

Of course the physicalist, or die-hard skeptic, would not be open to the possibility that there's any truth to such reports. But this might *not* have been the case for Aquinas had the body of anecdotal evidence that we have today been available to him. If it had, I wonder if his view would have been different. Moreover, as discussed previously, Aquinas really had no biblical basis for his view—only a wildly speculative hypothesis. Therefore, any case made by theologians that the animal soul does not retain consciousness after the death of its body appears indefensible.

9.4 Feeble Theoretical Objections to Animal Immortality by Atheists

Atheist John W. Loftus argues that the theologian advocating an "animal heaven" is beset with significant problems. In a series of questions ("a collage of rhetorical barbs"[54]), Loftus identifies what he believes are a number of them:

> What kinds of bodies will each creature have in heaven? Will a bear or a shark or an eagle still be carnivorous? Will a mosquito or leech still need to suck blood? Since their bodies have a direct bearing on who they are, if they lack these bodies will they be the same creatures in heaven? Will they also need to live in the same kind of habitat? Will there be both cold and hot regions in heaven? Will there be wetlands and deserts? Mountains and oceans? Will all species of animals even be in heaven, or just a select few, Lewis's "tamed animals"? Would we really want scorpions, alligators, ticks, snakes, spiders, and skunks in heaven with us? Will all parasites be there? What rational criteria can distinguish between animals that will be in heaven from those that aren't there? Or would there be separate heavens for each species?[55]

A response to the questions may begin with an explanation of a two-phase life for animals (terrestrial-celestial), and an extradimensional hypothesis (conceptions for humans that are discussed in chapter 3). As with humans, the natural animal body fulfills its functions at its death. The surviving soul leaves the body and begins its second phase of life. It enters the celestial spatial dimension(s) wherein at an appointed time it could receive a celestial body that is imperishable. Like the caterpillar that becomes a butterfly, each animal could enter an afterlife that is developmentally higher and involves remarkably different life experiences.

At least some higher animal souls in an afterlife could experience SPS (see chapter 3) that is fully active in their celestial life (as with humans). If so, then they would be able to communicate by way of telepathy or remote viewing, for example, with each other, humankind, angels, or God. This, of course, could radically transform instinctual thinking that would forever end all behavior of a parasitical, carnivorous, or reproductive kind. If so, then there could be safe and peaceful interaction between celestial humans and celestial animals (that were formerly ferocious or menacing). People might literally sit down with a lion, a wolf, or a lamb, reminiscent of the metaphorical depictions in Isaiah (35:9, 65:25).[56] A glimpse of the docility of the celestial animals might come through in the story of Daniel in the den of lions. An angel showed up and "shut the mouths of the lions," and Daniel survived the night unharmed in the den with the lions (Dan. 6:22).

Moreover, life in heaven may also be harmonious if different species are separated one from another in either one world (or dimension) or a multitude of dimensions, each with a celestial habitat suited for each animal species. Each could dwell in a perfectly controlled climate and terrain. One dimension, for example, could contain an ocean to which all celestial sea creatures go and dwell in eternal bliss.

Humans, however, would prefer a dimension comfortable to them. Perhaps a place of green fields and beautiful flowers where they play with whatever animal they call into their world. Or perhaps some people in heaven cross into the dimension of another habitat and interact on some telepathic level with (formerly wild) celestial animals. It seems plausible, then, that celestial humans would feel no qualm about sharing a dimension with sharks, tigers, scorpions, alligators, ticks, snakes, spiders, or skunks.

Opponents of Christianity typically snicker after asking Christians if there is a heaven for mosquitos, or the Symbion pandora (a 0.5 mm wide microscopic animal that dwells on the mouth parts of Norway lobsters). It is presumed that an animal afterlife requires a soul with a significant mind. If so, then there wouldn't appear to be an afterlife for such tiny creatures as these.

However, because we do not know what exactly constitutes a soul, and because we do not know how or why a soul survives death, Christians are without sufficient information to know if the Symbion pandora would be in an animal "heaven." A creature with a soul would appear to need a significant mind, but how significant the Bible doesn't say. For all we know the Symbion pandora *has* a soul that survives the death of its body.

But supposing that significant intelligence is necessary for an afterlife, how far down the chain of animal life a significant mind extends may be much farther than we realize. I find the studies of the intelligence of bees brought out by Scot S. Smith enlightening:

> James Gould, a Princeton ethologist, has documented a certain bee behavior which looks to be intelligent. The bee's "waggle dance" is supposed to indicate how the others can locate a source for honey and as he studied it, he hit on an idea to test the insect's ability to "think." Gould would put sugar water near a hive and the bees would go to it to save having to find flowers. Then he would move it further away in a calculated ratio each time. The bees began to anticipate his moves, flying past him to wait at the place where he would be moving it next.[57]

Smith also mentions the 1995 Discovery Channel documentary on ants. "They play, build complicated homes, they wage war, they take slaves, they clean each other, they have dozens of signals to communicate, and a complex social organization."[58]

But whether tiny creatures go to an animal "heaven" poses no problem. If a creature has a mind that can experience suffering, it would appear to also have a soul that could experience a celestial life of blissful glory and so be compensated for its suffering.

9.5 How Much Do Animals Suffer?

In defending God's character regarding animal pain and suffering, another point should be considered in the discussion. The point is that the degree or extent of the suffering of animals from pain, fear, loneliness, or bereavement is often not of the severity imagined. This is not to suggest any notion that animals do not suffer, such as that attributed to the French philosopher René Descartes (1596–1650).[59] On the contrary, certainly the higher animals really experience pain, fear, distress, loneliness, and bereavement.

However, according to scientific theories that explore the nature of animal pain and suffering, it appears the intensity for animals is significantly inferior to that of humans. Animals experience pain, but not in the same way we do. For example, animals may experience a "blind pain" in which the animal is not mentally aware that it is in a state of pain, because it lacks a higher order of thought that one is, oneself, in a first-order state, or lacks the mental ability to regard the state of being in pain as undesirable or unpleasant, or mildly undesirable or unpleasant.[60]

We have a tendency to imagine that what a mammal experiences when it cries out is the same as we would experience. But such imaginings rest on the assumption that the cries are primarily due to the animal's mental state of unpleasantness, which does not reasonably follow from an evolutionary standpoint. More likely the animal screeches because reacting this way has proven to be adaptive, and it can be completely detachable from any feelings of unpleasantness that may attend the mental state that generates the screeching. "Thus, if the prey seeks to escape the predator, to cower, to whimper, etc., it does so because such behaviors have, for whatever reason, proven to be adaptive, or to be related to adaptive capacities the organism possesses. But this is true whether or not the mediating mental states are regarded as pleasant or not."[61] Theist philosopher Marilyn McCord Adams argues that most animals lack the cognitive and affective capacities, such as "self-consciousness and the sort of transtemporal psychic unity required to participate in horrors."[62]

Loftus tells us that we can see for ourselves that animals experience pain when an insect or arachnid convulses and tries to run away as it is sprayed with an insecticide, or when a mouse grimaces, squeaks, or has increased breathing rates.[63] He is correct that we can observe signs of distress and pain suffered by some animals, but much of the reaction to an antagonist, or something potentially injurious, is probably mostly, and in some cases entirely (e.g., snails and jellyfish), adaptive, and therefore is not an actual reflection of the degree of suffering that an animal experiences.

The mistake that is made is anthropomorphizing[64] the suffering of animals. We have a pervasive tendency to presume what an ape is experiencing, for example, when it is thrown by another ape against a tree trunk because we can imagine what it would feel like for *us*. This tendency leads us to falsely attribute mental states to animals that they do not have. Consequently, animal suffering often appears worse than it actually is.

Opponents of Christianity (e.g., Richard Dawkins) capitalize on this using caricatures of animals grotesquely ripped apart by predators depicted with anthropomorphic flare.[65] Popular examples were mentioned at the beginning of this chapter, such as caterpillars that are eaten alive from within by wasp larvae, or a doe eaten alive by wolves.

Such caricatures of animal suffering exaggerate it by giving the impression that animal killing is normally horribly violent. People imagine, for example, lions killing their prey by tearing them to shreds with their powerful jaws and sharp teeth. Actually, lions usually kill their prey by strangulation.[66] Situations where mammals are ripped apart while alive are probably comparatively few, or rare.

The animal suffering that occurs in the world is also exaggerated by telling us that there have lived trillions of animals over the course of a few billion years that have suffered intensely. The reality is that the span of time that there have existed animals capable of experiencing significant pain and suffering has most likely been around one seventh of the time life has existed on Earth. We do not find organisms with even a rudimentary nervous system (first vertebrates) until the earliest period of the Paleozoic Era, roughly five hundred million years ago (the Cambrian Period). However, these organisms lacked nervous systems needed for sentience. Sentient animals (e.g., reptiles) did not begin to appear until around the Carboniferous Period, roughly three hundred million years ago. These organisms likely lacked the ability for substantial pain and suffering. Then, roughly 250 million years ago, organisms emerged with sentience and mental states for experiencing significant pain, albeit diminished pain compared to the pain experienced by animals that appear later with a cerebral cortex, and far diminished compared to those with a mammalian neocortex (Mesozoic Era). Mammals with the neural capacity to experience pain in a more profound way, including apes, began to appear roughly thirty million years ago. Thus, animals with mental states capable of significant or intense suffering actually make up a very small fraction of the total population of the animal kingdom, and a tiny fraction of the time in which animals have existed on Earth (roughly 1/126).

Taking account of this is not meant to trivialize the suffering of animals. Rather, it is a matter of taking an honest look at the actual extent of it. If the investigator is interested in a fair assessment of the problem of animal pain and suffering, he is going to need to show at least this much intellectual rigor.

Another important factor to take into account is that the higher degree of pain that an animal is capable of experiencing, the higher the degree of *pleasure* it is also capable of experiencing. On the whole, then, the degree of suffering of an animal is counterbalanced by the pleasure it enjoys. Most animals are not suffering continuously during an entire lifetime. The life of most higher animals is marked by times of discomfort, and times of comfort, as well as times of significant pleasure. Thus, taking account of the quality of life of most animals on the whole, the suffering experienced is probably much less than what critics of Christianity make it out to be.

Again, this is not to suggest that animal suffering is somehow canceled out by times of comfort or pleasure. It merely assists us in our effort to weigh the amount of animal suffering that occurs in the world against any good that God is said to bring out of it by offering an accurate conceptualization, rather than an exaggerated one.

9.6 Was the Fawn's Suffering Pointless?

So far Christian justification for animal suffering includes a reasonable and believable argument that it could be God's plan from the beginning to create the OEC world in which animals serve a vital role in a kind of biological "great chain of being" that would eventually produce a species with the capacity for a consummate relationship with God (versus a mediocre relationship) to advance the overall degree of goodness in existence to the greatest possible degree. A byproduct of this creation process is that some animals suffer from pain, fear, distress, loneliness, or bereavement. However, each animal is compensated for its suffering in an afterlife of eternal bliss in a celestial state in an alternate spatial dimension of animal "heaven." Therefore, the existence of animals that suffer is not pointless, and God is morally justified in allowing animals to suffer.

Still, it might seem that there are instances of animal suffering that occur that God could prevent without depriving us of significant divine hiddenness, nomic regularity, or compatibility-determining free will needed to have a consummate relationship with God. Such is argued to be the case for the instance of the fawn (introduced earlier) that suffers with pain from burn wounds for several days without a human observer until it dies.

Loftus argues that God could have prevented the fawn's suffering without losing an outweighing good by either: (a) intervening to stop the fire from starting, (b) keeping the fawn from being burned by the fire, or (c) quickly ending its life. Therefore, the pain that the fawn suffered for several days was pointless, which is something God would never allow.⁶⁷

However, it appears plausible that any one of the proposed ways of preventing the fawn's suffering could thwart God's plan. Considering the first one (intervening to stop the fire from starting), as mentioned in chapter 7: if the quantity and extent of forest and grass fires were less than they have been, growth inhibitors would accumulate in the soils, resulting in poor soil nitrification that would make animal life and human life impossible. Also, there would be insufficient charcoal production for adequate soil water retention and absorption of certain growth inhibitors. Obviously God would not be able to carry out his plan without mammal life, and so he is obliged to allow a certain number and extent of forest fires to occur. Perhaps the number and extent are exactly the number and extent necessary to fulfill God's plan.

The critic may balk at this and retort that one less forest fire would not cause a chain of events that would lead to the end of mammal life on the planet. However, as brought out earlier, the slightest change in events in the world—even events as seemingly insignificant as that of a motion of one butterfly—can, and do, have a profound effect on the lives of thousands of mammals. Factors that could be altered include local ecosystems, the global ecosystem, animal reproduction and migration, and various species populations. If, for example, the honey bee population in the world were to become extinct (and this is a present scientific concern), there would be a sharp decline in pollination and fruit and vegetable reproduction, which would likely lead to a massive shortage of food in the world necessary to sustain mammal life—especially human life. Consequently, the nonoccurrence of even one forest fire that otherwise God would've allowed to occur could possibly have a profound adverse effect of ending mammal life.

Although the critic could argue that God could've started a forest fire in a different forest and spared the fawn that way, and soil nitrification and charcoal production would not be significantly affected. This might seem to present a viable alternative until we realize that starting a fire in another forest could cause another mammal, or a greater number of other animals, to be badly burned and suffer. Because forests are not all the same (they differ in size, terrain, and makeup), a fire in another forest might not burn as extensively. If multiple "other forests" are burned during a span of millions of years, charcoal production and soil nitrification could go down a slippery slope that would make human life impossible; or enough vegetation could be destroyed that could wipe out certain animal species populations that would alter the evolutionary process, thwarting the emergence of humankind. Or perhaps a fire in another forest might burn more extensively, causing other changes that would have the eventual result of bringing about less than the greatest possible good. Therefore, moving the locations of fires to avoid animal injury could still likely cause the loss of the outweighing good of a human population capable of being among the heavenly community in consummate relationship with God.

The second way (keeping the fawn from being burned by the fire) would also likely have caused the loss of outweighing good. This is because the critic is not actually arguing that God would keep the fawn from being burned by the fire. Rather, the critic is arguing that God would prevent *all* instances of mammal pain of a degree that is relatively similar to that of the fawn, without a human observer—whether by fire, another kind of natural catastrophe, harsh climate, predation, accident, or disease. If one such instance of animal suffering is pointless to permit, then any and all of them are, and God is perfectly willing and able to prevent any and all of them. But, that kind of intervention would likely radically alter local ecosystems, the global ecosystem, animal reproduction and migration, food supplies, various species populations, et cetera, and the emergence of human life might never happen. A result of these changes alone could substantially alter the actual (versus theoretical) phylogenic tree, and humans capable of being among the consummate community might never emerge.

Even if humans appear on Earth as they have, there could've been other changes in the food chain that could've caused large populations of mammals to suffer from starvation. Moreover, the level of divine intervention to prevent all instances of substantial mammal suffering from harsh climates, predation, accidents, or diseases would likely break down the degree of divine hiddenness, and perhaps nomic regularity, to an extent that there'd be significant loss of compatibility-determining free will.

The third suggested way of preventing the fawn's suffering (quickly ending the fawn's life) would also likely have caused the loss of outweighing good. This is because, as said previously, the critic is not actually arguing that God would quickly end the fawn's life. Rather, the critic is arguing that God would quickly end the lives of all mammals that suffer pain comparable to that of the fawn. For the past thirty million years, millions of mammals around the globe with severe injury, or severe illness, would have suddenly died. Because many mammals that suffer from severe injury or illness continue moving and interacting with other animals (i.e., predators), it is possible that the sudden deaths of millions of mammals would have altered events and evolutionary processes such that the (actual) phylogenic tree is altered and humans never emerge.

Moreover, even supposing that the (actual) phylogenic tree remains the same, and that humankind appears on Earth just as it did, divine hiddenness and nomic regularity would likely be altered to a significant extent which, in the human era, would cause significant diminishment of compatibility-determining free will. The quick deaths of injured mammals, unexplainable by repeatable and reproducible scientific experiments, would so strongly reinforce the Christian claim of the existence of God that our awareness of his existence and will to reward or punish would likely cause significant loss of divine hiddenness to generate a coercive environment.

In summary, contrary to the assertions of critics, Christians *do* have a plausible explanation for why God did not intervene to prevent the fawn from suffering pain for several days. God cannot intervene any more than he does without loss of good that is of outweighing value. It is unfortunate that the fawn suffered, but its suffering was not anywhere near as bad as that of a human with a comparable burn injury, and it shall be more than compensated for its days of suffering in postmortem bliss for eternity.

Conclusion

Critics of Christianity argue that there is no greater good that would require God to allow a world in which animals suffer. But they do not consider the possible and quite plausible explanation that having animals capable of suffering is necessary if God is to bring about the greatest possible good by way of a heavenly community in consummate relationship with God. It would be necessary if animal suffering is an unavoidable byproduct of creating the OEC world that is: (a) nomically regular; (b) hides God's existence and will to reward or punish to a necessary extent; and (c) has a divinely orchestrated evolutionary process that results in a long prehuman pedigree or biological "great chain of being" that serves as a catalyst (among other purposes) for the ultimate emergence of the human species capable of joining with the heavenly community in a consummate relationship with God for the greatest possible expressions of love and goodness.

Such a purpose of the animals does not treat them as a means to an end without due regard for their intrinsic value, because God has in store a celestial life for animals of blissful glory. There is strong theological underpinning for this being God's plan. As such, the pain and suffering of animals is defeated by making their life experience on balance worth having.

Taking into account that God is working out a plan to accomplish the greatest possible good by way of animals that unfortunately suffer, but are more than compensated with an eternal life of bliss, it appears that animal suffering is justifiable, and there's no contradiction between the existence of God and the animals in the world that sometimes suffer.

I conclude that the "Darwinian Problem of Evil" has been met, and solved. I remain cognizant that, for some reason unknown to me at this time, the theodicy presented here might not hold up under a reasonable and intellectually honest examination. And if so, then I'll adjust my conclusion accordingly.

NOTES to Chapter 9

1. Gary Paulsen, *Woodsong* (New York: Simon & Schuster, 1990), as quoted in John W. Loftus, *Why I Became an Atheist: A Former Preacher Rejects Christianity* (Amherst, NY: Prometheus Books, 2008), 238.

2. An oft-repeated quote from Alfred Tennyson's poem.

3. John W. Loftus, "The Darwinian Problem of Evil," in *The Christian Delusion: Why Faith Fails*, ed. John W. Loftus (Amherst, NY: Prometheus Books, 2010), 238.

4. William L. Rowe, "The Problem of Evil and Some Varieties of Atheism," in *The Improbability of God*, eds. Michael Martin and Ricki Monnier (Amherst, NY: Prometheus Books, 2003), 253.

5. John W. Loftus, *Why I Became an Atheist*, 234–235.

6. Young earth creationists believe that the universe, Earth, and all life on Earth were brought into material being in an instantaneous fashion inside of six consecutive twenty-four-hour days (Gen. 1), and that the author of Gen. 5 and 11 intended to record complete (or near complete) chronological genealogies. Some YECs have made a Bible chronology that indicates that the world began to exist roughly six thousand years ago. Other YECs, however, feel that there is room in a Bible chronology for the world beginning roughly ten thousand or more years ago.

7. Proponents of theistic evolution vary in their beliefs about God's involvement in evolution. Some believe he created the natural laws and let evolution run its course, while others believe God was actively involved in the evolution process (http://www.oldearth.org).

8. Stasis in this context is a condition in which no macro changes in the makeup or structure of a species occur such that there is no observable transition from one species to another. Stasis in the fossil record documents the stasis of many species that lasts longer than one million years, which creationists believe presents a challenge to the theory of gradual transitions from species to species.

9. Progressive creationists accept that God created each species of animal as a somewhat unique creation, by periodical occurrences of divine intervention to effect macro (or mega) changes in offspring, during a span of approximately 3.8 billion years (http://www.oldearth.org).

10. Paul Copan, *That's Just Your Interpretation: Responding to Skeptics Who Challenge Your Faith* (Grand Rapids, MI: BakerBooks, 2001), 150–152. In Psalm 104, for example, God gets the credit for creating the lion to prey upon other animals (vv. 20–21, 24, 27–28) and their prey killed for food is called "good" (v. 28), which, as explained later in the chapter, indicates a functioning order in creation as God intended without intimation as to the quality of animal life, animal diet, or animal immortality. The conception of animal suffering and death as the result of Adam's sin appears to be a mistaken interpretation that developed after the Old Testament writers. While some believe the apostle Paul taught that animal suffering and death were a result of Adam's sin (Rom. 5:12), careful exegesis shows that sin resulted in human spiritual death in the world. The Bible writers would've considered the Greek word for death (*thanatos*) to mean a literal bodily death, but it was used metaphorically "as a symbol of final separation from God, which we might describe . . . as spiritual death" [Charles H. Dodd (1884–1973), *The Epistle of Paul to the Romans* (London: Hodder and Stoughton, 1932), 81]. The use of the word "death" metaphorically as spiritual death is discussed briefly in chapter 10.6. See also Gary R. Habermas and J. P. Moreland, *Beyond Death: Exploring the Evidence for Immortality* (Eugene, OR: Wipf and Stock Publishers, 2004), 305–306.

11. Old earth creationism is held by a growing population of Christians who have adjusted their view of Genesis chapters 1, 2, 5, and 11, in light of the evidence for an ancient universe, a 3.8 billion year span of life on Earth, and a recent advance in methodology for Bible exegesis which incorporates comparative studies of ancient Near Eastern literature.

12. http://reasons.org/articles/notable-christians-open-to-an-old-universe-old-earth-perspective, accessed on March 2, 2015. N. T. Wright, Bruce Waltke, Tremper Longman III, Francis Collins, and Davis Young were not listed on the reasons.org website.

13. For an introduction to the framework view see *The Genesis Debate: Three Views on the Days of Creation*, ed. David G. Hagopian (Mission Viejo, CA: Crux Press, 2001), 217–256.

14. Conrad Hyers, *The Meaning of Creation: Genesis and Modern Science* (Atlanta, GA: John Knox Press, 1984); "The Fall and Rise of Creationism," in *The Christian Century*, April 24, 1984, pages 411–415 (found at http://www.religion-online.org/showarticle.asp?title=1917); "Comparing Biblical and Scientific Maps of Origins," in *Perspectives on an Evolving Creation*, ed. Keith B. Miller (Grand Rapids, MI:

William B. Eerdmans Publishing Company, 2003), 19–33. Hyers received his PhD in theology and philosophy of religion from Princeton Theological Seminary. He was an American writer, lecturer, and ordained Presbyterian minister, and, before retiring, was professor of comparative mythology and the history of religions at Gustavus Adolphus College, St. Peter, MN.

15. John H. Walton, *The Lost World of Genesis One: Ancient Cosmology and the Origins Debate* (Downers Grove, IL: InterVarsity Press, 2009); *The NIV Application Commentary: Genesis* (Grand Rapids, MI: Zondervan, 2001), 65–161; *Ancient Near Eastern Thought and the Old Testament: Introducing the Conceptual World of the Hebrew Bible* (Grand Rapids, MI: Baker Academic, 2006), 165–199.

16. Gordon J. Wenham, "Genesis 1-11 as Protohistory," in *Genesis: History, Fiction, or Neither?: Three Views on the Bible's Earliest Chapters*, gen. ed. Charles Halton, series ed. Stanley N. Gundry (Grand Rapids, MI: Zondervan, 2015), 73–97; *Word Biblical Commentary, Genesis 1–15*, Vol. 1, gen. eds. David A. Hubbard, Glenn W. Barker, Old Testament ed. John D. W. Watts (Grand Rapids, MI: Zondervan, 1987), 5–40.

17. Geologists, including Christian geologists, are overwhelmingly in agreement that 4.55 billion years is the most acceptable age of planet Earth [Davis A. Young and Ralph F. Stearley, *The Bible, Rocks and Time: Geological Evidence for the Age of the Earth* (Downers Grove, IL: InterVarsity Press, 2008), 156. Many tens of thousands of repeated cross-testings of carbon-14 dates and radiometric dates confirm their validity and accuracy. Age estimates have been cross-tested (often in rival labs) by using different isotope pairs, and the results of different techniques continually confirm each other within approximately 1-2 percent chance of error, which is highly accurate (http://www.oldearth.org/radiometricdating.htm).

18. Sometime between 3.5 and 4.1 billion years ago [Neil A. Campbell, *Biology*, third ed. (Redwood City, CA: The Benjamin/Cummings Publishing Company, Inc.,1993), 506].

19. Davis A. Young and Ralph F. Stearley, *The Bible, Rocks and Time: Geological Evidence for the Age of the Earth* (Downers Grove, IL: InterVarsity Press, 2008), 243–287; Paul Copan, *That's Just Your Interpretation: Responding to Skeptics Who Challenge Your Faith* (Grand Rapids, MI: BakerBooks, 2001), 150.

20. John Hick, *Evil and the God of Love* (New York: Palgrave MacMillan, second ed. 2007), 316.

21. Michael A. Corey, *Evolution and the Problem of Natural Evil* (Lanham, MD: University Press of America, 2000), 152–156

22. Kenneth R. Miller, *Finding Darwin's God* (New York: HarperCollins, 1999), 290. Miller received his ScB in biology from Brown University and his PhD in biology from the University of Colorado at Boulder. He has taught at Harvard University and is also the author of *Only a Theory: Evolution and the Battle for America's Soul* and (with J. Levine) *Biology: The Living Science*.

23. Michael A. Corey, *Evolution and the Problem of Natural Evil*, 153. Emphasis in the original.

24. Ibid., 154. Emphasis in the original.

25. Michael J. Murray, *Nature Red in Tooth and Claw: Theism and the Problem of Animal Suffering* (New York: Oxford University Press, 2008, paperback ed., 2011), 180. Murray is the senior visiting scholar in philosophy at Franklin and Marshall College.

26. Some Christian readers may be thinking that this creates a contradiction. If conversion of the world to Christianity deprives too many of compatibility-determining free will, why would Jesus in Matt. 28:18–20 command his disciples to go around the world making disciples in all nations? If the conversion of the world to the faith is a bad thing, why would God command it? In response, there is no contradiction here at all. God knows that conversion of the majority of the world's population in a postscientific-industrial-technological-information age would substantially reduce his hiddenness and generate a coercive environment, but, as explained in Part 1, a major objective of creating this world is the temporary process of self-determination of our eternal destiny by significant compatibility-determining free will. If world conditions change in such a way that this free will would be lost, God is expected to intervene to alter the world's conditions to prevent that from occurring by either altering the world's conditions so that a freewill world would continue, or bringing the world to an end by revealing himself to all the world in the appearance of Jesus Christ in great power and glory to resurrect the dead, translate the living, and separate the people who inherit hell from those who inherit heaven, as foretold in Scripture (Matt. 24:14, 27, 30–31; 25:31–34, 41, 46; 1 Thess. 4:16–17; Rev. 1:7; 20–22). If the vast majority of the world was to convert to biblical creationism and Christianity, it would usher in Christ's return and the end of the world, which is consistent with Bible prophecy.

27. Michael J. Murray, *Nature Red in Tooth and Claw*, 179.

28. Put forth by Philip Henry Gosse (1810–1888) in his book *Omphalos* in 1857.

29. Michael J. Murray, *Nature Red in Tooth and Claw*, 183.

30. H. W. Beecher, *Evolution and Religion* (New York: Fords, Howard, and Hurlbert, 1885), 116, as quoted in Michael J. Murray, *Nature Red in Tooth and Claw* (New York: Oxford University Press, 2008, paperback ed., 2011), 183.

31. Such as: Job 38:39–40; 39:28–29; 41:1, 10, 14; Ps. 104.

32. John H. Walton, *The NIV Application Commentary: Genesis* (Grand Rapids, MI: Zondervan, 2001), 115, 187. Nowhere in the Bible does *tob* ("good") indicate a perfectly idyllic being or circumstance, as the following verses affirm: Gen. 24:16; 50:20; Num. 14:7; Eccl. 3:13; Lam. 3:27. Therefore, the interpretation that the "good" creation of Gen. 1 is idyllic and free of pain and death would appear to result more from eisegesis than exegesis, from reading a concept into the text, rather than drawing the writer's intended meaning out of the text.

33. John H. Walton, *The NIV Application Commentary: Genesis*, 134–136; 341–343. Contrary to the thought that Gen. 9:3 teaches that humans were permitted to begin eating animal meat after the flood, the text most likely indicates that in addition to domesticated animals, God's people in Noah's day were granted the privilege of also

eating wild animals that travel in herds, which is similar to his blessing in Gen. 1:29–30 with the privilege of adding wild vegetation to their diet.

34. Charles H. Dodd, *The Epistle of Paul to the Romans* (London: Hodder and Stoughton, 1932), 81.

35. See also Gary R. Habermas and J. P. Moreland, *Beyond Death: Exploring the Evidence for Immortality* (Eugene, OR: Wipf and Stock Publishers, 2004), 305–306.

36. The "great chain of being" is a concept derived from the works of Plato, Aristotle, Plotinus, and Proclus. It was developed during the Middle Ages (fifth to the fifteenth centuries) and reached its fullest depiction in modern Neoplatonism (nineteenth century). It details a strict, religious hierarchical structure of all matter and life, believed to have been decreed by God [Arthur O. Lovejoy, *The Great Chain of Being: A Study of the History of an Idea,* thirteenth ed. (Cambridge, MA: Harvard University Press, 1936, 1984); *The Blackwell Dictionary of Western Philosophy*, eds. Nicholas Bunnin and Jiyuan Yu, 2004, accessed at http://www.blackwellreference.com/public/book.html?id=g9781405_9781405106795, on March 7, 2015].

37. Michael J. Murray, *Nature Red in Tooth and Claw*, 156–157, 167–168.

38. Reasons why God would create some animals that feed on flesh may not be fully understood until the afterlife, but may include: (1) it is necessary to maintain a delicate balance of ecosystems necessary for the emergence and survival of humans; (2) it is a necessary driver of evolution for the emergence of humans; (3) it plays an indispensable role in population control; (4) it is a necessary component for the best human neurological development in the "great chain of being" for a consummate relationship with God; (5) it provides important moral lessons that can impart a disposition of trust, courage, responsibility, repentance, et cetera, as well as make occasion for acts of love that are greater or more diverse than acts of love in a world without any carnivores, all of which are needed if the human mind and disposition is to maximally express love and goodness; (6) carnivorous attacks are judgments held in readiness (Deut. 32:24; Ezek. 5:17) that could operate in a manner that would help maintain divine hiddenness (versus a multitude of judgments in the form of fire balls that strike from the sky); and/or (7) in a postscientific era in which future scientific discovery could point further to God's existence, it adds a necessary element to preserve divine hiddenness.

39. "The Darwinian Problem of Evil," in *The Christian Delusion: Why Faith Fails*, ed. John W. Loftus (Amherst, NY: Prometheus Books, 2010), 257.

40. Martin Luther, as quoted in Michael Murray, *Nature Red in Tooth and Claw*, 124.

41. New Living Translation (NLT), except for verse 20, which is from the New International Version (NIV). Emphasis added.

42. John Calvin, in *Calvin's Commentaries: The Epistles of Paul the Apostle to the Romans and to the Thessalonians*, eds. D. W. Torrance and T. F. Torrance (London: Oliver and Boyd, 1961), 173, as quoted in Michael J. Murray, *Nature Red in Tooth and Claw*, 124.

43. *Matthew Henry's Commentary on the Whole Bible* (Peabody, MA: Hendrickson Publishers, 1991), 1770.

44. Wesley's sermon "The General Deliverance," as quoted in Michael J. Murray, *Nature Red in Tooth and Claw*, 123. Wesley was a Church of England cleric and Christian theologian, and he is credited with founding the Methodist movement. Wesley's theological view was Arminian (as opposed to Calvinist). It is interesting that animal immortality was recognized by prominent Christian thinkers in both Calvinism and Arminianism.

45. Keith Ward, *Rational Theology and the Creativity of God* (New York: Pilgrim, 1982), 201–202. Ward, a British philosopher and theologian, is an ordained priest of the Church of England. His main topics of interest are comparative theology and interplay between science and faith. He received his MA and DD degrees from both Cambridge and Oxford and an honorary DD from the University of Glasgow. Ward is the author of over twenty books, including *Why There Almost Certainly Is a God: Doubting Dawkins* and *The God Conclusion*.

46. Peter Kreeft, *Everything You Ever Wanted to Know About Heaven—But Never Dreamed of Asking* (San Francisco: Ignatius Press, 1990), 45–46.

47. C. S. Lewis, *The Problem of Pain* (New York: HarperCollins Publishers, 1940, 1996), 140–147.

48. Aquinas' argument is discussed by Habermas and Moreland in *Beyond Death*, 106–108; and by Michael J. Murray in *Nature Red in Tooth and Claw*, 123.

49. John H. Walton, *The NIV Application Commentary: Genesis*, 131–139; Paul Copan, *Is God a Moral Monster?: Making Sense of the Old Testament God* (Grand Rapids, MI: Baker Books, 2011), 29.

50. Jason Offutt, *Darkness Walks: The Shadow People Among Us* (San Antonio, TX: Anomalist Books, 2009), 137. Offutt is a writer and college journalism instructor. At various times in his career, he has also been a newspaper editor, general assignment reporter, photographer, newspaper consultant, and the mayor of a small Midwestern town. His books include *Haunted Missouri: A Ghostly Guide to the Show-Me State's Most Spirited Spots* and a collection of parenting humor entitled *On Being Dad*.

51. Scott S. Smith, *The Soul of Your Pet: Evidence for the Survival of Animals After Death* (Edmonds, WA: Holmes Publishing Group, 1998), 12. Smith is an investigative reporter who, in the early 1990s, asked readers of several magazines to send him letters of any experiences which might have a bearing on the subject of an afterlife for animals. He was stunned by the response. "Rather than 'ghost stories' you could dismiss as the result of overworked imaginations, the reports which came in were amazing in their variety, complexity, and credibility. Skeptics who would be eager to debunk the encounters as the result of the wishful thinking of grieving pet owners will be sorely disappointed. Experiences were sometimes lengthy and multi-sensory, occurring to perfectly normal people who usually did not have supernatural experiences of any kind" (p. 7).

52. Brad Steiger, *Shadow World: True Encounters with Beings from the Dark Side* (San Antonio, TX: Anomalist Books, 2007), 150–152.

53. Scott S. Smith, *The Soul of Your Pet: Evidence for the Survival of Animals After Death*, 43–51.

54. Applying Paul Copan's phrase from his book *Is God a Moral Monster?: Making Sense of the Old Testament God* (Grand Rapids, MI: Baker Books, 2011), 17.

55. John W. Loftus, "The Darwinian Problem of Evil," in *The Christian Delusion*, 258–259.

56. Isaiah's animal metaphors are briefly discussed in chapter 10 of this book.

57. Scott S. Smith, *The Soul of Your Pet: Evidence for the Survival of Animals After Death*, 118.

58. Ibid.

59. In this view, "animal pain and suffering has such a radically different character that it has no moral significance whatsoever." It is reputed that Descartes "held that animals do not experience pain and suffering, or indeed any sentient state. Thus, Descartes and the Cartesians are reputed to have been seen torturing animals and marveling at how well their behavior mimicked the behavior of organisms, like ourselves, who *really do* experience pain and suffering" [Michael J. Murray, *Nature Red in Tooth and Claw*, 42. Emphasis in the original].

60. Michael J. Murray, *Nature Red in Tooth and Claw*, 52–58; C. S. Lewis, *The Problem of Pain*, 134–137.

61. Michael J. Murray, *Nature Red in Tooth and Claw*, 57. Murray has a summarization of possible mental states of animals with respect to the nature and degree of animal pain and suffering in chapter 2 of his book.

62. Marilyn McCord Adams, *Horrendous Evils and the Goodness of God* (Ithaca, NY: Cornell University Press, 2000), 28. Adams received her PhD from Cornell University, her ThM from Princeton Theological Seminary, and her DD from the University of Oxford. She is distinguished research professor of philosophy at Rutgers University. She is the author of *William Ockham* and coeditor of *The Problem of Evil*.

63. John W. Loftus, *Why I Became an Atheist*, 238.

64. Anthropomorphizing is attributing human characteristics and feelings to nonhuman things or beings.

65. Richard Dawkins, *River out of Eden: A Darwinian View of Life* (New York: HarperCollins, 1996), 131–132; John W. Loftus, *Why I Became an Atheist*, 238.

66. Gus Mills, "About Lions—Ecology and Behavior," African Lion Working Group. Http://www.african-lion.org/lions_e.htm, accessed on March 3, 2014.

67. John W. Loftus, *Why I Became an Atheist*, 234–235. This is an argument presented by William L. Rowe in "Evil and Theodicy," *The Improbability of God,* eds. Michael Martin and Ricki Monnier (Amherst, NY: Prometheus Books, 2003), 272.

Part 3
The Problem of Suffering in Hell

10
Would a Loving God Torture People in Hell?

Synopsis

Critics of the view of hell as a place of literal fire and torture argue that its punishment is pointless, revengeful, and too severe for any crime we could commit. Therefore, hell is a place that a perfectly loving and good God would neither create, nor allow.

A Christian response is that the critics are correct that the literal torture chamber view of hell is not something God would create or allow, but such a view of hell is not biblical, as it does not hold up under exegetical analysis. As such, a hell of flaming tortures should not be in the discussion about whether the punishment of hell is consistent with a perfectly loving and good God.

Many opponents of Christianity are eager to point out what they believe are several problems with the Christian concept of a hell. Hell seems to them to be purely retributive. They point to the Bible verse that says, "'It is mine to avenge; I will repay,' says the Lord" (Rom. 12:19) and think the punishment is inflicted in the spirit of moral outrage, or personal vengeance. Hell seems to them to make God out to be a spiteful retaliator, deriving satisfaction from making people suffer, and suffer intensely—emotionally and physically—for eternity.

Further objection to hell stems from the idea that it is a ghastly and gloomy realm without any hope in which the condemned writhe in pain from both imaginable and unimaginable tortures that make a medieval dungeon look almost humane. How could even the wickedest of people, such as Nero, Hitler, or Saddam Hussein, deserve hell? We no longer subject even the worst criminals to medieval tortures, so, it is argued, shouldn't we expect God to be at least as humane as we (sinners) are? Is it any wonder, then, that they call the idea of hell ludicrous, preposterous, or "morally absurd"?[1] Atheist George H. Smith says it is to be "the most vicious and reprehensible doctrine of classical Christianity."[2]

Atheist (and former Christian) David Mills not only finds the idea of hell to be "sadistic" and "barbaric," but also "pointless," as it is torturing for the satisfaction God would get from torturing—"a purposeless, vengeful end in itself."[3] As discussed previously, any suffering that does not serve to bring about a greater good is pointless. God and pointless suffering cannot coexist. This is because God is good and therefore not willing for anyone to suffer unnecessarily, or unproductively, and he is all-able to prevent any such suffering. Therefore, if the suffering in hell isn't necessary, there would be a major contradiction in Christian teachings.

Not only does hell seem to the critics to be pointless, but also unjust. The punishment does not appear to fit the crime. Never-ending suffering, some of which may be torture, they argue, seems far too horrendous a punishment for the meager offense of not believing in God, especially when God makes it so difficult to believe due to his so-called hiddenness and bizarre Bible stories of talking animals, the parting of the Red Sea, and so forth.

Moreover, the critics argue, since hell is so final, shouldn't the condemned get a second chance after death? After all, it appears that since most people have no idea of the potential consequence of hell befalling them, they could not make an informed choice for heaven or hell. As atheist Keith M. Parsons says, "Surely, nobody has actually weighed the two options: 'Hmmm . . . eternal bliss or eternal torment? Which will it be?' . . . Only a lunatic would consciously choose eternal torment over eternal bliss."[4]

All of the criticism can be boiled down to an argument that the punishment in hell goes against the character of God because the suffering in hell is: (1) pointless; and (2) disproportionate to the crime. In this chapter, and in the next, I tackle these issues by uncovering the actual hell of the Bible and exposing the myths. I explain why hell is not actually pointless. I compare the actual punishment to the actual crime and show why the punishment isn't really disproportionate.

10.1 Is Hell a Torture Chamber?

During the European Dark Ages, Christian literature reflects a predominantly held view of hell as a place of literal darkness, fire, beatings, and rotting corpses. The souls of the unsaved at death leave their bodies (the disembodied state [Hades]) and undergo a life review followed by irrevocable judgment and suffering from the pain and horror inflicted by the punishments of hell.

The literature embellishes on Scripture with all sorts of imagined horrors.[5] Following a misunderstanding of the "eye for eye, tooth for tooth" principle of punishment (Ex. 21:24; Lev. 24:20), called *lex talionis*, and a principle of a proportional measure of punishment for the measure of every sin, a variety of bizarre tortures was invented. Damned murderers are in pits being bitten by reptiles and their bodies filled with worms. Women who had abortions sit neck deep in the excretions of others. Those speaking evil either hang by their tongues or have their mouths filled with hot coals. Adulterous women dangle over boiling mire. "Idolaters are driven up cliffs by demons where they plunge to the rocks below, only to be driven up again. Those who turned their backs on God are turned and baked slowly in the fires of hell."[6]

The conception of hell as a torture chamber was codified in the fourteenth century by Dante Alighieri's *Divine Comedy* that depicted it as a place of heavy darkness and dense gloom where people suffer nightmares of stark terror.[7] Some of them boil in blood while others run from hoards of biting snakes, and still others are trapped inside lead cloaks. People scream and wail and writhe in horror and excruciating agony.

Despite rising concerns by many Protestant reformers, a number of Protestant theologians and ministers of the eighteenth and nineteenth centuries saw hell as a literal lake of fire and brimstone where the unsaved would burn and wail forever and ever. They interpreted the Bible to teach that in the final judgment (Rev. 20:11–13), condemned souls are resurrected[8] and cast into a realm of blackest darkness[9] and a lake of fire (*Gehenna* or *tartarus*) (Rev. 20:14–15) where they forever weep and grind their teeth[10] and writhe in agonizing pain from beatings,[11] burnings by fire,[12] and the nightmare of rotting while being eaten by worms.[13]

We find the likes of New England theologian Jonathan Edwards (1703–1758), who taught that God personally tortures the damned in hell, fearfully and painfully, with liquid fire that sears every part of the body and soul so that they suffer extreme horror, pain, and inexpressible torment:

The God that holds you over the pit of hell, much in the same way as one holds a spider, or some loathsome insect, over the fire, abhors you, and is dreadfully provoked; his wrath towards you burns like fire. . . . You hang by a slender thread, with flames of divine wrath flashing about it and ready every moment to singe it, and burn it asunder. . . . Consider this, you that yet remain in an unregenerate state. That God will execute the fierceness of his anger implies that he will inflict wrath without any pity . . . you shall be tormented. . . . There will be no end to this exquisite horrible misery.[14]

Edwards elaborates:

To help your conception, imagine yourself to be cast into a fiery oven, all of a glowing heat, or into the midst of a blowing brick-kiln, or of a great furnace, where your pain would be as much greater than that occasioned by accidentally touching a coal of fire, as the heat is greater. Imagine also that your body were to lie there for a quarter of an hour, full of fire, as full within and without as a bright coal of fire, all the while full of quick sense; what horror would you feel at the entrance of such a furnace! And how long would that quarter of an hour seem to you! . . . And how much greater would be the effect if you knew you must endure it for a whole year, and how vastly greater still if you knew you must endure it for a thousand years! O then, how would your heart sink, if you thought, if you knew, that you must bear it forever and ever! . . . That after millions of ages, your torment would be no nearer to an end, than ever it was; and that you never, never should be delivered! But your torment in Hell will be immeasurably greater than this illustration represents.[15]

Nineteenth-century British preacher Charles H. Spurgeon (1834–1892) also taught the literal view of hell:

Thine heart beating high with fever, thy pulse rattling at an enormous rate in agony, thy limbs cracking like the martyrs in the fire and yet unburnt, thyself put in a vessel of hot oil, pained yet coming out undestroyed, all thy veins becoming a road for the hot feet of pain to travel on, every nerve a string on which the devil shall ever play his diabolical tune.[16]

10.2 Interpretation

By the twentieth century, however, civilized societies were going through changes in laws, education, medicine, economic opportunities, and customs such that leaders, philosophers, and then the general population came to see the unnecessary torture of humans (and animals) as immoral. With the widespread belief that unnecessary pain in *this life* is wrong, it became all too clear that tortuous pain and burning flesh for eternity in hell had to be the worst of all imaginable evils. Contrasted with this belief about hell was the picture in the Bible of a perfectly loving and good God. Consequently, the idea of God inflicting such torture didn't make sense.

Preachers who've struggled with the dichotomy either stopped sermonizing on hell or stayed away from any horrific details.[17] Sermon time for preaching about hell was instead filled with more preaching about God's love and grace.

While there were fewer and fewer sermons on the torturous pain of hellfire, theologians reexamined the underlying exegesis of Bible passages on hell. Exegesis is the interpretation of a text that follows a systematic method of a multiplex of critical analyses. The theologian who has completed a properly accredited doctorate program in the principles, rules, and techniques of biblical exegesis has the education to be an expert in exegesis. Such theologians are sometimes called exegetes (the writers of Bible commentaries or articles in theological journals).

Exegetes utilize specific methods of critical examination of a text to uncover the meaning most likely intended by the writer, without (ideally) bias from doctrinal beliefs. All analyses can fall under three headings: literary analysis, cultural-historical analysis, and theological analysis. Within each of these are subcategories of various kinds of analyses. Literary analysis, for example, includes lexical analysis, which includes various forms of analysis, such as etymological, semantic, and syntax analyses; literary analysis also includes the study of: derivation, usage, sociolinguistic distinctions, genres, compositional structure, grammar, context, word forms, figures of speech, metaphors, similes, hendiadys, hyperbole, overstatement, synecdoche, metonymy, and euphemism.

A cultural-historical analysis is vital to the interpreter to find the meaning of a text. It includes background studies in the literature and world views of the ancient Near East that cover ancient Near Eastern history, traditions, cosmology, geography, cosmography, astronomy, architecture, technology, etc.[18] Theological analysis includes interpreting a text in light of the broader context and system of exegetically derived doctrines concerning God (his characteristics and character), our relationship to God, and God's plans for humankind. The exegete (Bible commentator) considers possible interpretations and, by a process of elimination, rules out the ones that conflict with the well-established definition of God, his conduct, and the big picture of his plans for creation.

The accuracy of the interpretation depends on the strength of the methods utilized. A strong system of methods includes a comprehensive and in-depth array of analyses. But some exegetes, unfortunately, utilize a significantly less comprehensive and less in-depth array of analyses and techniques, and thus follow a weak method for interpretation. The result is the existence of some published commentaries and articles that are exegetically unreliable in a pursuit of truth.

For example, with respect to genre analysis, the exegete should consider that each genre of Scripture (e.g., narrative, prophecy, poetry, letter) has a different set of rules of interpretation. This is because each genre has a different degree of figurative language, metaphor, narrative prose, allegory, etc. Thus, prophetic or apocalyptic writings have a higher degree of figurative, symbolic, or allegorical language than narrative prose writings. Recognition of such differences can avoid the mistake of interpreting a text literally that was meant by the Bible writer to be understood metaphorically, and thus miss the intended meaning.

This is why it is important to choose your Bible commentary carefully. I've examined many commentaries, checking for indications of a comprehensive and in-depth body of work that is inclusive of the widest and deepest span of different kinds of analyses and background studies, and the most intelligent theological mooring. And I usually compare commentaries when studying any given Bible text, in addition to using various study tools, such as a lexicon, a theological wordbook, a concordance, or a Bible dictionary.

With regard to the views of hell, unlocking the truest understanding is a matter of an exegete's utilization of the greatest comprehensive and in-depth multiplex of analyses that enables the exegete to better classify words intended by the Bible writers (under inspiration) to have metaphorical meaning versus literal meaning. In the following, it becomes clear that the strongest exegetical analysis and interpretation leads us to understand that hell's fire was not intended to be literal—that hell is not a torture chamber of literal fiery pits, burn wounds, beatings, pitch black darkness, and rotting corpses.

10.3 Metaphorical Terms for Heaven Imply Metaphorical Terms for Hell

As discussed, the issue is whether the verses on hell that mention fire, darkness, rotting corpses, beatings, etc. are literal or metaphorical. Metaphor is a figure of speech in a word or group of words that ordinarily designates one object or action that is applied to another object or action to which it is not literally applicable or is symbolically representative, thus making an implied comparison. The implied comparison characterizes the main object or action, or conveys deeper meaning or concepts that are more effectively understood and remembered.

Metaphors are used extensively in ancient Near Eastern literature and in the Bible. Many biblical examples could be listed. "Eating" and "drinking" are metaphors for learning from revealed truth. Various forms of vegetation and animals are metaphors for aspects of human character (Matt. 3:10; 7: 6, 15, 17-19; 10:16; 12:33; Acts 20:29). Popular animal metaphors include: lion, wolf, snake, ox, pig, dog, and eagle. To emphasize Herod Antipas' (20 BC–AD 39) craftiness or to characterize him as crafty, Jesus referred to him as a "fox" (Luke 13:32). Both a "lion" and a "lamb" are a few of the metaphors for the messiah Jesus (Rev. 5:5–6, 8, 12–13; 19:7; 21:9). Metaphors for God include a "rock" (Deut. 32:4), a "father," and a "shepherd" (Ps. 23:1). A "bride" is a metaphor for God's organized people (church) on Earth (Rev. 19:7; 21:2, 9–10; 22:17). Jesus referred to himself as the "bread" of life from heaven (John 6:32–35, 41, 48, 50–51, 58). The Bible is so replete with metaphors, I would need more space than this chapter just to *list* them.

The theologian believing in a literal hellfire recognizes the fact that the Bible is full of metaphors, but insists that the verses on hell happen to be verses in which there aren't any metaphors. A more comprehensive and in-depth literary analysis, however, provides us with several reasons why we can be sure that *all* of the Bible verses on hell about fire, darkness, beatings, and rotting bodies are metaphorical.

One reason is that Bible verses on *heaven* are nearly unequivocally metaphorical, and, if the texts on heaven are metaphorical, then we should expect that texts on hell are also metaphorical. A clear metaphor on heaven is in Isaiah 65: "'The wolf and the lamb will feed together, and the lion will eat straw like the ox, but dust will be the serpent's food. They will neither harm nor destroy on all my holy mountain,' says the Lord" (v. 25). Isaiah is not revealing to us that there will be animals in the heavenly life, at least not directly (which does not suggest that there is no immortal life for animals, as discussed in chapter 9). Rather, this passage is a metaphorical promise of a future heavenly community in which there is complete peace, safety, restfulness, and blessing. God will do away with the "beast" in his true people (in heaven) and all "lions" shall behave as "oxen." The types of animals are carefully chosen in light of known animal behaviors that metaphorically represent sinful characters. It is also apparent that the animal types are chosen in light of the ceremonial laws concerning clean and unclean animals (Lev. 11; Deut. 14). Christian apologist Paul Copan says the Israelites "were to avoid the unholy activity of preying [like a beast] upon the vulnerable in society."[19] By depicting unclean animals dwelling with the clean in the new earth (heaven), further depth of meaning might be implied that God's salvation was meant to be offered to all peoples, the clean and unclean, the holy and unholy, the Jew and the Gentile.

An even clearer example of metaphor regarding heaven is in Revelation 21–22, where John also speaks of heaven using metaphors in order to characterize the heavenly life. In Revelation 21, he tells of a new heaven/earth without any "sea" (*thalassa*) (v. 1) that is fully lighted by God's presence that dispels away any darkness of night (vv. 11, 23; Rev. 22:5). This is significant because the ancient Israelites associated the sea (cosmic sea[20]) and darkness as elements of chaos and a natural threat to God's creation of an orderly and functional cosmos.[21] The dark of night was also associated with robbers and rapists. But a fully lighted city was an image of a life without fear or harm. Thus the absence of the cosmic sea and darkness suitably symbolize John's epithet of a new life of peace, security, well-being, and blessing.

To add to his depiction, John describes a floating holy city (v. 2) with dimensions that form a perfect cube (v. 16), with impenetrable walls 1,400 miles (2,200 kilometers) high (v. 12) and two hundred feet (sixty-five meters) thick (v. 17), and with twelve foundations (v. 14) and twelve open pearly gates (vv. 12–13, 21, 25) attended by twelve angels (v. 12). To the ancient Israelite, such a city would indeed seem to be absolutely unassailable—a fitting metaphor for a life of perfect peace and security. It is quite expected, then, metaphorically, for the first century writer to depict heaven as an impenetrable and everlasting structure. Every strong city known to them had high, sturdy walls. But literal walls would not protect anyone from supernatural beings that could pass through them (Luke 14:30–31; John 20:19; Acts 12:5–7). To further depict heaven's safety, the city is pictured with gates always open, suggesting there will be no combatants for them to contend with.

John's depiction of the new life as a life of well-being and blessing in the new heaven/earth also tells of feasting (Rev. 19:7–9). Many in the ancient Near East worked hard from dawn to dusk just to survive. So the imagery of a bountiful wedding supper fit for princes and princesses was a picture of the richest blessing, inheritance, and honor.

The new heaven/earth has crystal clear water (Rev. 22:1), the tree of life (Rev. 22:2), and "no longer any curse" (Rev. 22:3). The tree of life for "the healing of the nations" (Rev. 22:2) aptly conveys the consummated psychospiritual condition discussed in chapter 3.1.

Inside the city is a great street of gold (Rev. 21:21) and the walls and foundations are decorated with every kind of precious jewel and precious metal (vv. 18–20), symbolizing the greatest of wealth, abundance, and blessing. Yet the most precious to us are the diamond and platinum, and these are conspicuously missing from the list. It is thought that diamonds are missing because they were too difficult to build with.[22] Platinum is obviously missing because it was not known of until the sixteenth century. Pearls, however, adorned the richest and most powerful of John's time. Yet John says the most impoverished of God's redeemed will be surrounded by unimaginable wealth.

Heaven is represented by the absence of a temple in the holy city (Rev. 21:22), as "they will see his face, and his name will be on their foreheads" (Rev. 22:4). The ancient Israelite was all too familiar with the need for a temple to bridge the gap between fallen humankind and a holy God. The absence of a temple, then, is a fitting metaphor for the end of the era of divine hiddenness and the terrestrial life, and the beginning of glorification in the celestial life in a direct "face-to-face" relationship with God.

The fact that John is writing about a vision (in Rev. 21–22) does not mean that the objects depicted should be interpreted as literal objects, as there are Bible passages that unequivocally show that images in vision are sometimes, if not many times, metaphorical images. For example, the prophet Daniel experienced a vision in which he saw strange-looking animals, including a lion with wings, a bear with three ribs in its mouth, and a leopard with four wings (Dan. 7). An angel later explained to Daniel that the animals he saw were metaphorical for nations (Dan. 8:20–25). The lion represented Babylonia, the bear represented Medo-Persia, the leopard represented Greece, and a terrifying and frightening beast represented Rome. Thus, God shows the future using objects that are not literal.

Another example of a vision of metaphorical things is in Acts 10. Peter experiences a vision in which "he saw heaven opened and something like a large sheet being let down to earth by its four corners" (v. 11). It contained various unclean animals that the Jews were forbidden to eat. A voice from heaven told Peter to kill and eat. But Peter, perhaps thinking this to be a test, affirmed his conviction to "never eat anything impure or unclean" (v. 14). But the voice then told him to not consider anything impure that God has made clean (v. 15). Peter affirmed his conviction two more times before the sheet was taken back to heaven. Then later he reflected on the vision and realized that God was reproving him for his favoritism against Gentiles. God wasn't telling Peter literally he could eat unclean animals. He was telling him metaphorically to share the gospel also with Gentiles. He exclaimed, "I now realize how true it is that God does not show favoritism but accepts men from every nation who fear him and do what is right" (v. 34).

To summarize, in the Bible passages about heaven there are many metaphorical terms, and few literal terms. It is apparent that the metaphors were meant to characterize heaven, rather than provide literal depictions of details. As such, there is strong indication that the Bible passages about hell have similar metaphorical terminology. Moreover, there are other textual confirmations in the Bible that terms for hell are metaphorical, as discussed in the remainder of the chapter.

10.4 Hell's "Fire"

Hell is depicted by eternal fire and smoke (Isa. 34:9–10; 66:24; Matt. 5:22; 18:8, 9; 25:41; Mark 9:44, 46, 47–48; Rev. 14:11; 20:10). Long before the time of Jesus, the ancient Israelites used "eternal fire" and "smoke" to metaphorically characterize condemnation. The Hinnom Valley (*ge-hinnom*) was a ravine south of Jerusalem that had a long history of evil and ruin. The deities of polytheism were worshiped there, and sometimes worship included child sacrifice (Jer. 7:31–32; 19:5–6; 32:35; 2 Chron. 28:3; 33:6). Jeremiah denounced such practices by saying that the Hinnom Valley would become the valley of God's judgment, a place of slaughter (Jer. 7:32; 19:5–7). King

Josiah put a stop to the Hinnom Valley sacrifices (2 Kings 23:10), and it came to be used as a place where human excrement and garbage were disposed of; worms could always be found there and sulfur fires burned continually.[23]

During a few hundred years before Christ, the Hebrew name *ge-hinnom* (Hinnom Valley) evolved into *gehenna* (hell) ("valley of whining" or "valley of lamentation").[24] The valley of gehenna was then widely used as a metaphor for the final punishment of the wicked,[25] although a small number of Jews failed to recognize the metaphor and thought the valley would literally become the place of hellfire and judgment (1 Enoch 27:1–2; 54:1–6; 56:3–4; 90:26–28; 4 Ezra 7:36).[26]

Later, around AD 28–30, Jesus shared his message about hell. He spoke of it as a celestial place not located on Earth (Matt. 25:34, 41; John 14:2; Heb. 11:16). Jesus used the old, familiar metaphor of the gehenna trash dump—a dump that most Jews had been using for generations, as it suitably characterized the awful ruin of the condemned soul in hell (Isa. 66:24) (Jesus also used the Hellenistic term that is translated "hades"[27]). The literary parallelism of the gospel of Matthew shows Jesus taught that the "judgment" (*krisis*) (condemnation) is synonymous with going into "the fire of hell" (*gehenna*) (Matt. 5:22).[28] Paul also speaks of fire metaphorically as the judgment (1 Cor. 3:13–15), as does James (James 3:6).[29] Thus, textual evidence is supportive of metaphorical use of terms for hell's fire.

When writing the book of Revelation, John didn't use the gehenna trash dump metaphor used by Jesus, but instead chose to depict hell as a lake (*limnē*) of burning sulfur (Rev. 19:20; 20:10, 14–15; 21:8). It may be that John adapted an ancient image from the Egyptian and Greek underworlds that contained fiery lakes and rivers (e.g., rivers Pyriphlegethon and Styx) (Coffin Texts[30]). An image in the Papyrus of Ani (ca. 1250 BC), a version of the Book of the Dead, has been described as follows:

> The scene shows four cynocephalous baboons sitting at the corners of a rectangular pool. On each side of this pool is a flaming brazier. The pool's red colour indicates that it is filled with a fiery liquid, reminding one of the "Lake of Fire" frequently mentioned in the Book of the Dead.[31]

Here again we see a Bible writer using an image familiar to his audience (in Asia Minor) to metaphorically characterize the fate of the wicked. In fact, the Bible writers used fire as a metaphor for a number of different things. In addition to fire being a metaphor for judgment (1 Cor. 3:13–15; Matt. 5:22), God is called a "consuming fire" (Deut. 4:24; Hebrews 12:29) ("God's burning holiness"[32]) who has a throne "flaming with fire" that has a "river of fire" issuing from beneath the throne (Dan. 7:9–10). In John's vision, the exalted Jesus has eyes like "blazing fire" (Rev. 1:14). Elijah was carried to heaven in a "chariot of fire" (2 Kings 2:11). Fire is also a metaphor for discord (Luke 12:49), boastful words (James 3:5–6), and sexual desire (1 Cor. 7:9). Jesus visibly appears in the sky in power and glory, metaphorically "in blazing fire" (2 Thess. 1:7) (perhaps a bright light).

Metaphorical fire is also used by extrabiblical Jewish writers. The Torah was said to have been written with "black fire on white fire" (Jerusalem Talmud, Shekalim 6:1, 49d), and the tree of life was described as gold looking in "the form of fire" (2 Enoch 8:4). There are mountains of fire (Pseudo-Philo 11:5), rivers of fire (1 Enoch 17:5), thrones of fire (Apoc. Abraham 18:3), lashes of fire (T. Abraham. 12:1)—even angels and demons of fire (2 Bar. 21:6; T. of Sol. 1:10).

Hell's fire is said to be eternal, unquenchable, and always continually burning (Isa. 34:9–10; 66:24; Matt. 18:8; 25:41; Mark 9:48; Rev. 14:11; 20:10). These descriptions were meant to metaphorically convey the irrevocability of God's judgment. By "unquenchable," the writers depicted an afterlife that was unstoppable or irreversible. This is important because some of God's judgments *were* stopped or quenched. For example, Moses interceded and pleaded with God to spare the rebellious Hebrews of the Exodus, and their destruction was stopped. Therefore, with regard to hell, it was important that the people be warned that no amount of intercession or pleading would stop or quench the coming judgment. To drive this warning home, the Bible writers used the examples in Jeremiah and Ezekiel as metaphors for an "irrevocable judgment," and in the case of hell an "irrevocable condemnation." It is no surprise, then, to find in Jude 7 that the destruction by "eternal fire" of the cities of Sodom and Gomorrah served as a metaphorical example of those who were condemned to hell. Obviously these cities are not burning still today, so a literal interpretation doesn't make sense. But as a metaphor, it makes perfect sense. The warning is that no amount of intercession or pleading would stop or quench the coming judgment and condemnation.

The image of the continually rising smoke in Isaiah (Isa. 34:9–10; 66:24) is echoed in the New Testament in the words of John: "The smoke of their torment rises for ever and ever" (Rev. 14:11; see also 18:9, 18; 19:3). The situation of the condemned is "for ever and ever." Thus, both the perpetually burning gehenna valley trash dump and the Egyptian lake of fire are appropriate metaphors of judgment's irrevocability.

Based on the foregoing discussion, it is apparent that the Bible texts associating hell with fire are probably speaking metaphorically to characterize hell. As such, textual support for a literal hellfire appears lacking.

10.5 Hell's "Darkness" and "Death"

Hell is also depicted as a place of darkness (blackest darkness or outer darkness) (Matt. 8:12; 22:13; 25:30; 2 Pet. 2:4, 17; Jude 6, 13). Darkness symbolically carries multiple meanings of God's judgment and wrath (Amos 8:9); being accursed (Rev. 22:3a, 5); cultivation of unrighteousness (Isa. 9:2; Matt. 4:16 Luke 1:79; John 3:19; Rom. 13:12; 1 John 1:5–7; 2;9, 11); ignorance of divine things and human duties (Rom. 2:19; 2 Cor. 4:6); loss of the richest inheritance available to humans (Matt. 8:12); and the power of Satan (Acts 26:18). Based on these metaphors, it seems likely that "blackest darkness" (Jude 13) metaphorically characterizes hell as a state of eternal unrest from sin, estrangement from God, and mediocrity (although, as discussed in chapter 11.1, the depictions about darkness may not be entirely metaphorical as the resplendent blessing of physical light in hell may be scarce from the lack of God's presence).

In contrast, light is a metaphor for the greatest gain, fellowship with God, the consummate life of holiness (Matt. 5:16), and God's revelation (Luke 2:32). Those in heaven live in the "light" of God (Micah 7:9), in the beatific relationship, as "God is light; in him there is no darkness at all" (1 John 1:5; 4:8).

In addition to the metaphors of "light" and "darkness" are the metaphors of "life" and "death." Life is a metaphor for heaven (John 1:4–5; 1 Tim. 6:17–19). By contrast, hell as "darkness" is closely associated with the metaphor of "death." For example, see Isaiah 9:2: "The people walking in darkness . . . those living in the land of the shadow of death," and Matthew 4:16: "Those people living in darkness . . . living in the land of the shadow of death" (see also Luke 1:79).

For Bible writers, "death" (*thanatos* in the Greek) meant a literal bodily death, but it was used metaphorically "as a symbol of final separation from God, which we might describe . . . as spiritual death,"[33] the disastrous state of those who are living "dead" in their sins in estrangement from God. Speaking to the Ephesian church, Paul said, "You were dead in your transgressions and sins, in which you used to live when you followed the ways of this world and of the ruler of the kingdom of the air [Satan]" (Eph. 2:1–2; see also Rom. 7:9–10; 8:6). And as Matthew Henry (1662–1714) says, "Sin is the death of the soul."[34]

The ultimate spiritual death is in hell (Acts 14:15). Jesus' disciples thought of it as the worst of all curses. This is evident in what Jesus taught: "Be afraid of the One who can destroy (*apóllymi*) both soul and body in hell" (Matt. 10:28). To the first century Israelite, the Greek word for destroy (*apóllymi*) does not mean annihilation, but rather to be rendered useless, ruined, lost, or to be put out of the way entirely.[35] Thus, "death" is a Bible metaphor for the "ruin and misery" of the unsaved soul. All such are "dead" in their terrestrial life (the first "death"), and if they continue to cultivate a selfish and malicious character and rejection of trust in God, their "death" is irrevocably sealed (the second "death") (Rom. 1:32; 2 Cor. 3:7; James 1:15; Rev. 2:11; 20:6, 14; 21:8, 11; Isa. 22:14).

Given the array of metaphorical uses of darkness and death in the Bible, it appears most likely that the Bible verses associating hell with darkness and death are speaking metaphorically to characterize hell, and not to describe it literally (although due to the lack of God's presence in hell the resplendent blessing of physical light may be scarce).

10.6 "Grinding of Teeth"

Some assume that people in hell are literally grinding their teeth because they are suffering excruciating physical pain from hellfire or beatings. The Bible verses cited are Matt. 8:12; 13:42; 22:13; 24:51; 25:30; and Luke 13:28. However, it is apparent that the gospel writers used an Old Testament metaphor of "weeping and grinding of teeth" to depict the awfulness of being condemned. In Zephaniah we read that "the great day of the LORD is near, it is near, and hasteth greatly, even the voice of the day of the Lord: the mighty man shall cry there bitterly" (1:14 KJV). The psalmist says, "The wicked man will see and be vexed, he will gnash his teeth and waste away; the longings of the wicked will come to nothing" (Ps. 112:10). According to theologian and lawyer Edward W. Fudge:

The expression "weeping and grinding of teeth" seems to indicate two separate activities. The first reflects the terror of the doomed as they begin to truly realize that God has thrown them out as worthless and as they anticipate the execution of His sentence. The second seems to express the bitter rage and acrimony they feel toward God, who sentenced them, and toward the redeemed, who will forever be blessed.[36]

The Old Testament metaphor is a fitting characterization of hell as a state of life in which there is bitter regret and deep sorrow. It seems most probable, then, that, instead of depicting a literal grinding of teeth, the gospel writers used the Old Testament metaphor for this purpose.

10.7 "Rotting Corpses"

Unburied and rotting dead bodies is another Old Testament metaphor for the ones condemned by God (Isa. 66:24; Jer. 9:22; 16:4; 34:20) that is echoed in the New Testament (Matt. 24:28; Mark 9:48; Luke 17:37). "And they will go out and look upon the dead bodies of those who rebelled against me; their worm will not die . . . and they will be loathsome to all mankind" (Isa. 66:24). Jesus echoed this metaphorical imagery when teaching about God's judgment that comes as a "thief in the night" (1 Thess. 5:2; see also Matt. 24:43; Luke 12:39; Heb. 9:27). At the end of the world, Jesus adjudicates all remaining cases and visibly appears in the sky in power and glory to separate the "sheep" from the "goats," the "wheat" from the "weeds," the saved from the unsaved. Some will be taken into the heavenly community while others will "go away to eternal punishment" (Matt. 25:46). Two will be grinding grain together; "one will be taken and the other left" (Luke 17:35). The disciples asked Jesus about the fate of those "left" behind and Jesus replied, "Where there is a carcass, there the vultures will gather" (Matt. 24:28; from Jer. 16:4); "where 'their worm does not die.'" (Mark 9:48).

The imagery of unburied dead bodies infested with worms was a fitting metaphor for the condemned, because in ancient Israelite culture, dead people not properly buried, "like refuse lying on the ground," were thought to be cursed by God (Jer. 9:22; 16:4).[37] Moreover, in the early first century there were thousands of animals being sacrificed weekly, and there was a sewage system for the blood and fat to flow outside, where it gathered in a pool. There were worms constantly ingesting that. It was a fitting image of the worst of curses. Thus, words or phrases of unburied and rotting bodies have appropriate metaphorical use in depicting the state of the ones judged for hell.

Today most literalists do not believe those in hell will literally have rotting dead bodies consumed by worms. This may be partly because it is impossible for a finite entity to decay or be consumed endlessly; a finite point in time must eventually be reached when there would be nothing left to decay or be consumed. The same reasoning can be applied to a body endlessly burning. Eventually a literal fire would completely consume a body capable of burning. Therefore, the Bible texts associating hell with unburied and rotting bodies are probably speaking metaphorically to characterize hell as the worst of all curses.

10.8 "Beatings"

Likewise, those in hell are not literally "beaten with many blows" (Luke 12:47). Jesus told a parable of the watchful servants (Luke 12:35–48). The main theme of the parable is that of preparing to meet Jesus when he visibly appears in the sky to carry out judgment on the world by laboring in loving service for the King. Peter asked Jesus if he was telling the parable to the Jews, or to the Gentiles, or both (v. 41). Jesus responded that his parable was for both the Jews *and* the Gentiles, but he made a distinction between the degree of suffering in hell for the unsaved Jew, who is "beaten with many blows" (v. 47), and the unsaved Gentile, who is "beaten with few blows" (v. 48). It was an allegorical story of a human master and his servants, so the punishment would be in the context of the story, such as receiving a beating. Therefore, there are no exegetical grounds for interpreting the punishment in hell as consisting of literal beatings. What is taught is that those with greater knowledge and opportunity (i.e., the Jews) will be tormented with worse regret for not seeking a true conversion to God (Matt. 7:21–23).

10.9 Confirmation from Textual Inconsistencies

Confirmation that the images of hell are metaphors comes from the textual inconsistencies that arise when we try to see hell as a place where all these things literally occur. For example, Jude says those in hell suffer "the punishment of eternal fire" (Jude 7) and never-ending "blackest darkness" (v. 13). But how could it be a place with literal fire and blackest darkness at the same time? A realm with a literal "lake of fire" (Rev. 19:20; 20:10, 14, 15; 21:8) would be well lit.

Moreover, the term "blackest darkness" in Jude is located at the end of a string of six phrases (vv. 12–13) that all Bible scholars agree are graphically metaphorical. Phrases such as "clouds without rain" and "wandering stars" are metaphorical descriptions of "godless men, who change the grace of our God into a license for immorality and deny Jesus Christ our only Sovereign and Lord" (v. 4). A similar string of metaphors is in 2 Peter, where the wicked "are springs without water and mists driven by a storm. Blackest darkness is reserved for them" (2:17).

In addition to the literal contradiction of fire and darkness, as mentioned previously, hell is a place where bodies can decay endlessly while burning (Isa. 66:24). How can it be both? But there is no problem if the images are metaphors. As metaphors, Matthew's depictions are not contradictory. It is both a place of "fire" (3:10; 12; 5:22; 7:19; 13:40, 42, 50; 18:8–9; 25:41) and "darkness" (8:12; 22:13; 25:30). The same is true of Jude's epistle and of other Bible writings. They can juxtapose as many terms to depict hell as they want metaphorically without contradiction.

Actually, this was common in extra-biblical Jewish writings (Qumran, 1QS 2:8; 4:13; 1 Enoch 100:9; 103:7; 2 Enoch 1:2; 10:2; Jerusalem Talmud, Shekalim 6:1, 49d; Judith 16:17; Sirach 7:17). The writers warn of "black fire" (2 Enoch 10:2), "blazing flames worse than fire" (1 Enoch 100:9), and a place where the wicked have a decaying body that burns eternally (Judith 16:17; Sirach 7:17).

Some literalists, however, suggest that such contradictions are solved by recognizing that hell is a supernatural realm. In such a realm natural law does not apply. The eternal hellfire was created for supernatural beings (Matt. 25:41) and humans condemned to hell receive supernatural bodies (Acts 24:15; 1 Cor. 15:35–50), so obviously hellfire, darkness, and bodily decay defy the laws of physics. Thus, the literalist argues, the damned can experience being in blackest darkness and with never-ending bodily decay while burning in a fire that produces physically felt pain but that doesn't emanate light.

This might seem to be a strong argument for the literal-traditional view, but it has a problem. The words to depict heaven are metaphorical, and unambiguously so (as discussed in section 10.3). Why, then, would the Bible writers speak metaphorically about heaven but literally about hell? "Fire" in the context of the eschatological does not appear to have been meant to be literal any more than heaven's 1,400 mile high wall decorated with precious jewels and metals (Rev. 21:18–20). But if there exists such an exception, it must be demonstrated, and I don't believe a literalist theologian has yet demonstrated it.

However John F. Walvoord (1910–2002) would disagree. He argues that there is an exception for interpreting hell's images as literal because of the "frequent mention of fire in connection with eternal punishment" and because the flames mentioned in the story of the rich man and Lazarus (Luke 16:19–31) seem to be like literal flames, because "thirst would be a natural reaction to fire, and the desire to cool his tongue would be in keeping with this description."[38]

This is a noble attempt by Walvoord, but it has fatal flaws. First, the mention of fire in connection with eternal punishment has barely more frequency in Scripture than do the metaphorical occurrences of darkness, corpses, or grinding of teeth. Thus, if frequency is the guide, the argument for a literal fire is not persuasive at all. But a greater problem for the literalist is that there is no exegetical rule that tips the scales in favor of a literal interpretation versus a metaphorical one if the frequency of occurrences in Scripture is higher. The higher frequency may correspond to a wider use of the metaphor of "fire" in the first century than, say, the use of the metaphor of "corpses." If so, then when the gospel writers compiled the sayings and teachings of Jesus and his disciples, the number of occurrences of fire just happened to outnumber each of the other metaphorical occurrences because it was more widely used.

Moreover, "darkness" is also frequently mentioned in connection with eternal punishment, yet it is undoubtedly metaphorical. This, as previously discussed, is evident by its placement in a string of unequivocally metaphorical terms in Jude and in 2 Peter.

Finally, Walvoord's argument that there is sufficient evidence that the fire is literal in the parable of the rich man who died unsaved (Luke 16:19–31) has problems. Walvoord assumes that the rich man's thirst and desire to cool his tongue are literal bodily desires. But if the rich man's body was seared in literal flames, why in the world would he ask for a few drops of water on his tongue? Why not ask that a bucket of ice water be poured on his head? Or, better still, why not ask for a pond of cold water to jump in? Furthermore, the rich man's tongue would never be literally cooled if Lazarus had dipped the tip of his finger in water and touched it (v. 24). Therefore, reading this story literally doesn't make sense.

Metaphorically, however, it makes complete sense. The rich man's request may have to do with the fact that in hell (actually *hadēs*) he could never taste "the water of life" (Rev. 22:17). "The water of life" is symbolic for fellowship with God, and, in the afterlife, is symbolic of the blessing of being among the consummate heavenly community in an everlasting state of consummate psychospiritual well-being. Thus, the rich man longed to have even a tiny taste of the blessings of heaven. Before he died he could have taken freely of the "water," but between heaven and hell is a "great chasm" (irrevocable judgment) that prevents those in hell from ever being among the heavenly community (Luke 16:26).

Another problem with trying to read this story literally is that the time the story takes place is during the rich man's disembodied state (*hadēs*) before the resurrection-translation at the end of the world (when the condemned receive their supernatural bodies and are then cast into hell [*gehenna* {Matt. 5:22; 10:28}]). Thus, the rich man should be bodiless. When he dies (Luke 16:22), his disembodied soul enters the celestial realm (*hadēs* [2 Pet. 2:9][39]) (Luke 16:23) where he undergoes life review (Luke 16:25). If the rich man is bodiless, so is Lazarus (who is at Abraham's side with God), therefore he does not have a finger to dip into water to cool the rich man's tongue, and the rich man doesn't have a tongue needing to be cooled (Luke 16:24). Since the story does not make sense literally, it would appear that the "fire" he is suffering in is metaphorical. "The flame tormenting him" is his bitter regret of the way he squandered opportunities in his earthly life.[40]

Conclusion

The literal hellfire view probably came about as a result of a deficient methodology for exegesis utilized by well-meaning theologians of a barbaric era, whose interpretation would go unchallenged until the Reformation, after which a reexamination of methods for interpretation uncovered the deficiency. Consequently, the literal torture chamber view of hell does not appear to be biblical. As such, the literal hellfire view should be set away from a discussion about whether the punishment of hell is consistent with the perfectly loving and good character of God.

But if the literal torture chamber of hell is not biblical, then what is hell's punishment? Is there bodily suffering? Is there mental torture? How bad is it? What can those who go to hell expect? Whatever the punishment is, is it necessary? Is it proportionate to the crime of rejecting God? These questions are addressed in the next chapter.

NOTES to Chapter 10

1. B. C. Johnson, *The Atheist Debater's Handbook* (Buffalo, NY: Prometheus, 1981), 116, as quoted in Gary R. Habermas and J. P. Moreland, *Beyond Death: Exploring the Evidence for Immortality* (Eugene, OR: Wipf and Stock Publishers, 2004), 286.

2. George H. Smith, *Atheism: The Case Against God* (Buffalo, NY: Prometheus, 1979), 299, as quoted in Gary R. Habermas and J. P. Moreland, *Beyond Death*, 286.

3. David Mills, *Atheist Universe: The Thinking Person's Answer to Christian Fundamentalism* (Berkeley, CA: Ulysses Press, 2006), chapter 8.

4. Keith M. Parsons, "Hell: Christianity's Most Damnable Doctrine," in *The End of Christianity*, ed. John W. Loftus (Amherst, NY: Prometheus Books, 2011), 238. Parsons earned a PhD in history and philosophy of science from the University of Pittsburgh and a PhD in philosophy from Queen's University (Canada). He is professor of philosophy at the University of Houston and author of several books, including *God and the Burden of Proof* and *Rational Episodes: Logic for the Intermittently Reasonable*.

5. Paul Johnson, *A History of Christianity* (New York: Simon & Schuster, 1976), 341.

6. William V. Crockett, "The Metaphorical View," in *Four Views on Hell*, series ed. Stanley N. Gundry, gen. ed. William V. Crockett (Grand Rapids, MI: Zondervan, 1996), 46–47. It is amazing to me that the inventors of such tortures saw humans receiving harsher punishment than demons, who are traditionally believed to be more culpable than the worst of human sinners.

7. Dante Alighieri, *Divine Comedy*, trans. Charles Eliot Norton (Chicago: University of Chicago, 1952), as discussed in William V. Crockett, "The Metaphorical View," *Four Views of Hell*, 47.

8. Dan. 12:2; John 5:28–29; Acts 24:15; Rev. 20:5.

9. Matt. 8:12; 22:13; 25:30; 2 Pet. 2:17; Jude 13.

10. Matt. 8:12; 13:42; 22:13; 24:51; 25:30; Luke 13:28.

11. Luke 12:47.

12. Isa. 66:24; Matt. 5:22; 18:8, 9; 25:41; Mark 9:44, 46, 47–48; Rev. 20:10.

13. Isa. 66:24; Mark 9:48.

14. Jonathan Edwards, sermon: "Sinners in the Hands of an Angry God," delivered in 1741, as quoted in John W. Loftus, *Why I Became an Atheist: A Former Preacher Rejects Christianity* (Amherst, NY: Prometheus Books, 2008), 392–393.

15. Jonathan Edwards, as quoted by Edward William Fudge, "An Introduction to Conditionalism," in *Two Views of Hell: A Biblical & Theological Dialogue* (Downers Grove, IL: InterVarsity Press, 2000), 19–20.

16. Charles H. Spurgeon, Sermon 66, *New Park Street Pulpit*, 2:105, as quoted by Edward William Fudge, "An Introduction to Conditionalism" in *Two Views of Hell*, 20.

17. William V. Crockett, "The Metaphorical View," in *Four Views on Hell*, 49.

18. Craig L. Blomberg has a brief introduction to a cultural-historical analysis in *Handbook of New Testament Exegesis* (Grand Rapids, MI: Baker Academic, 2010), 63–92. John H. Walton discusses cultural-historical analysis inclusive of comparative studies of extra-biblical literature in *The NIV Application Commentary: Genesis* (Grand Rapids, MI: Zondervan, 2001), 21–35, 44–48; and in *Ancient Near Eastern Thought and the Old Testament: Introducing the Conceptual World of the Hebrew Bible* (Grand Rapids, MI: Baker Academic, 2006), 15–40, as does Charles Halton in "A Desiccated Finger and the Study of Genre," in *Genesis: History, Fiction, or Neither?: Three Views on the Bible's Earliest Chapters* (Grand Rapids, MI: Zondervan, 2015), 13–21.

19. Paul Copan, *Is God a Moral Monster?: Making Sense of the Old Testament God* (Grand Rapids, MI: Baker Books, 2011), 84.

20. The ancient Israelite cosmography included a cosmic sea believed to surround a disc-shaped earth [John H. Walton, *Ancient Near Eastern Thought and the Old Testament: Introducing the Conceptual World of the Hebrew Bible* (Grand Rapids, MI: Baker Academic, 2006), 176–177].

21. John H. Walton, *The NIV Application Commentary: Genesis*, 73–74, 100–103, 343–345.

22. William V. Crockett, "The Metaphorical View," in *Four Views of Hell*, 55–56.

23. *The Zondervan NIV Bible Commentary, Volume 2: New Testament*, consul. eds. Kenneth L. Barker and John R. Kohlenberger III (Grand Rapids, MI: Zondervan Publishing House, 1994), 173.

24. *Holman Concise Bible Dictionary* (Nashville, TN: Broadman & Holman Publishers, 1997), 269; William D. Mounce, *Complete Expository Dictionary of Old and New Testament Words* (Grand Rapids, MI: Zondervan, 2006), 331.

25. *The Expositor's Bible Commentary*, gen. ed. Frank E. Gaebelein, consul. eds. James Montgomery Boice and Merrill C. Tenney, Vol. 10 (Grand Rapids, MI: Zondervan Publishing House, 1976), 188; William V. Crockett, "The Metaphorical View," *Four Views on Hell*, 58.

26. Hans Bietenhard, "Hell," in *The New International Dictionary of New Testament Theology*, ed. Colin Brown, Vol. 2 (Grand Rapids, MI: Zondervan, 1976), 208.

27. Matt. 11:23; 16:18; Luke 10:15; 16:23.

28. *The Zondervan NIV Bible Commentary, Volume 2: New Testament*, 221–222.

29. Ibid., 1030; *The Expositor's Bible Commentary*, 188; *Matthew Henry's Commentary on the Whole Bible* (Peabody, MA: Hendrickson Publishers, 1991), 1938.

30. Coffin Texts are a collection of ancient Egyptian funerary spells written on coffins beginning approximately around 2100 BC. These texts emphasize subterranean

elements of the afterlife ruled by Osiris in which there are threatening beings, traps, and snares with which the deceased must contend. The spells in the texts were believed to allow the deceased to protect themselves against these dangers and against dying a second death. A theme recorded in the texts is the concept that all people are judged according to their deeds in this life by Osiris and his council.

31. Eva Von Dassow, Raymond Faulkner, Carol Andrews, Ogden Goelet, and James Wasserman, *The Egyptian Book of the Dead: The Book of Going Forth by Day—The Complete Papyrus of Ani* (San Francisco: Chronicle Books, 1994), 168.

32. John Phillips, *Exploring 1 Corinthians: An Expository Commentary* (Grand Rapids, MI: Kregel Publications, 2002), 76. Phillips received his DMin degree from Luther Rice Seminary. He served as assistant director of the Moody Correspondence School as well as director of the Emmaus Correspondence School, one of the world's largest Bible correspondence ministries. He also taught in the Moody Evening School and on the Moody Broadcasting radio network.

33. Charles H. Dodd, *The Epistle of Paul to the Romans* (London: Hodder and Stoughton, 1932), 81. See also Gary R. Habermas and J. P. Moreland, *Beyond Death*, 305–306.

34. *Matthew Henry's Commentary on the Whole Bible*, 1848.

35. William D. Mounce, *Complete Expository Dictionary of Old and New Testament Words* (Grand Rapids, MI: Zondervan, 2006), 423; James Strong, "A Concise Dictionary of the Words in the Greek Testament," in *The New Strong's Exhaustive Concordance of the Bible* (Nashville, TN: Thomas Nelson Publishers, 1990), 14.

36. Edward W. Fudge, *The Fire That Consumes: A Biblical and Historical Study of the Final Punishment* (Houston, TX: Providential Press, 1982), 112. Fudge received his BA and MA from Abilene Christian University and his JD from the University of Houston College of Law. Fudge has been called "one of the foremost scholars on hell" by *The Christian Post*.

37. *Holman Concise Bible Dictionary* (Nashville, TN: Broadman & Holman Publishers, 1997), 164.

38. John F. Walvoord, "The Literal View," in *Four Views of Hell*, 28.

39. Gary R. Habermas and J. P. Moreland, *Beyond Death*, 289–290.

40. Herbert Lockyer, *All the Parables of the Bible* (Grand Rapids, MI: Lamplighter Books, 1963), 295.

11

Is Hell's Suffering Pointless and Unjust?

Synopsis

Critics of the doctrine of eternal separation from God in hell argue that the punishment is pointless, revengeful, and too severe for any crime we could commit. Some Christians find an eternal hell difficult to accept and reinvent it to either be a place of temporary, rehabilitative punishment (universalism) or a blazing fire that annihilates the condemned (annihilationism).

A Christian response is that an eternal hell of separation from God is not based on revenge, but rather on justice (principle of accountability), and is not unjustly severe, being proportionate to the ultimate crime. Moreover, universalism and annihilationism do not hold up under philosophical or exegetical scrutiny.

The conclusion of the previous chapter was that the view of hell as a literal torture chamber doesn't hold up under exegetical scrutiny and is therefore not actually biblical. This means that the unsaved are not cast into a flaming pit to suffer physical pain from burning fire. Even so, the Bible is clear that the unsaved are irrevocably confined to hell without hope of ever being reconciled to God in heaven.

Critics of hell usually argue that even though it isn't a torture chamber of a literal hellfire, suffering eternally in hell is still far too severe a punishment for any crime any of us could commit. Billions of hell's inhabitants suffer without hope, without restoration, without rehabilitation, and without end. It is too final, too horrendous and cruel to be an equitable or fair punishment, it is argued. This seems especially so since many are of the opinion that sins committed during a finite lifetime should be met with *finite* punishment—not *infinite* punishment.

As atheist John W. Loftus says, "No matter what conception of eternity without God the Christian proposes, the fact that most all human beings will suffer this fate is incompatible with the theistic conception of a good God. Such a punishment simply does not fit the crime"[1] Even a hell without literal fire, Loftus says, is "still a horrible fate for a loving God to inflict upon human beings" and "does not fit the crime, period. No thinking person should believe this is what our so-called sins deserve."[2]

Theologian Clark H. Pinnock (1937–2010) would agree. He argues that, based on the Old Testament standard of justice, and the apparent disparity between finite sins committed in our terrestrial life and infinite punishment in hell, an eternal hell is unjust:

> An eye for an eye and a tooth for a tooth (Exod. 21:24). Did the sinner visit upon God everlasting torment? Did he cause God or his neighbors everlasting pain and loss? Of course not; no human has the power to do such harm. Under the Old Testament standard, no finite set of deeds that individual sinners have done could justify such an infinite sentence. . . . It would amount to inflicting infinite suffering upon those who have committed finite sins and goes far beyond an eye for an eye and a tooth for a tooth. It would create a serious disproportion between sins committed in time and the resulting suffering experienced forever.[3]

Critics of hell also argue that no good purpose is served by unending suffering. As Pinnock says, "Unending torment would be utterly pointless, wasted suffering that could never lead to anything good."[4] Therefore, it is argued, eternal punishment could only be motivated by vindictiveness, spiteful retaliation, and satisfaction in making people suffer. Since eternally suffering in hell is pointless, it is argued, a loving and good God would not have it.

Some Christians, trying to avoid this apparent contradiction, remove both the finality and the infiniteness of hell by making it have a redemptive punishment. They see the afterlife in hell as conscious misery where the Holy

Spirit continues to minister for as long as it takes for the wicked to learn to appreciate a right relationship with God and be welcomed into the heavenly community. Ultimately, all go to heaven, leaving the realm of hell empty. This is the universalism view (or postmortem evangelism view). It is argued by a minority of scholars (its most notable proponents include: Morton Kelsey [1917–2001], Marilyn McCord Adams, and George T. Knight).

Other Christians, however, also struggling to reconcile an apparently unjust and pointless hell with God's character, interpret hell differently. They interpret it in a way that allows it to still be final, but with a finite duration of suffering. In this view, God ends the conscious existence of the unsaved with a destroying fire (euthanizing them). This view is called annihilationism and it is argued by a minority of scholars (its most notable proponents include: Clark H. Pinnock, John Wenham, John Stott, P. E. Hughes, Stephen Travis, and the Seventh-day Adventist church).

As a Christian, I too used to struggle to reconcile the finality and severity of an eternal hell with a perfectly loving and good God. I used to think of infinite suffering as disproportionate to a finite life of sin. I tended to think that either of the alternate views (annihilationism or universalism) must be Christianity's solution to the apparent disparity between God's goodness and hell's absolute awfulness. But as a result of my investigative study, I discovered that the solution to reconciling hell with God's character is not found by adopting an alternate view of hell, as neither view solves the apparent doctrinal contradiction, nor is clearly taught in the Bible. Rather, the solution to reconcile an eternal hell with God's character is found by understanding: (a) the actual nature of the punishment, and (b) the crime said to be worthy of hell.

11.1 The Nature of the Punishment

Two New Testament passages provide the clearest depiction of hell. The first tells us that the condemned "will be punished with everlasting destruction and shut out from the presence of the Lord and from the majesty of his power" (2 Thess. 1:9). The other passage speaks of the judgment when God "will say to those on his left, 'Depart from me, you who are cursed, into the eternal fire prepared for the devil and his angels.' . . . Then they will go away to eternal punishment" (Matt. 25:41, 46).

From these (and other) verses, it is apparent that the punishment in hell is the consequence of a genuinely broken and spoiled relation to God that results in permanent exclusion from communion with God and his people in relationship with him.[5] The "presence of the Lord" is the beatific communion. The condemned are "everlastingly" "shut out from" it. And "what he shuts no one can open" (Rev. 3:7). The nature of the punishment as exclusion from heaven is consistent with other Bible verses (Matt. 8:12; 22:13; 25:30; Luke 13:27–28).

A result of the exclusion in hell is a very poor situation. One of the reasons for this is that the fundamental need to feel loved[6] will not be fulfilled to an ultimate degree, as nothing but intimately knowing God in eternity, in beatific vision, could do that. This is "eternal life" (John 17:3), the "rich and satisfying life," promised to believers (John 10:10 NLT). This is the "life that is truly life" (1 Tim. 6:19). The community of hell never attains it, and without it, continues in a poor psychospiritual condition.

Another reason hell is a very poor situation is the lack of God's presence and hence a scarcity of God's resplendent blessings. Physical light and other aspects of an environment amiable to human living may be scarce or absent. The atmosphere may be somewhat dark. The climate may be somewhat inhospitable. Any vegetation may be partially or completely lifeless. The air may smell foul.

Another reason for a very poor situation in hell is that loving and good conduct is scarce or absent. One may wish to be respected or left alone, but there are probably times of harassment, oppression or attack. Notwithstanding, the community of hell is subdivided into communities according to the caliber of the disposition, and so rules of conduct might be established for mutual benefit, although it is likely that they would sometimes be broken.

Persons in hell are stuck with the sin-plagued disposition that was forged in this life. The beatific vision eliminates the pull of the sinful nature to sin, so the heavenly community never struggles against that nature. But in hell, if that struggle continues at all (versus surrendering to the sinful nature entirely), it would continue forever. Because each forges his or her own disposition to take into hell, the degree of regret of the loss of heaven is worse for some than for others. Thus, the ones responsible in this life for cultivating a violent, or especially selfish, disposition would be most tormented, while the ones who've cultivated enough of the principles of love and goodness to be considered by society as a "good" person (because of the Holy Spirit's ministry) would be far less tormented.

The whole situation in hell is amplified by a lucid consciousness and fully active SPS (supernatural powers of the soul) (see chapter 3 on SPS). God's creation plan from the beginning was that humans would be among the heavenly community in a consummate relationship with God, with a lucid consciousness and fully active SPS to receive the greatest blessings. But such consciousness and powers among the community of hell would likely magnify the suffering. On the other hand, fully active SPS might also bring moments of joyless pleasure. Nonetheless, feelings of regret, loneliness, sorrow, or anger may at times be intense.

A biblical example of the intensity of such feelings is in the previously discussed story of the condemned man in Luke 16:19–31. He feels intensely tormented (not tortured) by regret (v. 25). He knows all too well the tragedy of his free choice to make himself into an unloving and malicious person, unfit for heaven. He was wealthy and had many invitations to choose to be loving and generous. But instead he cultivated greed and malice, thereby shutting and locking the door to the Holy Spirit's repeated calls to him. The intense feelings of his fate are a heavy burden that otherwise could have been completely lifted had he responded to divine light shown in his life by cultivating love and a trusting relationship with a loving and good God.

Feelings in hell might also be compounded by the situation of having a celestial (supernatural) body.[7] Feelings may be felt bodily,[8] much like, for example, feeling "sick to the stomach." Although, as Habermas and Moreland advise, "We should be cautious in trying to picture in detail what life will be like then" because a celestial body is much different from a terrestrial body.[9]

It should now be evident that contrary to what critics of hell think, it is not a realm created for the purpose of inflicting suffering as God's way of satisfying some urge to get back at evildoers. It is not a place where God takes his revenge in retaliation for the way he has been offended. Rather, it is the situation that naturally occurs when the relation to the greatest and most loving person is freely and genuinely broken and spoiled. This is a matter of retribution—not spiteful revenge.

Revenge is taken without authority against another and is motivated by an emotional urge to strike back. But retribution is carried out by a "properly constituted authority" that carries out punishment for the purpose of accomplishing true justice.[10]

The best hope for a perfectly fair and just motive for hell's punishment is in God. He alone could deliver what is truly fair and right. This is because he is all-powerful, all-knowing, and perfectly loving and good. His judgment, therefore, is just, as he honors the choice of a person who has freely and genuinely chosen to become the kind of person who is against being in a direct, intimate, and eternal relationship with God. C. S. Lewis most famously proposed this in his book *The Great Divorce*, saying, "There are only two kinds of people in the end: those who say to God, 'Thy will be done,' and those to whom God says, in the end, 'Thy will be done.'"[11]

By honoring the ultimate, negative choice, God "hands them over" to the consequence of their choice.[12] Doing so is in accord with his perfect and immutable law or principle of justice through accountability[13] and is consistent with perfect love and goodness. Thus, they "bring judgment on themselves" (1 Tim. 5:12a). He respects their choice to become the kind of person incompatible with the beatific relationship, which ends in self-exclusion from the beatific relationship. It is in this sense that hell is retributive.

Honoring the ultimate, negative choice in our earthly life is a matter of respecting and dignifying the individual by treating the choice as significant.[14] Thus, the judgment is based on love and goodness—not vindictiveness. Hell is a very undesirable place to be, but it is the most appropriate place for the unsaved that respects them as persons and honors their free will.

Moreover, God doesn't feel spiteful satisfaction that people are suffering in hell (Ezek. 18:32; 2 Tim. 2:4; 2 Pet. 3:9), and neither do the redeemed. The offensive idea held in centuries past by some that God and heaven enjoy witnessing the suffering of the people in hell[15] isn't biblical. The Bible says love "doesn't revel when others grovel" (1 Cor. 13:6).[16] Perhaps God's only satisfaction concerning hell is that it accomplishes what is right, fair, loving, and good.

In summary, contrary to what critics of hell think, the nature of the torment (not torture) does not derive from a place where people are made to feel deep emotional pain as payback for evil doings out of spite. Rather, the punishment in hell is banishment from the heavenly community due to a freely and genuinely broken and spoiled relation to God that God honors. This causes those in hell to suffer because outside of the beatific relationship is a mediocre existence made fully apparent by a lucid consciousness and fully active SPS.

11.2 Quality of Life in Hell

Many people imagine living (existing) in hell as being completely and continually miserable without any intermission. It is seen as suffering intensely, nonstop, without any sense of pleasure or satisfaction at all. But there may be reasons for believing otherwise.

God is the perfect judge and he perfectly loves and respects the inhabitants of hell. As such, God would ensure that the conditions in hell are perfectly fair and just. It is reasonable, then, to suppose that the quality of life in hell is proportionate to the degree of a person's rejection of the divine light shown in the earthly life by the Holy Spirit. And this appears to be taught in the Bible.

Scripture tells us that judgment is according to the disposition and beliefs cultivated in this life.[17] The people of heaven experience varying degrees of blessing according to how they've lived (Matt. 16:27; 2 Cor. 5:10). Likewise, the quality of life in hell is also said to correspond to works done in the terrestrial life (Matt. 11:20–24; 23:23; Luke 12:47–48). In the story in Luke 12:35–48, it is said that the greater sinner with greater knowledge and opportunity (v. 47) receives worse punishment than the lesser sinner with less knowledge and opportunity (v. 48). Thus, it should be expected that hell "will be more bearable" for some than others (Matt. 11:22, 24), as the quality of life in hell corresponds to the degree of sin cultivated in this life.

From this we may postulate that the realm of hell consists of a multitude of levels or realms — varying from the one that is the least lacking in resplendent blessings to the one that is devoid of resplendent blessings. Thus, the lack of resplendence of the sky and land in each realm varies from the least unpleasant to the horrible. The persons in the least unpleasant realm are the least of the scoundrels, while the persons in the most horrible realm are extremely vile. I find it interesting that the concept that hell has multiple levels (dimensions?) agrees with some near-death experiences (NDEs).[18]

If this is true, then there may be people in hell who are thankful (to God) that their life in hell isn't as bad as it could've been had they been a worse sinner. Keeping this thankfulness in mind might alleviate an otherwise completely dismaying situation — some way of making it bearable. It is probably an existence to which the condemned are able to grow accustomed; there are likely to be periods of misery, but on the whole, it may be a bearable existence — a just consequence in accord with the principle of justice through accountability, and proportionate to the degree of rejection of God.

An additional point about the quality of living in hell is that time may run differently. If time is experienced differently in the afterlife, the intensity of the suffering in hell could be substantially less than we might imagine. (It is interesting that some NDErs say that time passes differently in the afterlife.)[19]

It might seem from all of this that life in hell is not severe enough to be called punishment. However, compared to the incommensurable reward of the consummate relationship with God in heaven, life in any level of hell is loathsome. It is loathsome in the sense that those in hell know that they have forever lost out on ever experiencing the greatest well-being and happiness. It is a "dreadful thing" to be in hell (Heb. 10:31).

The thought of what was missed will torment the mind at times when circumstances bring this loss into perspective. But there may be shifts of mental focus on things that bring moments of some pleasure, although at least a trace of suffering will likely always be present. This is because in hell, committing sin is inevitable, which perpetuates the torment of heaven lost. Paul may have alluded to this in his letter to the Roman Christians where he says, "There will be trouble and distress for every human being who does evil" (Rom. 2:9). The Greek word for "distress" (*stenochōria*), also translated as "anguish" (KJV), suggests a narrow place where there is nowhere to turn for relief. But even a scintilla of suffering is dreadful if there is no end to it.

In summary, the nature of the punishment in hell entails a quality of life that varies depending on how life was lived on earth. Hell might be somewhat bearable by way of adjustment to the new life by finding things with which to occupy the mind that might bring bearableness to the situation. In this way, for some, at least, life in hell might have some relative tolerability. But there is never escape from being tormented by regret (in varying degrees) over heaven lost.

11.3 Why Hell's Punishment Is Irrevocable

The Bible tells us that hell is "everlasting" (2 Thess. 1:9) and "eternal" (Heb. 6:2). Just as the saved consciously experience endless life in the consummate relationship, the unsaved consciously experience endless life outside of the consummate relationship (Matt. 25:41, 46[20]). This is consistent with several other Bible verses, including those that mention the "eternal" condemnation (Mark 3:29), which is metaphorically characterized as "eternal" or "unquenchable" fire (Matt. 3:12; 18:8; 19:16; Luke 3:17), and which is the opposite of the "eternal" reward in heaven (Matt. 19:16; 19:29; Mark 10:17, 30; 18:30; John 3:16).

The concept that hell is the result of an unchangeable and irreversible judgment was important to the Bible writers because some of God's judgments in Israelite history have been averted, or changed, following repentance toward God. But we are repeatedly told in Scripture that the judgment to hell is not one of them. It is the one judgment that is definitely said to be irrevocable. It is no wonder, then, why God's prophets warned of it with strong language.

The reason hell is irrevocable has to do with the conditions that make experiencing a conversion for salvation possible. The salvation experience is marked by faith in and love for God, and it is sometimes called the "born again" experience. The Bible tells us that such an experience is necessary if one is to be reconciled to God for heaven. As Jesus says, "Very truly I tell you, no one can see the kingdom of God unless he is born again [or born from the Divine]" (John 3:3). It is necessary for salvation because only a salvation experience demonstrates a genuine choice for a permanent membership in the community in direct fellowship with God. Only a genuine choice is accepted, because to do otherwise would neither honor free will nor be consistent with perfect love and goodness, as said previously. (The subjects of salvation and judgment are discussed in the next chapter.)

Contrary to what many people think, the salvation experience (by free will) cannot happen in any kind of environment. It requires an environment in which there is compatibility-determining free will and divine hiddenness, because the salvation experience entails a significant degree of faith[21] and genuine love for God. But such faith and love are not possible when there is substantial fear of punishment. In such an environment, no seed of significant faith or genuine love for God could possibly germinate (1 John 4:18).[22]

It is for this reason that God placed us in a world of divine hiddenness. In a world of divine hiddenness we have the kind of free will needed to experience significant faith and genuine love for God that constitute a genuine choice for heaven.

As discussed in chapters 3 and 4, at death the soul leaves the terrestrial life of divine hiddenness behind. With lucid consciousness, fully active SPS, and the ability for interdimensional travel, the soul is extraordinarily aware of God's existence and will to reward or punish. Consequently, compatibility-determining free will is precluded, as well as the opportunity to exercise a substantial degree of uncoerced faith in and genuine love for God necessary for an actual conversion.

Because conversion requires such faith, love, and free will, it is not possible after death in hell (or Hades) for a person to experience a saving relationship with God. The environment of hell itself makes it impossible for condemned souls to be saved. Thus, they are forever stuck there. This is why hell is irrevocable and why there's no second chance for salvation.

This is by far the single strongest argument against the universalist view (or postmortem evangelism view) of salvation after death. Christians of the universalist view believe that a loving and good God would give the unsaved in hell a second chance.[23] Hell, to them, is a form of purgatory, where the Holy Spirit's ministry continues to try to convert the heart for as long as it takes until eventually every soul in hell is converted and welcomed into heaven. But, as was just discussed, conversions in hell are not possible. Any submission of the will to God's will could only occur by *coercion*. Obedience would be predominantly motivated by fear of further punishment—not love. It is wrong—even unloving—to force bad people to become good.[24] Thus, a soul that goes into hell without a saving faith in and love for God can never later come to have such faith and love. This points to the fatal flaw with the universalist view of hell. It does not take into account that, despite the greatness of God's love and mercy, there can be no genuine conversion or "born again" experience in hell.

To summarize, the nature of the punishment in hell is everlasting banishment from the consummate relationship with God due to a genuinely and permanently broken and spoiled relation to God. A result of the situation is indeed a poor quality of existence.

It is irrevocable. There's no second chance for redemption for a condemned soul because the coercive conditions in the afterlife are prohibitive of having the free will, faith, and love that are entailed in the only response to God's grace by which we must be saved.

Now that we've looked at the nature of the punishment, it's time to look at the crime. Then we can compare them to determine if the crime fits the punishment.

11.4 The Real Crime

Notwithstanding the punishment in hell just described, many critics of the doctrine believe that none of our sins could be bad enough to be worthy of it. They argue that we may be deserving of a hell that is temporary, but not a hell without any hope of reconciliation or end. For even heinous sins, such as the ones mentioned in the previous chapters (e.g., heinous abuse and murder of children), deserve only a finite punishment in hell. This seems especially so because of the fact that many decent people who do not believe in God are bound for hell. Some of them do not believe because of the unfortunate circumstance of never having an opportunity to hear the gospel, or misunderstanding a Christian creed, or being raised in a non-Christian religion (e.g., Islam, Buddhism) that makes the gospel too implausible for a diligent seeker to find acceptable. Many of them lead a relatively good life of devotion to moral principles and prayer. Thus, their sins appear to be far too light to make them worthy of an eternal hell.

However, contrary to what opponents of the doctrine of hell think, no one goes to hell for such sins as theft, adultery, con schemes, wife beating, illegal drug dealing, or even abusing or murdering children. Yes, hell is reserved for those who practice such conduct, but this is because such sins are the manifestation of the *real* crime for which one is consigned to hell. The real crime is a genuine and ultimate rejection of God.

Also contrary to what opponents of the doctrine of hell think, genuine and ultimate rejection of God *is* an option available to *everyone*. It matters not where or when a person is born or the worldview of the family in which one is raised. It matters not if there is no opportunity to encounter a missionary from which to receive a hearing of the gospel. It does not matter if a Christian creed is misunderstood, or if the gospel is too implausible to reasonably accept because of lack of education. Regardless of our circumstances in this life, everyone is afforded fair opportunity to either accept or reject a direct, intimate, and eternal relationship with God.

The Holy Spirit ministers to everyone by various general and special modes of revelation (chapter 12.2 discusses the Holy Spirit's ministry). Such modes include: our observation of the created world, material blessings, the conscience, conviction of what is wrong and what is right, mental impressions, dreams, visions, an encounter with an angel (holy or evil), or even an encounter with the resurrected Jesus.

Everyone receives some light of the Divine, and, if it is found to be palatable, greater light is imparted. The palatable light is met with convictions and changes in lifestyle and beliefs. More light is then given by the Holy Spirit until the seeker has enough to experience faith in and love for a loving and good Divinity sufficient to appropriate the grace of God through Christ for salvation.

As discussed in chapter 12.3, there are plenty of examples of people from various cultures and religions who've reported just such an experience. Recently an elderly Hindu priest was led step-by-step to greater light until he was introduced to the gospel of Christ he never before knew existed. He embraced the Christian faith and was baptized. Similar stories are told by former tribal polytheists, Buddhists, Muslims, Jews, etc.

But people who do not find the divine light appealing end up closing the door on the channel by which they would be enlightened. Their minds are set on beliefs that allow them to indulge the sinful nature (Acts 26:20; Rom. 8:5). Such beliefs include worship of a deity that suits the desire to be an adulterer, deceitful, greedy, unmerciful, or cruel.

Consequently, their unloving spirit closes the door in the face of the Holy Spirit, without whom they are lost (Eph. 4:30; Heb. 10:26–29). They never find their way out of whatever culture, faith, philosophy, or mindset shapes them into the kind of person that isn't compatible for heaven. This is not because they were unfortunate to have been born in the wrong place or time. Rather, this occurs because they rejected whatever amount of light was shown. As a result, they remain in darkness and spend their whole life cultivating the kind of character that reflects a genuine and ultimate rejection of God.

Such a rejection of the Holy Spirit is only possible in a life without significant coercion. There must be significant compatibility-determining free will in a world of divine hiddenness. Such are the conditions of our life, which means that by simply living our life we either genuinely and ultimately choose God, or genuinely and ultimately reject him. Thus, rejection doesn't have to be as obvious as completing a series of Bible studies and telling the instructor, "I completely understand who God is and how he desires to save me from sin and hell, but I love sin too much to accept Jesus Christ as my personal savior." Rather, it can be as imperceptible as a lifetime of using people for selfish gratification and sexual encounters without accepting responsibility for any of the diseases spread or the children spawned—even without ever having been introduced to the Bible's teachings.

Because the rejection occurs in an environment such as ours with its maximal free will, the rejection could never be truer. Honoring what is true makes such a rejection irreversible and irrevocable. It is also an irrevocable experience of the rejected. God gets to live with the truest, most genuine and ultimate rejection forever. Because God is the consummate lover, his pain from the loss is intense (although not to the point of crushing him).[25] God was "grieved" and "his heart was filled with pain" when he was rejected in the time of Noah (Gen. 6:6). Time and again God is depicted as suffering with grief and vexation because of the rebellion of the Israelites (Ps. 78:40–41; Jer. 31:20; Hos. 11:8–9). The rejection "grieves" him (Eph. 4:30). The Greek word translated as "grieve" (*lypeō*) is used elsewhere to convey "distress" (Matt. 14:9; 18:31) and being thrown into sorrowful grief (Matt. 17:23; 1 Thess. 4:13).

His grief is not only over the loss of the fellowship of those in hell, but also of the loss of the expressions of love and goodness that could have been. As discussed earlier, God's creation plan is to bring about an ever greater degree of love and goodness through persons in consummate relationship with him. But rejection of God goes against his creation plan. And God grieves forever over this tragic loss.

Ultimate Crime, Ultimate Punishment. According to Christian theologians, a genuine and ultimate rejection of God is the ultimate and most reprehensible sin. Matthew Henry (1662–1714) tells us that the Holy Spirit "is graciously given to men, and that works grace wherever it is, . . . this Spirit they have grieved, resisted, quenched, yea, done despite to him, which is *the highest act of wickedness*, and makes the case of the sinner desperate, refusing to have the gospel salvation applied to him."[26]

When asked to guess what the ultimate crime, or sin, is, most people don't think about God, and so rejection of God doesn't make the list of contenders. Rather, they guess such sins as the cruelest abuses of children, destruction of the habitability of the environment, or genocide. Such crimes are inarguably horrible and reprehensible. But, as theologian J. P. Moreland says, "They pale in light of the worst thing a person can do, which is to mock and dishonor and refuse to love the person that we owe absolutely everything to, which is our Creator, God himself."[27]

Besides God himself, reciprocating love and goodness with God is *the* thing of ultimate value. God is love and goodness (1 John 4:8). To reject this by turning away from life's opportunities to choose to express and receive love and goodness, we turn away from the ultimate and most valuable person in existence—God. Because the thing rejected is of ultimate value, rejection of it is intensified to an ultimate extent, making it the ultimate and most reprehensible sin. The only punishment worthy of the ultimate sin is the ultimate punishment in hell previously discussed. Therefore, the crime does indeed seem to fit the punishment. "At the very least," say theologians Habermas and Moreland, "such a scheme is not clearly immoral and unjust."[28]

11.5 Is an Endless Hell Pointless?

Critics of hell argue that no good purpose is served by confinement to unending suffering, and therefore, God's motivation for an eternal hell stems from spiteful vindictiveness. One such critic, Keith Parsons, argues that the punishment is "purely retributive, and purely retributive punishments are merely expressions of spite and vindictiveness and so are wicked."[29] Atheist David Mills argues that hell is pointless because it is God's infliction of suffering for the satisfaction of making people suffer, which is "a purposeless, vengeful end in itself."[30]

However, God's motivation for the retributive punishment of an unending existence in hell has nothing to do with anger, spite, or vindictiveness. Theologians Jeffery, Ovey, and Sach describe the distinction between retribution and revenge in their book, *Pierced for Our Transgressions*. As they say, revenge is exacted by people who do not have a properly constituted authority to punish and who care little, if at all, about whether the measure of punishment is disproportionate to the crime. The avenger feels delight in the pain of the offender, whereas "retribution is motivated by the solemn demands of justice—thus God can tell us in Ezekiel 18:23 that he takes no pleasure in the death of the wicked, while assuring us in the very next verse that he will serve the death penalty as justice requires."[31] Moreover, the human avenger feels satisfaction of a selfish nature, while God's retribution, even if motivated by his "desire to satisfy his own sense of justice, cannot be 'selfish' in any negative sense, because it is right for God to put himself and his will at the center of the universe in a way that would be wrong for anyone else to do."[32] This may explain why the apostle Paul warned church members not to try to exact retribution themselves, but to leave it to God (Rom. 12:19).

Another problem with the argument that an eternal hell is pointless was brought out previously. Hell lasts forever, not because God's desire for payback is insatiable, but rather because the circumstances of the afterlife make having a salvation experience in hell impossible. The salvation experience involves significant, uncoerced faith in and genuine love for God. But such faith and love require a free will that is of the compatibility-determining kind, and we no longer have this kind of free will in the afterlife. Therefore, the condemned are stuck (by their own doing) in an eternal situation.

11.6 The Failure of the Universalist View of Hell

Despite the discussion of the previous sections, it is still felt by some that a hell that never ends is either unjust or pointless. Some theologians try to rectify this by removing the finality of hell by giving the ones in hell a second chance to eventually get to heaven. They see hell as a rehabilitative punishment, for a time, while the Holy Spirit continues to minister to draw the unsaved to God until each eventually experiences conversion and is welcomed into heaven. In this view, God's desire that all be saved comes true, and hell becomes an empty realm. Hell's punishment has a discernable purpose, and it wouldn't appear to be so severe as to be unjust. This view falls within the universalist view of salvation/hell. Bible texts cited in an argument for universalism are: Acts 3:21; Rom. 5:18-19; 11:32; 1 Cor. 15:22–28; Eph. 1:10; and 1 Tim. 2:4.

To many Christians, this view has much appeal. But it has major problems, the chief of which was briefly discussed in section 11.3. The divinely appointed response to God's grace for salvation is an experience of significant, uncoerced faith in and genuine love for God. Such faith and love require having compatibility-determining free will, which is possible only in an environment of divine hiddenness. But the environment of the afterlife precludes divine hiddenness, and, consequently, compatibility-determining free will. Thus, a salvation experience in hell is not possible. This impossibility complements Jesus' teaching that none in hell can cross over into the realm of heaven (Luke 16:26). Therefore, there can be no possible second chance for anyone in hell. The only chance is in this terrestrial life.

Moreover, as argued by philosopher Michael J. Murray, the idea proposed by universalists that the Holy Spirit ministers to souls in hell, to wear down their resistance to his love to the point of submission (which would be a ministry of coercion), robs them of autonomy and dignity as a person and purges any (or nearly any) meaning out of their free will.[33] Again, this way of treating the unsaved is not consistent with a perfectly loving and good God. And if the person who chooses to become the kind of person who is incompatible with heaven isn't excluded from it, then there would hardly be any point to having compatibility-determining free will, or this earthly life. Therefore, a postmortem evangelism by the Holy Spirit is not consistent with perfect love and goodness, because it would be coercive and disrespectful, and it would undermine the purpose of the terrestrial life.

Now, the universalist may complain that the irrevocability of hell somehow is a defeat of God, or his desire that all be saved. But it is not clear why God would be defeated. God desires that all be saved. For souls entering the afterlife, being saved means being in consummate relationship with God, which, as discussed in chapter 4, is only possible if one has compatibility-determining free will in the earthly life. Thus, while God desires that all be saved, he obviously has a greater desire that compatibility-determining free will be honored, as it plays a role in bringing about the greatest possible good. And if he honors such free will by consigning some souls to an irrevocable hell, God's greater desire is met. How, then, could God be defeated? Clearly he could not.

Philosophically and theologically, the universalist view appears bankrupt. But what of the Bible texts cited by universalists? Do any of them indicate that salvation is possible in hell?

On close examination, the verses cited do not support universalism at all. This is because the verses do not describe an ultimate reconciliation of all people, neither in this life nor in the next. Rather, the texts teach either what God's desire is without affirming what will happen, or the restoration of God's rulership over all beings.

The Bible verse that is probably most cited by universalists is Romans 5:18–19. It reads: "Consequently, just as the result of one trespass was condemnation for all men, so also the result of one act of righteousness was justification that brings life for all men. For just as through the disobedience of the one man the many were made sinners, so also through the obedience of the one man the many will be made righteous."

Whether Paul intended a universalist message here depends on how the terms "all men" (v. 18) and "the many" (v. 19) are interpreted. If he meant literally every human being, then he would be saying that every human being will ultimately be justified by virtue of Christ's sacrifice, if not in the earthly life, then in hell (postmortem conversion and justification).

Universalists argue from this that every person is eventually justified for heaven through the ministry of Christ, just as every human is condemned because of being born with a sinful nature to which each of us submits (Rom. 3:23). But each of us is "in Adam" not by the nature we are born with, but rather by the universal fact that each of us at one time or another chooses to be controlled by that nature. The reason the result of the trespass of Adam was "condemnation for all men" is not because of the nature we are born with, but rather because each person lets that nature control him (Rom. 8). As such, we are not condemned "in Adam" by birth, but by choice. The solution that Paul is preparing his readers to see is that just as all are condemned by submission to a nature we inherited from Adam ("in Adam"), we can also be saved by submission to the Spirit through a relationship with Christ ("in Christ"). Or, said succinctly, "as 'all who are in Adam' die, so 'all who are in Christ' will live (cf. 1 Cor. 15:22)."[34]

Furthermore, it might appear that Paul's wording (i.e., "all men") was to remind the church in Rome that the Jews had no right to brag about being superior to the Gentiles, as all are saved on the same basis (Rom. 2:17; 5:27–30). Therefore, it is apparent that at the least, Rom. 5:18–19 does not provide a clear indication that anyone would be justified while in hell. And considering the absence of any clear Bible text on the matter, it seems most likely that none of the Bible writers believed in a universalist view of hell.

Another text cited by universalists is 1 Cor. 15:22–28. Verse 22 says, "For as in Adam all die, so in Christ all will be made alive." Universalists argue that, like the Rom. 5:18–19 passage, this one also reveals a secret that the ones in hell will eventually experience a saving repentance and obedient faith in God. However, Paul's message here is essentially what he told the Romans—that being "in Adam" is a life choice, just as being "in Christ" is a life choice, and not a matter of being born a descendant of Abraham. The people who are "in Christ" are the ones "who belong to him" by faith (v. 23), as all of the churches to which Paul ministered should know (Rom. 6:1–10; 7:1–17; 2 Cor. 5:17; Eph. 2:8–10). Therefore, as with the Rom. 5 text, 1 Cor. 15:22–28 also does not indicate that anyone would undergo conversion and justification in hell.

Another text cited by universalists is Acts 3:21. It says Jesus must remain in heaven until the time comes for God to "restore everything." Somehow "restore everything" is interpreted to mean "reconciles all sinners to God." The most glaring problem for universalists is that nowhere in Scripture is it suggested that when Jesus appears at the end of the world in the sky with great power and glory, the wicked, as well as the righteous, will be reconciled to God. On the contrary, the Bible is unmistakable that Jesus will return to destroy the antichrist (2 Thess. 2:1–12), separate the "sheep" from the "goats" (Matt. 25:31–46), take some to heaven (1 Thess. 4:16–17), and leave some behind (Matt. 24:41; Luke 17:35), who "go away to eternal punishment, but the righteous to eternal life" (Matt. 25:46). So either Acts 3:21 is mistaken about Jesus remaining in heaven until the time of reconciliation (of everything), or the phrase "restore everything" should not be interpreted to mean "save everyone." Therefore, Acts 3:21 really doesn't support the universalist view.

Another text that universalists claim is supportive of the universalist view is Eph. 1:9–10. It reads, "And he made known to us the mystery of his will according to his good pleasure, which he purposed in Christ, to put into effect when the times will have reached their fulfillment—to bring all things in heaven and on earth together under one head, even Christ." Universalists interpret this to mean that eventually every soul in hell will be brought together under Christ's rulership in heaven. But notice that it does not mention anyone in hell being brought to heaven. It says all things in heaven and on earth. "Heaven and earth" phrases in the New Testament refer to the human cosmos, which has been disharmonious since humankind's chosen estrangement with God. When at the end of the world all cases for heaven or hell are decided and Jesus Christ reveals himself to all the world in power and glory, harmony of the human cosmos is restored, as every man, woman, and child from all ages who would be "in Christ" is glorified with a celestial body (the resurrection-translation of the redeemed) and is forever removed from the potential influence of Satan and his angels. The "war against the flesh" will be at an end. Therefore, this text doesn't reveal a postmortem salvation in hell.

The final verse cited by universalists is 1 Tim. 2:4. It simply says that God "wants all men to be saved and to come to a knowledge of the truth." But as discussed previously, it is wrongly assumed that God's desire that all be saved is his *greater* desire. His greater desire is that compatibility-determining free will be honored, as this preserves the dignity of souls by respecting their freedom of choice, which is fully consistent with God's character and plays a role in bringing about the greatest possible good. Thus, by consigning unrepentant souls to an irrevocable hell, God's desire that all be saved never comes to pass, but his greater desire is fully met.

Furthermore, nowhere in the Bible is there even one verse that tells us of a postmortem evangelism. Of all of the verses that mention hell, not one intimates there being hope of being justified and reconciled to God after death.

In summary, while universalism has strong emotional appeal, it does not work theologically or exegetically. A postmortem salvation experience without compatibility-determining free will is not possible. Moreover, it would go against

God's perfectly loving and good character, as well as his creation plan to accomplish the greatest possible good by way of free will and the heavenly community in a consummate relationship with God. Close inspection of the Bible verses cited in support of universalism do not reveal a belief held by Jesus' disciples that all who reject God will ultimately experience a genuine conversion and be reconciled to heaven. This is confirmed by Bible texts that contradict universalism, such as: Matt. 8:12; 25:31–46; John 5:29; Rom. 2:8–10; and Rev. 20:10, 15.

11.7 The Failure of the Annihilationist View of Hell

Other Christians, also feeling that an eternal hell is unjust, or pointless, correctly interpret hell as being irrevocable, but the suffering in hell is viewed as extremely short, as its inhabitants are annihilated by a literal fire. This view is the annihilationist view of hell. Annihilationists argue that annihilating the unsaved is more just than eternal torment. As Jonathan L. Kvanig argues in his book *The Problem of Hell*, it is most loving, merciful, and just that God annihilate the unsaved "as a sort of rational suicide when all other alternatives are too painful and/or hopeless."[35] In this view, hell's fire is a literal fire that burns flesh, soul, and spirit completely out of existence.

According to annihilationists, this view is morally superior and is actually what the Bible writers intended to teach. However, close inspection shows that it is neither morally superior nor biblical. There's not enough room here for a complete discussion, but the following touches on the more critical points of the failure of the annihilationist view.

Perhaps annihilationism's strongest argument is that it is morally superior, as God is not subjecting hell's inhabitants to punishment that might be viewed as overly severe or pointless. The ethic behind this view is similar to that of quality-of-life advocates (euthanizers) who argue that it is more humane, and thus morally superior, to extinguish the consciousness of the sufferer. The same sort of ethic underlies the arguments of advocates of abortion of less than normal fetuses and of euthanizers who believe it is right to take the life of those with a low quality of life due to illness or injury. The belief is that God would do the same. Therefore, instead of subjecting the condemned to an unending consciousness that no one can terminate, God either annihilates them one by one as each eventually loses any will to go on, or he immediately annihilates them regardless of whether they would prefer to continue with a conscious existence in hell.

While at first this view might appear to theologically solve the moral dilemma, there are a few problems. First, this view presupposes that the suffering in hell is unbearably extreme, either by physical pain from fire wounds, emotional pain only, or both, and this much pain causes the inhabitants of hell to cry out to be annihilated. But as discussed in sections 11.1 and 11.2, the suffering does not appear likely to be bad enough that the inhabitants of hell would wish for annihilation. That being the case, annihilation would seem unnecessarily cruel, and therefore inconsistent with perfect love and goodness.

Second, immediately annihilating the inhabitants of hell regardless of whether they would prefer to continue with a conscious existence is also inconsistent with perfect love and goodness. This is because it treats them as things without intrinsic value, as merely a means to an end (see chapter 9.2). Moreover, it disrespects their free choice to live in self-exclusion from the heavenly community. According to Habermas and Moreland, a God who respects and dignifies those made in his image

> Treats their choices as significant by allowing them to choose against him, not just for him. . . . Hell is the result of God's respect for persons. It is reasonable to argue that it is wrong to [annihilate] the type of intrinsic value humans have. If God is the source and preserver of values, and if persons have the high degree of intrinsic value Christianity claims they have, then God is the preserver of persons. He would be wrong to [annihilate] something of such value just because it has chosen a life it was not intended to live. Thus, one way God can respect persons is to sustain them in existence and not annihilate them.[36]

Therefore, whether God annihilates the inhabitants of hell one by one as each loses any will to go on, or he immediately annihilates them regardless of whether they would prefer to continue with a conscious existence in hell, annihilationism's so-called claim to moral superiority is actually morally inferior to the traditional view of eternal, conscious punishment.

Not only does the annihilationist's view of hell fail theoretically, but also biblically (exegetically). Annihilationists interpret hell's fire as literal. But as discussed in chapter 10, the most comprehensive and in-depth exegesis shows that the fire is not literal. It is a metaphor for the awful regret over a life foolishly lived and deserving of an irrevocable exclusion from the community in beatific relationship with God. Therefore, there is no literal fire spoken of

Is Hell's Suffering Pointless and Unjust?

in the Bible with which to annihilate the unsaved.

Annihilationists also think that when the Bible says the souls in hell are "destroyed" they are annihilated. They cite Matt. 10:28 (and others[37]): "Be afraid of the One who can destroy both soul and body in hell." While annihilation might seem (to Western readers) to be the most plausible meaning, a literary analysis shows that this is not the case.

The Hebrew and Greek words for "destroy" and "destruction" in the Bible have an array of meanings (uses), each of which can negate a meaning of annihilation: to be lost, to be marred, to be ruined, to perish, to die, to be destroyed.[38] Thus, while the unsaved are "destroyed" (Ps. 143:12), so was Israel (Hos. 13:9; cf. Isa. 9:14), yet Israel wasn't annihilated. Another example in which the thing "destroyed" is not annihilated includes the parable of the lost sheep in Luke 15:4. The Greek word for "lost" (*apóllymi*) in the parable is the same word for "destroyed" (*apóllymi*) in Matt. 10:28. Likewise, in the parable of the "lost" (*apóllymi*) coin in Luke 15:8, the coin was obviously not annihilated.

Moreover, one of the Greek words for the "destruction" (*apōleia*) in hell (Matt. 7:13; 2 Pet. 3:7) has the root verb *apóllymi* (Matt. 10:28), which can mean separating away, or "shut out" from entirely, as in 2 Thess. 1:9.[39] Thus, there is no legitimate reason to insist that the word for "destroy" in Matt. 10:28 means annihilation. Rather, it appears most likely that Jesus taught that in hell both body and soul are separated from (*apóllymi*) the Source of eternal blessing.

In response to the foregoing, annihilationists typically argue that the *context* governs the interpretation of the word, and the context is annihilation. They believe this because: (a) the fire of hell is believed to be a literal fire; and (b) many annihilationists believe the soul cannot consciously exist after death; thus, once the body is annihilated, so is the conscious soul (a belief held by Seventh-day Adventists).

Regarding the belief that the fire of hell is literal, according to annihilationists, common sense tells us that any consumable substance (e.g., a body) that is thrown into a literal lake of fire (Rev. 19:20; 10:14–15; 21:8) is annihilated. But the previous chapter discussed why the fire of hell is metaphorical. As such, there is no stated method for annihilating the unsaved in the Bible—no stated context of an annihilating hellfire. And since God does not do anything significant without first warning his people by his prophets

(Amos 3:7), it appears even less likely that annihilation would be the fate of the unsaved.

Regarding the view of some Christians that the soul is mortal and ceases to exist at death, this is the teaching of non-immortality of the soul, or conditional immortality. In this teaching, there is no conscious soul that survives the death of the body, because a conscious soul cannot exist apart from a living body. Thus, when a body dies, consciousness ceases and the soul no longer exists. So when the unsaved, who are resurrected in the final judgment, are then engulfed in literal flames, their bodies are annihilated, which annihilates the soul. This is the "second death" (Rev. 2:11; 20:6, 14; 21:8), the final annihilation, according to annihilationists.

There's not enough room here for a full discussion (several chapters would be needed), but the following points are sufficient to show that it is not biblical. To begin with, in Matt. 10:28 Jesus alludes to the concept that the killing of the body does not cause the conscious soul to cease to exist. "Do not be afraid of those who kill (*apokteinó*) the body but cannot kill (*apokteinó*) the soul." The point of the text is that what the worst people can do to us does not match the worst God can do, and thus, God should be respected above all others. But with this, as Matthew Henry (1662–1714) points out, is an allusion to the concept that "the soul does not . . . fall asleep at death, nor is deprived of thought and perception; for then the killing of the body would be the killing of the soul too. The soul is killed when it is separated from God and his love, which is its life."[40]

Annihilationism has a big problem with its interpretation methodology. The first step is to interpret a few Old Testament texts (wrongly) to teach non-immortality of the soul (e.g., Eccl. 9:5-6, 10; Ps. 115:17; 146:4; Ezek. 18:20). Then New Testament verses that appear contradictory (to speak about the soul's immortality) are explained away so as to make the New Testament on the afterlife harmonize with their ill-constructed view of non-immortality of the soul.[41] This is particularly problematic because the Old Testament books, written by God's earlier prophets, contain almost no information received from God on the nature of the afterlife.[42] This should be no surprise to Christians familiar with the doctrine of progressive (cumulative) revelation. God progressively revealed concepts to humankind over the course of many centuries so that obscure revelatory concepts recorded by the earlier prophets are, at appropriate times in the future, fleshed out and made clear. This is the Apostle Paul's understanding of revelation (Rom. 16:25; Col. 1:25–27). It is no wonder, then, that it is acceptable to most modern conservative biblical scholars,[43] including the renowned theologian Charles Hodge (1797–1878):

> What at first is only obscurely intimated is gradually unfolded in subsequent parts of the sacred volume, until the truth is revealed in its fullness. This is true of the doctrines of redemption; of the person and work of the Messiah, the promised seed of the woman; of the nature and office of the Holy Spirit; and of *a future state beyond the grave*.[44]

One example of progressive revelation on the subject of the afterlife is that of the truth of the corporate resurrection-translation that is prophesied to take place at the end of the world. From the time of Abraham until the time of Daniel (roughly 1,500 years) there is no intimation in Scripture of the corporate resurrection-translation, and even what Daniel relates tells very little (Dan. 12:2). Then, some five hundred years later,[45] Jesus expounds on the subject in detail, resulting in numerous passages in the New Testament.

Another problem for the teaching of non-immortality of the soul is that Old Testament prophets believed in a conscious, or at least semiconscious, ghostly existence after death (a kind of soul immortality). Their conception of an afterlife was fairly compatible with their ancient Near Eastern neighbors' concept of a literal netherworld (underworld) of the dead.[46] The netherworld (*sheol*[47]) was seen by the ancient Hebrews as a gloomy, shadowy mode of existence (Job 10:21–22; Ps. 143:3) lying deep under the surface of the earth (Ps. 88:6; Ezek. 26:20; 31:14–15; Amos 9:2) where the dead are conscious, or semiconscious, spirits or "shades" (*rehaim*[48]) who can communicate in some sense (Isa. 14:9–20; Ezek. 32:21) and where they can no longer experience God's favor and blessings in the land of the living (Ps. 6:5; 88:12; Eccl. 9:10). With some variance, this conception was universally accepted in the ancient Near East, and textual evidence in the Old Testament tells us that until the first century, God's people believed it.

Some Christians are uncomfortable with the idea that the ancient Hebrews would believe in the existence of a mistaken view of the afterlife, such as the netherworld, as it would seem to go against biblical inerrancy by the inspiration[49] of the Holy Spirit. They find it difficult to accept that if Scripture is "God-breathed" (2 Tim. 3:16), God would not have diverted his penmen away from such a belief by some new revelation. However, there are several conservative biblical reasons why the netherworld concept in the Old Testament does not go against biblical inerrancy by inspiration.

According to 2 Tim. 3:16–17, 2 Pet. 1:20–21, and other texts,[50] the

Holy Spirit's superintendence or steering or "carrying along" of the writer ("God-breathed" [*theopneustos*]) extends to ensuring that what is written is useful (which necessitates being true, correct, and reliable) "for teaching, rebuking, correcting and training in righteousness, so that the man of God may be thoroughly equipped for every good work." In other words, the Bible is inerrant in the truths that equip one to be "completely ready to meet the demands of discipleship," such as how to cultivate an appropriate disposition and lifestyle for a saving relationship with God.[51] According to conservative scholarship on inspiration and inerrancy (e.g., Geisler, Boice, Packer, Sproul, and Wenham), from this we should garner a rule that the Holy Spirit would not allow untrue conceptions or beliefs into Scripture *except* in some instances[52] when overriding purposes warrant allowing man to write something inconsequential that may not be completely accurate or true. This is not a theory of partial inspiration or partial inerrancy, but rather a *qualified* inspiration and inerrancy for God's overriding purposes.[53]

One such exception is the overriding necessity of progressive revelation. Two necessary purposes for a progressive revelation are effective communication and God's providential plan for the unfolding of a history that accomplishes the greatest possible good. There was an overriding necessity to effectively communicate revelatory material in terms that the ancient audiences would understand and embrace as a people. This required packaging truths in ancient cultural conceptions that would not grossly countermand worldviews to an extent that the messages would be seen as too objectionable. This was a matter of providential timing that was sensitive to certain mindsets, cultures, and traditions in order to bring about events to move the human race forward in a world of divine hiddenness according to God's plan.

This way of revealing truth took a multitude of generations, over the course of several thousand years. This is evident by comparing the earliest Bible writings (e.g., the book of Job or Ecclesiastes) to later writings (e.g., the book of Daniel or the books of the New Testament). By comparing, it is easy to see that a younger Israelite nation possessed less knowledge of God's nature, the messianic ministry, details of redemption, Satan, and the eternal afterlife than the first-century writers.[54]

Textual evidence, then, supports a progressive method of revelation by the Holy Spirit. This means that it was God's plan to allow the earlier prophets to continue to hold onto certain untrue beliefs. This is not misleading them,[55] but it does entail keeping some truths secret from earlier generations, which meant that some of their erroneous (or pagan) beliefs were allowed to continue, for a time.

Such is the case with the ancient belief in a netherworld. By this, the Spirit is not relinquishing the authority or credibility of Scripture. Rather, he is withholding correction of the mistaken belief until the time of the messiah, when it would be properly replaced by the greatest revelation in the first century setting. Revelation does not correct earlier revelation; rather, revelation supplants earlier *non-revelatory* conceptions.[56]

Although while the concept of the netherworld as a whole is untrue, it was not without a kernel of truth with respect to the concept of an eternally existing consciousness (even if only a semiconsciousness) that survives the death of the body. Thus, there actually is a revelatory component within the netherworld concept. This component (soul immortality) is affirmed in the New Testament: Matt. 14:26; Mark 6:49; Luke 16:19–31; 23:43; 2 Cor. 5:1–8; Phil. 1:23; Rev. 6:9–11. Therefore, Christians need not be uncomfortable with the idea that the ancient Hebrews would believe in the existence of the netherworld.

Still, annihilationists object to the idea that the ancient Hebrews believed in a literal netherworld. They argue that the term *sheol* always refers to the grave and never to the netherworld.[57] But as Hebrew scholar John H. Walton points out, passages like Psalms 55:15; 139:8; and Amos 9:2 go against this.[58] In Ps. 139:8, for example, the psalmist observes: "If I make my bed in the depths (*sheol*), you are there." The psalmist is talking about the impossibility of a conscious person being able to flee to any location to get away from God, including the netherworld, which is appropriate because God has access to *sheol* (netherworld) (Job 26:6; Prov. 15:11; Amos 9:2). But the verse makes no sense at all in the view by annihilationists that consciousness ceases at death. It can only make sense if consciousness, or semiconsciousness, continues after death.

An exception to this would be if it were meant as figurative hyperbole to emphasize the idea that there's *nowhere* on earth, or sea, that a person can go to escape God. But it is difficult to believe *sheol* here was meant figuratively because of the references to literal places in the cosmos (v. 8–9) and the many references to a literal three-tiered cosmos consisting of the solid sky dome, the earth, and the netherworld in the Old Testament.[59] Moreover, the author of Job seems to see the netherworld as a literal place of conscious existence (Job

10:18–22). Therefore, at the least, we can feel sure that the ancient Israelites believed in a conscious state after death, and that it was likely wrapped up in the non-revelatory but commonly accepted conception of a literal netherworld.

In addition to the previously-discussed problems of the teaching of non-immortality of the soul are two other problems worth mentioning. One is no continuity of self. If the soul is derived completely from the natural body, as annihilationists argue, then when the body dies and decomposes, the soul would cease to exist. An immortally existing soul could only occur if a body is subsequently recreated (resurrected) with conscious being. The problem with this is there is no continuity of self and identity. The recreated person would not be the same person.

The other problem for the teaching of non-immortality of the soul is the voluminous collection of evidence that the conscious soul survives the death of the body discussed briefly in chapter 3.3. Many thousands of people— even unbelievers in the supernatural, or unbelievers in soul immortality— report having an out-of-body experience and observing things that would be impossible to observe if our consciousness does not continue after death.

In sum, the premises of a literal hellfire and non-immortality of the soul (conditional immortality) would make the context of hell one of annihilation if they were biblical. But because they lack biblical support, a context of annihilation for hell is unwarranted. In the absence of a context of annihilation, interpreting the "destruction" of the unsaved in the Bible as separation from the heavenly community is by far the most plausible interpretation.

Another reason annihilationism does not hold up exegetically is that being judged and consigned to hell is "everlasting." The Greek word describing hell's duration that is translated as "everlasting" (*aionios*)[60] appears in the New Testament seventy-one times. While the word can mean either an age or a very long period of time, it most often means eternity. Whether it means an age or eternity is determined by the context in which it is used. Out of the seventy-one times the word appears, sixty-four of these (or about 88 percent) are in an eternal context.[61] The context of life in heaven is clearly a context of eternity (rather than a very long period of time), so the occurrences of the Greek word (*aionios*) with regard to texts on heaven[62] mean eternity. The Greek word also occurs in reference to hell.[63] Because most of the occurrences indicate a meaning of eternity (rather than a very long period of time), and because all of its uses with regard to heaven indicate eternity, it is reasonable to suppose that hell lasts eternally.

Further support for this comes from the analogous states of an eternal heaven and an eternal hell in Daniel 12:2 and Matthew 25:41, 46. In Daniel 12:2, "Multitudes who sleep in the dust of the earth will awake: some to everlasting (*olam*) life, others to shame and everlasting (*olam*) contempt." In Matthew 25:41, 46, Jesus taught that the unsaved will be cast "into the eternal (*aionios*) fire prepared for the devil and his angels. . . . Then they will go away to eternal (*aionios*) punishment, but the righteous to eternal (*aionios*) life." ("Eternal life" is a term symbolizing an intimate relationship with God in heaven irrespective of an issue of consciousness versus no consciousness).[64] The structure of the verses suggests that the states of the saved and the unsaved are analogous. That is, both have eternal consciousness—the saved are blessed with God eternally, and the unsaved are cursed without God eternally.

In sum, some Christians struggling to reconcile an eternal hell with a loving and good God interpret hell as being a brief period when the unsaved are extinguished by a literal fire. This is thought to be morally superior and what is taught in the Bible. However, it turns out that it is actually morally inferior and cannot be legitimately derived from what the Bible teaches.

Conclusion

Critics of hell argue that the unending punishment in hell is needless and unfruitful, and therefore could only satisfy the anger of a spiteful and retaliating God. Moreover, the punishment is too severe to be justly proportionate to the crime.

A Christian response is that hell may seem pointless and unjust because the punishment and the crime are misunderstood. The souls consigned to hell have affirmed, by their lives lived, that they genuinely prefer to keep their relation to God irrevocably spoiled and broken. In accord with his law of justice through accountability, God honors this by handing them over to their life choice. He does not do this out of spite or anger, but out of his respect for the intrinsic value of life and free will.

Suffering in hell results from a poor quality of life due to the circumstance of being outside of heaven. This loss overshadows all thoughts and makes for some very unpleasant experiences. But it is probably not an existence without some times of light suffering, particularly in the levels of hell made for the least of God's rejecters, although even a life with the mildest suffering that never ends is a very awful situation.

This is a fair punishment because it is the reward for the ultimate crime. Rejecting the thing of greatest value intensifies the rejection to an ultimate extent, making it the ultimate and most reprehensible sin. The only punishment worthy of the ultimate sin is the ultimate punishment, which is life in hell outside of the heavenly community.

Despite the foregoing, some theologians reinterpret hell to conform to either a universalist view or an annihilation view of hell. But each alternate view fails on theoretical, as well as exegetical, grounds.

The conclusion, then, is that given the previously discussed view of the punishment, and the nature of the crime, a reasonable inference can be made that the punishment is proportionate to the crime. Therefore, hell appears to be just, which makes God appear to be just for consigning anyone to it, and there is no apparent inconsistency between the existence of hell and the existence of a perfectly loving and good God.

NOTES to Chapter 11

1. John W. Loftus, *Why I Became an Atheist: A Former Preacher Rejects Christianity* (Amherst, NY: Prometheus Books, 2008), 256.

2. Ibid., 388.

3. Clark H. Pinnock, "The Conditional View," in *Four Views on Hell*, series ed. Stanley N. Gundry, gen. ed. William V. Crockett (Grand Rapids, MI: Zondervan, 1996), 152. Pinnock argues in favor of the annihilationist view of hell. Pinnock received his PhD at Manchester University, England.

4. Ibid.

5. *Zondervan NIV Bible Commentary, Volume 2: New Testament*, consul. eds. Kenneth L. Barker and John R. Kohlenberger III (Grand Rapids, MI: Zondervan Publishing House, 1994), 878.

6. Gary D. Chapman, *The Five Love Languages: The Secret to Love That Lasts* (Chicago: Northfield Publishing, 1992), 21–22.

7. Matt. 5:22; 10:28.

8. Gary R. Habermas and J. P. Moreland, *Beyond Death: Exploring the Evidence for Immortality* (Eugene, OR: Wipf and Stock Publishers, 2004), 289.

9. Ibid., 290.

10. Steve Jeffery, Michael Ovey, and Andrew Sach, *Pierced for Our Transgressions: Rediscovering the Glory of Penal Substitution* (Wheaton, IL: Crossway Books,

2007), 252.

11. C. S. Lewis, *The Great Divorce* (New York: HarperOne, 1946, 2009 ed.), 75.

12. Ps. 78:50; 81:12; Ezek. 20:25; Rom. 1:28; Acts 7:42; 1 Cor. 5:5; 1 Tim. 1:20.

13. For a brief discussion of the principle (law) of justice through accountability see appendix D.

14. Gary R. Habermas and J. P. Moreland, *Beyond Death*, 295.

15. Two notable examples are: Catholic priest Thomas Aquinas (1225–1274), and Scottish church leader Thomas Boston (1676–1732) [Paul Johnson, *A History of Christianity* (New York: Simon & Schuster, 1976), 341–342]. Modern opponents of Christianity typically bring up this idea in their attacks. One such opponent is Keith Parsons in "Hell: Christianity's Most Damnable Doctrine," in *The End of Christianity*, ed. John W. Loftus (Amherst, NY: Prometheus Books, 2011), 235.

16. Eugene Peterson, NIV/ *The Message Parallel Bible* (Grand Rapids, MI: Zondervan, 2004), 1873.

17. Matt. 16:27; Rom. 2:6; Rev. 18:6; 20:12–13; 22:12.

18. P. M. H. Atwater, *Dying to Know You: Proof of God in the Near-Death Experience* (Faber, VA: Rainbow Ridge Books, 2014), 40–41.

19. One NDEr who reported time passing differently in the afterlife is Don Piper [Jonathan Bernis, *A Rabbi Looks at the Afterlife* (Shippensburg, PA: Destiny Image Publishers, 2014), 209].

20. In verse 46 the author uses the same Greek word (*aiōnios*) to describe the duration of the punishment in hell as he does for the duration of the reward in heaven.

21. Heb. 11:1–3, 6, 13; Eph. 2:8.

22. *Zondervan NIV Bible Commentary, Volume 2: New Testament*, 1103; *The Expositor's Bible Commentary*, gen. ed. Frank E. Gaebelein, consul. eds. James Montgomery Boice and Merrill C. Tenney, Vol. 10 (Grand Rapids, MI: Zondervan Publishing House, 1976), 346; *Matthew Henry's Commentary on the Whole Bible* (Peabody, MA: Hendrickson Publishers, 1991), 1970; Gary D. Chapman, *The Five Love Languages*, 101.

23. Morton T. Kelsey, *Afterlife: The Other Side of Dying* (New York: Paulist, 1979), 247.

24. Gary R. Habermas and J. P. Moreland, *Beyond Death*, 295, 296.

25. Paul Copan, *That's Just Your Interpretation: Responding to Skeptics Who Challenge Your Faith* (Grand Rapids, MI: Baker Books, 2001), 136.

26. *Matthew Henry's Commentary on the Whole Bible* (Peabody, MA: Hendrickson Publishers, 1991), 1923. Emphasis added.

27. J. P. Moreland, as quoted in Lee Strobel, *The Case for Faith: A Journalist Investigates the Toughest Objections to Christianity* (Grand Rapids, MI: Zondervan, 2000), 181.

28. Gary R. Habermas and J. P. Moreland, *Beyond Death*, 307.

29. Keith Parsons, "Hell: Christianity's Most Damnable Doctrine," in *The End of Christianity*, ed. John W. Loftus (Amherst, NY: Prometheus Books, 2011), 242.

30. David Mills, *Atheist Universe: The Thinking Person's Answer to Christian Fundamentalism* (Berkeley, CA: Ulysses Press, 2006), chapter 8.

31. Steve Jeffery, Michael Ovey, and Andrew Sach, *Pierced for Our Transgressions*, 252.

32. Ibid.

33. Michael J. Murray, "Heaven and Hell," in *Reason for the Hope Within*, ed. Michael J. Murray (Grand Rapids, MI: Wm. B. Eerdmans Publishing Co., 1999), 310–312.

34. Douglas J. Moo, *The NIV Application Commentary: Romans* (Grand Rapids, MI: Zondervan, 2000), 193; *Zondervan NIV Bible Commentary, Volume 2: New Testament*, 548.

35. Jonathan L. Kvanig, as quoted in John W. Loftus, *Why I Became an Atheist*, 391.

36. Gary R. Habermas and J. P. Moreland, *Beyond Death*, 295–296.

37. Matt. 7:13; Rom. 9:22; Heb. 10:26–27.

38. James Strong, "A Concise Dictionary of the Words in The Hebrew Bible," p. 7, and "A Concise Dictionary of the Words in the Greek Testament," pp. 14 and 51, in *The New Strong's Exhaustive Concordance of the Bible* (Nashville, TN: Thomas Nelson Publishers, 1990); William D. Mounce, *Complete Expository Dictionary of Old and New Testament Words* (Grand Rapids, MI: Zondervan, 2006), 423.

39. *Vine's Expository Dictionary of Old & New Testament Words* (Thomas Nelson, 1997), 165; cf. John 11:50; Acts 5:37; 1 Cor. 10:9–10; Jude 11; William D. Mounce, *Complete Expository Dictionary of Old and New Testament Words*, 423; James Strong, "A Concise Dictionary of the Words in the Greek Testament," in *Strong's Exhaustive Concordance of the Bible*, 15.

40. *Matthew Henry's Commentary on the Whole Bible*, 1321.

41. This methodology is clearly evident in Samuele Bacchiocchi's book *Immortality or Resurrection?: A Biblical Study on Human Nature and Destiny* (Berrien Springs, MI: Biblical Perspectives, 1997).

42. Charles H. Dodd, *The Epistle of Paul to the Romans* (London: Hodder and Stoughton, 1932), 81.

43. Progressive revelation is even affirmed in Article V of The Chicago Statement on Biblical Inerrancy of 1978. Contributing scholars include: Norman L. Geisler, James Montgomery Boice (1968–2000), James I. Packer, Robert C. Sproul, and John Wenham.

44. Charles Hodge, *Systematic Theology*, Vol. 1 (Peabody, MA: Hendrickson Publishers, 1981, 1999 reprinted ed.), 446. Emphasis added.

45. The more persuasive argument for the date of the writing of the book of Daniel has it around 530 BC, although some scholars (perhaps due in part to difficulty believing in long-range prophecy) date it at around 150 BC.

46. John H. Walton, *Ancient Near Eastern Thought and the Old Testament: Introducing*

the *Conceptual World of the Hebrew Bible* (Grand Rapids, MI: Baker Academic, 2006), 166, 177–178, 313–329; J. Edward Wright, *The Early History of Heaven* (New York: Oxford University Press, 2000), 85–88; Gary R. Habermas and J. P. Moreland, *Beyond Death*, 289.

47. While a few occurrences of *sheol* refer to the grave (e.g., Isa. 28:15), most occurrences refer to the netherworld.

48. Job 26:5; Ps. 88:11; Prov. 2:18; 9:18; 21:16; Isa. 14:9; 26:19.

49. The plenary-verbal view of inspiration is the orthodox view. The word *plenary* means "complete" or "full," and *verbal* means "the words of Scripture." Thus, the Holy Spirit moves on the writer in the writing process to the extent that the meaning of every word scribed is scribed by God's approval (2 Tim. 3:16–17; 2 Pet. 1:21). Although while *all* Scripture is inspired, authoritative, and useful, revelation is progressive, meaning that God communicates incompletely or partially. A result of this is that later prophets have more light than earlier prophets. Moreover, the knowledge of the writers was limited (as the Holy Spirit intended) to the contexts of literary genre, or culture, to address immediate concerns that played a significant role in God's grand scheme for humankind. Thus, we are to adapt to genres, literary styles, and conventions in order to properly interpret Scripture. "Inspiration does not eliminate the need for the hard work of interpretation" [Mark L. Strauss, "The Inspiration of the Bible," in *The Baker Illustrated Bible Handbook*, eds. J. Daniel Hays and J. Scott Duvall (Grand Rapids, MI: BakerBooks, 2011), 995–1005].

50. 2 Sam. 23:2; Mark 12:36; 1 Cor. 2:11–13; Rev. 1:1–2, 10–11; 2:7, 11, 19, 29.

51. *Zondervan NIV Bible Commentary, Volume 2: New Testament*, 915. According to Craig Blomberg, at most, 2 Tim. 3:16 tells us "that every *book* of Scripture, and perhaps every major unit of thought within those books, has theological significance [Craig L. Blomberg with Jennifer Foutz Markley, *A Handbook of New Testament Exegesis* (Grand Rapids, MI: Baker Academic, 2010), 237. Emphasis in the original].

52. Such as progressive revelation, literary conventions with inherent untrue elements (i.e., parable), phenomenal language, generalizations, nonliteral language, etc. [Mark L. Strauss, "The Inspiration of the Bible," in *The Baker Illustrated Bible Handbook*, eds. J. Daniel Hays and J. Scott Duvall (Grand Rapids, MI: BakerBooks, 2011), 1000, 1003].

53. John H. Walton, *The NIV Application Commentary: Genesis* (Grand Rapids, MI: Zondervan, 2001), 88. Walton affirms the fact that there are non-revelatory areas in Scripture. However, non-revelatory material in the Bible does not imply any sort of theory of partial inspiration, or partial inerrancy, but rather a qualified inspiration and inerrancy for God's overriding purposes ("biblical inerrancy" should not be confused with "biblical literalism").

54. Ibid., 211.

55. Ibid., 88.

56. In addition to revelatory conceptions of transcendent metaphysical realities received directly from God (1 Cor. 2:11–13; 2 Pet. 1:20–21), there are non-revelatory conceptions in the Bible—conceptions of men (e.g., naturally occurring eyewitness

testimony of events in the gospels, Paul's quotes of the writings of non-Christians [Acts 17:28; 1 Cor. 15:33; Titus 1:12], and Jude's quotes from extrabiblical Jewish literature [Jude 9 and 14] [the Testament of Moses {or Assumption of Mosel} and the First Book of Enoch {and possibly also the Apocalypse of Moses}]).

57. R. L. Harris, "The Meaning of the Word Sheol as Shown by Parallels in Poetic Texts," in *Bulletin of the Evangelical Theological Society*, December 1961: 129–135.

58. John H. Walton, *Ancient Near Eastern Thought and the Old Testament*, 320.

59. Some of the Bible verses include: Exod. 24:10; Deut. 32:22; Job 9:6–7; 22:14; 26:7, 10; 36:27; 38:4–6, 19; Pss. 8:3; 24:2; 104:3; Prov. 8:27; Isa. 40:22; Ezek. 1:22. For discussion, see John H. Walton, *The NIV Application Commentary: Genesis*, 87, and *Ancient Near Eastern Thought and the Old Testament*, 165–178.

60. Matt. 18:8; 25:41, 46; Jude 6–7, 13; Rev. 14:11; 20:10.

61. Gary R. Habermas and J. P. Moreland, *Beyond Death*, 304.

62. John 6:27; 6:40, 47; 12:50; Acts 13:46; Rom. 6:22; Gal. 6:8; 1 Tim. 1:16.

63. Matt. 18:8; 25:41, 46; Jude 6–7, 13; Rev. 14:11; 20:10.

64. John 17:3; 10:10; 1 Tim. 6:19.

Part 4

The Problem of Those Who Have Never Heard

12

Is Hell Unjust for People Who Had Never Heard of the Gospel?

Synopsis

Critics of Christianity argue that God is either not all-loving or not all-powerful, because a large number of people die without the opportunity to know about the gospel and be able to properly respond to God for salvation from hell. If God can ensure that all hear the gospel, but he is unwilling to give the opportunity for some to hear it, he wouldn't be all-loving; or if God is willing to give the opportunity for all to hear the gospel, but he is unable to, he wouldn't be all-powerful. Either way, the situation in the world does not reflect the existence of God.

A Christian response is that despite the apparent lack of opportunity for salvation for a large number of people, God gives everyone access to gospel knowledge and the ability to properly respond to God for salvation, by natural and supernatural means, regardless of where or when a person is born or the religion a person inherits. Therefore, the fact that millions die without hearing about the gospel is consistent with God's willingness for all to have the opportunity to be saved, as well as his ability to make it so.

A few years before renouncing my belief in Christianity, I attended a board meeting as one of the leaders of my church. Midway into the meeting we switched to the topic of evangelism. The pastor, sensing a need to motivate the members to come up with new ideas of how to reach our community with the gospel, interjected, "We've got to work harder to get the gospel message to those who've never heard it. God will hold us accountable for neglecting the work. Woe to us if a person ends up in hell because we didn't reach him with the gospel."

Rife with frustration over my consternation with this notion, I faced the pastor and said, "I've heard members say people are necessarily lost who never hear the gospel. But I can't see how or why God, who is concerned for the salvation of everyone, would place that responsibility on people he knows will fail to accomplish the task. It is an impossible responsibility for us to bear. And it makes God appear irresponsible for leaving salvation up to our limited and frail ability, and unloving for not caring whether some have a chance to be saved."

The pastor, looking caught off guard, thought for a moment and said, "Well, that is the traditional view of the church . . . The apostle Paul seemed to believe that way. You yourself know, Dan, as it says in John 14:6 and Acts 4:12, that no one is saved by the Father except by faith in Christ.[1] Anyway, we are called and commanded to get the message out. We can talk about this some other time; we need to get on with church business."

I agreed to get on with the meeting. We never made time to discuss the matter further.

The view to which I was voicing objection is called restrictivism. It is held by some evangelical Christians and believed in a variety of denominations. It is, essentially, that no one can properly respond to God and thus be accepted by God without such a response being based in knowledge of the gospel tenets. The gospel tenets refer to the need to be saved from sin and hell for holiness and heaven by way of the person and work of the messiah (Jesus Christ). All who die without this knowledge cannot properly respond to God for salvation, and end up in hell. Several New Testament texts are cited in support of this view. The texts are discussed in appendix E.

I hadn't studied the view in any depth, but it did not seem to be theologically sound. And, over a span of several years, I had developed considerable objection to it. I would roll my eyes every time I'd hear Christians fret about getting the gospel to those who would most certainly have no chance for heaven without it; millions of people who live in places where the gospel is never introduced would all, without exception, be lost. This did not seem fair.

Years later when my faith was crumbling, due in large part to the challenges that seemed to debunk Christianity listed in chapter 1.4, I added restrictivism to my list of reasons to renounce my belief in God. I couldn't see how anyone could believe in a God who condemns people to hell who never had a chance to learn about the gospel and so have a chance to be saved.

The problem is sometimes referred to as the problem of evil concerning the unevangelized, or the soteriological[2] problem of evil. God is said to be perfectly loving and good and all-powerful (and all-knowing). Such a God desires the salvation of all and is powerful enough to make salvation universally accessible to all people. But if God predetermines that a large portion of the human population never hears the gospel and is lost to hell, then he is either not perfectly loving and good or not all-powerful. God could not be both, which poses a doctrinal inconsistency.

God's options are to either: (a) make no access to salvation for any sinner, (b) make salvation accessible to some and not others, or (c) make salvation accessible to every sinner. Option (a) (make no access to salvation for any sinner) would not conflict with God's character, because sinners are undeserving of, and not entitled to, reconciliation and heaven according to the principle of justice through accountability. This dictates that all conduct ultimately be made to meet its just consequence—that there must be a reaping of what is sown.[3] The just consequence for sinful conduct is separation from God, ultimately for a mediocre life in hell, as there can be no fellowship between God and a person who chooses a mindset in rebellion against God's disposition (God's law). Therefore, God would be just and fair if he had not initiated his messianic plan of salvation and let all sinners reap the consequence of their sins in hell. But (thankfully) God closed the door to this option when he made an oath to save humankind that is manifest in the ministries of the Holy Spirit and Jesus Christ (see appendix D). This leaves God with options (b) and (c).

In option (b) God would provide a chance to be saved to some and provide no chance to others. The ones with no chance would be unable to respond to God to avoid hell. This is the option some Christians believe God has chosen. The idea is that because sinners do not deserve heaven, it would be consistent with a loving and good God to exercise inscrutable judgment that is "uninvestigatable" to humans to make heaven a possibility for some, while an impossibility to others. Among the proposed reasons for why some would not be given a chance are that the limit of God's mercy means he'll seek to save some and not others, or God's judgment is an eternal mystery. However, there are problems with this view.

The first is that it is not consistent with God's disposition, because a deity that makes salvation possible for some and impossible for others shows favoritism. According to at least twelve Bible texts,[4] showing favoritism goes against a principle (law) of love and goodness with respect to treatment of persons, and is therefore a sin. "God does not show favoritism," especially with regard to the judgment (Rom. 2:11). It's not consistent with a God "who loves so indiscriminately that he sends sun and rain on both the righteous and the unrighteous."[5]

Second, with regard to God's judgment being inscrutable and uninvestigatable, this goes against a point made in chapter 4 that a consummate relationship with God in heaven *depends* on God's adjudication and judgment being fathomable and searchable, which is consistent with the investigative nature of the judgment (Dan. 7:9–10; 1 Cor. 6:2–3; Rev. 20:11–15), in which the redeemed get to find out why some were not saved.[6] So this idea that God's adjudication is to forever be a mystery doesn't appear theologically sound, as such an eternity is liable to fracture the integrity of the heavenly community's relationship with God.

Another problem is that in at least six verses the Bible directly states that God desires heaven for all sinners[7] — God, "not wanting anyone to perish, but everyone to come to repentance" (2 Pet. 3:9). It therefore doesn't make sense that he would choose to make a path to heaven impossible for some sinners. Making it impossible doesn't seem to accord with his desire. Although, I suppose it could be argued that God foreknew that if they were given a chance, they'd reject it, which takes us to the problem of the previous paragraph.

Moreover, if God creates a portion of humankind that has no opportunity for salvation, then he would create beings for the express purpose of condemning them to hell. Such evil and suffering would be an unnecessary and gratuitous perpetuity of God. As pointed out in chapter 7.2, the glaring problem of the existence of pointless evil and suffering is that it does nothing to bring about a greater good (or prevent a greater evil) and thus is not logically consistent with the existence of God. Such a deity is very different from the Deity who does not want anyone to be lost.

Finally, if God is intentionally making it impossible for some to be saved, he would be setting up a situation in which some are under coercion to sin, which would rob them of compatibility-determining free will. If their only chance for salvation comes by divine intervention and that intervention is withheld, how could the sinner really make a genuine choice to be the kind of person compatible with hell? The restrictivist might argue that God would foreknow the choice they'd make, but such a choice *would not be demonstrated*, which returns us back to the problem of an inscrutable and uninvestigatable judgment that would thwart God's plan for the consummate community of heaven.

Because of these theological problems, option (b) doesn't appear to be the one God would choose. The only one remaining is option (c): extend the opportunity to be saved to everyone. But, atheists and restrictivists alike argue that it is evident that God did not choose this option, as salvation is dependent upon having certain knowledge of the gospel tenets, and it is a fact that millions of people died before learning about them. If God is extending the opportunity to be saved to all, the situation in the world would have to be very different.

So how might the soteriological problem be solved? After spending years studying the Bible on the topic of salvation, including study of the views of Calvinism,[8] Molinism,[9] Arminianism,[10] predestination, universalism,[11] pluralism,[12] Catholicism, Eastern Orthodox, etc., I propose that the solution comes from the resolution of a two-part issue of whether God makes salvation possible for all.

The first part of the issue concerns the fact that millions of people die before learning about the gospel message of the need to be saved from sin and hell that is made possible through Christ. In light of this fact, many are of the opinion that God is parsimonious, unloving, arbitrary, and unjust, because his neglect of the human situation ensures that a multitude of people will remain lost to hell. But such opinion is based on the erroneous assumption that if God allows a person to die without learning of the gospel, he has denied the person a chance for conversion and salvation. The following section discusses how God provides an opportunity for salvation to everyone, including the multitude that dies before learning of the gospel.

The second part of the issue concerns what sort of information and knowledge is required in order for a sinner to properly respond to God for acceptance into heaven. Does one have to understand all of the gospel tenets—the concepts of salvation from sin and hell through God's grace by the work of Jesus? Or could one experience a saving response to God while having little or no knowledge of these truths? The answer essentially comes down to the biblical conception of the basis on which God makes a decision to accept a sinner for heaven or reject a sinner for hell (God's adjudication). This is discussed in section 12.2.

12.1 How God Provides Opportunity for Salvation to Everyone

The Bible is clear that it is by God's grace that any of us are accepted into the heavenly community. His grace manifests in three vitally important ways. One way is in the person and ministry of Jesus Christ, who makes acceptance into heaven possible by satisfying the immutable principle of justice through accountability on behalf of sinners. Unless that principle has been upheld, God the Father (representing the three persons of God) cannot remain perfectly righteous while extending mercy to save any sinner. But Jesus' substitutionary death satisfies and upholds it, so the Father has a green light, so to speak, to extend mercy to reconcile any of us to him, and to heaven. The Father's merciful judgment is another manifestation of God's grace. (See appendix D for further discussion.)

Another such manifestation is the ministry of the Holy Spirit and his angels. Their job is to: (a) impart knowledge that facilitates the existence of a saving relationship with God; (b) preserve the existence of significant compatibility-determining free will in humans by (1) keeping the abilities and influences of lost angels at bay to a necessary extent (Job 1:9–12) and (2) providentially balancing incentives in each person's life to do good and bad things to preserve optimal free will (as discussed in chapter 4); and (c) provide power to overcome temptation and sin in accord with the will that is genuinely surrendered to obedience to the principles of love and goodness.

With the three manifestations of God's grace in operation, the human will, despite its sinful nature, has the God-given ability for a free and proper response to God for salvation. But while the ability is given, it's up to each of us to properly respond.

Rays of Information That Light a Pathway to Salvation Are Indiscriminately Given to All (by Common Grace). The pertinent role of the Holy Spirit is that of universal, supernatural evangelist, revelator, and instigator of faith. He loves all souls unconditionally. The Bible tells us that directly, and indirectly, through the ministering community of his angels,[13] the Spirit imparts rays of metaphysical conceptions to each and every human mind[14] to light a path that, if walked, would lead to greater light,[15] by which a person could enter into a saving relationship with God. According to Acts 17:26–27:

> From one man he made every nation of men, that they should inhabit the whole earth; and he determined the times set for them and the exact places where they should live. God did this *so that men would seek him and perhaps reach out for him and find him*, though *he is not far from each one of us* (emphasis added).

The passage informs us that God is providentially working out a plan by which each person of the whole world is given rays of divine light that illuminate a path in life for a *journey* that enables her or him to ultimately find God.

The rays come to us by the works of the Holy Spirit and his angels. They utilize various modes, whether natural or supernatural, to reveal light of the Divine. Among the natural modes are the created world, and human observation and reaction to it.

In a prehistoric time there arose a conception that order was a righteous virtue, as the gods were thought to generally place value on order, justice, and security in the human realm.[16] The cosmos was seen as orderly because of its functionality, the functioning ecosystem, the world's cycles of seasons, and the apparent movements of stars, planets, and the sun and moon across the sky. Thus, in the ancient polytheistic world, the cosmos was seen to reflect the righteousness of its originator(s), or creator(s).

The Old Testament prophets claimed to have special revelation on this universal conception that the cosmos declared the glory and righteousness of the one, true God. In the Psalms we read,

> The heavens declare the glory of God; the skies proclaim the work of his hands. Day after day they pour forth speech; night after night they display knowledge. There is no speech or language where their voice is not heard. Their voice goes out into all the earth, their words to the ends of the world (Ps. 19:1–4a).

And, "the heavens proclaim his righteousness, for God himself is judge" (Ps. 50:6). While this was a truth revealed by God, the underlying primitive conception was universal throughout the polytheistic world.

In the New Testament, Paul makes a point in his discourse to the Roman Christians while referring to the primitive conception that polytheists who've never heard of the Mosaic law, or of Christ, have no excuse for leading sinful lives. As Paul says, since the beginning of the world,

> What may be known about God is plain to them, because God has made it plain to them. For since the creation of the world God's invisible qualities—his eternal *power* and *divine nature*—have been clearly seen, being understood from what has been made, so that men are without excuse (Rom. 1:18–20; emphasis added).

They are without excuse because even pagan cultures taught that the orderly cosmos itself testified to a call to righteousness. In this, Paul says, God speaks to all, and calls all out of sin.

Paul's missionary friend Luke suggests that even in the polytheistic world, a caring and divine creator is perceivable from the gentle dew, the blossoming flower, sunshine and rain, food, water, and air to breathe. As he says in Acts 14:16–17, God's kindness is shown by giving rain, good crops, times of plenty of food, and joyfulness. The apparent divine superintendence of all these things, and more, adds to the cumulative reasoning that there may be a caring creator behind it all. Divine providence is also perceivable when people unexplainably escape from otherwise certain injury or death.

Sixteenth century theologian John Calvin (1509–1564) seems to expand this conception for believers where he says that God "daily discloses himself in the whole workmanship of the universe. . . . Upon his individual works he has engraved unmistakable marks of his glory . . . wherever you cast your eyes, there is no spot in the universe wherein you cannot discern at least some sparks of his glory."[17]

Today some scientists suggest that data points toward the existence of a super intelligent designer of the universe and life. From outer space to inner space, from the big bang of the universe to the immensely complex machinery within living cells—all are said to be suggestive of a creator. The properties of the universe and the timing and interaction of planetary bodies and elements are so mind-blowingly precise to allow life to be possible that the probability of the origination of complex life on Earth by pure natural accident is nearly zero (see chapter 1.5). All these observations of the natural world are believed to declare that there is a God who wishes to be sought.

Of course, atheists argue back that God and his character are not evident in nature at all. They think there's no evidence for answered prayer (which I discuss in chapter 5.4), no evidence of supernatural occurrences (which I discuss in chapter 3.3), and no evidence that the universe and life needed a God to come into existence. The ones seeing anything about a God in nature are superstitious.

Atheists argue that the universe and life can exist without God, but the fact is that a purely naturalistic, atheistic universe that sustains life is highly unlikely. Still, atheists who argue that the natural world doesn't seem to declare the glory or power of God to a large portion of the human population have a valid point. But, as discussed in previous chapters (particularly 3, 4, and 9), a world that appears obviously created by God would go against God's plan to bring about the greatest possible good through divine hiddenness, nomic regularity, and compatibility determination by free will. Thus, it is God's plan to leave for us *subtle* marks, or clues, to be found by the ones tuned in by appreciation for the principles of love and goodness. Such receive insights through observation of the natural world that play a role in lighting a walkable pathway to truth. But the person who doesn't have the "radio dial" of his heart tuned in to pick up the divine "radio waves" sees no divine light in nature. Nonetheless, he or she is the recipient of common grace (prevenient grace) by a different ray of light—the conscience.

Our conscience is said to be another mode of the Holy Spirit's revelation (Rom. 2:14–15). Everyone with the ability to reason and with healthy mental faculties is morally conscious of conduct identified in the Bible as good and evil. All have an intuitive sense of right and wrong. All have a sense of the principles of divine love and the wellness it creates, as well as selfish maliciousness and the harm *it* creates.

When the conscience functions in unison with reason from observations of nature, a person has a significant amount of revealed insight of the Divine. There can be reasonable inference of the existence of a loving and good Divinity and conviction of sin (John 16:8). Of course there can also be a *lack* of conviction of sin due to a conscience that has been "seared as with a hot iron" (1 Tim. 4:2) from the continual cultivation of sinful habits.

In addition to the natural modes of revelation are the supernatural ones. These include: mental impressions,[18] dreams,[19] words directly to the mind, either consciously or subconsciously, an audible voice,[20] visions,[21] encounters with angels,[22] and encounters with the resurrected-translated Jesus.[23]

Some Christians think that the supernatural modes are reserved for rare cases in which God communicates to his chosen prophets in particular times and places. The idea is that supernatural modes are limited to special occasions and therefore are considered to be "special revelation." However, both the Bible and human experience teach that the supernatural modes are not restricted to God's Bible prophets, but rather are operating generally in the lives of people on every continent, in every human era, regardless of religion, belief, education, or even lifestyle.

Take, for example, Nebuchadnezzar, the king of Babylon (Dan. 2). He wasn't a chosen prophet of God. Likely he had not been properly educated about God and the Abrahamic/Mosaic covenants. If he had been told about God's compassion and mercy toward people in the lowest stations in society, Nebuchadnezzar probably would've cast God off as a weak and useless deity. Yet we are told the Holy Spirit supernaturally ministered to him (and through him) in his dreams, which opened a way for a meeting between the king and the prophet Daniel.

Another example is the Pharaoh of Egypt in the time of Joseph. Likely he, too, had little or no appreciation of God. Yet he also received supernaturally revealed information in dreams (Gen. 41). The revelation imparted to him paved the way for an opportunity for the Pharaoh to learn about God from Joseph (another one of God's missionary prophets).

Another example is Abimelech, the polytheistic Philistine ruler over the town of Gerar. Scripture says God came to him in a dream one night and warned him that the woman he had taken was already married (Gen. 20:3–7).

We also have modern-day examples of nonbelievers receiving divine light by supernatural modes. One comes by way of a Hindu priest in 2012 who was devoted to his faith all his life. One night he had a dream of a God who reigned over all other gods. The dream stayed with him and he longed to know this God. Several days later, missionaries arrived who showed the film *Jesus*. The priest attended the showing of the film and, while watching, he determined that the Jesus in the film was the God in his dream. At the end of the film, the Hindu priest approached the missionaries and told them about his dream. Then he began believing and trusting in the God of the Bible. He and his family committed themselves to God and began attending church.[24]

A relatively high number of formerly loyal Muslims also report having had an extraordinary dream or a vision of the resurrected Jesus followed by conversion to the Christian faith. These are devout Muslims, living in places where dissemination of the Christian gospel is strictly outlawed. In these cases, conversion comes with the threat of severe persecution, imprisonment, or a death sentence. Given the high cost, it is difficult to believe the stories of the visions are made up. They could've experienced a naturally occurring hallucination, but given the totality of available evidence of supernatural occurrences (a fraction of which was mentioned in chapter 3.3 and notes), the stories are not beyond the range of reasonable believability.

Decades ago a nine-year-old Iranian girl, by the name of Noor, first learned of Jesus by supernatural means. In her village there were no churches, missionary programs, or satellite television or radio ministries from which she could have learned of the stories of Jesus. One day Noor prayed, "God, if you are real, show yourself to me." Months later Noor began having unusual and vivid dreams of a deeply loving man in white who would come near, sit down, and tell her stories of his experiences with his friends, one of whom was named Peter. In one of the stories the man and his friends were in a boat and crossing a lake when a great storm began. He commanded that the storm cease, and the wind stopped blowing and the lake became calm.

For six months the dreams continued. One night in a dream she asked the man, "Who are you? Why are you appearing to me in my dreams? Why are you telling me these stories?" He told her that he had been showing himself to her in her dreams in response to her prayer that God reveal himself to her.

A few months afterward the man stopped appearing in her dreams and Noor came into possession of a Bible. When she read Matthew, Mark, Luke, and John, she discovered that the stories in the gospels were the same stories the man told in her dreams. Then Noor believed in the God of the Bible. When she grew up she immigrated to the United States. She has since helped produce televised evangelism programs for SAT-7 PARS that are broadcast into Iran.[25]

Other experiences of the commonality of supernatural modes of revelation include reports of personal encounters with people believed to be angels because of some supernatural event associated with the encounter.[26] This is consistent with the biblical admonition to not forget to be hospitable to strangers, "for by so doing some people have entertained angels without knowing it" (Heb. 13:2).

Another supernatural mode prevalent among humankind is SPS (ESP) ability that is mostly dormant in the earthly life. As discussed in chapter 3.3, there are a plethora of reports by thousands of people in every human culture and educational background of experiences involving SPS. SPS ability in the earthly life is predominantly dormant, but may be activated at times by the Holy Spirit, or any of his angels, to communicate a metaphysical conception of truth. By clairvoyance, for example, a person could see events of the life of another person in another time, an angel of God (or an angel of Satan), or Jesus himself.

Integrally related to SPS experiences are OBEs (out-of-body experiences) and NDEs (near-death experiences). Given the available evidence, it appears that sometimes some people are in a type of celestial vision (NDEs) or experiencing a temporary departure of the soul from the body (OBEs) (see chapter 3.3 and notes). Some Christians mistakenly interpret a claim of an OBE in which there is reported to be travel to heaven and back as a soul's journey to heaven. But when the soul leaves the body its SPS is fully active, and thus is able to be *shown* celestial realities, such as what it is like to travel to heaven, be in heaven, or even talk with God (2 Cor. 12:1–4). Biblically, and experientially, then, NDEs and OBEs are supernatural modes of the Holy Spirit to communicate truth.

And not unrelated to these types of experiences are the sightings of intangible or ethereal beings of various humanoid shapes, whether angels, spirits, ghosts, or shadow people. These reports are indiscriminate of worldview, culture, religion, race, nationality, age, education, or career and span the entire record of human history. Some of the reports are made by scientists who are skeptical of the existence of God or the supernatural, and who are leery of stories by people with an overactive imagination. In some cases, two or more people and animals all simultaneously see an apparition. (See chapter 3.3 and notes.)

Such sightings could be revelations orchestrated by the Holy Spirit in activating human SPS ability to perceive things beyond the natural senses. He may intend that the sightings play a key role in his ministry to reveal truths (2 Kings 6:14–17). Perhaps one purpose behind them is to open the mind that is otherwise closed to the Divine because of the influences of metaphysical naturalism or scientism,[27] or atheism.

Obviously, supernatural experiences of celestial beings are not common. But revelatory experiences that are common and involve probably the entire human population at some point in a lifetime are the subtle and ordinary supernatural experiences, such as a mental impression, subconsciously received messages, an extraordinary dream, or even a discussion with a trusted friend who claims to have had a profound supernatural experience.

Appreciation of Partial Light Is Rewarded with Greater Light. By both the natural and supernatural modes, the Holy Spirit and his angels cast partial light upon a path or life course that is apparent to each of us at one time or another. The path is marked by principles of love and goodness. By this, everyone has the opportunity to demonstrate appreciation of the principles, or lack thereof. Everyone has a chance to respond to light. A life choice is involved, which is free and true concerning God, as he is light (1 John 1:5). The ones appreciative of the principles make their way to the path, while the ones who don't appreciate them turn away.

Walking the path is a journey in which there is cultivation of the principles. As the journey is continued, greater light is given—new metaphysical conceptions—to light the way ahead. As the Bible says, "To those who use well what they are given, even more will be given, and they will have an abundance" (Matt. 25:29 NLT; see also Matt. 13:11–15;[28] Mark 4:25; Luke 8:18).

Along the way, a point is reached where a person has enough truth and belief to properly respond to God's gracious offer of fellowship and acceptance into the heavenly community. The promise is that those who "hunger and thirst after righteousness" can expect to be "filled" (Matt. 5:6). As theologian Matthew Henry (1662–1714) says, "To him that has, and to him that asks, shall be given; to him that uses and improves what he has, and that desires and prays for more of the knowledge of Christ, God will give more."[29]

In proportion to true appreciation, greater knowledge of the Divine is imparted until the true seeker has sufficient knowledge of the truth for a proper response to God for salvation. But the ones who do not appreciate the partial light shut the door on receiving the greater light. "From those who do nothing, even what little they have will be taken away" (Matt. 25:29 NLT). As theologian F. F. Bruce (1910–1990) says, "Those who refuse the light, in whatever fashion it shines on them, pronounce sentence on themselves."[30] It is pointless to impart information necessary for a proper response to God to those who truly do not wish to (Matt. 7:6–11; Luke 11:9–13;[31] 2 Cor. 4:3–4[32]). Consequently, except for whatever light might happen to filter in by the works of human missionaries, information about the gospel is not given. The ones unappreciative of the light remain in darkness in polytheism, pantheism, Hinduism, or atheism, etc. (truth seekers in non-Christian religions are not in total darkness, as the Spirit's ministering work leaves glimmers or traces of light in each,[33] except religions on par with the Church of Satan).

Incidentally, this allows the Christian to draw an interesting inference. Atheists argue that nonbelief in God's existence (arguably because of a lack of evidence for it) is inculpable, and thus, if it turns out that God actually exists, such nonbelief would be justifiable. Most often my response is that the nonbelief of atheists who reject Christianity is culpable because it follows a shallow or incomplete investigative study of biblical claims (evident by books written by atheists to debunk Christianity that lack thorough study in both sides of a debate, or lack studies in the Bible, theology, and exegesis). But, in view of the work of the Holy Spirit, it appears that unbelief may not be a result so much from inadequate study as one's lack of appreciation of the partial light bestowed. "The man without the Spirit does not accept the things that come from the Spirit of God, for they are foolishness to him" (1 Cor. 2:14). As such, there would be no such thing as inculpable or justifiable nonbelief in God's existence.

The Holy Spirit is grieved by their rejection (Eph. 4:30), but being perfectly respectful, he honors it. He honors it by not imparting revelation that would actually be an imposition. Where the gift of Truth (John 14:6) is not appreciated, it is not given. Consider, for example, the instance in the gospel of John where Jesus spoke before a crowd of people and said he would glorify the Father's name. Just then some in the crowd heard thunder, while others heard a voice from heaven speaking words (John 12:28–29). The greater manifestations of the revealing of truth are reserved for people who've truly cultivated a saved heart. Human missionaries are not in a position to make such a distinction, but nonetheless are to use their judgment to determine the ones who are obstinate and hard-hearted[34] after first sharing the gospel indiscriminately (Mark 16:15–16).

But the people who are appreciative of whatever light is given have made their way to the path shown. The first steps of it are attended by lifestyle change, no matter how small. As the journey is continued, there is cultivation in the heart of several significant principles of love and goodness (Matt. 25:34–40). Additional light is given. If the journey does not come to a stop with rejection of the light imparted, additional light is promised, followed ultimately by gospel light.

Such a journey is promised to the prehistoric hunter-gatherer, the African sky god worshiper, the devoted Hindu, or the Buddhist. Consider, for example, the Iroquois of America prior to the arrival of Europeans. They had never been introduced to the Judeo-Christian gospel. Yet their beliefs suggest that many of them had received light from the Holy Spirit sufficient to cultivate many Christian principles of love and goodness.

According to the unevangelized Iroquois, it was right for an Iroquois husband to be faithful to his wife,[35] to be sexually pure, to not rape, to not steal, to be honest, to be humble, to be patient, to be friendly and hospitable, to not defame others, to be sympathetic, to not practice witchcraft, and to teach children to be good.[36] They were slow to become angry. They did not know what foul language was.[37] They believed in caring for others, sharing food and shelter, and caring for the sick and injured.

Crimes were very infrequent (although punishment was harsh). They believed it to be wrong to take human life except in self-defense or in times of war, when killing a warrior of another tribe. They believed it to be wrong to break any treaty or agreement made at the council fire when the peace pipe had been smoked or after parties making the treaty had partaken of food together. To them it was wrong to kill animals for any purpose other than food and covering, and for the protection of growing crops and human life. They believed it was wrong to neglect the elderly in any way. They believed it was wrong to make fun of the handicapped.[38]

Given the moral ideals of the unevangelized Iroquois, it appears that some had made their way to the lighted path (that would ultimately lead to salvation) and had traveled some distance along it. This is an example of the journey, making productive use of what is given. More light is then imparted to show more of the path ahead. (But, whether any of them had received enough divine light for salvation before the missionaries had arrived is unknown to us.)

Consider also the apparent light imparted by the Holy Spirit to the Inca people. Among the pantheon of their gods was Viracocha, the all-powerful and good god who made all things. About a century before the arrival of Europeans (Spanish conquistadores), the Inca king Pachacuti (1438–1471) described Viracocha as supreme and uncreated, manifesting himself as a trinity when he wishes, surrounded by angels. He is the creator of all peoples and spirits. He provides for humankind. He brings peace and order. He pities men's wretchedness and enables them to combat their evil tendencies. He alone judges and forgives.[39]

The Inca idea of evil and good may be reflected by the moral code of the people. The Inca code for living was simple: Do not steal, be honest, and do not be lazy. According to one source, "those who followed these simple precepts eventually enjoyed eternity living in the warmth of the Sun while those who failed to follow these simple rules would spend eternity on the cold earth."[40] The moral code of the people and their metaphysical conceptions might not be much different than those of Abraham (see appendix F).

There are two speculations as to how they could've received such divine light. It is said Pachacuti's father, Hatun Tupac, had a dream in which Viracocha reminded him that Viracocha was truly the creator of all things. If true, it might appear that the Inca people were on a supernaturally lighted journey in the direction of the greater light and, potentially, salvation. Although, if their conceptions of the Divine did not come from Tupac's dream (in addition to nature, conscience, reason, etc.), then perhaps human migration brought these concepts to the Inca people from the Middle East through Asia, and across the Alaskan land bridge created by the last ice age into the Americas (11,000–25,000 years ago). If so, then some of the basic concepts of God's characteristics and character would date back to prehistoric times, which would be consistent with old earth creationism[41] (i.e., Adam living many tens of thousands of years ago, and God's revelation to Noah around the year 5600 BC regarding a coming cataclysmic flood that would destroy agricultural societies now submerged in the Black Sea, landing Noah in Ararat territory [Urartu] and creating a diaspora in that region of the planet[42]).

To summarize, by the common grace of the Holy Spirit and his angels, and both natural and supernatural modes of revelation, God shines various kinds of rays of light on a pathway for each individual for a journey that leads to reception of greater light, and ultimately gospel light. Each of us has an opportunity to decide to start the journey or walk a different way. Therefore, as a result of the partial light given, God provides access to salvation to everyone, no matter where or when born, religion or world view grown up with or married into, or educational background.

12.2 Information for a Proper Response to God for Salvation

This brings us to the second part of the issue introduced at the beginning of the chapter. How much light of the Divine is sufficient to properly respond to God's offer of acceptance into heaven? What metaphysical concepts must a person hold before he is able to properly respond for salvation?

Let's first consider what constitutes a proper response to God for salvation.

Is Hell Unjust for People Who Had Never Heard of the Gospel?

Some Christians blurt out that it's having faith in God, or having love for God, or being in Christ, or obedience to God. Others point to Bible verses, such as: John 3:16, "Whoever believes in him [Son of God] shall not perish but have eternal life;" John 14:23, "If anyone loves me [Jesus Christ], he will obey my teaching. My Father will love him and we will come to him and make our home with him;" Romans 8:1, "There is now no condemnation for those who are in Christ Jesus;" and Ephesians 2:8, "You have been saved, through faith . . . not by works."

While Bible verses such as these are helpful, it's best to understand them as pieces to a puzzle. A puzzle picture is barely discernable by looking at a few pieces. But when all are in place, there is a synthesis that forms a complete picture (an elementary approach to Bible study lost on atheist Michael Martin).[43] The synthesized picture of the human response to God for salvation may be expressed as follows.

God offers forgiveness for reconciliation and ultimate acceptance into heaven. As discussed previously, whether we know it or not, this offer is extended individually to everyone, regardless of where or when born or religious beliefs taught since childhood. Heaven is offered when the Holy Spirit lights a path for a human journey toward greater light. Thus, the Buddhist unaware of the existence of the Abrahamic covenant, Judaism, or Christianity is offered reconciliation to God and salvation in heaven.

The human response is a response to whatever partial light is shown. If it is to lead to salvation, the responder must follow the lesser light and make sincere use of it. The promise to the follower is that the Holy Spirit will, by natural or supernatural modes, equip her with sufficient light for a changed heart for a relationship with God.

In such a relationship one becomes the kind of person compatible for acceptance into an everlasting fellowship with God and the heavenly community. There is a connection between the sinner and God, a relationship, companionship, significant shared desires, and trusting obedience. In this there is the demonstration of a disposition that will follow through in glad acceptance of what heaven is about.

In my studies, I found there to be two basic views on the metaphysical conceptions a person needs to believe for a transforming and saving relationship with God. One view is what I call the short list. This is a set of beliefs based in part on studies of Bible passages concerning the patriarchs of Genesis who are said to be saved (e.g., Noah and Abraham), but appear textually to be without understanding of the God-man messiah's role in salvation. See appendix F for a discussion in favor of the short list being sufficient for salvation.

The short list includes:

1. Belief/trust that a loving and good Divinity exists (Heb. 11:6).
2. Belief/trust that the Divinity hears prayers.
3. Trust of the Divinity's word and guidance, which produces obedience[44] and acceptance of divine blessings (e.g., grace and fellowship).
4. Love of the Divinity.

Other theologians, however, believe a longer list is needed for a transforming and saving relationship with God. They insist that a person cannot be in a relationship with God that sufficiently transforms the heart to become the kind of person that is compatible for acceptance into heaven unless it includes the messianic gospel tenets. The long list includes the following:

1. Belief/trust in the existence of a divine judgment against sin and consequential consignment to hell (per the principle of justice through accountability).
2. Belief/trust that all humans are sinners deserving of hell.
3. Belief/trust in the existence of a God-man-messiah who satisfies the principle of justice through accountability so that God has the "green light" to forgive sinners (see appendix D).
4. Belief/trust that heaven exists.

The argument as to why a person's beliefs must match the long list for a transforming and saving relationship with God seems to be that without such knowledge and beliefs, a person is unable to have such a relationship. He is powerless to "die" to sin, to live by the Spirit, and thus to overcome a sinful disposition sufficient for heavenly compatibility (Rom. 1:16; 6:1–14; 8:1–17; 12:2). But if the metaphysical conceptions and beliefs of the patriarchs who are saved for heaven are similar to the short list, then it would appear that one can overcome a sinful disposition sufficiently to be accepted into the heavenly community without the long list of beliefs inclusive of the messianic gospel.

Having examined both sides of the debate, it appears more likely to me that the shorter list of beliefs is sufficient. If so, then knowledge of the person, ministry, and death of Christ would not be necessary to be saved (although certainly beneficial). But even if the beliefs of the patriarchs were similar to the long list that included the messianic God-man gospel, the soteriological problem of evil can be considered solved.

It can be considered solved because whether the journey to salvation is short or long matters not, since *access* to a path for the journey is individually given to all, as previously discussed. If the long list of knowledge is required, and God allows a person to die before receiving it, it would be because the person didn't appreciate whatever partial light was given, thereby closing the door to receiving the greater light of the gospel (on the long list) that is needed to be saved. As such, God is making salvation accessible to everyone, and the soteriological problem is solved. Whether a person dies without learning of the gospel is irrelevant.

Mistakenly thinking that it is relevant, Michael Martin argues that there are people without access to salvation because they lack an opportunity to learn of Jesus Christ and thus aren't given a chance to be saved.[45] They were "born in the wrong time or the wrong place. A Chinese woman in the second century BC, a native American living in the eighth century AD, and a black living in Africa in the second century AD would have had no opportunity to be saved." But, by common grace and the promise of greater light to true seekers, God creates an opportunity for every individual to receive metaphysical conceptions of a good God and salvation from sin and hell through Christ. As such, the millions of people who die before learning of the gospel that are consigned to hell are not in hell because they were "born in the wrong time and place," or weren't fortunate enough to have been evangelized to the gospel message, or because God didn't love them enough to give them the gospel so that they'd have a chance for heaven. Rather, they died ignorant of the greater light of the gospel and have a mediocre life in hell because they did not appreciate the partial light given, in whatever fashion it shined on them, that would've led them on a journey to reception of the greater light, to which they could've responded properly to God for acceptance into heaven.

NOTES to Chapter 12

1. Other Bible passages cited are 1 John 5:11–12; John 3:18; and Rom. 10:9–10, 14 as well as several texts in the book of Acts with regard to the disciples' motivation for missions: Acts 2:38; 13:46; 16:30–34; 20:26–27; 26:17–18.
2. Soteriology is the study of religious doctrines of salvation.

3. Prov. 22:8; Gal. 6:7.

4. Lev. 19:15; Deut. 10:17; 2 Chr. 19:7; Matt. 22:16; Acts 10:34; Rom. 2:11; Gal. 2:6; Eph. 6:9; Col. 3:25; 1 Tim. 5:21; James 2:1-9; 1 Pet. 1:17.

5. *Zondervan NIV Bible Commentary, Volume 2: New Testament*, consul. eds. Kenneth L. Barker and John R. Kohlenberger III (Grand Rapids, MI: Zondervan Publishing House, 1994), 29.

6. Not to be confused with the investigative judgment teaching of the Seventh-day Adventist church.

7. Ezek. 18:23, 32; 33:11; John 12:32; 1 Tim. 2:4; 2 Pet. 3:9.

8. I recommend for study: Robert A. Peterson and Michael D. Williams, *Why I Am Not an Arminian* (Downers Grove, IL: InterVarsity Press, 2004). I've also read articles by Calvinists on the Internet.

9. Molinism (named after Luis de Molina) is a kind of offshoot teaching from Calvinism in which three types of God's knowledge are understood in a way that reconciles God's election of some people to become saved believers and some people to never become saved believers with human free will. While this might alleviate issues surrounding human free will and God's sovereignty, it leaves a problem unresolved that was discussed in chapters 3 and 4. A perception by the heavenly community that God's adjudication is a mystery, secretive, inscrutable, or uninvestigatable opens a door to a seed of belief that God is arbitrary and unjust, which would result in a perception of God's disposition and personality befitting a mediocre relationship with God and consequential loss of the degree of expressions of love and goodness by the community that would otherwise result if God were to take all measures to build and inspire trust in him, inclusive of a transparent adjudication made possible by compatibility determination (see chapter 4). Moreover, an uninvestigatable adjudication or judgment doesn't appear consistent with the investigative nature of the judgment (Dan. 7:9–10; 1 Cor. 6:2–3; Rev. 20:11–15) (not to be confused with the investigative judgment teaching of the Seventh-day Adventist church).

10. I recommend for study: Jerry L. Walls and Joseph R. Dongell, *Why I Am Not a Calvinist* (Downers Grove, IL: InterVarsity Press, 2004). I've also read articles in defense of Arminianism against Calvinism on the Internet.

11. The universalist view meets with failure—theologically, philosophically, and exegetically (see chapter 11.6)—and it contradicts the texts that clearly affirm that God's decision for heaven or hell is according to actions done in the mortal life (2 Cor. 5:10; Heb. 9:27) and not actions done in the afterlife. In the universalist view, every sinner is eventually justified by God and accepted into heaven. The Holy Spirit and Christ continue their saving ministries on those in hell to draw them to him until eventually they are converted to genuine fellowship with God and taken out of hell and into heaven. In the universalist view, hell serves the purpose of rehabilitating sinners (who choose to learn the hard way) and salvation is universal for all. God's desire that all be saved (1 Tim. 2:4) is realized, and God and his love triumph over all rebellion and everybody lives happily ever after. Bible texts cited in support of this view include: Matt. 10:32–33; Mark 16:15–16; John 3:18, 36; 1 Peter 3–4; 1 Cor. 15:19, John 5:25–29; 10:16.

12. The pluralist view is clearly not biblical. This view states that all religions are valid ways of seeking an ultimate, metaphysical reality that is not sufficiently revealed to the human race; Jesus Christ is not God; Jesus is not the only savior; Jesus unfolded one piece of the ultimate reality; other religions hold other pieces of the same metaphysical reality; all of the world's religions are on par with each other; none have a monopoly on truth; and all are legitimate avenues to salvation. This view requires throwing out core biblical Christian doctrines.

13. Heb. 1:14; Rev. 1:1b.

14. Matt. 5:45b.

15. "Light" is a biblical metaphor for metaphysical realities, conceptions, and perceptions revealed by God for salvation from sin and hell.

16. John H. Walton, *Ancient Near Eastern Thought and the Old Testament: Introducing the Conceptual World of the Hebrew Bible* (Grand Rapids, MI: Baker Academic, 2006), 306.

17. John Calvin, as quoted in Alvin Plantinga, *Warranted Christian Belief* (New York: Oxford University Press, 2000), 174.

18. A modern example of a mental impression is that of the person who has a strong impression to not get on an airplane that ends up crashing or being hijacked.

19. Gen. 20:3; Num. 12:6; Job 33:13–18; Dan. 2; 4; 7:1; Joel 2:28–29; Acts 2:16–18.

20. Matt. 17:5; 3:17; see also Ex. 33:11; Isa. 6:8; Acts 9:4–7.

21. Gen. 15:1; Num. 12:6; Job 33:13–18; Dan. 2:28; 4:34–37; Acts 9:10–16; 10:1–6.

22. Matt. 28:2–7; Luke 2:10–11; Acts 10:1–6, 30.

23. Matt. 28:9–10; Acts 9:1–7.

24. Testimony of missionaries of The Jesus Film Project, http://www.jesusfilm.org/updates/120913, accessed on September 13, 2012.

25. SAT-7 PARS is a channel on the SAT-7 Arabic and Farsi Christian Satellite Television Network. I learned of Noor's experience in a letter from Dr. Rex Rogers, president, SAT-7, dated November 19, 2012.

26. James Stuart Bell, *Heaven Touching Earth: True Stories of Angels, Miracles, and Heavenly Encounters* (Bloomington, MN: Bethany House Publishers, 2014); *Angels, Miracles, and Heavenly Encounters: Real Life Stories of Supernatural Events* (Grand Rapids, MI: Bethany House Publishers, 2012); John Geiger, *The Angel Effect: We Are Never Alone* (New York: Weinstein Books, 2013); Judith MacNutt, *Angels Are for Real: Inspiring, True Stories and Biblical Answers* (Grand Rapids: MI, Chosen Books, 2012); James W. and Michael Ann Goll, *Angelic Encounters: Engaging Help from Heaven* (Lake Mary, FL: Charisma House, 2007). A reasonable investigator reads the anecdotes and wonders if they've been made up. But, taking into account the totality of proposed evidence of supernatural occurrences (a fraction of which was briefly mentioned in chapter 3 and notes), it would be reasonable to believe that more likely than not at least some of them actually occurred.

27. Adherents of metaphysical naturalism (the natural sciences reveal all of the elements and principles that exist) and scientism (a sense of which holds that truth is

discovered by science alone) tend to hold a dogmatic commitment to a materialistic philosophy that dismisses nonmaterialist or non-naturalist possibilities, a priori, leaving the only naturalistic explanations as real possibilities, such as naturally occurring hallucination, psychopathology, deception, overactive imagination, or false positives of cameras and videos made by lens flares, double exposure, light reflections, shadows from natural light sources, etc.

28. *The Wycliffe Bible Commentary*, eds. Charles F. Pfeiffer and Everett F. Harrison (Chicago: Moody Press, 1990), 952; *Zondervan NIV Bible Commentary, Volume 2: New Testament*, 65–66.

29. *Matthew Henry's Commentary on the Whole Bible* (Peabody, MA: Hendrickson Publishers, 1991), 1576.

30. F. F. Bruce, *The Gospel of John: Introduction, Exposition, and Notes* (Grand Rapids, MI: William B. Eerdmans Publishing Company, 1983), 92. Bruce (1910–1990) was Rylands Professor of Biblical Criticism and Exegesis at the University of Manchester, England. He wrote more than forty books and commentaries. He served as general editor of the New International Commentary of the New Testament from 1962 to 1990.

31. *The Wycliffe Bible Commentary*, 941, 1048; Craig S. Keener, *The IVP Bible Background Commentary: New Testament* (Downers Grove, IL: InterVarsity Press, 1993), 64; *Zondervan NIV Bible Commentary, Volume 2: New Testament*, 35–36, 252.

32. *Zondervan NIV Bible Commentary, Volume 2: New Testament*, consulting eds. Kenneth L. Barker and John R. Kohlenberger III (Grand Rapids, MI: Zondervan Publishing House, 1994), 672–673.

33. Earl Schipper, *Religions of the World* (Grand Rapids, MI: Baker Book House, 1982), 10–14.

34. Prov. 23:9; Matt. 7:6; 1 Cor. 2:15; Rev. 22:15. *Matthew Henry's Commentary on the Whole Bible*, 1305.

35. Morris Wolf, *Iroquois Religion and Its Relation to Their Morals*, (New York: Columbia University Press, 1919), 62.

36. Ibid., 64.

37. Ibid., 90.

38. Ibid., 88–91.

39. Don Richardson, *Eternity in Their Hearts* (Ventura, CA: Regal Books, third ed., 2005), 34.

40. http://www.heatoftheinitiate.com/taxonomy/term/339, assessed on September 13, 2012.

41. Old earth creationism was defined in chapter 9.

42. William Ryan and Walter Pitman, *Noah's Flood: The New Scientific Discoveries About the Event That Changed History* (New York: Simon & Schuster Paperbacks, 1998); Ian Wilson, *Before the Flood: The Biblical Flood as a Real Event and How It Changed the Course of Civilization* (New York: St. Martin's Press, 2002).

43. Michael Martin, *The Case Against Christianity* (Philadelphia: Temple University Press, 1991), 197–212. Martin argues that the Bible shows four different conflicting routes to salvation. Assuming that Martin is intellectually honest in his book, he appears clueless as to how to study the Bible or make a case against Christianity on the basis of what the Bible teaches about salvation.

44. Rom. 1:5; 1 Thess. 1:3; 2 Thess. 1:11.

45. Michael Martin, *The Case Against Christianity*, 204–205.

Appendix A
Responses to Arguments for Less Divine Hiddenness

Argument One. Chapter 4.2 mentioned two things that could rob our will of the freedom needed for significant compatibility determination: (1) too much awareness of God's existence; and (2) too much awareness of God's will to reward or punish. If this is so, an argument goes, why couldn't God make evidence of his existence sufficiently clear for reasonable belief in *his existence alone*, while keeping the facts about divine punishment and reward under wraps? This way there could be undeniable evidence of God's existence so that many more people would believe, but since awareness of his will to reward or punish would be kept hidden, we'd remain significantly free to engage in compatibility determination. In other words, even though evidence of God's existence would be dialed up, this would be counterbalanced by a dialing down of evidence of his will to reward or punish. The net effect would arguably be the same unfettered maximal degree of compatibility-determining free will that we now have, but in a world in which many more people would believe that God exists.

Response. The argument suggests that bringing about the greater good need not call for God to leave us with so little (if any) observable evidence of his existence. Thus, a substantial degree of hiding of evidence of God's existence and presence is unnecessary and unjustified, in which case a theodicy dependent upon this kind of divine hiding would fail. However, the argument has a few fatal flaws.

One of the flaws is that it creates a contradiction regarding God's character. Keeping facts hidden about God's will to reward or punish would also keep facts hidden about God's character, moral guidance, and even his plan of salvation. We would have plenty of evidence that there exists a creator, but we'd have little or no information as to whether the creator is good or evil (as in deism). Such a scenario is clearly not consistent with a God who perfectly loves humankind. As philosopher Michael J. Murray says:

> The problem here is that it is hard to see how such a scenario is one that could be favored by a loving God at all. Surely it would not be an act of love of God towards creatures to keep facts about human flourishing tucked safely behind the counter simply in order to make his existence clearly known.[1]

Moreover, the scenario wouldn't actually result in a net effect of an unfettered maximal degree of compatibility-determining free will, because it would provide overpowering incentives for *bad* conduct which would prevent compatibility-determining free will. People would likely believe *a* god exists, but they would have little or no reason to believe that it would resemble the God of the Bible. Consequently, each and every society would make its own moral rules as to what is right and what is wrong without a divinely revealed standard. Assuming that the revelation through the patriarchs and Israelites was necessary to preserve the right balance of incentives to do good and bad, eliminating such revelation would create an imbalance that would significantly deprive the world of compatibility-determining free will.

Argument Two. Christians retain their moral freedom despite being convinced that God exists and rewards those who seek him and punishes those who reject him. They have a great deal of information about these things in the Bible and claim to "know" that these things are true. Yet they retain plenty of freedom to get entangled in sin, and even seriously so (Matt. 7:21–23). Moreover, the prophets and disciples of Jesus observed and performed eye-popping miracles and yet they still struggled with temptation. The apostle Paul even brought a man back from death (Acts 20:9–10) and received many visions from God.[2] Yet all this divine disclosure did not overpower incentives for Paul and the other disciples to engage in bad conduct (Rom. 7:14–24).

If the knowledge and miracles of the first century disciples did not preclude them from having compatibility-determining free will, why should we think that increasing observable evidence of God's existence and will to reward or punish would? Don't these examples prove that a substantial degree of God's hiddenness is not necessary to preserve compatibility-determining free will?

Response. The argument might at first appear to expose a major flaw in the theodicy. However, there are a few things to consider that shed light on the fact that the Christian life and the lives of Jesus' disciples and prophets do not decrease God's hiddenness to the extent that they would be deprived of significant compatibility-determining free will.

Christians may speak of what they "know," but they live by faith, not by sight,[3] which means there is always room for doubt and a mitigated awareness of God's existence and will that keeps the will free of significant coercion. The Christian lives in a multi-environment of widening circles. The believer's most inner environment in which there is Bible study, prayer, and fellowship with other believers may at times intermittently raise one's awareness of God's existence and will somewhat, but this is counterbalanced by the day-to-day life that at times takes them into the outer environments of nonbelief (e.g., in a job, in school, during sleep, and through association with nonbelievers), where the mind is fed messages of nonbelief (whether consciously, subconsciously, or subliminally). Moreover, even in the believer's most inner environment, there are messages of nonbelief from prayers unanswered, thoughts of the attitudes of nonbelievers in the world, atheistic philosophies, the presence of nonbelievers in the home or in school, nonbelieving visitors, and worldly and atheistic media, all of which play a role in attenuating the Christian's awareness of God's existence and will.

Furthermore, there are times in the Christian life when God's hiddenness seems very pronounced. The psalmists of the Old Testament expressed their angst and dismay over Gods silence. "O my God, I cry out by day, but you do not answer" (Psalm 22:2). "Why, O Lord, do you stand far off? Why do you hide yourself in times of trouble?" (Psalm 10:1). "Why do you hide your face and forget our misery and oppression?" (Psalm 44:24). Some of the believers struggling with divine hiddenness include Jews who've survived the Holocaust.

Therefore, with regard to the Christian life, despite having faith and knowledge of the divine, God is evidently still substantially hidden to the extent that believers have significant compatibility-determining free will. But what about the prophets of the Bible who experienced numerous clear miracles? Do such events significantly diminish divine hiddenness for them? Wouldn't such divine disclosure significantly interfere with their compatibility-determining free will?

While the clear, stupendous miracles that are claimed to have occurred in the Bible might attenuate a degree of divine hiddenness temporarily for the witness of the miracles, there are at least two reasons why they do not raise awareness of God's existence and will to the extent that would wipe out significant compatibility-determining free will.

First, an astute Bible student can see that the disciples seldom witnessed or performed miracles. The time lapse between them is sufficient to allow messages of nonbelief, ordinary events, and many unanswered prayers (2 Cor. 12:7, 9) to create the needed counterbalance that sufficiently attenuates awareness of God's existence, presence, and will. Some get the impression from reading the gospels that the disciples must have seen a miracle every day during the three and a half years they were with Jesus. This is because the gospel writers chose to write about the most significant events of Jesus' life and ministry, and many such events included overt miracles. But we forget that the writers left out of the story the vast number of comparatively insignificant and ordinary events of the three and a half years (John 21:25). As a result, we get a warped view of what the life of Jesus' first-century disciples/prophets was like. The same is true of the great Old Testament characters. Genesis records only eight supernatural revelations experienced by Abraham during his whole long life. So with regard to overt miracles, the lives of Jesus' disciples were nearly as ordinary as those of average Christians today.

Second, it is reasonable to infer that some people can be the recipients of a greater degree of divine disclosure than that which is common. Some have a higher threshold of indifference to the threat of punishment than others. There may be a certain psychological or psychospiritual makeup behind this. Therefore, certain people could retain significant compatibility-determining free will despite the greater abundance of divine evidence. But the vast majority of the world's population would not be capable of retaining significant compatibility-determining free will under the same circumstances. As Murray says, "God *will* provide such revelations to those who can receive them and still remain free in the required way. . . . The theist might actually *expect* that there would be such cases. What the theist can deny, however, is that such powerful revelations would be *common*."[4]

This may explain (in part) why few individuals are the chosen recipients of miraculous experiences. The Bible is clear that prophets were not necessarily chosen because they had superior faith or appreciation for godly virtues. When God initially called Isaiah to serve in a prophetic role, his response was, "'Woe to me!'. . . 'I am ruined! For I am a man of unclean lips, and I live among a people of unclean lips, and my eyes have seen the King, the Lord Almighty'" (Isa. 6:5). Paul thought himself the worst of sinners (1 Tim. 1:12–15) when God initially called him to serve in a prophetic role in which he would perform miracles.

In sum, the compatibility-determining free will of God's prophets was not likely inhibited because: (a) stupendous miracles occurred infrequently, and (b) those chosen by God to witness or perform such miracles probably had a higher tolerance, or indifference, to threat than most people, and could thus handle such experiences without their compatibility-determining free will being significantly affected. Therefore, the nature of the lives of Christians and the prophets does not prove that a substantial degree of God's hiddenness is not necessary to preserve compatibility-determining free will.

Argument Three. Atheist philosopher John L. Schellenberg argues that unless people know with *certainty* that a coercer exists and will carry out his threat (or reward), they cannot be coerced to behave accordingly, because anything less than certainty leaves room for self-deception. Being less than certain and engaging in self-deception about God's existence and will could sufficiently attenuate awareness of the divine such that the will is significantly free for compatibility determination. If this is so, then it would appear that God need not hide a substantial amount of evidence of his existence and will.[5] Moreover, perhaps the evidence could be dialed up to such a degree that no one in the world could have reasonable unbelief in God's existence.[6]

Response. According to Murray, it can be sufficiently demonstrated that a degree of belief that is less than "certain" is sufficient to deprive a person of significant compatibility-determining free will.[7] Murray uses an illustration of a man in Manhattan at night approached from behind by a man who sticks a small cylindrical object into his back and demands his money or else he will shoot him. The man being robbed is *not certain* that this threat can be carried out, as he is not certain the cylindrical object in his back is a pistol or a piece of a pipe or something else. Even if the man thought the probability that the mugger had a gun was extremely low, he would not dare risk it; he would not gamble with his life. Suppose the man had seen news reports that most of the muggers in the city were using water pistols instead of guns. More likely the object in his back is a water pistol, but there is a chance it could actually be a gun and so he's pressured to hand over his wallet. Despite his knowledge that most muggers in the neighborhood have water pistols, which creates his *uncertainty* that the mugger has a gun, the man is still coerced into handing over his wallet.

The point of the illustration is that it does not take a lot of divine disclosure to coerce the will, and the threshold of coercion is reached while a person does not know with certainty that God exists and will carry out his threat (or reward). Thus, a world in which God's hiddenness is significantly less than it is in the present world likely would deprive people of compatibility-determining free will. It may be true that the degree of divine disclosure that Schellenberg has in mind may not preclude compatibility-determining free will for some people, as tolerance or indifference to divine threat varies from person to person. But it is very likely that the coercion of some would, over centuries, transform the world environment to the extent that it would exert a coercive influence over the rest of the population (see chapters 7.1 and 8.1), and a significant number of people would not be capable of compatibility-determining free will. Therefore, it seems likely that the degree that God is hidden from us in the present world is the degree that is most appropriate to maximize the number of people with compatibility-determining free will, to maximize the resulting good of the heavenly community in consummate relationship.

NOTES to Appendix A

1. Michael J. Murray, "Deus Absconditus," in *Divine Hiddenness: New Essays*, eds. Daniel Howard-Snyder and Paul K. Moser (New York: Cambridge University Press, 2002), 76. Emphasis in the original.

2. Acts 9:3–7; 16:9–10; 18:9; 26:19; 1 Cor. 12:6–7, 12.

3. 1 Cor. 5:7; Heb. 11:1.

4. Ibid., 77. Emphasis in the original.

5. John L. Schellenberg, *Divine Hiddenness and Human Reason* (Ithaca, NY: Cornell University Press, 1993), 121–124.

6. It is unclear from Schellenberg's explanation what exactly "reasonable nonbelief" is, so it is difficult to determine the degree of divine disclosure that he has in mind.

7. Michael J. Murray, "Deus Absconditus," in *Divine Hiddenness: New Essays*, 73.

Appendix B
Suffering with Value

The evilness of suffering is often thought to be much worse than it actually is, because many people do not take into account the good things that result from it or come out of it. One of the good things that can arise from some instances of suffering is the facilitation of the experience of repentance from sin. Another is the facilitation of an increase of faith in God.

Suffering Facilitates Repentance. Repentance is a change of attitude with convictions in favor of the principles of love and goodness, and in favor of God, that make a saving relationship with God possible (Acts 20:21; 26:20). There are various experiences that lead to repentance. Some popular examples include: listening to preaching (Matt. 21:32); the perception of being a recipient of God's kindness (Rom. 2:4); harsh rebuke that causes sorrow for sin (2 Cor. 7:8–10); and gentle instruction (2 Tim. 2:25). But the not-so-popular experiences are those which involve suffering. They are undesired but necessary when suffering is the only effective way to reach people who've chosen to learn the hard way, or who've cultivated an insensitivity to divine light and the principles of love and goodness. As philosopher Peter Kreeft says,

> One purpose of suffering in history has been that it leads to repentance. . . . Only after suffering, only after disaster, did Old Testament Israel, do nations, do individual people turn back to God. Again, let's face it: we learn the hard way. To quote C. S. Lewis: "God whispers to us in our pleasures, speaks in our conscience, but shouts in our pains. It is his megaphone to rouse a deaf world."[1]

Some people tune out messages of the divine, whether verbal, nonverbal, subtle, or not so subtle, which can leave significant suffering as the only remaining viable option in God's arsenal to attack our stubbornness and lead us to repentance. Some people are so entrenched in patterns that drive a wedge between them and God that the only thing that effectively arrests the attention and diverts thoughts in a productive direction is some kind of temporal harm or distress. Sometimes the mindsets we get ourselves into are like an incurable sickness which can only be cured by way of suffering a money crisis, injury, or illness. As Kreeft says,

> [C. S. Lewis] pointed out that we're not just imperfect people who need growth, but we're rebels who need to lay down our arms. Pain and suffering are frequently the means by which we become motivated to finally surrender to God and to seek the cure in Christ. That's what we need most desperately.[2]

Jesus likened the unsaved heart to being ill. "It is not the healthy who need a doctor, but the sick. . . . I have not come to call the righteous, but sinners" (Matt. 9:12–13). Sometimes the medicine to cure us is unpleasant and even agonizingly painful. But the alternative is worse (a greater evil). So the loving Physician administers the necessary treatment, as a matter of caring for our highest good. God's message to us is: "Those whom I love I rebuke and discipline. So be earnest, and repent" (Rev. 3:19).

Some critics of Christianity, however, argue that suffering is almost entirely ineffective to lead to repentance. In an online article titled "Human Suffering and the Acceptance of God" (1997), atheist Michael Martin argues that "if God's aim was to have the maximal number of people believe in God . . . he has not been successful. Billions of people have not come to believe in the theistic God."[3] And as atheist John W. Loftus argues, if the purpose of suffering is to cause us to turn to God, "God has done a poor job of this. The pain and the question of human suffering account for more defections from theism than probably any other cause. What else can explain why the problem of evil is the most serious one for Christians?"[4]

A Christian response can be twofold. First, the number of converts can be misleading when judging whether suffering works to lead to repentance. This is because a higher purpose of this world is the experience of compatibility determination and a free-will decision for or against God. Therefore, suffering can only provide knowledge and perspective—a way of communicating divine light unlike any other—to which the free agent responds (either negatively or positively). It is an experiential sermon, and as with any sermon, we can respond by either putting up our hands or casting down our idols; we can either continue to cultivate arrogance, bitterness, or lust or we can let humility settle in and surrender to the way of love; we can continue in the mentality of a victim, or we can choose not to be a victim and make the most of a situation. But the potential for repentance is there for anyone. As Kreeft says,

> I believe all suffering contains at least the opportunity for good ... but not everyone actualizes that potential. Not all of us learn and benefit from suffering; that's where free will comes in. One prisoner in a concentration camp will react quite differently from another, because of the choice each one makes to respond to the environment.[5]

Theoretical physicist and cosmologist Stephen Hawking (1942-2018) suffered from a progressive motor neuron disease related to amyotrophic lateral sclerosis (ALS) and was mostly paralyzed. As difficult as it may be to imagine, his condition afforded him perspective, knowledge, and experience that had, in concert with other means in God's ministerial arsenal, facilitated a path to repentance toward God. But, judging from what is commonly known of his beliefs about the Christian God, it appears he had avoided the path. This is not because suffering doesn't work, but rather because of the kind of disposition and character he forged in his life by his free will (before his disease began, and after). It could have been otherwise. If there were ten "Hawkings" in the world, one or more of them might be a committed Christian.

Second, Loftus argues that many have abandoned their trust and belief in God because of suffering, suggesting that it does not work. However, the Bible is clear that from time to time God's professed people are to be shaken like wheat and chaff in a sieve to separate one from another (Amos 9:9; Matt. 3:12; Luke 22:31[6]). The Bible teaches that God employs suffering to bring about, or maintain, a certain degree of purity versus hypocrisy among God's professed believers so that the church body fulfills its intended role in God's comprehensive creation-redemption plan. Therefore, the people who have renounced belief in God due to an instance or condition of suffering are in most cases probably those whom God has shaken out because of an artificial devotion to God. Although, this does not mean that all people shaken out will not enter heaven. In some cases, the defectors later reaffirm their profession of fellowship with God with a *genuine* devotion to him. In light of this, the number of defectors, or the number of converts, does not provide a clue about whether suffering leads to repentance toward God.

Suffering Facilitates the Building of Good Character. Jesus and his disciples believed that the building of good character advances goodness in the world. This would bring about greater evangelism and a larger populace of Christian disciples in the world, not to mention more nations and cultures that value the golden rule and the principles of God's commandments on how to treat one another. Consequently, in the world there would be a greater degree of love, respect for others, humility, peacemaking, faithfulness in marriage, sexual purity, honesty, self-sacrifice, etc.

It is a well-established fact that suffering can serve to build good character. The concept dates back to ancient polytheistic philosophy[7] and the Old and New Testaments.[8] Ancient Hebrew fasting, for example, is self-induced suffering for the purpose of shaping character. One example of such fasting is found in Esther 4:16: "Go, gather together all the Jews who are in Susa, and fast for me. Do not eat or drink for three days, night or day. I and my maids will fast as you do. When this is done, I will go to the king even though it is against the law. And if I perish, I perish." Here, fasting (with prayer[9]) was to prepare their character to stand in a life or death trial. There are several kinds of fasts, but the central idea is simply to deprive oneself of a comfort or a pleasure as a form of training, the building of discipline, mental conditioning, and adjustment of attitude.

The Old Testament also talks of suffering from various calamities allowed by God to purge professed believers from disobedience to God's commandments. "I know, O Lord, that your laws are righteous, and in faithfulness you have afflicted me" (Ps. 119:75). "Blessed is the man whom God corrects; so do not despise the discipline of the Almighty. For he wounds, but he also binds up; he injures, but his hands also heal" (Job 5:17–18). "My son, do not despise the Lord's discipline and do not resist his rebuke, because the Lord disciplines those he loves, as a father the son he delights in" (Proverbs 3:11–12).

The concept of character growth through suffering continues in the New Testament. It was the case with the Corinthian Christians that it was said that God permitted sufferings to come upon them as a merciful means of dealing with their failures. The suffering was intended to save them from continuing in transgression. Paul informed them that "when we are judged by the Lord [undergo discipline through suffering], we are being disciplined so that we will not be condemned with the world" (1 Cor. 11:32). It was better to have their life course steered to the direction of heaven by suffering than to let them continue on their course that would have potentially led them away from heaven.

Illness, disability, hardships, and persecutions provide the opportunity for believers to undergo rapid growth in right thinking, trust, and obedience. While suffering is very unpleasant at the time, later on "it produces a harvest of righteousness and peace for those who have been trained by it" (Heb. 12:11). Suffering happens to each of us, but the true wisdom-seeking Christian has a worldview that allows her to be trained by it.

Paul suffered from an illness or disability, and he wanted to be healed. Some scholars believe he may have been suffering from failing eyesight because in his letter to the Galatian church he mentions writing with "large letters" (Gal. 6:11). Whatever the infirmity, Paul believed that it helped keep him from becoming arrogant and conceited (2 Cor. 12:6–10).

Often believers filled with independence, strength, or accomplishment, or submerged in what Christians call "worldliness" (1 John 2:15–17), tend to get blinded to their pride, indifference, unforgiveness, disrespect, or lust. Such believers can undergo training by way of suffering in order to regain a state of complete renunciation of self-authority/pride (1 Cor. 2:3–5), which enables the believer to get free of "everything that hinders and the sin that so easily entangles" and run with perseverance the race marked out for them (Heb. 12:1). As explained by some theologians,

> The Christian paradox is that occasions of weakness may be transformed into occasions of strength. Defeat can always be turned into victory. Real strength of character grows out of weakness, which, in distrust of self, is surrendered to the will of God. A man strong in his own strength tends to be self-reliant instead of relying on God, and often does not realize his need of divine grace. The great heroes of the Bible learned the same lesson, men such as Noah, Abraham, Moses, Elijah, Daniel. Only those whose weakness and insecurity have been completely submerged in the blessed will of God know what it is to possess true power.[10]

In sum, despite the pain, distress, and negative reaction of some people to suffering, suffering indeed can lead to repentance and salvation for those who will allow themselves to be changed by it in a positive way. In this respect, suffering itself would appear to be valuable when considered in this context. Even medical treatment that causes suffering can be thought to be valuable if it saves a life (e.g., amputation). Character building through suffering, though unpleasant and painful, is also effective for those who allow themselves to be trained by it. And it may help facilitate the making of Christian disciples (but not to the extent that significant moral free will is lost).

In response to this, skeptics are quick to point out that some of the suffering that Christians (or even non-Christians) endure does not build good character, but actually tears people down and away from God. Senseless and heinous evils sometimes cause unbearable suffering, which can lead to a crushed spirit followed by binge drinking, drug use, divorce, abandonment of the faith, and sometimes even suicide. In such cases suffering doesn't seem to be productive at all and, in fact, appears to be pointless. What the skeptics are referring to here is called pointless, spirit-crushing suffering. This is discussed in appendix C.

NOTES to Appendix B

1. Peter J. Kreeft, as quoted in Lee Strobel, *The Case for Faith: A Journalist Investigates the Toughest Objections to Christianity* (Grand Rapids, MI: Zondervan, 2000), 44. Kreeft quotes from C. S. Lewis, *The Problem of Pain* (New York: Macmillan, 1962), 93.

2. Ibid.

3. Michael Martin, "Human Suffering and the Acceptance of God" (1997), as quoted in John W. Loftus, *Why I Became an Atheist: A Former Preacher Rejects Christianity* (Amherst, NY: Prometheus Books, 2008), 248.

4. John W. Loftus, *Why I Became an Atheist*, 248.

5. Peter Kreeft, as quoted in Lee Strobel, *The Case for Faith*, 45.

6. See also Matthew 7:21–27; Mark 4:3–20.

7. Peter J. Kreeft and Ronald Tacelli, *Handbook of Christian Apologetics* (Downers Grove, IL: InterVarsity Press, 1994), 140.

8. 2 Sam. 12:23; 1 Kings 11:2; 21:12; 2 Chron. 20:3; Ezra 8:21; Esther 4:16; Ps. 69:10; Isa. 58:4-5; Jer. 14:12; 36:6, 9; Dan. 9:3; Joel 1:14; 2:12, 15; Jonah 3:5; Zech. 7:3; Matt. 4:2; 6:16-18; 9:14–15; Mark 2:18–20; Luke 2:37; 5:33–35; 18:12; Acts 13:2; 14:23; 27:9.

9. Prayer usually accompanied fasting in distressful times and was presumably a part of this fast as well (see Judg. 20:26; 1 Sam. 7:6; 2 Sam. 12:16; Ezra 8:21–23; Neh. 9:1–3; Isa. 58:3; Jer. 14:12; Joel 1:14; 2:12–17; John 3:6–9).

10. *Seventh-day Adventist Bible Commentary*, Vol. 6 (Washington, DC: Review and Herald, 1956), 921.

Appendix C
Spirit-Crushing Suffering

As discussed in chapter 7.3, despite negative reactions by some sufferers, suffering can play a pivotal role in the facilitation of repentance and character growth. But opponents of Christianity are quick to point out that some Christians (or even non-Christians) are in situations of evil and suffering that do not build good character, but actually tear people down and away from God. In these situations, the victim and/or the victim's loved ones are often dumbfounded, distressed, or shocked, and, eventually, drained of hope and faith. Many times there is heavy drinking, drug abuse, divorce, or even suicide. For these victims, the evil and suffering do not seem at all effective to facilitate spiritual growth. Instead, spirits are crushed, minds are numbed, and faith is abandoned.

An example of this is told by theologian Gregory A. Boyd:[1]

A number of years ago I learned of a couple who discovered that their seven-year-old daughter had a rare and untreatable genetic disorder that was beginning to deteriorate her brain. Over the course of several years, the doctors informed them, these parents would have to helplessly watch their previously bright and creative child gradually lose all her mental capacities. It would ultimately leave her in an almost vegetative state. The news was understandably life-shattering.

What made the scenario even more nightmarish, however, was that this particular genetic disorder was hereditary. Any subsequent children of this couple would most likely grow without any abnormality for the first five to seven years of their lives but would then begin to deteriorate as their older sister had. It so happens that in the previous year this couple had given birth to a beautiful set of twins.

As predicted, the first child began to deteriorate mentally over the course of the next several years. All the while her sister and brother were growing normally, sometimes asking about their older sister, who now spent her days in a special home, rocking back and forth and staring into space. The emotional strain on this couple as they lovingly raised these two beautiful children, all the while knowing their probable fate, was unbearable.

They and their friends persistently prayed and struggled to hope for a miracle. But a miracle never happened. Around the age of six both siblings began the same slow, torturous process of deterioration that their older sister had gone through. Some time in the second year of this macabre process the mother suffered a nervous breakdown. When she recovered she found that she had completely lost her faith. The husband's faith followed suit several years later. With their faith went all hope and eventually most of their character. The last I heard of the two, they had gone through a bitter divorce, both had become heavy drinkers, and the father had been fired from his previously successful career.

There are many other such instances where Christians are emotionally and spiritually ruined. Situations such as this destroy faith because it is thought that if God exists, he would intervene to keep a situation from getting so bad that faith is destroyed. However, the idea that God would intervene in this manner overlooks a few facts.

The first fact is that prior to each situation of intense suffering, there are multitudes of moral choices made—not only by the one suffering intense evil, but also by his loved ones (e.g., friends, family, pastor, elders, deacons, deaconesses, and church members). Too often in such situations they make uncaring choices that cause the afflicted to suffer a higher degree of strain and sense of hopelessness that makes a bad situation much worse. In other words, very often a situation that would otherwise be a faith-building experience is turned into a spirit-crushing situation due in significant part to the unloving conduct of family, friends, or the church. Thus, to a significant extent, spirit-crushing suffering can result from bad use of free will, even if significant suffering is from a natural source (e.g., a congenital disease).

Spirit-Crushing Suffering

With this in mind, let's take another look at the situation of the parents with the three children afflicted by the untreatable genetic disorder. Assuming they belonged to a church group, there were many people who had the opportunity and means to intervene to mitigate the parents' ordeal and play a role in preventing their destructive course. Visiting schedules could've been organized and implemented (or implemented better). Perhaps a buddy system could have been implemented (if it hadn't been). Preventative psychological care was needed. The church could've raised money (or more money, if some had been raised) to cover psychological or psychiatric care expenses and other needs. If necessary, the members could've sold possessions or made cutbacks in household expenses for luxuries and entertainment (Acts 2:45; 4:32–36). More members could've sacrificed more of their time. The parents needed special Bible classes, and they needed to be taught from the best books on dealing with evil and suffering. Perhaps the members could've also assisted the parents with the care of the children to alleviate some of the strain. The parents could've been brought to support group meetings. With this sort of Christian intervention alone, it is doubtful that the chain of events would have occurred that led to the mother's nervous breakdown and heavy drinking (which so often leads to wrecked lives and loss of faith).

But the success of such intervention depends on whether the one suffering from intense evil has a will surrendered to God. At a minimum, this involves cooperation with church intervention. At a maximum, it involves "taking up a cross," letting go of pride, ego, or whatever attitude stands in the way of listening to good counsel, cooperating with relief efforts, and receiving assistance or money. This might involve agreeing to see a qualified psychologist (at church expense if necessary), attending support group meetings, letting friends visit more often, attending special classes, etc.

Surrender to God during an intense ordeal also depends on one's use of time and degree of devotion to God *prior* to being hit by a situation of intense evil and suffering. To allegorically teach this point, Jesus shared a parable of a farmer who sowed seed in various kinds of soil (Mark 4:3–20). Some of the seed was scattered on a heavily traveled path, some on rocky or shallow soil, some among thorns, and some on good soil. Each of the soil types is a metaphorical type of a cultivated disposition or belief in response to divine light. The first three soil types represent negative dispositions and beliefs that lead to spiritual ruin. One represents complacency in sin or never letting go of cherished sin. Another represents the worries ("thorns") of this life and the deceitfulness of wealth which can choke a relationship with God to death. Still another soil type represents having no "root," or not seriously cultivating a deep-rooted faith. "When trouble or persecution comes . . . they quickly fall away" (Mark 4:17). But the seed scattered into good soil represents Christians who "hear the word, accept it, and produce a crop—thirty, sixty, or even a hundred times what was sown." Such are the ones who are preparing themselves to walk *with God* through a future crisis (instead of walking through it alone). They've cultivated deep roots and guarded their soul against "stinkin' thinkin'" and the worries of this earthly life, the deceitfulness of materialism, or an anti-Christian culture. Such Christians are more likely to be trained by pain and tragedy (Heb. 12:11), whereas all others are more likely to be drained of hope and faith (2 Tim. 3:2–5).

Often believers filled with independence, strength, or accomplishment or submerged in what Christians call "worldliness" (1 John 2:15–17) tend to get blinded to such faith killers as pride, selfishness, lust, indifference, and an unforgiving attitude. Such believers make themselves unready to be trained by suffering that would lead them to serious renunciation of self-authority/pride (1 Cor. 2:3–5), which enables the believer to get free of "everything that hinders and the sin that so easily entangles" and run with perseverance the race marked out for them (Heb. 12:1).

The skeptic, however, could object to this, arguing that no Christian could be trained by suffering that is unbearable. God is supposed to know what a person can handle and temper the degree of evil and suffering so that the Christian does not get overwhelmed and lose faith. This is said to be a promise of God: "God is faithful; he will not let you be tempted beyond what you can bear" (1 Cor. 10:13). But a problem with the objection is that it misunderstands the Bible promise. The second half of the verse (v. 13) says God will not let Christians be tempted beyond what they can bear—not only because he adjusts the degree of his intervention to somewhat accommodate the believer's level of spiritual growth, but also because he provides the means and opportunity that the believer is to take hold of by trusting in God so that he can stand up under affliction. In the midst of an intense situation there are choices to be made, relief aid to be received, and cooperation with the interventional efforts of the church. There is a way, made by God, to keep from being wrecked and faithless. And no Christian need end up that way.

As Matthew Henry (1662–1714) says,

He will take care that we be not overcome, if we rely upon him, and resolve to approve ourselves faithful to him. We need not perplex ourselves with the difficulties in our way when God will take care that they shall not be too great for us to encounter. . . . There is no valley so dark but he can find a way through it, no affliction so grievous but he can prevent, or remove, or enable us to support it, and in the end overrule it to our advantage.[2]

Am I unrealistic about this? Am I being insensitive? In chapter 1 I mentioned something of my years-long plight in which I was drained of hope and eventually abandoned my faith in God. I've experienced spirit-crushing suffering. But looking back, I realize that it didn't have to happen that way. I made it happen. I played the victim. I refused to take hold of the available means and opportunities by faith so that my relationship with God would hold up under the strain. I and my Christian friends made negative choices, which made the weight of it too heavy for me. God didn't break his promise in 1 Cor. 10:13. Rather, I did not claim it.

The skeptic may recognize that I have an insider's perspective on spirit-crushing suffering, but object that I've overlooked the real issue, which is that many victims are caught off guard and unwittingly sink into a depression that overpowers faith. However, basic psychology teaches us that depression results from negative views or beliefs of our experiences. Negative perceptions of our self, the world, our place in the world, and the future make us vulnerable to internalizing stress and succumbing to depression. According to experts in psychology, "It is not bad things happening to us that is upsetting; it is our *interpretation* of them that makes all the difference."[3] Indeed, "it seems clear that our beliefs about ourselves and our relationships with others make us more or less vulnerable to depression when buffeted by life's inevitable stress."[4] Thus, depression is an end product of previously cultivated beliefs about themselves and their relationship with God and others. The depression doesn't just happen to us or arise from a vacuum. It's a result of free moral choices long before the depression begins.

It is true that they can be traced to the culture born into, upbringing, genetic makeup, chemical imbalances, or the harms that strike us. But they can also be traced to a multitude of free moral choices. Examples include choices against praying, being taught from the Bible, personal Bible study, congregating or fellowshipping with Christians, and reading books on apologetics, as well as engaging in personal worship, devotion, spiritual fasting, and intermittent rededication to faith and obedience. Christians are to fortify their faith so that they are not "caught off guard" by putting on the whole armor of God (Eph. 6:10–18). Choices against such things often include choices that get a person tangled up in anti-Christian entertainment, pleasure seeking, and abuse of alcohol or drugs. Christians are warned about this (1 John 2:15–17). All of these things set the Christian up for failure. They set into place certain beliefs about oneself and the world which have the potential of ensnaring one into a tendency to internalize stress and anger and cultivate depression. Then when a catastrophe strikes, mood disorders are more likely to take hold.

Nevertheless, mood disorders do not automatically spell doom for faith. As previously discussed, the *active* Christian is among fellow Christians who can intervene and offer assistance. And the faithful sufferer is to cooperate with the assistance offered. The end of a story of intense suffering doesn't have to be the loss of faith. It wasn't this way for me, and I had felt almost no supportive Christian love toward me from believers (in part because I had distanced myself from them). The same is possible for all who abandon their faith.

Any given situation of potential spirit-crushing suffering is surrounded by a vast multitude of free moral choices by at least several people, if not many people, over a course of a significant percentage of each of their lives. Given the wide range of free moral choices, it is not difficult to imagine why intervention by a free-will–preserving God would be so limited as to allow them to get that bad. If God were to intervene to that extent, coercing Christians into certain courses of action, there would be too much coercion and a great deal of compatibility-determining free will would be lost. If each of these persons is to have such free will, God must not intervene to the extent that prevents every Christian from being crushed and faithless. Actually, doing so would diminish life's challenges to the extent that there would be little character growth. Overall this could have a ripple effect that could alter God's plan to bring into being the greatest possible good.

NOTES to Appendix C

1. Gregory A. Boyd, *Satan and the Problem of Evil: Constructing a Trinitarian Warfare Theodicy* (Downers Grove, IL: InterVarsity Press, 2001), 260–261.
2. *Matthew Henry's Commentary on the Whole Bible* (Peabody, MA: Hendrickson

Publishers, 1991), 1810.

3. Benjamin B. Lahey, *Psychology: An Introduction*, eighth ed. (New York: McGraw-Hill, 2004), 556. Emphasis in the original.

4. Ibid., 557.

Appendix D
Notes on a Tripersonal Reconciliation

According to the Bible, the disobedience of humankind (sin) created a broken relationship with God and unfitness for fellowship with him and his heavenly community (Gen. 3). Unless God intervenes, the appropriate place in the second phase of life for all is exclusion from communion with God, which is a mediocre life at best (hell). But God has loved humankind[1] and has desired to give opportunity to everyone to freely choose to be reconciled and made fit for heavenly fellowship.[2] The giving of this opportunity is manifest in a plan that uniquely involves a tripersonal ministry by a triune God.

God is three persons, each one equal to the others in essence, or nature, and each with a distinct will that is ultimately expressed as the one will of God.[3] Their minds allow each to fully know each other; know each other's will, purposes, plans, and actions; and be in an undividable bond of unity. Thus, the action of one of the persons completely reflects the will of the other two persons. And, being three persons, they may establish distinct roles in whatever endeavor they desire, including their endeavor to save lost humankind.

The Role of the Father. One of the three persons of God assumes the role of the triune God, representing the triune will of the three. He is referred to in Scripture as the "Father." In his representative role as the triune God, the Father sends his servants, including the other two persons of God (the Son and Holy Spirit) who've assumed salvific roles in the world.

Prior to humankind's unfitness for fellowship with God, the Father, in his representative role, solemnly promised (made an oath or covenant) to save all who would be saved. He always has been, and always will be, faithful to his word.[4] This is poignantly affirmed in the words of the hymn *Great Is Thy Faithfulness*: "Great is Thy faithfulness, O God my Father, There is no shadow of turning with Thee; Thou changest not, Thy compassions, they fail not. As Thou has been, Thou forever wilt be."[5]

The Role of the Son. God is perfect, immutable love (1 John 1:5; 4:8), which necessarily includes his perfect commitment to perfect justice (all circumstances considered in the scheme of eternity). A loving person must be committed to justice or else he is not loving. Thus, God cannot be God if he is not perfectly committed to perfect justice. This dictates that all conduct ultimately be made to meet its just consequence—that there must be a reaping for what is sown.[6] The just consequence for sinful conduct is separation of the one generating it from God, ultimately in hell, as there can be no fellowship between God and a person who chooses a mindset in rebellion against God's disposition (God's law). Therefore, because of God's perfect commitment to justice, God has a red light, so to speak, against treating sinners as if they are entitled to fellowship with him, which ultimately includes exclusion from heaven, unless there is a way for God to treat them as if they are sinless while upholding his vitally necessary commitment to the principle of justice through accountability.

Fortunately for sinners, there is a way by means of a "messiah" who is fully God and fully man. With these two natures, he is able, as God and as a sinless man (2 Cor. 5:21; 1 John 3:5b), to justly have the consequence (punishment) for sinful conduct carried out on him on behalf of sinners. If he were not sinless, it would be impossible for the punishment to be carried out on him on behalf of other sinners. Thus, a sinless human life of the "messiah" is vital.

By the unique person and work of Jesus Christ, God's vitally necessary commitment to justice can be fulfilled. The disciple Matthew tells us that Jesus came to fulfill the law (Matt. 5:17). In this way God has a "green light" to save sinners. This is why Scripture says that "without the shedding of blood" there can be no forgiveness for salvation (Heb. 9:22).

Before humans first walked the earth God had a plan to uphold the principle of justice through accountability while being merciful to save those undeserving of heaven.[7] The plan involved one of the persons of God volunteering[8] to take the role of the incarnate[9] "Son" (Heb. 1:4) to satisfy

God's vitally necessary perfect commitment to justice by carrying out sin's penalty on him. At a point in the stream of humanity (Ps. 2:7; Heb. 1:5), the Son would manifest his role by becoming the perfect human to satisfy the law for all who would be saved. At the perfect time in human history (Gal. 4:4), the Son of God would enter the human world as a baby (Luke 1:26–38; 2:7), and, as a grown man (and fully God), willingly suffer the consequence for sin instead of penitent sinners. In this, the principle of justice through accountability for sin is upheld (God's commitment to justice remains perfect), vindicating God from any suggestion (by Satan) that he had not done so when he forgave sinners (Rom. 3:25–26).[10]

The Son made a solemn promise (oath) with the Father[11] to one day be our propitiation[12] regarding God's necessary position to uphold the principle of justice through accountability for sin. By the Son's oath, the Father had the "green light" to reconcile penitent sinners to himself and for heaven—even before the transgressions of Adam and Eve. Thus, at the time of the fall of man, God's vindication for being merciful and forgiving of their sins (and everyone's sins since) was already set to be fulfilled by the promise of the Son. This is why despite the sin of Adam and Eve, it was right for God to seek them in the garden and ask, "Where are you?" (Gen. 3:9). Without God's oath, God could not have initiated such reconciliation and remain perfectly righteous.

Because of God's oath in the beginning, people living in all of the ages before the crucifixion of Jesus may have received forgiveness by virtue of the curse he promised he would bear. This includes such men as Enoch,[13] Noah,[14] and Job.[15] They were saved thanks to the person and work of Jesus. Martin Luther (1483–1546) acknowledges this: "He forgave them [the patriarchs in BC times] their sins . . . in view of the promised atonement to be made by Christ."[16] This is referred to as the retrospective effect of Christ's substitutionary death (Rom. 3:25b). The prospective effect of Christ's death applies to all living since (Rom. 3:26a).

The fulfillment of the Son's promise occurred while he was arrested, flogged, and torturously executed outside of Jerusalem. There, he was treated by the Father (who represented the triune God) as if he were a sinner by carrying out the consequence for sin on Jesus. He was treated in a nonreconciliatory fashion and was relationally forsaken and allowed to be brutally treated. Signs of the relational break include the Son: being arrested; being flogged; being crucified; enduring the three hours of darkness in the land (Mark 27:46); crying to God, who had forsaken him (Matt. 27:47); and his death. He felt forsaken in the final hours of his life. After his death he continued to feel forsaken as a disembodied soul, which was exclusion from communion with God in beatific vision (which lasted approximately forty hours).

To understand the separation from God that Jesus suffered, it is helpful to recognize that (under theories of Christology) Jesus had two spheres of consciousness: a human sphere and a sphere as one of the three persons of God. He interacted between the two, but for his terrestrial mission he had given up access to his divine consciousness. Thus, when Jesus was forsaken, he experienced this as a human soul with a first-century mind, but the pain was also felt by his divine sphere of consciousness, which, due to the unity of the three persons of God, was also felt by the Father and the Spirit[17] (which makes the suffering from this event far worse than the suffering of any created being in hell).

A key accomplishment of "the cross" was its demonstration that God had always and would always uphold the principle of justice through accountability for sin (stay true to his perfect commitment to justice), even while treating sinners in a way that suggests that he wasn't upholding it. As such, God is vindicated when he doesn't hold repentant sinners accountable for sin and reconciles them to himself in the earthly life and in the afterlife in heaven.

Some critics of the atonement argue that it is never moral to inflict suffering on someone as punishment for something he or she did not do. Therefore, as the argument goes, it is immoral for God to punish Jesus, even if he is a volunteer. But the problem with this is that it is based on a misunderstanding of the incarnation and the atonement. Jesus Christ is one person with two natures: divine and human. As God, he is lawmaker, the definer of sin, the law giver, the judge, the prosecutor (with prosecutorial discretion), and the definer of perfect justice. On the other hand, as a created human, he is subject to God and his law, but innocent of any wrongdoing. As God, he has the prerogative of upholding his perfect commitment to justice by having the consequence of sin carried out on him. Christ's dual nature makes "the cross" judicially unique. As such, the ship carrying the argument that "the cross" is unjust runs aground. No other human (or angel) has this prerogative, so for God to have called any other human to the task would've been morally wrong. But Jesus' divine nature gives him alone this divine prerogative, which makes having the consequence for sin carried out on him morally right. Not only is it right for

Jesus alone to do this, but it is also effective only if *he* does it, as he alone can absorb the consequence because he is without sin.

The Role of the Holy Spirit. The ministerial role of Jesus Christ would save no one if not for the ministerial role of the Holy Spirit. The Holy Spirit's role in salvation is indispensable. The indispensability of their roles is summed up in Ephesians 2:18: "All of us can come to the Father through the same Holy Spirit because of what Christ has done for us" (NLT).

The Spirit's role is that of the universal, supernatural evangelist; revelator; and instigator of faith. The Spirit imparts salvific knowledge (divine light) to which we may respond by faith in a loving and good God. Each of us receives divine light by various modes—both natural and supernatural. Rays of light are imparted from: our observation of, and experiences in, nature; inspired Scripture; our conscience; a mental impression; a dream; words direct to the mind (subconsciously or consciously); an encounter with an angel (either in disguise or not in disguise); a vision; or an encounter with the resurrected Jesus. As discussed in chapter 12, the more extraordinary or supernatural modes are not restricted to God's prophets, but, according to the Bible, happen to some nonbelievers. Moreover, today there are reports in various places in the world by people who've converted to Christ from a non-Christian religion because of a kind of supernatural experience. The Spirit employs only as much of the extraordinary and supernatural modes as necessary to ensure that none of the persons excluded from heaven have an excuse. (The ministry of the Holy Spirit is discussed in chapter 12.1.)

The Holy Spirit desires the salvation of all, and, accordingly, imparts rays of divine light to all—"both the good and the bad" (Matt. 22:10)—which are sufficient to lead the interested person to salvation. But while everyone receives some ray of salvific knowledge, some receive more than others. This is not because the Spirit loves some more than others. Rather, it is because the degree of divine light imparted is in proportion to the measure of human desire to know a loving and good Divinity. There is no purpose in giving salvific knowledge to those who would rather not have it (Matt. 7:6). But those who "hunger and thirst after righteousness" will be "filled" (Matt. 5:6). In other words, God reveals himself according to the measure of earnestness and zeal shown by those who seek him. People who perceive and make practical use of the salvific knowledge imparted will be given more (Matt. 13:11–15; Mark 4:25).

Even in non-Christian cultures, if a person genuinely seeks a loving and good Divinity, the Spirit will make a way for greater knowledge to be imparted. He will employ any one of the modes of revelation, whether directly or indirectly, or by a human missionary, or by a combination of supernatural ways without a human missionary.

For we read in Acts 17:26–27:

From one man he made every nation of men, that they should inhabit the whole earth; and he determined the times set for them and the exact places where they should live. God did this so that men would seek him and perhaps reach out for him and find him, though he is not far from each one of us.

It is God's plan that each person is providentially assigned a place of birth where he or she is ministered to by the Holy Spirit in a variety of ways in hope that a loving and good Divinity would be sought. Regardless of culture or religion, the Spirit is within reach of each of us, so salvation is accessible to everyone.

By imparting knowledge and conviction of sin, the Spirit is the instigator of faith in God. He provides all the means necessary. It is up to us as to how we respond to it. If the will starts to lean in God's direction, the Spirit accompanies it with his providential intervention to help fulfill it (he cooperates with a surrendered will). He may intercede in small ways or big ways to give power over the addictive pull of sin or steer a person away from temptation, and thus aid in altering the course of the life. But the Spirit does nothing to coerce the will toward salvation.

NOTES to Appendix D

1. John 3:16; 1 John 4:8; 1 Cor. 1:3.

2. Gen. 12:3; Ezek. 18:23, 32; 33:11; Matt. 18:14; John 12:32; Acts 3:25; Gal. 3:8; 1 Tim. 2:4; 1 Pet. 3:9.

3. Paul Copan, *That's Just Your Interpretation: Responding to Skeptics Who Challenge Your Faith* (Grand Rapids, MI: Baker Books, 2001), 125.

4. Gen. 6–8; 12:1–3; Deut. 29:12–15; James 1:12; 2:5, 25; 1 John 2:25.

5. Hymn *Great Is Thy Faithfulness* by Thomas Chisolm (1866–1960). Published in 1923 with musical score by William Runyan.

6. Prov. 22:8; Gal. 6:7.

7. Eph. 1:3–5; 2 Thess. 2:13; Titus 1:1–2; Rev. 13:8.

8. John 10:11, 15, 17–18; 1 John 3:16.

9. John 1:14; 1 Tim. 3:16.

10. Anders Nygren, *Commentary of Romans*, trans. Carl C. Rasmussen (Philadelphia: Muhlenberg Press, 1949), 159–160. Additional commentary on Rom. 3:25–26 explaining this vital point is found in: *Matthew Henry's Commentary on the Whole Bible* (Peabody, MA: Hendrickson Publishers, 1991), 1761; Charles H. Dodd (1884–1973), *The Epistle of Paul to the Romans* (London: Hodder and Stoughton, 1932), 59; David Martyn Lloyd-Jones, *The Cross: The Vindication of God* (Carlisle, PA: The Banner of Truth Trust, 1976), 14; *The Wycliffe Bible Commentary*, eds. Charles F. Pfeiffer and Everett F. Harrison (Chicago: Moody Press, 1990), 1192–1193; Douglas J. Moo, *The NIV Application Commentary: Romans* (Grand Rapids, MI: Zondervan, 2000), 128–130, 135–136; *Zondervan NIV Bible Commentary, Volume 2: New Testament*, consul. eds. Kenneth L. Barker and John R. Kohlenberger III (Grand Rapids, MI: Zondervan Publishing House, 1994), 538; Steve Jeffery, Michael Ovey, Andres Sach, *Pierced for Our Transgressions* (Wheaton, IL: Crossway Books, 2007), 81, 211; *The Expositor's Bible Commentary*, gen. ed. Frank E. Gaebelein, consul. eds. James Montgomery Boice and Merrill C. Tenney, Vol. 10 (Grand Rapids, MI: Zondervan Publishing House, 1976), 44.

11. Heb. 6:12–18; 9:26; Rev. 13:8; 17:8.

12. Some opponents of the atonement believe the doctrine of salvation is incoherent because the Father, Son, and Holy Spirit are all equally God, which should suggest that each of the Godhead must be appeased (propitiated) and not just the Father. Additionally, it would seem absurd to think that Christ would appease himself by his own sacrifice. But a problem with this argument is that it is based on an incorrect understanding of the doctrines of salvation, the incarnation, and the Trinity, as well as a lack of recognition of the ministerial roles of the Father and Son. God's wrath against sinners consists of upholding the principle of accountability for sin. When this principle is upheld, the divine "wrath" is appeased or propitiated. The will of all three of the persons of God is to uphold the principle, so the person of God in the role of the Son *was* propitiated. However, Scripture speaks of the persons of God with respect to their ministerial roles and therefore does not specifically talk about the propitiation of the Son and Spirit. The Father represents the wills of the Son and Spirit, so when he is propitiated, so are the other two. Moreover, it is not accurate to say Jesus appeased himself. Jesus had two spheres of consciousness: a human sphere and the divine sphere. In his mission, he had given up access to his divine consciousness. Thus, Jesus did not appease the will of his human consciousness, but the will of his divine consciousness.

13. Gen. 5:24; Heb. 11:5.

14. Gen. 6–8.

15. Job 1:1, 8; James 5:11.

16. Martin Luther, *Commentary on Romans*, trans. J. Theodore Mueller (Grand Rapids, MI: Kregel Publications, 1976), 79.

17. Paul Copan, *That's Just Your Interpretation*, 133–136.

Appendix E
Discussion of Texts Cited to Support the Long List (Restrictivism)

As was said in chapter 12.2, in my studies I found there to be two basic views on the knowledge and beliefs necessary for a transforming and saving relationship with God. The view that less knowledge and beliefs are needed I called the short list. The view that more are needed, including the knowledge of and belief in the gospel of Christ, I called the long list. The additional tenets of faith of the long list are as follows:

1. Belief/trust in the existence of a divine judgment against sin and consequential consignment to hell (per the principle of justice through accountability).
2. Belief/trust that all humans are sinners deserving of hell.
3. Belief/trust that there exists a God-man-messiah who has satisfied the principle of justice through accountability so that God could have the "green light" to forgive sinners (see appendix D).
4. Belief/trust that heaven exists.

Advocates of the long list argue that the following New Testament texts support the long list (restrictivist) view of salvation: John 3:18; 14:6; 20:30–31; Acts 2:38a; 4:12; 13:46; 16; 20:26–27; 26:17–18; Rom. 1–3; 10:13–14; 1 John 5:11–12. This appendix discusses the texts and shows that the Bible doesn't clearly teach that the long list is necessary for a transforming and saving relationship with God. Before beginning this discussion, however, I offer a preliminary word on a fallacy inherent in the view.

E.1 A Problem in the Long List (Restrictivist) Interpretation

Many long listers (restrictivists) rely on the following reasoning for their view:

There are Bible verses that state that all who respond to imparted messianic gospel knowledge by faith in God is saved (all RGKF are S), which necessarily means that the group of people who are saved could only be those with messianic gospel knowledge who exercise faith in God (thus people without messianic gospel knowledge who exercise faith in God are not saved) (all S are RGKF).

That everyone who responds to imparted messianic gospel knowledge by faith in God are saved (all RGKF are S) is self-evident by unequivocal statements in the Bible that relate this. However, it does not follow that this necessarily means that the group of people who are saved could *only* be those with messianic gospel knowledge who exercise faith in God (all S are RGKF). It could *possibly* be true, but it is not *necessarily* true. Therefore, this reasoning employed by some restrictivists is fallacious.

The following provides clarification. All mothers in a given group are necessarily female, but not all females in a group are necessarily mothers. While it is possible that all females in a given group are mothers, it is also possible that at least one of them isn't. Therefore, an argument that all females in the group are mothers because all mothers in a given group are necessarily female is fallacious.

Likewise, it is not necessarily so that all S are RGKF just because all RGKF are S. Or, spelled out, it is not necessarily so that the only saved people are those who respond to messianic gospel information by faith in God just because there are Bible texts that relate that all who are familiar with the gospel and who respond by faith in God are saved. Therefore, texts that relate that anyone who receives gospel knowledge and responds to it by faith is saved should not be construed on that basis as teaching that the only people who have a chance of being saved are those who learn about the gospel prior to death.

Some restrictivists (long listers) acknowledge the bad reasoning, but insist that their view is based on certain Bible passages. The following section discusses the Bible passages and why they do not clearly teach that the long list is necessary to be saved.

Discussion of Texts Cited to Support the Long List (Restrictivism)

E.2 Texts Cited to Support the Long List View (Restrictivism)

Rom. 10:13–14

"Everyone who calls on the name of the Lord will be saved." How, then, can they call on the one they have not believed in? And how can they believe in the one of whom they have not heard? And how can they hear without someone preaching to them?

Restrictivists say the Bible passage teaches that people living since the time of Jesus' crucifixion and resurrection cannot have a saving belief without having knowledge of the gospel of Christ brought by a human missionary. Therefore, people not evangelized prior to death have no chance of having a proper relationship with God for salvation. However, with a proper exegetical background study of the passage, it becomes apparent that Paul meant to teach something quite different.

Beginning at verse 1 of Romans 10, Paul expresses his "desire and prayer to God for the Israelites . . . that they may be saved." The Jews, as Paul explains, were stuck on the disastrous doctrine of righteousness by the law (Rom. 10:2–3, 5). It was disastrous because it would instill a delusional sense of confidence in being safe from condemnation. And such surety often led to self-justification of cherished sins detrimental to one's compatibility for salvation.[1] As a result, some were doing the same malicious, deceitful, and lustful practices that many of the Gentile polytheists were doing (Rom. 2:1–6, 17–25). Paul warns that righteousness by the law leads ultimately to hell. But God had the antidote to the inappropriate confidence in righteousness by the law—the gospel of Christ, by which one can overcome self-justification and cherished sins (Rom. 10:4, 8–13). In this regard, a hearing of the gospel of Jesus *is* necessary to help the Israelites avoid the dangerous influence of righteousness by the law (by replacing a nonworking covenant with one that would work).

To reinforce his admonition, Paul leaves his audience with no justifying excuse for holding onto righteousness by the law (and rejection of Christ). In Rom. 10:14–21 he meets each excuse head-on using a series of rhetorical questions. Paul asks what conditions are necessary for "calling on the Lord," and he then shows that these conditions have been fulfilled: Have the preachers of the gospel been sent, so that all the Jews may have an opportunity to believe (v. 14)? Yes, the gospel had been sufficiently preached in Israel, as Isaiah had foretold (Isa. 52:7) (v. 15). Does the fact that all of the Jews have not believed prove that they have not heard (v. 16a)? No, because Isaiah also had foretold that some would not receive the message (vv. 16b–17). Is it possible that some of the Jews may not have heard (v. 18a)? This could not be, because by that time (about twenty-seven years after Christ's crucifixion) the gospel had been proclaimed widely enough that Jews on the whole had heard (v. 18b). Paul continues. Even if it is true that Israel heard the gospel, is it possible that they did not grasp its significance (v. 19a)? This also could not be, for, as Moses and Isaiah have said, even the less privileged and less knowledgeable Gentiles have been able to understand Christ's role in God's salvation (vv. 19b–20). Therefore, the Jews cannot plead a lack of understanding of the gospel as an excuse for rejecting Christ. The fact is that, as Isaiah has said, the reason for the Jews' rejection of the gospel of Jesus is that they are a "disobedient and obstinate people" (v. 21).[2]

This is Paul's conclusion. God did his part and fulfilled his promise to send to Israel his message of justification by faith in him apart from the possession of the law. Thus, Israel should have known from Scripture and the preaching of the apostles that righteousness by the law is spiritually dangerous. Yet, Israel refused to submit to it, rather holding fast to its own false view of justification, that of justification by virtue of their possession of a law they could not fully obey.[3] Thus, God's rejection of Israel would be just.

The conclusion that this leads to is that Rom. 10:13–14 is not teaching that a universal response to God is required for salvation, per se. He is not suggesting that all who die unevangelized have no chance of experiencing a saving belief. Therefore, it appears that the Bible passage does not support a restrictivist long list view of salvation.

Nonetheless, some fail to see this, in part due to a misunderstanding of verses 11–13, which are thought to convey a universal requirement to acquire gospel knowledge: "As the Scripture says, 'Anyone who trusts in him will never be put to shame.' For there is no difference between Jew and Gentile—the same Lord is Lord of all and richly blesses all who call on him, for, 'Everyone who calls on the name of the Lord will be saved.'"

However, in these verses Paul is setting the stage for his message to the Jews by declaring God's promise to send Israel his message of justification by faith for *all peoples*.[4] For his Jewish audience, Paul references Isaiah 28:16 (in verse 11) and Joel 2:32 (in verse 13). He acknowledges a promise of God to all evangelized people (Jews and Gentiles) that any who love the Lord receive the ever-rewarding salvation of God. By this, Paul is affirming his teaching of a universally *available* justification by faith that he had laid down in chapter 3 (which is evident from the passages in the book of Isaiah that Paul cites in Rom. 10:14–21).

Such a promise of God would be empty unless the Jews were given the opportunity of being its beneficiaries. If God made the promise, he must orchestrate the conditions so that the Jew could avail himself of it. But, as explained, the Jews could argue that they did not have fair opportunity to have God's promise fulfilled in them. This led Paul to address any excuses in the series of rhetorical questions (vv. 14–21). Therefore, taking verses 11–13 to mean that every individual Jew and Gentile on the planet must hear the gospel and believe in the Lord to be saved is taking these verses out of the context of a message aimed at dealing with God's just rejection of Israel for its stubborn refusal to accept the gospel of Christ.

Another reason for concluding that verses 11–13 are merely setting forth God's promise so that Paul can deal with the danger inherent in righteousness by the law is because to read them as saying no unevangelized person is saved contradicts Paul's statements made in Rom. 2:6–15. In this part of the epistle, Paul tells us that people unaware of the truths of Scripture may be justified (v. 13) as a result of a positive response to revelations by the Holy Spirit to form a disposition and beliefs concerning a loving and good Divinity compatible for eternal reconciliation.[5]

John 14:6 and Acts 4:12

Jesus answered, "I am the way and the truth and the life. No one comes to the Father except through me."

Salvation is found in no one else, for there is no other name under heaven given to men by which we must be saved.

Restrictivists tell us that these verses affirm that salvation is in being evangelized so as to have belief in Christ. The unevangelized, unfortunately, have no such opportunity, and are certainly lost.

However, these verses only underscore the ontological necessity of the person and work of Jesus Christ for salvation. In other words, the fact that Christ satisfied the need to fulfill the principle of accountability (demand of justice/law) is critical if God is to forgive any of us (this is discussed in appendix D). Christ gives God the "green light" to save. Thus, no one enters heaven except by what Jesus has done.

Moreover, neither of the verses speaks of a saving response to God that is universal, or of the kind of knowledge of the Divine that is universally necessary for a saving belief. They do not speak of an epistemological necessity of Christ. Therefore, these texts provide no answer to the question of whether people who die unevangelized have no chance for salvation.

Rom. 1:18–32 and 3:10, 23

Restrictivists refer to these verses in Romans in an argument that "general revelation" alone is insufficient to cultivate a disposition and beliefs compatible for salvation. A disposition and beliefs compatible for salvation require being evangelized to a messianic gospel by "special revelation."

According to restrictivist Ronald H. Nash (1936–2006),

> Paul makes it plain that general revelation does not and cannot save. . . . General revelation serves only to condemn man, not to save him. . . . Paul's teaching that no human being succeeds in living up to the light of general revelation implies that general revelation cannot save; special revelation is required for that result.[6]

In response, it is first of all worth noting that nowhere in this passage does Paul address the question of whether the information of general revelation is sufficient for salvation.[7] Paul does not actually teach that no human being succeeds in living up to the light of general revelation. This is not a point made anywhere in the text. Rather, he simply mentions general revelation for his argument that neither Jew nor Gentile have excuse for the sinful conduct he lists in verses 24–32. Therefore, the argument that the text implies that general revelation cannot save is without foundation.

But whether general revelation is insufficient to impart enough knowledge for salvation does not matter. As discussed in chapter 12.1, the Holy Spirit touches every mind with subtle forms of special revelation without being taught from Scripture. Everyone is given sufficient light to demonstrate either rejection of that light or desire for more. Those who desire more are given more. And the mode by which more light is imparted may not involve a human missionary, as biblical and extrabiblical examples show (see chapter 12.1). Ultimately, unevangelized people who would embrace an eternal fellowship with God are given enough salvific knowledge to lead them there, whether that includes learning of a messianic gospel or not (as in the case of Abraham).

What we can rightly imply from Rom. 1:18–32 is that generally most people do not find whatever divine light they are given palatable. Consequently, the Holy Spirit lets them remain in the darkness they desire. "God gave them over in the sinful desires of their hearts" (Rom. 1:24). But if any would demonstrate a heart that would be led to God, the Holy Spirit would reach them—by various modes, and in an amount of light that corresponds to a person's desire for the truth.

Therefore, the people of Rom. 1:18–32 were not lost because they hadn't been instructed about a messianic gospel from Scripture. Rather, they were lost because they did not find the light given to be palatable. And because they didn't find the light they received to be palatable, they wouldn't have cultivated an enduring and saving surrender of the heart to God if a missionary had taught them the gospel of Christ. The conclusion, then, about Rom. 1:18–32 and 3:10, 23 is that there is no clear indication that knowledge of messianic gospel tenets is required for a saving disposition and beliefs.

John 3:18; 20:30–31; 1 John 5:11–12

John 3:18 reads: "Whoever believes in him [Jesus] is not condemned, but whoever does not believe stands condemned already because he has not believed in the name of God's one and only Son."

Restrictivists seem to interpret "whoever" as meaning "any and every person regardless of *any* circumstances, including the circumstance of being unevangelized." But the context implies that "whoever" means "whoever is presented with the gift of the light of the gospel of Christ." The ones who do not believe in the name of Christ have a negative attitude toward the light received because of cherished sin.[8] Therefore, the text does not speak on the situation of the unevangelized and should not be cited in support of a restrictivist view of salvation.

John 20:30–31 reads: "Jesus did many other miraculous signs in the presence of his disciples, which are not recorded in this book. But these are written that you may believe that Jesus is the Christ, the Son of God, and that by believing you may have life in his name."

Some restrictivists say that their view is so apparent in this text that it "speaks for itself."[9] However, it might seem obvious only until the context is examined, as well as a few key phrases. John's hope was that the evangelized believer in God (Jews and God-fearers) would have a new and enduring relationship with God by believing that Jesus is the messiah, the Son of God, and by living "life in *his* name."[10] John recorded the evidences of Jesus' divine messiah-ship in his book to present "those that read and hear the gospel" with the "duty to believe, to embrace, the doctrine of Christ, and that record concerning him." Therefore, it was not intended to relate a universal requirement for salvation. It does not address the question as to what happens to people who reach the end of their life without having been evangelized and should not be cited in support of a restrictivist view of salvation.

1 John 5:11–12 reads: "And this is the testimony: God has given us eternal life, and this life is in his Son. He who has the Son has life; he who does not have the Son of God does not have life." This admonition is essentially an echo of John 20:30–31, and thus involves the same context of an address to evangelized believers in God (Jews and God-fearers). It says nothing about the situation of those who've never heard of the God of the Jews.

E.3 The Book of Acts and the Motivation for Missions: Acts 2:38a; 13:46; 16; 20:26–27; 26:17–18

Restrictivists believe that a long list view of salvation is the motivation for missions, as is apparent in the book of Acts. They ask: If people could be saved by God apart from learning of the messianic gospel from a human missionary, why the strong emphasis in the book of Acts on taking the gospel into all the world? Isn't the motivation for sharing the gospel to bring a message to people who would otherwise be eternally lost if they did not hear it? Wasn't this the motivation of Peter and Paul, evident by their extraordinary zeal?

The apostles lived lives of extraordinary sacrifice, perseverance, and suffering in order to preach the gospel of Jesus. There were times when Paul and some of his companions were arrested, severely flogged, and imprisoned.[11] Some had their property confiscated (Heb. 10:34). Paul was pummeled with rocks (Acts 14:19), suffered a shipwreck from a hurricane (Acts 27:13–44), suffered from hunger, suffered with illness (2 Cor. 12:7), and suffered from insults, hardships, beatings, distress, persecutions, and difficulties (2 Cor. 12:10). In one of his letters Paul tells us something of what his life was like:

> I have worked much harder, been in prison more frequently, been flogged more severely, and been exposed to death again and again. Five times I received from the Jews the forty lashes minus one. Three times I was beaten with rods, once I was stoned, three times I was shipwrecked, I spent a night and a day in the open sea, I have been constantly on the move. I have been in danger from rivers, in danger from bandits, in danger from my own countrymen, in danger from

Discussion of Texts Cited to Support the Long List (Restrictivism)

Gentiles; in danger in the city, in danger in the country, in danger at sea; and in danger from false brothers. I have labored and toiled and have often gone without sleep; I have known hunger and thirst and have often gone without food; I have been cold and naked (2 Cor. 11:23–27).

The pertinent question is: Is all this extraordinary zeal (or fanaticism, as some might call it) a reflection of a belief that people without knowledge of Jesus have no chance of experiencing salvation?

To answer this question, we first go to Paul. Theologians gather from his second epistle to the Corinthian Christians that his adversaries had reproached him concerning his zeal in preaching the gospel (2 Cor. 5:13). If there is any place in Paul's epistles where we should reasonably expect a defense of a restrictivist (long list) motivation for preaching, it is here. If people have no chance of salvation if not for learning of the gospel by a human missionary, here is where Paul should remind the church. But instead, he says his motivation for his extraordinary zeal is a profound attitude of selflessness inspired by Christ's love for the glory of God and the good of the church (2 Cor. 5:13–14).

This attitude prompted Paul's obedience to Jesus' command to go and teach the gospel and make disciples (students) of people in all nations (Matt. 28:18–20a; Acts 1:8). According to theologian Matthew Henry (1662–1714) the purpose behind Jesus' proclamation (the great commission) is to advance God's kingdom in the world, to take ground away from darkness and grow the kingdom of light.[12] This is a fulfillment of the prayer in Matt. 6:9–10: "Our Father . . . your kingdom come, your will be done on earth as it is in heaven."

Paul's zeal was also in large part due to a specific kind of mission given directly to him by God (Acts 9:3–16; 26:12–20). But every Christian should be strongly motivated to play a part in the increase of a population empowered to love others according to Jesus' example. And this was some of Paul's motivation: that more of the world would be saved from sin[13] and its destruction. Christians desiring an end to violence, insecurity, deceit, and heartache have plenty of motivation indeed to spread the word to advance the kingdom.

A part of Paul's mission included bringing the gospel to the Jews that had fallen into sin because of righteousness by the law (discussed earlier). Paul points to the only saving solution to changing the course of a disposition molded by righteousness by the law—acceptance of the gospel of Christ. It was in this sense that preaching the gospel to the Jews and Gentile converts was vitally needed to divert them from the spiritual danger.

Finally, there should be strong motivation to share the gospel because of the joy and the more dramatically changed lives witnessed in those who accept it. Paul said the message of the gospel brings power from God for transformation of mind and life (Rom. 1:16; 12:2). Christians will undoubtedly feel strongly about the message reaching the ears and eyes of the world. It gives hope like no other. Anyone with the right attitude about God and love and goodness will naturally find herself sharing the gospel with the unevangelized.

But, the restrictivist responds, what about the passages in the book of Acts that suggest that people who die without knowledge of the messianic gospel have no chance of salvation? Restrictivists claim that the following texts reveal this view, if only indirectly: Acts 2:38a; 13:46; 16; 20:26–27; 26:17–18.

In response, close inspection of the passages reveals that there really is no allusion to a restrictivist view of salvation. In the context of Acts 2:38a, Peter is preaching the gospel of Christ to a group of Jews (vv. 5, 11, 22). They were then "cut to the heart and said to Peter and the other apostles, 'Brothers, what shall we do'" (v. 37). Being in spiritual danger from righteousness by the law, *they* had only one choice that would save *them*—"Repent and be baptized, every one of you, in the name of Jesus Christ for the forgiveness of your sins" (v. 38a).

Despite the fact that Peter was speaking to the Jews, restrictivists read into this text that Peter's admonition is a universal requirement that extends to people who've never heard of Judaism, Christ, or baptism. Reading it this way seems to be justified by either applying the reasoning discussed in section E.1 (all RGKF are S = all S are RGKF) that was shown to be fallacious, or assuming that the restrictivist view is clearly taught elsewhere in the Bible.

However, as discussed in appendix F, there are people named in the Bible who are saved without knowledge of a messianic gospel. Moreover, it was shown earlier that the Bible texts cited by restrictivists do not actually teach the restrictivist view of salvation. This is further supported by Rom. 2:14–15, which indicates allowance for the possibility that at least a small percentage of Gentiles without gospel knowledge could cultivate a disposition and beliefs compatible with heaven.[14] Therefore, the restrictivist view of salvation

Discussion of Texts Cited to Support the Long List (Restrictivism)

appears to be without biblical foundation. While Acts 2:38a affirms that a saving response to the gospel of Christ necessarily entails repentance and faith toward God (Acts 20:21) followed by baptism (if possible), it is silent on the question of whether a person without knowledge of the gospel of Christ has a chance of being saved. As such, it does not provide a biblical basis for restrictivism.

In Acts 13:46 the apostle Paul preaches the gospel of Christ in Pisidian Antioch to an audience of Jews and Gentile converts to Judaism, who were rejecting Christ: "We had to speak the word of God to you first. Since you reject it and do not consider yourselves worthy of eternal life, we now turn to the Gentiles." Restrictivists read this text as saying that the Gentiles are lost to hell because acceptance of the person and work of Christ is required for salvation, and the Gentiles hadn't yet heard the gospel. Thus, if any of the Gentiles were to die before the arrival of the apostles with their message, they would certainly have been lost without hope.

Reading it this way, however, has problems. The verse speaks of two groups of people: a group that rejects the gospel of Christ, and, by such rejection, demonstrates its lostness, and a group yet to learn of the gospel and thus acquire the same opportunity to accept it (or reject it). There is no statement that the Gentiles who are yet to hear the gospel are lost. Lostness is said to be the plight of an evangelized person who rejects Christ. The text is silent on the situation of the unevangelized. Therefore, it should not be cited in support of the restrictivist view of salvation.

In Acts 16, a Philippian jailer asks Paul and Silas: "Sirs, what must I do to be saved? They replied, 'Believe in the Lord Jesus, and you will be saved—you and your household. Then they spoke the word of the Lord to him and to all the others in his house. At that hour of the night the jailer took them and washed their wounds; then immediately he and all his family were baptized. The jailer brought them into his house and set a meal before them; he was filled with joy because he had come to believe in God—he and his whole family" (vv. 30–34).

To interpret this as indicating that people who die without learning about Christ have no chance of salvation, you would need to employ the fallacious reasoning discussed in section E.1. It does not logically follow that the jailer is saved after hearing the gospel and responding in faith (RGKF are S) or that the jailer was lost at all times prior to hearing the message from Paul (all S are

RGKF). Believing in the Lord Jesus was the jailer's best assurance of having an enduring, saving faith. But we cannot know from the text whether the jailer was unknowingly justified by Christ's atoning work and a positive response to the Holy Spirit prior to the time when Paul and Silas arrived in town. The fact that he responded to the message so eagerly could suggest that his heart had already been made compatible for heaven (e.g., God fearers). Therefore, Acts 16 doesn't actually have any clear support for the restrictivist view of salvation.

Another text cited by restrictivists is Acts 20:26–27: "Therefore, I declare to you today that I am innocent of the blood of all men. For I have not hesitated to proclaim to you the whole will of God." Restrictivists think this text tells us that if Paul had not been faithful in proclaiming the gospel to the people at Ephesus they would all be lost, and then he would've been responsible for their condemnation.

However, restrictivists misinterpret the text because they fail to account for its context. The context is of Paul's farewell address to the elders of the church at Ephesus (v. 28). He was leaving them, never to return. Paul was concerned about the danger of "false teachings" coming into the church, or arising from within the church, that could lure them away from a proper understanding of Jesus Christ (v. 29–32) or away from true fellowship with God and his community of believers (see Ephesians). Paul had similar concern for other churches. For example, to the Thessalonians he warned, "Stand firm and hold to the teachings we passed on to you, whether by word of mouth or by letter" (2 Thess. 2:15).[15] Thus, Paul had fortified the Ephesian elders with his careful instruction "the whole will of God."

With this context as our backdrop, it is easy to see why Paul would declare that he would not bear any fault if the church apostatizes. He spent an enormous amount of effort and time teaching them the truth. Now Paul leaves them, never to return.[16] So they are on their own. After his departure, if the church embraces false teachings it would not be the fault of Paul. With a correct understanding of the passage, it is apparent that it does not suggest that those who die unevangelized have no chance of being saved.

The final text in Acts cited by restrictivists is Acts 26:17–18. It recounts Paul's "vision from heaven" (v. 19) on the road to Damascus. In the vision, Jesus speaks to him in Aramaic, telling him he is sending him to Jews and Gentiles "to open their eyes and turn them from darkness to light, and from

Discussion of Texts Cited to Support the Long List (Restrictivism)

the power of Satan to God, so that they may receive forgiveness of sins and a place among those who are sanctified by faith in me" (v. 18).

To see this text as suggesting a restrictivist view of salvation, one has to rely on either:

1. The fallacious reasoning discussed earlier (all RGKF are S = all S are RGKF);
2. The idea that all of the people in the Bible said to be saved had messianic gospel knowledge;
3. The idea that the Bible elsewhere teaches restrictivism; or
4. The notion that Paul and Luke did not use generalizations in their writings in a context about salvation.

First, nothing further needs be said about misinterpreting a text from reliance on the fallacious reasoning discussed earlier (that it is not necessarily so that all S are RGKF just because all RGKF are S). Second, it is discussed in appendix F why there is no textual evidence to support the idea that all of the people in the Bible said to be saved possessed messianic gospel knowledge. Third, the previous discussion shows why none of the texts cited by restrictivists contain no clear teaching of restrictivism.

Finally, the idea that the writers of the New Testament did not use generalizations, even in the context of salvation, is patently false. We know from Paul's epistles that it was common to speak generally about people groups being lost when in fact it is known that a minority within the lost group is saved. For example, in Paul's epistle to the Romans he makes a generalization that the Jews had all rejected Christ, even though he knew that a minority had accepted him.[17] Thus the people yet to hear Paul's message are not necessarily lost or powerless to cultivate a disposition by a positive response to the Holy Spirit that could be justified by the substitutionary atonement of Christ. Therefore, this passage in Acts doesn't actually provide a supportive statement for restrictivism.

NOTES to Appendix E

1. Anders T. S. Nygren, *Commentary of Romans*, trans. Carl C. Rasmussen (Philadelphia: Muhlenberg Press, 1949), 119.

2. Charles H. Dodd, *The Epistle of Paul to the Romans* (London: Hodder and Stoughton,

169–172; Anders T. S. Nygren, *Commentary of Romans*, 384–388; Douglas Moo, *The NIV Application Commentary: Romans* (Grand Rapids, MI: Zondervan, 2000), 342–345; *The Seventh-day Adventist Bible Commentary, Vol. 6*, (Hagerstown, MD: Review and Herald Publishing Association, 1956), 599–600.

3. Anders T. S. Nygren, *Commentary of Romans*, 388.

4. Douglas Moo, *The NIV Application Commentary: Romans* (Grand Rapids, MI: Zondervan, 2000), 343.

5. Rom. 2:6–15 asserts that the human response for justification is a disposition and beliefs that produce loving and good conduct compatible with eternal fellowship in direct relationship with God. While Paul does not explicitly state in Rom. 2 that the good works of the redeemed are produced by "belief," "trust," or "faith," this is properly assumed because he specifically stated this in Rom. 1:5 and in other epistles, and the phrasing of the human requirement appears to coincide with what is taught by Jesus and his disciples (Matt. 16:27; 2 Cor. 5:10; Rev. 2:23; 18:6:20:12–13; 22:12). The view of the passage that people uninformed of the old covenant (and by extension the new covenant) may be justified by virtue of the atoning work of Christ if they by faith cultivate a disposition and beliefs compatible with an eternal relationship with God is supported by the following: Martin Luther, *Commentary on Romans*, trans. J. Theodore Mueller (Grand Rapids, MI: Kregel Publications, 1976), 58; *Matthew Henry's Commentary on the Whole Bible* (Peabody, MA: Hendrickson Publishers, 1991), 1757–1758; Charles H. Dodd, *The Epistle of Paul to the Romans*, 33–37, 41; Anders T. S. Nygren, *Commentary of Romans*, 121–125; *The Wycliffe Bible Commentary*, ed. Charles F. Pfeiffer and Everett F. Harrison (Chicago: Moody Press, 1990), 1188–1189; *Zondervan NIV Bible Commentary, Volume 2: New Testament*, consul. eds. Kenneth L. Barker and John R. Kohlenberger III (Grand Rapids, MI: Zondervan Publishing House, 1994), 530–532.

6. Ronald H. Nash, "Restrictivism," in *What About Those Who Have Never Heard?: Three Views on the Destiny of the Unevangelized*, ed. John Sanders (Downers Grove, IL: InterVarsity Press, 1995), 111. See also *The Expositor's Bible Commentary*, gen. ed. Frank E. Gaebelein, consul. eds. James Montgomery Boice and Merrill C. Tenney, Vol. 10 (Grand Rapids, MI: Zondervan Publishing House, 1976), 23; and *Zondervan NIV Bible Commentary, Volume 2: New Testament*, consul. eds. Kenneth L. Barker and John R. Kohlenberger III (Grand Rapids, MI: Zondervan Publishing House, 1994), 527.

7. James D. G. Dunn, *Word Biblical Commentary*, Vol. 38A, Romans 1–8, eds. Ralph P. Martin, David A. Hubbard, and Glenn W. Barker (Dallas: Word Books, Publisher, 1991), 57.

8. *Zondervan NIV Bible Commentary, Volume 2: New Testament*, consul. eds. Kenneth L. Barker and John R. Kohlenberger III (Grand Rapids, MI: Zondervan Publishing House, 1994), 306.

9. Ronald H. Nash, "Restrictivism," in *What About Those Who Have Never Heard?*, 127–128.

10. *Zondervan NIV Bible Commentary, Volume 2: New Testament*, 371; *Matthew*

Discussion of Texts Cited to Support the Long List (Restrictivism)

Henry's Commentary on the Whole Bible, 1642.

11. Acts 16:22–24, 37; 24:27; 26:10, 30; Rom. 16:7; Heb. 11:36.

12. *Matthew Henry's Commentary on the Whole Bible*, 1413.

13. 2 Thess. 2:13; Rom. 5:10; 1 Cor. 1:18; 2 Cor. 2:15.

14. The phrase "the requirements of the law are written on their hearts" is used to identify saved Christians, therefore, Rom. 2:14–15 leaves open the possibility that some Gentiles without gospel knowledge could be saved (without suggesting whether that is likely). See also note 5 above.

15. See also 1 Cor. 11:2; 1 Thess. 5:21; 1 Tim. 6:20–21; 2 Tim. 4:15.

16. Unknown to Paul at that time, though, he was later able to return to Ephesus (2 Tim. 4:9–13).

17. Douglas J. Moo, *The NIV Application Commentary: Romans,* 327. Such generalizations, by the way, do not violate the doctrine of inerrancy, as a generalization is one of the exceptions to the rule [Mark L. Strauss, "The Inspiration of the Bible," in *The Baker Illustrated Bible Handbook,* eds. J. Daniel Hays and J. Scott Duvall (Grand Rapids, MI: BakerBooks, 2011), 1003].

Appendix F
Discussion in Favor of the Short List

As was said in chapter 12.2, in my studies I found there to be two basic views on what metaphysical conceptions a person needs to believe for a transforming and saving relationship with God. One view is what I called the short list. Recall that the short list includes:

1. Belief/trust that a loving and good Divinity exists (Heb. 11:6).
2. Belief/trust that the Divinity hears prayers.
3. Trust of the Divinity's word and guidance, which produces obedience[1] and acceptance of divine blessings (e.g., grace and fellowship).
4. Love of Divinity.

This set of beliefs is derived in part from studies of Bible passages concerning the patriarchs of Genesis who are said to be saved (e.g., Noah and Abraham), but who appear textually to be uninformed of the God-man messiah's role in salvation. The following discusses the Bible passages and the knowledge the patriarchs had for their saving relationships with God.

Abraham's Covenant Knowledge. Abraham comes from a family of Mesopotamian polytheists (Josh. 24:2, 14).[2] Scholars assume he shared their beliefs. He may have worshiped the god of the moon.[3]

God speaks to Abraham on several occasions,[4] sometimes as an angelic representative.[5] Once God appeared to him in a vision (Gen. 15:1), and another time in what appears might be a dream (Gen. 15:12–16).

Regarding the divine realm, God gradually reveals to Abraham a sense that God is the only God he needs, as God is "filling all the roles of deity," thereby making any other deity irrelevant.[6] This revelation about the divine realm would transition Abraham into a practical monotheism, but it would not likely bring about the philosophy that the deities he had worshiped with his father did not actually exist.

We may speculate why God would withhold a clear command against worshipping other deities or direct revelation that there are no other gods. The mindsets of humankind are very lost, and God has a very big picture in view. God adapts his ideal to accommodate flawed attitudes and perceptions by not giving information that would discourage the believer from taking more steps in his direction.[7] God wouldn't impose information that would choke Abraham's progress. God sometimes leads by small steps. Perhaps this was God's method with Abraham. Perhaps a clear command against polytheism or a revelation of philosophical monotheism would have choked Abraham's progress. Whatever God's reasons were, the cultural seed for strict monotheism appears to have been planted in Abraham, but it did not spring up until centuries later in Moses.

Abraham believed God to be the "creator of heaven and earth [the cosmos]" (Gen. 14:19, 22; 24:3, 7). He saw God as "almighty" (Gen. 17:1), all-powerful (Gen. 18:14), and eternal (Gen. 21:33).

With regard to God's character, Abraham saw God as righteous. But Abraham's understanding of righteousness falls considerably short of the righteousness defined in the fuller revelation of the New Testament. Abraham's understanding of righteousness is within the bounds of natural, moral law that had been framed by the expectations of Mesopotamian society.[8] Societal expectations in Abraham's time entailed maintenance of order, security, and justice, and protection of the weak against the powerful. Righteous virtues included respect and care for others, honesty, sexual purity, and self-control. Wickedness included murder, rape, adultery, stealing, and breach of contract.

The gods were thought to generally place value on order, justice, and security in the human realm.[9] Abraham would believe God valued the same. The "wickedness" of the Sodomites was "against the Lord" (Gen. 13:13). Thus, God would be seen as being in favor of societal virtues to maintain order, security, justice, and protection of the weak against the powerful.

To summarize, Abraham would likely have perceived God as honest, faithful,[10] trustworthy, having integrity, being respectful of people of low status, protecting the weak against the powerful, caring for the well-being of humankind, and desiring order and justice. Abraham believed God had compassion and mercy in his heart (Gen. 16:11; 18:23–33; 19:16). He believed that God cared about what was important to Abraham (i.e., fathering a subsequent generation). He believed God cared about all peoples (Gen. 12:3). And Abraham believed that God listened to prayers and that in accord with his wisdom sometimes intervened (Gen. 14:20; 24:12).

Regarding Abraham's view of an afterlife, ancient Mesopotamians unquestionably believed there was eternal life after death, but the afterlife was in the netherworld, a dark and gloomy place located deep beneath the surface of the earth (the subject of the netherworld was briefly discussed in chapter 11.7). It was the destination of all humans, both the righteous and the wicked. The netherworld had a social and political structure much like the urban life of Mesopotamia. Here the deceased continued as they did in their earthly life, although among gloomy surroundings. The quality of life in the netherworld depended on a person's status in the earthly life, as well as on the amount/quality of grave goods provided by the family and how dutiful they were in performing the funerary cult.[11]

The writer of Genesis gives us sufficient indication that Abraham likely held this view of the afterlife. Abraham's grandson, Jacob, expected to join his deceased son at death in the netherworld (*sheol*) (Gen. 37:35). Nowhere in Genesis is the concept of a heavenly afterlife (or an afterlife in hell) introduced. Rather, God's rewards to Abraham are earthly oriented. The blessings promised to Abraham were all temporal, such as help to make a name to be remembered by successive generations or, most importantly, beget the next generation. It would therefore make sense that Abraham believed God was blessing him with high status in his earthly life and with a great number of descendants who could provide grave goods and perform the funerary cult. God did say to Abraham, "I will make you into a great nation and I will bless you; I will make your name great" (Gen. 12:2); and "Look up at the heavens and count the stars—if indeed you can count them.... So shall your offspring be" (Gen. 15:5).

In addition to blessing Abraham with a comparatively better life in the netherworld, perhaps we may speculate that he also thought God would bless him in the afterlife in a way that would involve God's access to the netherworld.[12] Regardless, Genesis provides no indication of Abraham believing that God was saving him from sin and hell so that he could enjoy a holy life with God in heaven.[13]

Some might disagree because of Heb. 11:16, which says Abraham was "longing for a better country—a heavenly one." However, according to Old Testament scholar John H. Walton, "Hebrews 11:16 does not bring in the concept of a heavenly country with regard to eternal destiny as a result of being saved from sin. It is a much more nuanced idea there that needs careful study within the context of Hebrews."[14] The adjective "heavenly" is used to simply connect God with the promised land, and with all it means to belong to God.[15] Other authoritative references also make no mention of God introducing to the patriarchs a concept of a heavenly abode similar to the one taught in the New Testament.

According to Walton, God's covenant to Abraham was not intended to address the sin problem or reconcile humankind's broken relationship with God. It was not an announcement of salvation or of a mechanism of salvation, such as a dying messiah. The first people to hope for a future messiah "developed around the concept of a future king of David's line."[16] There is no such hope in Scripture prior to that time. A few pre-Davidic verses are cited as messianic (e.g., Gen. 49:10; Num. 24:17), but it is apparent that their focus is on the destiny of the tribe of Judah.[17]

Rather than reveal a messiah, God's covenant to Abraham was to reveal a significant aspect of what God is truly like—amid the babble of misconceptions of deity. This was a vital step of many steps toward God's ultimate goal of imparting knowledge generations after Abraham that would be needed to conceptualize a redemptive relationship by way of the messiah.[18]

To summarize, the Bible does not appear to indicate that God informed Abraham of the messianic plan. Abraham was unaware of the future incarnation in a man (Jesus Christ)[19] who would play an indispensable role in the mechanism of Abraham's salvation. Thus, Abraham's covenantal knowledge appears to be more likely consistent with the short list of beliefs that do not include beliefs concerning Christ.

Rebuttal by Advocates of the Long List. Advocates of the long list have difficulty with this for a few reasons. The first reason is the notion that, based on the story of God's command to sacrifice his son Isaac (Gen. 22; Heb. 11:17–19), God revealed the planned ministry of the messiah and the mechanism of his salvation to Abraham. However, there is no indication in the text (or in the rest of the Bible) that Abraham would have understood the command to sacrifice Isaac as "a picture of a father's pain in sacrificing his son, as God eventually did in offering up Jesus."[20] The command to sacrifice Isaac may instruct later generations who've studied the Old Testament or New Testament of the Father-sacrificing-his-Son model. But we lack textual support that *Abraham* had such instruction.

Another reason some advocates of the long list have difficulty accepting that Abraham was ignorant of a future messiah comes from a statement by Jesus in John 8:56. Jesus said, "Your father Abraham rejoiced at the thought of seeing my day; he saw it and was glad." Long listers interpret this to reveal that the whole concept of the God-man messiah, including Jesus' future birth, ministry, substitutionary atonement, and crucifixion, was revealed to Abraham.

However, the context of the passage is of the Jews' stubborn opposition to Jesus' claims about himself and consequently the divine blessing received by those who would listen to him. To paraphrase, Jesus essentially says, "You who oppose me call yourselves children/followers of Abraham. However, God promised Abraham that his descendants would become the channel of divine blessing to all peoples (Gen. 12:3). Abraham was full of joy while imagining his many descendants filled with divine blessing. I am the embodiment of that blessing, and yet you reject me and you refuse to listen to my word."[21] While Abraham knew his nation of descendants would receive divine blessing, it is conjecture[22] to read John 8:56 as saying Abraham had received a vision of the distant future birth, ministry, travels, crucifixion, death, and resurrection-translation of Jesus.

Even if Abraham had been miraculously shown a pictorial of Jesus in ministerial action, would he have perceived the mechanism of his salvation? Prophets were shown many pictorials, some of which they did not understand. Daniel, for example, generally had considerable difficulty understanding things he saw in vision (Dan. 8:15–17). He prayed for understanding concerning one of his visions, but was told he would live out the rest of his life without understanding the vision (Dan. 12:8–9, 13). Thus, even if Abraham had seen Jesus in a vision, it is plausible that Abraham would've been unaware of the mechanism of atonement in Christ. Abraham imagined a blessed people. But there is no textual indication of God imparting to Abraham knowledge of a dying messiah as the mechanism of his salvation.

Advocates of the long list also reference Gal. 3:6–8 to support the assertion that the messianic gospel had been preached to Abraham. The text reads: "Consider Abraham: 'He believed God, and it was credited to him as righteousness.' Understand, then, that those who believe are children of Abraham. The Scripture foresaw that God would justify the Gentiles by faith, and announced the gospel in advance to Abraham: 'All nations will be blessed through you.'" The phrase "announced the gospel in advance to Abraham," it is argued, affirms that the messianic gospel had been revealed to Abraham.

However, many read this passage assuming that the "gospel" announced to Abraham is the same gospel of Christ that Paul was preaching to the Galatians, which is mistaken. The Greek term translated "announced the gospel in advance" (*proeuaggelizomai*) means to announce or promise beforehand news that causes happiness.[23] God proclaimed news that causes happiness ("gospel") to many people in the Bible about things having nothing to do with a promise of a messiah (e.g., 2 Sam. 18:31; Isa. 52:7; Nah. 1:15). Consequently, there are many "gospels" in the Bible related to one kind of "salvation" or another that have nothing to do with salvation through Christ. The way to determine which gospel is being discussed is to look at the context of the passage. Noah's "gospel" was God's word to him to save him and his family from the coming flood. There is no textual evidence that Noah knew he needed to be saved from sin, or that he knew of the atoning mechanism of salvation by way of a future dying messiah. Just because Christians since the first century have perceived Noah's animal sacrifices as foreshadowing Christ's crucifixion doesn't mean that this was apparent to Noah.

Abraham's "gospel" was God's word or promise that many peoples would be blessed through him and his descendants (Gen. 12:3). This is exactly what Paul tells us in Gal. 3:8: "God . . . announced the gospel in advance to Abraham: 'All nations will be blessed through you'" (Paul is quoting Gen. 12:3). Paul leaves *no room for ambiguity*. The gospel proclaimed to Abraham is God's promise that a multitude in the world would be blessed by way of Abraham's descendants. From Abraham's son Isaac, to David, to Jesus, the promise was fulfilled. But there is no suggestion that *Abraham* knew that the blessing involved a mechanism of a future atoning sacrifice of the messiah so that humankind could be saved for heaven.[24] Again, just because Christians since the first century have perceived Abraham's sacrifice of Isaac as foreshadowing Christ's crucifixion doesn't mean that this was apparent to Abraham. And such a notion does not appear to be the thrust of Paul's point in Gal. 3:6–8. Rather, what Paul is doing by referring to Abraham and quoting Gen. 12:3 is breaking down the barriers between Jews and Gentiles by pointing out that Gentiles, who do not have the law of Moses but trust God, as Abraham did, are "children of God." As Paul says, "Those who have faith are blessed along with Abraham, the man of faith" (Gal. 3:9; see also v. 17).

Still, advocates of the long list argue that Gal. 3:6 reveals that Abraham understood the messianic mechanism of his salvation, because the verse says, "Consider Abraham: He believed God, and it was credited to him as righteousness." Paul here references Gen. 15:6, which indicates Abraham was justified by his faith, and, long-listers argue, justification implies an understanding of a substitutionary sacrifice by a messiah.

But actually, while Gal. 3:6 affirms the fact that Abraham was justified, there is no indication from Paul concerning Abraham's beliefs or whether Abraham had understood the mechanism of substitution by a messiah for his justification. He knew God had declared him righteous, but nowhere does the Bible tell us that Abraham understood that his justification was by virtue of the divine promise of a future dying messiah.

In sum, in Gal. 3:6–8 Paul refers to Abraham's experience to help him make his point to the Galatians that people are saved (declared righteous) by trusting in God's promise to bless, and not by having the Mosaic law. Paul is not indicating that Abraham understood justification by faith in the blood of the messiah. Abraham was declared righteous by faith in God, and God's promise to bless him and all peoples through him. There's no textual evidence that Abraham understood the mechanism of his justification. The "gospel" preached to him was simply God's promise to bless in return for Abraham's trust.

Even so, long-listers further argue that there is evidence in Jewish tradition that Abraham understood the Christocentric mechanism of salvation, as it emphasized that he had been shown the messianic era.[25] In response, first of all, being shown "the messianic era" does not necessarily mean being shown the person of Jesus performing miracles, affirming his messiahship to his followers, being crucified, and being resurrected-translated. Even if "messianic era" implies this, we can only speculate whether Abraham would have understood how he was justified because of the substitutionary death of Christ.

Second, the Christian does not recognize Jewish tradition as being authoritative. Jewish tradition is one of the tools in the Bible student's arsenal, but it can lead astray. Teachings in Jewish tradition sometimes contradict each other, and the Bible. The Bible is the authority for Christian doctrine. It does not explicitly tell us that Abraham knew of Christ's ministry, or that he had placed his faith in the messiah for his salvation for heaven.

To summarize, the Bible doesn't appear to provide us with textual support that Abraham knew of a judgment to hell for unrepentant sinners, or of a salvation from hell for repentant sinners. Abraham had not been introduced to the messianic gospel, and the Abrahamic covenant, per se, was not a *messianic* gospel covenant (although it served a vital role in connecting the Davidic-messianic covenant to the New Testament messianic covenant). But, despite Abraham's ignorance (and according to the Bible), Abraham was saved for heaven.[26] Apparently the comparatively little knowledge (short list) that Abraham had was sufficient[27] for a faith that would demonstrate his compatibility with an eternal relationship with God and God's acceptance of him for heaven.[28]

If Abraham's ignorance of the messianic gospel did not prevent him from a saving discipleship, then it would appear that people who never hear the gospel, but have faith and knowledge of the Divine, like Abraham, are accepted by God and justified by virtue of the person and work of Christ (and the person and work of the Holy Spirit). If so, then knowledge of Christ is not necessary in order to be saved. Noah is another example of a patriarch in a saving relationship with God, but without knowledge of a future messiah to save him from sin and for heaven. There is no Bible verse intimating that Noah knew of a promised dying messiah for his salvation.

Advocates of the long list disagree, however, claiming that Noah received a story of a messianic gospel by oral tradition from his ancestors that can be traced back to Adam and the first messianic prophecy in Gen. 3:15. God declares to the serpent: "I will put enmity between you and the woman, and between your offspring and hers; he will crush your head, and you will strike his heel." The verse is interpreted by long-listers as revealing a promise of Christ's defeat of Satan by "crushing his head."

While many Christians believe this is the first messianic prophecy in Scripture, in-depth verbal analysis by exegetes of the past few decades, such as Gordon J. Wenham and John H. Walton, shows a different meaning.[29] It has been thought that the "he" who crushes the serpent's head is Christ and that the "you" who strikes his heel is Satan. But in Genesis, singular pronouns are typically used for collective nouns (see Gen. 28:14). Thus we should not think the pronoun "he" in "he will crush your head" is necessarily referring to one representative from among the woman's descendants (i.e., Jesus Christ). The consensus is that it most likely refers to humankind (the woman's offspring). Moreover, for the same grammatical reason, the "you" in "you will strike his heel" does not refer to the serpent (or Satan), but rather to the powers of evil. If it were referring to Satan, why mention the serpent's offspring? So the players in the verse are actually most likely humankind and the powers of evil, thus there isn't clear indication of it being messianic.

Further textual evidence against it being messianic comes from analysis of the strikes between humankind and the powers of evil. The verbs for "strike" and "crush" "are now properly identified as belonging to the same root, šwp. We must therefore conclude that the actions performed are "comparable" and "fairly generic" and thus a "crush" blow is not necessarily more damaging than a "strike" blow. Therefore, the phrase "he will crush your head, and you will strike his heel" could be translated: "he will strike a blow to your head, and you will strike a blow to his heel."[30] While we would normally think of a "head" strike as more damaging than a "heel" strike, the writer most likely intended that they be equally damaging, because a poisonous bite to a human foot by a viper (the most likely type of snake in view here) is deadly. Thus, the verse portrays potentially mortal blows being exchanged between the powers of evil and humankind. Given the exchange of potentially mortal blows and the repetition of the verb (for "crush" and "strike"), Walton suggests that the verse probably depicts an unending struggle from generation to generation without allusion to any eventual outcome.[31] Although, according to Wenham, it could be that the writer intended to offer the hope that humankind would eventually defeat the powers of evil.[32]

In rebuttal, however, long-listers point out that Gen. 3:15 should be interpreted as a messianic prophecy because the New Testament seems to understand it in a messianic sense, as in Rom. 16:20 and Gal. 3:16. Rom. 16:20 says, "The God of peace will soon crush Satan under your feet." Long listers say this is an interpretation of Gen. 3:15 under the inspiration of the Holy Spirit, which proves that Gen. 3:15 is the first messianic prophecy of Christ crushing Satan. But notice that while Rom. 16:20 does allude to Gen. 3:15, Paul is telling us that the ones crushing Satan are Eve's offspring, the church at Rome. The church's feet are crushing Satan, not Christ's. Therefore, Rom. 16:20 does not affirm that Gen. 3:15 is the first messianic prophecy.

Gal. 3:16 also does not affirm that Gen. 3:15 is messianic. Gal. 3:16 reads,

"The promises were spoken to Abraham and to his seed. The Scripture does not say 'and to seeds,' meaning many people, but 'and to your seed,' meaning one person, who is Christ." This verse doesn't refer to Gen. 3:15 and it doesn't refer to Eve's offspring. Paul is talking about Abraham's seed (Gen. 12 and 17), so there is no authority in Gal. 3:16 for interpreting Gen. 3:15. What Paul was likely doing, as Walton points out, was using a lesson in Hebrew grammar to teach of Christ's representation concerning Israel. "Just as the grammatical collective represents one standing for many, so Christ is one who represents the many. But in this passage Christ's representation of the many concerns Israel, not all humankind, so it tells us nothing about Genesis 3:15."[33]

Since it appears that Gen. 3:15 does not contain a promise of a messiah, we have no textual support for a messianic promise proclaimed to Adam that could have been passed on to any of the patriarchs. The conclusion, then, is that God's covenants with the patriarchs did not include an explicit element of a promised God-man messiah. From Adam to Abraham, there is no textual evidence that any of the patriarchs knew of the gospel of Christ.

NOTES for Appendix F

1. Rom. 1:5; 1 Thess. 1:3; 2 Thess. 1:11.

2. John H. Walton, *The NIV Application Commentary: Genesis* (Grand Rapids, MI: Zondervan, 2001), 428; *The Expositor's Bible Commentary*, gen. ed. Frank E. Gaebelein, consul. eds. James Montgomery Boice and Merrill C. Tenney, Vol. 10 (Grand Rapids, MI: Zondervan Publishing House, 1976), 456; *Zondervan NIV Bible Commentary, Volume 2: New Testament*, consul. eds. Kenneth L. Barker and John R. Kohlenberger III (Grand Rapids, MI: Zondervan Publishing House, 1994), 721.

3. Nahum M. Sarna, *Understanding Genesis: The World of the Bible in the Light of History* (New York: Randon House, Inc., paperback ed., 1995), 98.

4. Gen. 12:1–3, 7; 13:14–17; 15:1–21; 17:1–22; 18:1–33; 22:1–2, 11–12, 15–18.

5. Gen. 18:1–33; 22:11–12, 15–18. In these texts the first person language of the angel is appropriate because such messengers of God were endowed by God with authority to speak for God and not for themselves (John H. Walton, *The NIV Application Commentary: Genesis*, 465).

6. John H. Walton, *The NIV Application Commentary: Genesis*, 428, 429, 516.

7. Paul Copan, *Is God a Moral Monster?: Making Sense of the Old Testament God* (Grand Rapids, MI: Baker Books, 2011), 57–69.

8. John H. Walton, *The NIV Application Commentary: Genesis*, 422; *Ancient Near*

Eastern Thought and the Old Testament, 287–311. The principles of natural, moral law can be found in the ancient Mesopotamian laws of King Ur-Nammu (2112–2095 BC), King Lipit-Ishtar (about 1930 BC), the city-state of Eshnunna (about 1700 BC) and King Hammurabi (192–1750 BC), as well as commandments 5–10 of the Ten Commandments (Exodus 20:12–17; Deut. 5:16–21). According to lexical studies of D. Reimer and John Walton, the righteousness (*tsĕdaqah*) that God accredited to Abraham in Gen. 15:6 is similar in character to natural, moral law.

9. John H. Walton, *Ancient Near Eastern Thought and the Old Testament*, 306.

10. Heb. 11:11.

11. J. Edward Wright, *The Early History of Heaven* (New York: Oxford University Press, 2000), 31, 41, 46–47, 49, 50–51; John H. Walton, *Ancient Near Eastern Thought and the Old Testament*, 313–329.

12. Regarding God's access to the netherworld, see Ps. 139:8; Amos 9:2; Prov. 15:11.

13. John H. Walton, *The NIV Application Commentary: Genesis*, 430 (see also page 429).

14. Ibid.

15. *The Expositor's Bible Commentary*, gen. ed. Frank E. Gaebelein, consul. eds. James Montgomery Boice and Merrill C. Tenney, Vol. 10 (Grand Rapids, MI: Zondervan Publishing House, 1976), 121; *Zondervan NIV Bible Commentary, Volume 2: New Testament*, 997.

16. John H. Walton, *The NIV Application Commentary: Genesis*, 234.

17. Ibid.

18. Ibid., 401.

19. Ibid., 429, 431.

20. Ibid., 514. Paul admonishes us to not go beyond what is written (1 Cor. 4:6).

21. The reference for the point that Jesus was referring to God's promise to Abraham in Gen. 12:3 is: *Zondervan NIV Bible Commentary, Volume 2: New Testament*, 327.

22. *Matthew Henry's Commentary on the Whole Bible* (Peabody, MA: Hendrickson Publishers, 1991), 1576.

23. James Strong, "A Concise Dictionary of the Words in the Greek Testament," p. 60, in *The New Strong's Exhaustive Concordance of the Bible* (Nashville, TN: Thomas Nelson Publishers, 1990).

24. John H. Walton, *The NIV Application Commentary: Genesis*, 428–432. The following sources on Gal. 3:6–8 say nothing about Abraham knowing about the messianic gospel: Matthew Henry (1662–1714), *Matthew Henry's Commentary on the Whole Bible* (Peabody, MA: Hendrickson Publishers, 1991), 1839; Craig S. Keener, *The IVP Bible Background Commentary: New Testament* (Downers Grove, IL: InterVarsity Press, 1993), 525; *The Wycliffe Bible Commentary* (Chicago: Moody Press, 1962), 1290; *The Expositor's Bible Commentary*, gen. ed. Frank E. Gaebelein, consul. eds. James Montgomery Boice and Merrill C. Tenney, Vol. 10 (Grand Rapids, MI: Zondervan Publishing House, 1976), 456; *The Zondervan NIV Bible*

Commentary, Volume 2: New Testament, consulting eds. Kenneth L. Barker and John R. Kohlenberger III (Grand Rapids, MI: Zondervan Publishing House, 1994), 997.

25. Craig S. Keener, *The IVP Bible Background Commentary: New Testament* (Downers Grove, IL: InterVarsity Press, 1993), 287.

26. Isaiah 29:22; Matt. 8:11; 22:32; Luke 13:28; 16:23–30; 19:9). We know from the New Testament that no human is saved without benefiting from the atoning sacrifice of Christ. Thus, Abraham was justified by the Father who had the "green light" to justify Abraham by virtue of the promise of Christ yet to be fulfilled. He was saved in Christ even though he was not aware of Christ's existence or ministry. For a discussion of the gospel mechanisms of salvation, see appendix D.

27. It is possible that knowledge requisite for salvation is less than that of Abraham, although such a possibility appears to lack biblical support. I think Christians should keep an open mind to the possibility that less knowledge is sufficient, tempered by Paul's admonition that we not go beyond what is written by God's penmen (1 Cor. 4:6).

28. Salvation occurs when there is a human response to God's ministry that entails a dispositional transformation to become the kind of person that is compatible with an eternal relationship with God in heaven (2 Cor. 6:14; 1 John 1:3, 5–7).

29. Gordon J. Wenham, *Word Biblical Commentary: Genesis 1–15*, Vol. 1, gen. eds. David A. Hubbard and Glenn W. Barker, OT ed. John D. W. Watts (Grand Rapids, MI: Zondervan, 1987), 80–81; John H. Walton, *The NIV Application Commentary: Genesis*, 225–226, 233–236.

30. John H. Walton, *The NIV Application Commentary: Genesis*, 226.

31. Ibid., 225–226, 233–236.

32. Gordon J. Wenham, *Word Biblical Commentary: Genesis 1–15*, Vol. 1, 81.

33. John H. Walton, *The NIV Application Commentary: Genesis*, 235.

INDEX

Subjects

afterlife
　human, 2, 8, 19n1, 22n18, 58, 61, 64, 80n37, 100, 101, 104, 105-106, 109n13, 111n37, 124, 163, 181, 200, 224n38, 240, 247, 250n30, 252, 257, 260, 264, 265, 266, 272, 273, 274, 279n19, 304n11, 332, 355
　animal, 65, 205-213, 216, 225n51
Earth, scientific age of, 6, 8, 15, 20n8, n10, 195, 199, 203, 222n17
agent, 110n22, 160, 174, 316
animals
　anthropomorphizing the suffering of, 214-215, 226n64
　exaggerating the suffering of, 213-216
　extrasensory perception in, 65, 81n39, 212
　ghostly apparitions of, 81n39, 209-210, 225n51
　immortality for, 35, 65, 191, 202, 205-213, 216, 220, 225n44, 225n51, 236
　suffering, 16, 30, 34, 35, 36, 37, 38, 39, 40, 41, 42, 45, 52, 146, 149, 150, 158, 160, 162, 165, 166, 167, 168, 169, 173, 175, 176, 184, 187, 189, 191-220, 221n10, 224n38, 226n59, 226n61, 233
　suffering before the fall of man, 6, 15, 30, 35-37, 45, 192, 194, 196, 199, 200, 202-205, 215, 219, 221n10, 224n38
annihilationism, 242, 251, 253, 269-278
Arminianism, 225n44, 289, 304n10
atheism, 8-12, 14, 23n23, n26, 113, 296, 297
beatific vision, 59, 63, 64, 65, 72, 74, 98-101, 103-107, 120, 139, 163, 186, 190n16, 241, 254, 256, 270, 332
big bang, 24n31, 201, 292
Buddhism, 7, 261
Calvinism, 225n44, 289, 304n8, n9, n10
challenges to the credibility of Christianity, 5-7, 12, 14-17
chaos theory, 156
clairvoyance, 63, 64, 73, 79n36, 190n16, 296
common grace, 290, 293, 300, 303. *See also* prevenient grace
community, God's eternal, 19n1, 42, 51, 59, 63, 65, 87, 89, 97-99, 101-102, 105, 106-107, 109n15, 118, 143, 149, 161-166, 169, 173-174, 178, 180, 183, 185-188, 190n22, 191-192, 194, 196-197, 199, 201-203, 205, 218-219, 236, 243, 246-247, 253-256, 259, 269-270, 276, 278, 288-290, 297, 301-302, 304, 314, 329

compatibility determination, 42, 59, 87-104, 107, 109*n10*, 122, 139, 157, 165, 167, 183, 186, 188, 190*n22*, 195, 203, 222*n26*, 293, 304*n9*, 309, 313, 316, 360

conscience, 261, 293, 300, 315, 333

consummate relationship with God, 42, 51, 53-59, 62-63, 65, 74, 87, 91, 92, 95, 98-99, 103, 105, 107, 109*n15*, 149, 161-163, 165-166, 168-169, 173-174, 178, 186, 188, 192, 195-197, 199-200, 203, 216, 218-219, 224*n38*, 255, 258, 260, 263, 266, 269, 288, 314

creationism,
   old earth, 35, 38, 46*n17*, 194, 202, 221*n11*, 300, 306*n41*
   young earth, 20*n6*, 38, 194, 195-202, 220*n6*

Darwinian problem of evil, 192, 220

day-age view of Genesis 1, 195

deism, 8, 17, 310

design
   God's, 35, 59-60, 62, 91, 103, 136, 141, 164, 192, 194, 201, 203
   intelligent, 24, 196, 292

devil, 6, 232, 253, 277. *See also* Satan and Lucifer

divine
   hiddenness, 23*n26*, 32, 42, 51-53, 59, 74, 75*n4*, 87, 92- 95, 98, 100-108, 109*n15*, 113-114, 122, 124, 127-128, 139, 142, 150, 152-153, 157-158, 164, 166-169, 170*n9*, 174, 178, 180-185, 187-188, 192, 195-200, 203, 216, 218-219, 223*n26*, 224*n38*, 230, 237, 259, 262, 265, 274, 293, 309-314
   image, 65, 94, 134, 135, 139, 141, 208, 270
   intervention, 5, 22*n14*, 30, 37, 40, 116-118, 121-124, 136, 138, 141-142, 150-153, 157, 160, 167-169, 170*n9*, 174, 177-181, 187-188, 189*n1*, 193, 216-219, 221*n9*, 223*n26*, 288, 322-324, 326, 329, 334, 355
   light, 52, 89, 103, 106-107, 108*n8*, 241, 255, 257, 261-262, 281*n49*, 290-301, 303, 305*n15*, 315, 316, 323, 333, 342-343
   purpose, 4, 30, 36, 63, 72, 88, 114, 115, 117, 122, 128, 160, 160, 177, 184, 189, 197, 219, 252, 264, 265, 268, 274, 281*n53*, 288, 296, 315-316, 329, 333, 345

epistemic distance, 40, 92-93, 97, 104, 110*n23*, 152, 180, 196, 198

eternal life, 58, 61, 89, 97, 118, 120, 164, 200, 220, 254, 268, 277, 301, 344, 347, 355

evidence
   for common descent, 6, 21*n11*
   of an afterlife, 18, 68-72, 76*n18*, 78*n22*, 80*n37*, 80*n38*, 111*n37*
   of the supernatural, 65-72, 76*n18*, 79*n36*, 80*n37*, 81*n39*, 100, 111*n37*, 124-128, 129*n17*, 130*n19*
   of God's existence, 17-18, 80*n37*
   of answered prayer, 18, 124-128, 130*n17*, *n19*, 292, 295

evidentiary argument, 31, 42, 146, 175, 186-187, 189

evil
   amount of, 23*n26*, 27, 37, 40, 107, 143, 145, 146, 149-150, 158, 159, 162, 168, 173, 188, 216
   angels, 22*n18*, 38, 73, 83*n52*, 86*n67*, *n74*, 100, 104, 261, 296
   definition of, 31
   evidentiary problem of, 31, 42, 146, 149-172, 173-190, 191-226. *See also* probabilistic problem of evil
   intense, horrific, 5, 27-28, 30, 36, 41, 42, 83*n52*, 137, 149-150, 158-159, 161, 162, 165, 166, 167, 168-169, 173-189, 229, 255-257, 262-263

logical problem of, 31, 42, 53, 133-148
moral, 28, 31-32, 34, 36-39, 106-107, 109*n15*,135, 139, 149-150, 157-158, 160, 168, 173
probabilistic problem of, 31, 32, 42, 146, 149-172, 173-190, 191-226, 187, 189. *See also* evidentiary problem of evil
soteriological problem of, 16, 33, 42, 287, 289, 303
spirits, 71, 73
evolution
biological, 13, 21*n11*, 199, 214, 224*n38*
divinely-guided, 38, 65, 194-197, 199, 204, 218-219, 220*n7*, 224*n38*
theory of, 6, 18, 20*n11*
exegesis, 13, 16, 19, 23*n25*, 35, 46*n17*, 202, 221*n10*, *n11*, 223*n32*, 233, 247, 249*n18*, 270, 298
exegete, 233-234, 306*n30*, 360
extrasensory perception, 18, 22, 63-64, 65, 67, 68, 79*n32*, 83, 86*n69*, *n74*, 295. *See also* supernatural powers of the soul
in animals, 65, 81*n39*, 212
fall of man, the, 6, 34, 35, 36, 38, 41, 52, 60, 202, 331
fine-tuning argument, 24*n31*, 154-156, 292
foreknowledge, 63, 64, 160, 201. *See also* precognition
forgiveness, 36, 96, 124, 301, 330, 331, 346, 349
fossil record, 6, 13, 20*n10*, 21*n11*, 196, 199, 221*n8*
framework view of Genesis 1, 195, 221*n13*
freewill
compatibility-determining, 88-89, 92, 95, 104,108*n6*, 122, 127-128, 134-136, 139, 143, 150, 152, 157, 166, 168-169, 173-174, 177-178, 180, 186, 188, 196-198, 203, 216, 218-219, 223*n26*, 259, 262, 264-266, 268, 288, 290, 309-314, 326
libertarian, 88, 104, 108*n6*, 150, 157
moral, 39-40, 59, 88, 92, 104, 107, 110*n17*, 135,149-151, 155-160, 167-169, 173, 188, 310, 320
theodicy, 37-39, 41, 159
ghostly apparitions,
of animals, 81*n39*, 209-210, 225*n51*
of humans, 18, 71, 85*n64*, *n67*, 210, 296
God
all-knowing, 32, 52, 75*n2*, 80*n37*, 111*n37*, 134,137, 139, 178, 185, 192, 256, 287
all-loving and good, 52, 80*n37*, 111*n37*, 134, 139-140, 256, 287
all-powerful, 32, 52, 75*n2*, 80*n37*, 111*n37*, 134, 178, 192, 256, 287
Christian, 12, 128, 317
Father, the, 32, 53, 97, 114, 118, 123, 161, 286, 290, 298, 301, 329-330, 331, 332, 333, 335*n12*, 341, 345, 357, 364
Holy Spirit, the, 46*n18*, 72, 73, 86*n67*, 89-90, 97, 109*n10*, 123, 164, 206, 252, 261-263, 265, 267, 274-275, 281*n49*, 287, 290-291, 294, 296-301, 304*n11*, 333-334, 335*n12*, 341, 342-343, 348-349
personal, 94, 262
Son, the, 111*n32*, 114, 117, 329, 331, 335*n12*, 343-344
God's image, 65, 94, 134, 135, 139, 141, 208, 270
gratuitous evil, 160, 166, 176, 288. *See also* pointless evil
heaven, 32, 37, 42, 57, 61-63, 73-74, 75-76*n9*, 77*n19*, 88-91, 94, 96-98, 103-104, 109*n13*, *n15*, 111*n40*, 118, 143, 205-206, 211-212, 230, 235-236, 238, 240-241, 245, 247, 254, 256-258, 265, 267-268, 276,

281n46, 286-288, 290, 296, 298, 301-302, 304n11, 318, 333, 337, 348, 364n28
hell, 16, 33, 42, 44, 77n19, 78n20, 86n67, 90, 105, 108n5, 112n43, 200, 223n26, 229-247, 251-278, 279n20, 285, 286-287, 289-290, 302-303, 304n11, 337, 347, 355, 360
hellfire, 233, 235, 239, 241-242, 245, 247, 251, 271, 276
hermeneutics, 19
hiddenness, divine, 23n26, 32, 42, 51-53, 59, 74, 75n4, 87, 92, 93, 94, 95, 98, 100, 101, 102, 103, 104, 105, 106, 107, 108, 109n15, 113, 114, 122, 124, 127, 128, 139, 142, 150, 152, 153, 157, 158, 164, 166, 167, 168, 169, 170n9, 174, 178, 180-185, 187, 188, 192, 195-200, 203, 216, 218-219, 223n26, 224n38, 230, 237, 259, 262, 265, 274, 293, 309-314
Hinduism, 7, 297
Holocaust, 311
immortality
  animal, 5, 65, 191, 202, 205-213, 216, 220, 224n44, 225n51, 236
  conditional, 269-277
  human, 9-11, 13, 76n18, 272, 273, 275
inerrancy of Scripture, 19, 35, 46n17, n18, 273-274, 280n43, 281n53, 351n17
infinite punishment, 252, 253
inspiration of Scripture, 8, 19, 25n35, 35, 46n17, n18, 273-274, 281n49, n51, n53
  plenary-verbal view of, 46n18, 281n49
intermediate state, 60, 77n20
interpretation methodology, 16, 19, 233-235, 272
Islam, 7, 261
Jesus
  resurrection of, 7, 15-16, 18, 22n14, 339, 357
  return of, 2, 76n9, 122, 142, 147n6, 223n26, 240, 243, 267, 268
judgment
  God's, 37, 44, 55, 80n37, 86n67, 98-100, 105, 111, 118, 142, 143, 147n6, 200, 224n38, 231, 238-241, 243, 244, 247, 253, 256-257, 258-259, 272, 287-289, 290, 302, 304n9, 337, 360
  human, 109n11, 143, 298
justice of God, 7, 33, 55, 58, 75n3, 76n15, 80n37, 98, 99, 101, 111n37, 251, 255-256, 257, 264, 278, 279n13, 287, 290, 302, 330-331, 332, 337, 341
Kalam cosmological argument, 18
Lucifer, 34, 42, 103, 104, 112n42. *See also* Satan
metaphysical naturalism, 17, 23n29, 65, 81n42, 296, 305, 306n27
Molinism, 289, 304n9
Muslim, 262, 294
mystery religions, 5, 14
natural,
  disasters, 5, 28, 31, 35-38, 45n2, 52, 153-154, 158, 160, 166, 169, 179, 191, 196
  evil, 30, 34-36, 38-40, 106, 107, 149-150, 153, 158, 168, 173, 187
  selection, 8, 42, 194, 197
naturalism, metaphysical, 17, 23n29, 65, 81n42, 296, 305n27
naturalistic,
  evolution, 18, 196, 293. *See also* evolution, atheistic/unguided
  explanation, 23n29, 71-72, 82n42, 305, 306n27
  theory, 180
near-death experience, 18, 65, 72, 76, 77n18, 80, 81n38, n39, 84n54, n55, n59, n60, n61, n62, 86n72, 100, 111n35, n36, 210, 257, 279n18, 296
  veridical, 18, 68-72, 80n37, 111n37

netherworld, 273, 275-276, 281*n47*, 354, 355, 363*n12*. *See also* sheol
nirvana, 9, 23*n19*
Noah, 263, 300, 301, 319, 331, 353, 358, 360
Noahic flood, 7, 15, 223*n33*, 300, 358
nomic regularity, 39, 40, 41, 42, 150, 151, 152, 153, 154, 157, 158, 166, 167, 168, 169, 174, 178, 180, 181, 187, 188, 192, 195, 203, 216, 218, 219
nonbelief, 33, 298, 311-312, 314*n6*
nonbeliever, 6, 41, 44, 187, 294, 311, 333
nontheist, 11, 23*n22*, 32
Omphalos hypothesis, 199
origin of Satan, 103-105
out-of-body experience, 65, 68-73, 80*n38*, 83*n48*, 84*n54*, *n61*, *n62*, 85*n63*, 86*n69*, 210, 276, 296
  veridical, 68-72
Pelagianism, 90, 108*n10*, 109
pluralism, 41, 289
pointless evil, 5, 30, 36-37, 42, 134, 146, 149-150, 158-160, 168-169, 173, 176-177, 180-181, 188-189, 191, 193, 216-218, 229-230, 251-253, 264-265, 269, 277, 288, 320. *See also* gratuitous evil
postcognition, 22, 64
prayer
  evidence of answered, 18, 124-128, 292, 295
  unanswered, 5, 30, 42, 52, 113-130, 311, 312
precognition, 63, 64, 73, 79*n36*, 190*n16*. *See also* foreknowledge
predestination, 289
preponderance of the evidence, 14, 23*n26*
presentiment, 67-68
prevenient grace, 90, 293. *See also* common grace
progressive creation, 194, 195, 221*n9*
propitiation, 331, 335*n12*
protohistorical view of Genesis 1-2, 195
psychic healing, 64, 79*n36*
psychokinesis, 64, 73, 79*n36*, 85*n64*
psychospiritual condition, 54-57, 74, 96-98, 101-102, 161, 169, 180, 185, 191, 196, 199-200, 203, 237, 247, 254, 312
Quran, 7, 22*n15*
redemption, 260, 273, 274, 317. *See also* salvation
reincarnation, 8, 9, 22-23*n18*, 41
responsibility, 28, 39, 55, 89, 94, 100, 107, 110*n22*, 144, 151, 224*n38*, 262, 286
restrictivism, 286, 337-351
resurrection,
  of Jesus, 7, 15-16, 18, 22*n14*, 339, 357
  of humankind, 8, 60-62, 77*n20*, 247, 268, 273
revelation
  general, 261, 342
  natural modes of, 261, 291-293, 297, 300, 333-334
  progressive, 46*n18*, 272-275, 280*n43*, 281*n49*, n52
  special, 261, 291, 294, 342
  supernatural modes of, 261, 291, 293-297, 300-301, 333-334, 343
Rowe's Noseeum Inference, 182
salvation, 259-260, 261, 264, 265, 285-307, 329-335, 337-351. *See also* redemption
Satan, 34, 38, 79*n32*, 99, 104-105, 116, 120, 147*n17*, 241, 242, 268, 274, 296, 298, 331, 349, 360, 361. *See also* Lucifer
  the origin of, 103-105
scientism, 17, 23*n29*, 65, 81*n42*, 296, 305*n27*
self-determination, 87, 108*n1*, 223*n26*
sentient beings, 31, 207, 215, 226*n59*
sheol, 273, 275, 281*n47*, 282*n57*, 355. *See also* netherworld
soteriology, 45*n9*, 303*n2*

soul making, 41, 53, 87, 108*n1*
spatial dimensions, 60, 62, 76*n9*, 79*n25*, 104, 151, 211, 216
suffering
  animals, 16, 30, 34, 35, 36, 37, 38, 39, 40, 41, 42, 45, 52, 146, 149, 150, 158, 160, 162, 165, 166, 167, 168, 169, 173, 175, 176, 184, 187, 189, 191-226, 233
  children, 5, 7, 15, 27-28, 30, 34, 36, 41, 45*n2*, 134, 137, 138, 146, 149-150, 160, 165-166, 168, 169, 173, 174, 175, 179, 187, 189*n1*, *n2*, 260-261, 263, 321-322
  pre-fall animal, 6, 30, 35-37, 45, 192, 194, 196, 199, 200, 202-203, 205, 215, 219, 221*n10*
supernatural
  body, 6, 18, 22*n14*, 61-62, 77*n20*, 206, 245, 247, 255
  modes of revelation, 261, 291, 293-297, 300-301, 333-334, 343
  powers of the soul, 63-74, 79*n32*, *n36*, 80*n37*, 81*n39*, 82*n43*, *n49*, 83*n50*, *n52*, 86*n67*, *n69*, *n74*, 96, 98, 100, 101, 103, 104, 107, 111*n37*, 181, 183, 187, 212, 255, 256, 259, 295-296. *See also* extrasensory perception
telepathy, 63, 64, 65, 73, 79*n36*, 190*n16*, 212
theistic evolution, 194, 195, 220*n7*
theodicy
  Augustinian, 20*n7*, 33, 34
  counter-part, 33, 35-36
  freewill, 37-39, 41, 159
  Hick's Irenaean, 37, 40-41, 92-93
  higher-order goods, 33, 35-36
  natural consequences, 36-37, 38
  natural law/nomic regularity, 37, 39-40, 41, 42, 150-158, 166, 168, 169, 174, 180, 181, 187, 192, 195, 203, 216, 218, 219
  punishment, 33-34
two-phase life, 42, 59-63, 74, 95, 98, 103, 105, 150, 167, 173, 211
universalism/universalists, 41, 251, 252-253, 260, 265-269, 278, 289, 304*n11*
Wicca, 7, 73, 79, 86*n73*
worlds, best of all possible, 153, 156, 157, 169, 170*n12*, 177-178, 189*n8*
Zoroastrianism, 7

Authors

Adams, Marilyn McCord, 214, 226, 253
Alighieri, Dante, 231, 248
Archer, Gleason, 194
Athanasius of Alexandria, 208
Atwater, P. M. H., 72, 77, 81, 84, 86, 111, 279
Bagans, Zak, 81, 85
Baumgardner, John, 194
Beecher, Henry W., 201, 223
Bietenhard, Hans, 249
Blocher, Henri, 46, 111
Blomberg, Craig L., 249, 281
Boyd, Gregory A., 45, 47, 89, 108, 144, 148, 321, 326
Branden, Nathaniel, 75
Busnot, Dominique, 171
Chamberlain, David, 22, 109
Chapman, Gary D., 108, 110, 278, 279
Collins, Francis, 195, 221
Collins, Robin, 24, 171
Colson, Chuck, 194
Copan, Paul, 21, 46, 47, 79, 195, 221, 222, 225, 226, 236, 249, 279, 334, 335, 362
Corey, Michael A., 42, 47, 108, 110, 135, 146, 164, 172, 196, 197, 222
Craig, William Lane, 18, 21, 24, 25, 42, 47, 75, 108, 117, 121, 129, 130, 153, 156, 158, 170, 171, 181, 182, 189, 190, 195
Crigger, Kelly, 81, 85
Crockett, William V., 47, 248, 249,

278
Cunningham, Scott, 86
Davies, Paul, 24, 171
Dawkins, Richard, 19, 22, 125, 129, 214, 226
Deem, Richard L., 130
Dodd, Charles H., 46, 77, 221, 224, 250, 280, 349, 350
Draper, Paul, 45, 161
Edwards, Jonathan, 231, 232, 248
Ehrman, Bart D., 5, 20, 45, 145, 148
Falwell, Jerry, 194
Fudge, Edward William, 242, 248, 249, 250
Geisler, Norman L., 194, 274, 280
Gish, Duane, 194
Godfrey, Robert, 195
Gosse, Philip Henry, 223
Griffin, David, 34, 144, 148
Habermas, Gary R., 46, 61, 64, 76, 78, 79, 84, 221, 224, 225, 248, 250, 255, 264, 270, 278, 279, 280, 281, 282
Ham, Ken, 20, 194
Hannergraff, Hank, 194
Harris, R. L., 282
Harris, Sam, 19
Hasker, R. William, 47, 171, 177, 189
Haught, John F., 208
Hawking, Stephen, 317
Henry, Matthew, 61, 78, 79, 104, 105, 111, 112, 129, 194, 201, 206, 208, 209, 224, 242, 249, 250, 263, 272, 279, 280, 297, 306, 324, 326, 335, 345, 350, 351, 363
Hick, John, 37, 40, 41, 42, 47, 92, 93, 108, 110, 196, 222
Hitchens, Christopher, 19
Hodge, Charles, 194, 273, 280
Howard-Snyder, Daniel, 45, 46, 47, 108, 110, 170, 182, 190, 314
Hume, David, 45
Hyers, Conrad, 195, 221, 222
Irenaeus, 208
John of the Cross, 208
Kaiser, Walter, 194

Kelly, Edward F., 76, 84, 85, 111
Kreeft, Peter J., 42, 47, 108, 135, 143, 146, 147, 148, 164, 172, 207, 208, 225, 315, 316, 317, 320
Krucoff, M. W., 130
La Croix, Richard R., 45, 139, 140, 141, 146, 147, 171
Lahey, Benjamin B., 76, 110, 327
LaFollette, Hugh, 45, 139, 146, 147, 171
Leibnitz, Gottfried W., 170, 189
Lewis, C. S., 47, 88, 108, 144, 148, 194, 208, 211, 225, 226, 256, 279, 315, 316, 320
Lockyer, Herbert, 250
Loftus, John W., 10, 11, 12, 23, 30, 45, 79, 119, 120, 123, 129, 143, 144, 147, 148, 157, 158, 159, 160, 171, 180, 184, 185, 190, 192, 193, 205, 211, 214, 216, 220, 224, 226, 248, 252, 278, 279, 280, 316, 317, 320
Longman, III, Tremper, 195, 221
Luther, Martin, 205, 208, 224, 331, 335, 350
McDaniel, Jay, 208
Metcalf, Thomas, 171
Mettinger, Tryggve N. D., 77
Miller, Keith B., 21, 221
Miller, Kenneth R., 196, 222
Mills, David, 10, 11, 13, 19, 23, 127, 130, 152, 153, 170, 230, 248, 264, 280
Mills, Gus, 226
Moreland, J. P., 46, 61, 64, 76, 78, 79, 84, 195, 221, 224, 225, 248, 250, 255, 263, 264, 270, 278, 279, 280, 281, 282
Murray, Michael J., 24, 42, 47, 94, 108, 109, 110, 150, 151, 158, 170, 171, 190, 197, 198, 199, 201, 223, 224, 225, 226, 265, 280, 310, 312, 313, 314
Mackie, John L., 45, 147, 171
Martin, Michael, 19, 45, 147, 161, 189, 220, 226, 301, 303, 307, 316, 320

Moltmann, Jürgen, 208
Morris, Henry M., 45, 194
Nash, Ronald H., 42, 47, 101, 108, 111, 147, 151, 170, 189, 190, 342, 350
Newman, Robert C., 194
Nietzsche, Friedrich, 32, 45
Offutt, Jason, 77, 79, 81, 85, 86, 225
Oppy, Graham, 45, 161
Packer, James I., 181, 190, 274, 280
Parsons, Keith M., 230, 248, 264, 279, 280
Paulsen, Gary, 192, 220
Penelhum, Terence, 158, 171
Peterson, Eugene, 279
Peterson, Michael, 151, 154, 170
Peterson, Robert A., 304
Phillips, John, 78, 250
Pinnock, Clark H., 252, 253, 278
Plantinga, Alvin, 47, 108, 305
Price, George McCready, 194
Purtill, Richard L., 158, 171
Radin, Dean, 66, 67, 68, 76, 80, 83, 130
Ramm, Bernard, 194
Reichenbach, Bruce, 47
Ross, Hugh, 25, 86, 155, 171
Rourke, Jack, 85
Rowe, William L., 30, 45, 147, 159, 160, 161, 175, 176, 182, 186, 187, 189, 190, 193, 220, 226
Sanders, John, 47, 350
Sarna, Nahum M., 362
Schaeffer, Francis, 194
Schellenberg, John L., 45, 75, 88, 108, 110, 313, 314
Schmicker, Michael, 82, 85
Scofield, C. I., 194
Seligman, Martin E. P., 76
Shermer, Michael, 65, 66, 68, 71, 82, 84
Singer, Peter, 19
Smith, George H., 230, 248
Smith, Scott S., 77, 81, 85, 213, 225, 226
Smith, Quentin, 45, 171
Snoke, David, 195
Southgate, Christopher, 208
Spurgeon, Charles H., 232, 249
Stearley, Ralph F., 20, 21, 222
Steiger, Brad, 77, 81, 225
Stenger, Victor J., 65, 71, 72, 86, 129
Strobel, Lee, 146, 148, 172, 195, 279, 320
Swinburne, Richard G., 46, 47, 75, 93, 110, 151, 170
Tacelli, Richard K., 47, 108, 146, 320
Targ, Russell, 66, 76, 80, 82
Tart, Charles T., 66, 70, 71, 76, 80, 84, 85
Tennant, Frederick R., 47, 75, 147, 151, 170
Trau, Mary Jane, 176, 189
Van Inwagen, Peter, 47, 151, 170, 171
Van Lommel, Pim, 76, 80, 81, 84
Waltke, Bruce, 194, 221
Walton, John H., 45, 77, 111, 195, 222, 223, 225, 249, 275, 281, 282, 305, 356, 360, 361, 362, 363, 364
Walvoord, John F., 246, 250
Ward, Keith, 207, 208, 225
Warfield, B. B., 194
Weisberger, Andrea M., 38, 45, 47, 159, 160, 171
Wenham, Gordon J., 195, 222, 360, 361, 364
Wennberg, Robert N., 208
Wesley, John, 207, 208, 209, 225
Whitcomb, Jr., John C., 194
Williams, Michael D., 304
Wright, J. Edward, 281, 363
Wright, N. T., 194, 221
Wykstra, Stephen, 47
Young, Davis A., 20, 21, 195, 221, 222
Zacharias, Ravi, 47, 108, 110